COMMONSENSE DIRECT & DIGITAL MARKETING

5th Edition

Drayton Bird

KOGAN PAGE

London and Philadelphia

Dedication

This book is dedicated to my mother,
who was able to succeed at an age when
most other people have stopped trying.

First published in Great Britain in 1982 entitled *Commonsense Direct Marketing*
Second edition, 1989
Third edition, 1993
Fourth edition, 2000
Fifth edition, 2007, entitled *Commonsense Direct and Digital Marketing*
Reprinted 2008, 2010, 2011

120 Pentonville Road
London N1 9JN
United Kingdom
www.koganpage.com

1518 Walnut Street, Suite 1100
Philadelphia PA 19102
USA

4737/23 Ansari Road
Daryaganj
New Delhi 110002
India

British Library Cataloguing in Publication Data

A CIP record for this book is available from the British Library.

ISBN 978 0 7494 4760 1

Library of Congress Cataloging-in-Publication Data

Bird, Drayton.
   Commonsense direct and digital marketing / Drayton Bird. – 5th ed.
      p. cm.
  Rev. ed. of: Commonsense direct marketing / Drayton Bird. 4th ed.
London ; $a Dover, N.H. : Kogan Page, 2000.
  Includes index.
  ISBN-13: 978-0-7494-4760-1
  ISBN-10: 0-7494-4760-5
 1. Direct marketing. I. Bird, Drayton. Commonsense direct marketing.
II. Title.
  HF5415.126.B57 2007
  658.8'72–dc22

                        2007011100

Typeset by Saxon Graphics Ltd, Derby
Printed and bound in Great Britain by Henry Ling Limited, Dorchester, Dorset

'Drayton Bird knows more about Direct Marketing than anyone in the world. His book about it is pure gold.'

David Ogilvy

'Remarkably personal, yet authoritative.'

Ed McLean, *DM News,* New York

'Everything the testimonials say, and a bargain at any price.'

Robert Heller, Editor in Chief, *Finance*

'The most stimulating book on marketing I have ever read.'

M E Corby, Mail Users' Association Ltd

'I have already got my money back at least a hundred times over.'

John Fenton, Founder, The Institute of Sales and Marketing Management

'So clear and concise that selective quotations fail to do justice to the richness of its texture. Read it.'

Campaign

'Perceptive, provocative and funny as hell.'

Robert Leiderman, The Leading Telemarketing Expert

'I recommend it to all my students.'

Dick Hodgson, The Top US Direct Marketing Teacher

'Without doubt the best direct marketing book which exists.'

Erik Van Vooren, BBDO Direct, Brussels

'I picked up your book Saturday night late – I put it down early Sunday! I am very grateful to you.'

John Fraser-Robinson, Author, *Secrets of Successful Direct Marketing*

'Commonsense in direct marketing makes sense after reading Drayton Bird's excellent book.'

Eddie Boas, Organiser, Pan-Pacific Direct Marketing Symposium

'If you can spare the time to read only one direct mail book – this is it. Beg, borrow or steal it.'

Graeme McCorkell, Founder, MSW Rapp & Collins

'… the best work on the subject I've ever read… and I've read them all!'

James A Mienik, Direct Marketing Reports, Tampa, Florida

'A definitive mini institute from one of the industry's greats.'

Mike Pitt, Time-Life International, Australia

'Great book! Clear, honest and relevant – it's a great guide on how to focus on the basics and get it right'

Alex Smirniotis, Combined Insurance, Australia

'If you read no other book on direct marketing you should find the time to read this one'

Direct Marketing International

'Witty and practical, but never boring. A great book to read and re-read and one that I wish I had read a lot earlier in my career.'

Joseph Sugarman, CEO, JS&A

'Among my most valued possessions, and easily among the greatest ever written on advertising, right up there with those by Caples, Ogilvy, Schwab, Reeves and Hopkins.'

Gary Bencivenga, cited as America's top copywriter

'I read the whole book through from cover to cover in one weekend – because it was well written (as you would hope!) but also because it was just so immediately useful.'

Rowan Gormley, Virgin Isles

Contents

Plate section can be found between pages 216 and 231 in Chapter 9

List of Plates

Plate section can be found between pages 216 and 231 in Chapter 9.

Acknowledgements

Although I am indebted to many people, I would like to thank in particular for their help, encouragement and ideas:

Tony Arau, Malcolm Auld, Michael Carpenter, Maria Caricato, Jon Epstein, Iain Goodman, Gary Halbert, Brian Halsey, Steve Harrison, Melanie Howard, Bill Jayme, Daphne Kelsey, Jos Krutzmann, Lisa Lee, Robert Leiderman, Graeme McCorkell, Stewart Pearson, Denise Rayner, Brian Thomas, John Francis Tighe, Glenmore Trenear-Harvey, Carol Trickey, John Watson, Rod Wright

1

Beginnings

'Learning teacheth more in one year than experience in twenty.'
Roger of Ascham

'The only purpose of advertising is to sell;
it has no other justification worth mentioning.'
Raymond Rubicam
Founder, Young & Rubicam Advertising

'When a man knows he is to be hanged in a
fortnight, it concentrates his mind wonderfully.'
Dr Johnson

In 1957 my situation was bleak. I was making £7.00 a week editing a small trade journal. Even in those dear, dead days when cigarettes cost the equivalent of 10p a packet this would not support a wife and child – even in the two-up two-down cottage with outside lavatory we lived in. I had to do something.

At the time, I was much taken by a smooth aristocratic friend who worked in advertising. He seemed to be making pots of money without too much effort and advised me to become a copywriter. It took six months using all my reserves of servile flattery to find a willing employer.

I had three qualities to offer, apart from desperation.

First, I was brought up in a northern pub with a widely varied clientele. Encountering very different kinds of people after they have had a few drinks is splendid education for life. One minute I might be serving a pint of best mild in the vaults to Alec, whose party turn was describing how his wife had gone out one day for a loaf of bread and never returned. The next I would be listening to a mottle-faced cotton magnate in the American Bar lamenting the Socialist government's determination to part him from all he possessed.

Second, I could write. You may consider this essential for the job I sought, but this is not apparent to many would-be copywriters. An alarming number cannot spell, punctuate or write long sentences – let alone tangle with such niceties as 'it's' versus 'its', 'compliment' as opposed to 'complement' and so on.

Third, I had read every book on advertising in Manchester Public Library – there were three – and enrolled in an evening course on the subject. You may also see these preparations as obvious, but not all agree: when I finally entered the industry, I discovered few of my colleagues had taken the trouble to study the subject, or were even clear about the *purpose* of advertising.

This ancient ignorance has yet to be entirely dispelled. Over 80 years ago the first and best definition of advertising – 'Salesmanship in print' (still valid if you allow for broadcast media) – was formulated. However, this fairly simple thought has not penetrated the skulls of many practitioners or their clients to this day. You find this hard to believe? A 1980 survey of senior British marketing people revealed that 80 per cent thought advertising had some primary purpose *other* than selling. And today many are led wildly astray by a will o' the wisp called 'brand building'.

Many see this as a comfortable state of affairs. If nobody knows what advertising should do, how can the content (or results) be evaluated? Under such circumstances it is relatively easy to make a fair living in the industry if you have a quick mind and an ingratiating manner.

THE AMATEUR APPROACH

I imagined this amateur approach to be peculiarly British until I read a piece headed 'Ignorance is bliss' in the 21 December 1992 issue of America's *Advertising Age*. It revealed that 1,003 senior executives had been tested on their knowledge of marketing principles with results so abysmal that they would have done better if they had answered 'Don't know' to every question.

Study the subject

This foolish sloth is pervasive. Over the years I have interviewed hundreds of prospective employees. I almost invariably ask: 'What books have you read on direct marketing or advertising?' A significant percentage have read none; few have read more than one or two. The following account gives you an idea of the problem.

Bird: 'What books ...?'
Young (but not inexperienced) art director: 'Well none, really. I don't believe in theory. It kind of, well ... I don't like to restrict my imagination.'
Bird: 'Really. Then how do you learn about the business?'
AD: 'Well, you know, you kind of pick it up by being around. You know, reading *Campaign* and that sort of thing.'

Bird (getting agitated): 'What sort of thing?'

AD: 'Well, working in a good agency, and watching what happens.'

Bird (restraining certain violent tendencies): 'Would you expect to pick up brain surgery by standing around the casualty department at University College Hospital?'

AD: 'Well, no. That's different, isn't it?'

Bird: 'Yes. *Everything* is different. But that doesn't mean you don't have to learn it properly.'

(Interview breaks up in disorder.)

Depressing, isn't it? Especially if you're trying to build up a business. You have to *educate* your staff before they become any use – by which time, I might add, they have become rare and coveted commodities on the employment market.

THE DIFFICULT APPROACH

Returning to my early experiences, I soon discovered that some clients had very clear views on advertising. That was because their businesses depended on it. Either they were mail order firms seeking agents and customers or they were selling products door to door, seeking inquiries from likely buyers.

Why results matter

They were often difficult people. They wanted *replies* – and lots of them. Their advertisements tended to be bloody, bold and resolute; intent on results at the right cost. They would tell you very quickly (and sometimes quite offensively) whether their advertising was working.

Few of my colleagues were keen on working for them. They preferred clients with vaguer objectives like 'spreading our good name'. Even better were those who simply spent the agreed advertising appropriation every year in the way they always had. Such clients assessed their advertising quite simply: did they like it?

To this day many advertisers spend vast sums in the same slapdash way. They and their agencies may claim their efforts increase sales, but it's not always easy to discover by what alchemy that happy result occurs. So many other factors intervene – like what your competitors are doing in terms of advertising, price and distribution – that establishing how sales are affected by advertising is very tricky. This gives occasion for many fanciful alibis on the part of agencies and marketers when the sales curve goes down instead of up.

A senior marketing man with one of the world's largest companies once told me they advertise simply to create *awareness*. Sales were somebody else's problem, I gathered. Many regard their advertising in isolation in this way; they 'uncouple' it from the rest of the marketing process.

Awareness vs sales

If you ignore the matter of sales, you can discover many things about your advertising. Did people notice it? Did they read it? Did they understand it? Did they remember it? Did they like it?

This last question in particular can mislead. Some advertising is *so* likeable it obscures the merits of the product. Forty-odd years ago, a New York beer company called Piels ran commercials so popular the public demanded they be recalled when they were taken off. Unfortunately, every time they did so, sales went down. Similarly, for some years Isuzu ran ads in the United States which won so many awards the client kept them running despite the fact they did nothing for sales.

A puzzle

Why then, you may wonder, are so many still unwilling to use the only fool-proof way of measuring whether a message makes people act? Namely a reply device, a coupon, phone number or email address, and many of those who do, fail to measure the replies – a sort of idiocy that defies analysis.

Customers prefer coupons

It is a bit of a puzzle, isn't it? It's a shame, too, because research conducted by Daniel Starch & Staff in the USA indicates that putting a coupon in your advertisements actually increases readership. All advertisers, no matter what their views, agree this is desirable.

There has been a remarkable amount of ill-informed comment about coupons and response devices. A great many sensitive art directors believe a coupon spoils your image. This poisonous myth was demolished for all time by research from Telelab in the UK on how customers – business or consumer – really feel about response devices.

There were 801 respondents. 38 per cent of consumers and 48 per cent of business people claimed they had responded to advertisements to request information. Interestingly, wealthier, better-educated readers are more likely to respond among consumers; and amongst business people, the more senior the executives, the more likely they are to have responded. A counterblast to those who imagine only poor, less-sophisticated people like direct response.

And what do customers think of response devices? 89 per cent of consumers and 94 per cent of business people believe 'companies should provide a direct means of response in all their advertising'. 77 per cent of consumers and 61 per cent of business people think the mere presence of a response device 'said something positive about a company'. 21 per cent of consumers weren't sure what effect a response device had, and 33 per cent of business people were uncertain.

So 2 per cent of consumers and 6 per cent of business people thought response devices said nothing about a company or made a negative impression. This information conveys a message which I will put flippantly as follows: people who don't use response devices are anywhere between 94 per cent and 98 per cent stupid.

A response device reveals whether people were motivated to *act* on your message. It tells how well each advertisement performed against others. And you can evaluate media by running the same message in different publications or on different channels or at different times. The Telelab research shows you can do all this whilst enhancing your image *and* giving your customers what they want. That can't be bad, can it?

Why do people fear results?

This reveals one important fact which few realise – apart from the fact that people like response devices. The response device actually improves your image. Moreover, it was revealed in August 2006 that Sky TV in the UK had discovered 93 per cent of viewers had pressed the red response button during commercials in the first six months of the year.

To be honest, I think both agencies and advertisers are insecure. They are frightened of discovering that what they do does not work. Yet how can knowledge be anything but good?

I formed that view very early on. I hated being judged on the basis of someone's opinion – be it the client, the client's spouse (the case with one famous soap company I worked for), or even the client's customers in research. I was dying to know if I was making people *buy*. Then, every time I learned something was working (or not) I could improve. This simple approach helped me become creative director of a well known London advertising agency at the age of 26, within five years of entering the business.

I became conceited. Soon I was sure I knew more than any of my clients, even the ones who counted their results. After all, it was my copy, was it not, that ensured their business success? Mere trivia like understanding management, or how much you should pay for a product – let alone the boring business of distribution – were far beneath my notice. I decided I would quickly make my fortune in the mail order business.

SOME VALUABLE DISCOVERIES

Over 200 years ago Daniel Defoe observed: 'The mariner to sail with is he who has been shipwrecked, for he knows where the reefs are.' I discovered several reefs when I set out on my first venture.

A friend of mine and I ran a £560 ad for ladies' hairpieces in the *Daily Mirror*. The ad ran on a Saturday. The following Monday we rushed round to our borrowed office, a little room at the top of a flight of narrow stairs. It was almost impossible to open the door. A huge pile of envelopes had jammed it shut from the other side – envelopes full of money.

Don't rely on others

We gutted them swiftly and worked out our likely results. Bingo! We calculated we should make £5,000 profit at least. Our fortunes were clearly made, since the fashion for hairpieces was just beginning. I knew this was the business for me: all the thrill of gambling, only you control the odds.

Having discovered how quickly we could make money by selling direct, we soon learned an important lesson: don't rely too much on other people. Our supplier left all the hair samples our customers sent in next to an open window. When the wind blew them all over the place, we had a fearful refund problem.

The supplier was not put off by this mishap. He could see what a good business it was and decided to cut us out and do it himself. Happily, he lost his shirt. He didn't realise that unless the advertisement was correctly prepared, it would not get replies. Accordingly, he produced one himself which flopped totally. This was probably the only good thing to emerge from this exercise. My partner and I were lucky to escape without losing money.

You might imagine this discouraging experience would quench my enthusiasm. Not at all: I couldn't wait to walk out of my safe job and try again. I went to work with a friend who had the rights to a bodybuilding device called the 'Bullworker'. I used it for 30 days and gained 14lbs in solid muscle. If it could work for somebody like me – the perfect 'Mr Before' – I was sure I could sell it. I was offered a share of the profits if I succeeded.

I worked like stink and within six months we were selling 1,000 of these gleaming instruments every week. Unfortunately (my second lesson), my friend was not good at arithmetic. We had sold every single one at a loss. The business had to be disposed of. Over the years I have come across a surprising number of people who seem unable to commit, or disinclined to do so. It is the high road to folly.

After this disaster I retreated to the safety of another well paid job in advertising, but remained in love with mail order. It appealed to someone like me who spends every penny he makes. You didn't need much money to set up. No costly premises were necessary to entice passers-by. You could run advertisements even if you didn't have any goods – buying them from the suppliers as you sold them. You could even get credit from advertising agents, who were usually so eager to get new clients they rarely checked your financial status.

Get your figures right

I continued to try – and fail – until through force of sheer repetition my enterprises started to do well. One in particular demonstrated the unwarranted self-confidence and extraordinary gall I must have possessed. It was a newsletter advising people presumably even more ignorant than myself on how to make money. It did well for many years.

Over the years since then I have engaged in a range of activities so wide that simply contemplating them makes me feel tired. I have written scripts, advised companies on marketing, run a franchise company, organised exhibitions, run a sales force (never again!), helped launch a research company: you name it. In the course of all this I have also been fortunate enough to learn from some very talented people.

I have worked with some of the world's largest (and smallest) companies. Most of my clients have had the sense to ignore my more foolish suggestions and accept my more intelligent ones. I have planned and written thousands of advertising campaigns and individual pieces. Almost every experience has taught me something valuable.

THE MYSTERIOUS RISE OF DIRECT MARKETING

In the early days, mail order – direct marketing's most obvious manifestation – was unfashionable, verging on squalid. It attracted the wrong people: those who liked selling something sight unseen which could therefore be described with a licence and disregard for truth matched only by estate agents, motor dealers, holiday firms and people selling virility by the inch on the internet.

In turn this attracted the wrong products; the kind even a street corner tout would disdain to touch. I well recall asking a Belgian mail order operator in 1962 if a product which promised to expand the size of your bust worked. He looked at me with contempt: 'If you ask me silly questions like that, I am going straight home.'

Despite this sort of thing (which still persists), perceptive observers had always found the logic behind direct communications inescapable. In the 1960s David Ogilvy commented: 'Direct mail was my first love – and secret weapon in the avalanche of new business acquisitions which made Ogilvy & Mather an instant success.' A few years later, Ed Ney, chief executive of Young & Rubicam, then the world's largest advertising agency, predicted: 'When you wake up in ten years from now, you will find direct marketing is beginning to take over. If you choose direct marketing, you will be entering the most vital segment of the economy for the next 50 years.'

The most vital sector of the economy

As time passed, the mail order and direct mail businesses crawled out of the gutter and became mysteriously transmuted into direct marketing. By the end of the 1970s over half the *Fortune* Top 100 Companies were either dabbling with direct marketing or were direct marketers, like *Reader's Digest* or *Time-Life*. Why this occurred is a principal theme of this book. Until you understand the reasons, you will never know how to make the most of direct marketing.

The potential of direct marketing is certainly appreciated by most senior marketing executives. A 1987 survey revealed that 60 per cent of the top 250 advertisers in the United Kingdom thought that direct marketing would be more important than general advertising by the end of the century. This is rather surprising when you realise that, according to another survey conducted by Ogilvy & Mather Direct, the average marketing executive saw direct marketing practitioners as a bunch of unprofessional cowboys. (Hearteningly, those who had actually dealt with direct marketing agencies had a more favourable view.)

To those of us who have been involved in this business for a long time, this new interest in our activities is quite heartening. Where once we muttered at smart parties, 'Er, mail order', when asked what we did for a living, we can now say confidently: 'Direct marketing'. And today, of course, firms like Dell Computers and Amazon rely entirely on direct marketing.

Ignorance of direct marketing

In 1976 a farsighted friend, John Watson, suggested to me that we start an advertising consultancy or agency specialising in direct marketing – especially since I knew more about it than most.

I mentioned this to another old friend, Glenmore Trenear-Harvey, and the three of us set up in business. We had no clients and no money (we couldn't even afford an office) but within three or four years Trenear-Harvey, Bird and Watson was the largest direct marketing agency in the UK. This sounds quite grand until you realise that compared with the big general advertising agencies, our 22-man business was the tiniest of minnows.

Nobody knew what direct marketing was

Despite its growth, few people had a clear idea of what direct marketing was (still true today). Of course, to survive, you had to discover what worked and what didn't. But most of the books on the subject were either out of date or long and tedious, however informative; and none was British.

In 1980 my partners suggested I write the first book on the subject in the UK. Thus emerged *Commonsense Direct Marketing*, in 1982. I was surprised at how well received it was, and thought I could relax, having made my contribution to the literature of the subject.

However, although the principles that govern direct marketing have not really changed in the years since, the discipline is being employed by organisations which were barely aware of it until recently. Moreover, it's being used for a much wider range of purposes than merely selling – for instance, to affect voters' decisions. As far back as the Eisenhower presidential campaign, direct mail was being used on a very large scale, whilst in the 1992 American Election, quite a range of direct marketing activities were employed. One Democratic hopeful, Jerry Brown, asked people to call him on a toll-free number to give their opinion after his broadcast.

Who uses it

This was so successful it was copied by the other candidates. All three presidential candidates, Perot, Clinton and Bush, mailed out video tapes directly to special interest groups. And there was an enormous weight of direct mail designed to raise funds and shift opinions. In the UK I have myself written copy for both the Conservative and Labour parties.

Since 1982 I have spent a great deal of time travelling to many countries, meeting and talking with direct marketers. I have learned a great deal about how it is being used in almost every sort of society. I believe its impact, not merely on business, but even on our world, could be considerable. (A sweeping observation, you may consider; but as you read these pages, you may come to agree.)

For these reasons I was persuaded I ought to revise my original book. In the process of doing so, the task became more than a revision – it became almost a complete rewrite, and now it is a seemingly never-ending series of them. However, I have incorporated most of the original book and my intention remains the same: to give you the *essentials* of direct marketing, entertainingly and memorably so as to inspire you to make correct and profitable decisions.

The idea of this book is simple. First, I want to define direct marketing and show where it should fit into your business; what role it should play. Business methods flourish when they work for you and your customers;

therefore I also want to explore the technological and cultural changes in our society which make direct marketing so relevant.

Second, I want to answer some questions. How should you best plan your direct marketing? How does it relate to your other promotional activities like general advertising, sales promotion, packaging and public relations? How should you implement your efforts and, of course, evaluate your results?

Third, I believe one example is worth a ton of theory. It's all very well isolating principles, laying down rules and issuing exhortations, but I have also incorporated a wide range of appropriate case histories culled from many countries and types of business. These, I hope, will bring the subject to life.

Just commonsense

Fortunately, direct marketing is not hard to understand, despite the efforts of a large number of half-baked theorists with a penchant for quasi-academic jargon. We all like to dignify our craft with a little mystery for the benefit of outsiders; this is particularly true of experts talking to potential customers with bags of money. But direct marketing is little more than commonsense, which is what led to the title of this book.

This book's purpose

Nonetheless, success does not come without great attention to detail. In few businesses can so many things go wrong so quickly if you don't pay attention.

I have already told you about my initiation into the wonderful world of hairpieces, and throughout this book I shall give you a fair selection of examples showing my rare ability to turn triumph into disaster in a number of businesses – sometimes even my present one. As a result of these little coups, I have proved to my own satisfaction that I am as likely as not to get things wrong.

But I consider myself fortunate to have made so many mistakes. We learn little from success. We are usually so delighted that all we do is break open another bottle of champagne. We rarely stop to analyse *why* we did so well, assuming instead that it is our uncommon skill and talent. On the other hand, if you make a mistake you are forced to examine what's gone wrong and compare with previous success to ensure you don't repeat the error. Daniel Defoe was right.

Mistakes are a blessing

I will tell you as much as I can of what I have learned, with the minimum of technical detail. Like me, you may find technicalities hard to follow. What I am trying to point out are the *principles,* not the minutiae. By following them, you should be able to avoid some of the nasty surprises I have had. And the important point is that they tend to apply in almost every country, with almost every kind of audience and every type of product or service – and they are not new: indeed they date back over a hundred years.

From ant farming to insurance

One of the books which originally inspired me to go into the mail order business was called – with a directness which appealed to the larceny in my soul – *How I Made a Million Dollars in Mail Order*. Here's a quote that really got me humming: '**I know of no business in the world that requires such a small investment to start, yet holds promise of such tremendous financial gains.**'

The writer, Joe Cossman, started his business about 60 years ago. Having little money, he started by working from his kitchen table. His staff was his wife. He sold some bizarre products, including lifelike shrunken skulls (which *still* sell, by the way), an ant farm, a garden sprinkler, a spud gun and wild animal heads made of plastic to hang on your wall like big game trophies.

Since the 1940s, our business has changed dramatically. Yet if you were to read Joe Cossman's book today, you might find his writing style a bit breathless but you would still be impressed by the sense he makes.

The principles have not changed

For though we now sell more expensive products and services, in far greater variety; and though we now use lasers and computers to print and distribute our messages; and though we have now reached the point where people can order direct from their TV or computer screens, the *thinking* you need to succeed in direct marketing hasn't changed at all. You can still start from your kitchen table and make your fortune. Indeed, in the USA, Joe Sugarman with his JS & A company did precisely that starting in the 1970s and is thriving to this day.

Joe Sugarman has sold some very sophisticated products, many electronic or in the health field. Most didn't exist when Joe Cossman set out to festoon America with shrunken heads. Sugarman's ads didn't even carry coupons, because the vast majority of his orders came through the telephone with his customers paying by credit card. (I've illustrated an example of his work elsewhere in this book – he is a master copywriter.) But Sugarman's principles are much the same as those advocated by Cossman. The potential that awaits you by following these principles has by no means yet been realised.

For example, finance is probably the largest single area in our business. Within that field the largest category is probably insurance.

A PARADOX

In 1970 an American friend suggested we go into business selling insurance direct. I didn't understand how this could be done. How could an intangible like insurance be sold in this way? It seemed too *complicated*, too. And therein lies one of the central paradoxes of the direct marketing business. For it is precisely *because* they are complex that many products sell so well this way – as you will see later in this book.

Three years after my 1970 conversation I went to New York and took a ride on a bus. Inside the bus I was surprised to see hundreds of 'take-one' leaflets hanging from little hooks. The leaflets invited you to insure yourself against the cost of hospital expenses. I was quite amazed.

In the first place, I had never heard of the product before. But what particularly surprised me was that the leaflets featured not the worry of hospital costs, but the large sums of money you would be paid if you did end up in hospital. This seemed to make no sense at all to me. Of course, I was wrong. The thinking behind these leaflets was based upon an important truth: people often like a benefit (money) more than a negative, scary thought.

I was equally amazed at finding these leaflets on a bus. A strange place, I thought, to sell a financial service. Looking back, once again, the reasoning is simple. *Everybody* is interested in money. *Everybody* thinks they'll probably have to go to hospital one day. So this policy appealed to virtually everyone – and where better to offer it than on a bus?

Since then this type of policy has been sold in most countries around the world.

Oddly enough, in 1984 at a business lunch I was sitting next to two British insurance experts who also expressed doubt that insurance could be sold through the post. At the same table were two Americans. Both had become millionaires by doing precisely that.

YOUR TIMING IS GOOD

For years I have listened – with growing impatience – to people telling me that direct marketing is a passing craze. In particular, they worry about too much direct mail or internet spamming. A recent survey found that, contrary to the suggestion that people don't read direct mail, only 15 per cent of mail from financial services is never opened, and the industry average is 22 per cent. This research produced a lot of 'junk mail shock horror' headlines from national papers, including the *Daily Mail*, which described this as an 'astonishing waste of paper and money'. Pretty hilarious, really, when we consider how much of the *Daily Mail* is ignored by the average reader, who has actually paid for it. It's even more hilarious when you consider that the streets of London are currently paved by papers produced by three free newspapers, including two from the owner of the *Daily Mail*. Of course what the press really means by these attacks is, 'Stop spending on mail, come back and spend again with us.'

According to the Direct Mail Information Service, direct mail volumes were down by 5.3 per cent in 2005 to 5.1 billion items, little more than one item per person per week. That is hardly an avalanche, and the reduction is due to two things: better targeting and a lot of clients turning to e-mail.

The same research revealed that 70 per cent of unaddressed mail is unopened, which is hardly surprising really. Who wants to hear from people who don't know them and can't be bothered to find out their names? And this, dear reader, is what this book is about: getting to know your customers so as to serve them better. Within Ogilvy & Mather, the advertising agency group I used to work for, the direct marketing arm was growing much faster than general advertising, and this growth is continuing as more and more companies put resources into this form of marketing. So there is a great and growing lack of people who take the trouble to understand the business. People like you, in fact. There could hardly be a wiser time either to enter direct marketing, or to learn how to exploit it better.

You may be, as I once was, a young copywriter – or an art director. Perhaps an account handler in a general agency thinking that direct marketing might offer a better future. You may be an experienced marketer with millions to spend who is facing an intractable problem and wondering whether direct marketing will help. Would direct mail build brand preference as well as television? Is it as memorable? Should you be spending more money on *retaining* customers through a direct loyalty programme than on trying to attract *new* ones? Can direct marketing help you motivate your salesforce?

Perhaps you have money to invest and are considering direct marketing as a way of setting up in business. Or you may already be running a successful direct marketing business and want to improve your results. For that matter, you may be working in charity or politics. Whatever you are trying to achieve that involves persuading other individuals to do what you want, you should find this book helpful. And I assure you that you will have far greater success by following the guidelines you read here than depending on judgement alone, or that most costly of commodities, *flair*.

Rules not sacred

There's no certainty you'll succeed. But I can assure you that you are likely to minimise the risk of failure. Marketing is as much an art as a science, because human beings are involved. Every principle does not always hold true. Indeed, you will see quite a number of examples throughout the book where the 'rules' many direct marketers adhere to so slavishly, with such monotonous results, have been successfully ignored.

In fact, just about the only sure thing about direct marketing is that you will be surprised – frequently. No matter how carefully you plan, based upon how people *ought* to behave, or *have* behaved in the past, they keep giving you nasty shocks. That's one reason why direct marketing is never boring.

One thing I do promise: what you will learn here is a bargain. For I learned it with millions of pounds of other people's money – and quite a few thousands of my own.

TO MAKE LEARNING EASIER

Your money back if you are not satisfied

Finally, in the best direct marketing tradition, let me offer you a guarantee. I have tried to cram into this book as many thoughts and instances as I can summon up. I hope you find them informative, and the book entertaining. But most of all, I hope I stimulate you into fresh thinking, to help you succeed. So if you don't find at least one idea (and many more, I hope) that pays for the book ten times over, return it and we will refund the money.

On the other hand, if you like the book or you have ideas for improvements (and I am sure it could be improved) then write and tell me. This latest edition has evolved very much with the help of comments made by readers such as you.

I didn't plan this book as a textbook, and I hope it doesn't read like one. Nor was it so fat 25 years ago. However, it has now put on weight, and many use it as a textbook – or, I sometimes fear, a doorstop. So, to make it easier, when you're swotting for that exam or in a rush to finish that report you'll find notes at the end of each chapter. When I read them I was surprised how simple they seem to make things. I hope you agree.

I have changed the title of this edition to incorporate the word 'digital' for two reasons. First, as I write, the phrase 'digital marketing' attracts more interest than direct marketing or CRM. (The latter has been fashionable in recent years to the point where firms set up CRM departments without being all that clear about what the initials imply.) And second, increasingly media that transmit information digitally – especially those related to the telephone and internet, and the two working together – are making vast inroads.

Why digital? Two reasons – with a comment

I must say, though, that the thinking behind this phrase is not helpful. It focuses on the *means* of communication rather than the aim, which is better marketing. This in itself has led this kind of marketing to be dominated by technical experts, rather than marketers, with dire and costly results. It is almost as though builders were to dominate architecture – and the precedents are not good, as much the same occurred when television advertising became fashionable, and again when marketers started to be interested in databases. In both cases, people who knew nothing (and cared less) about selling took control, with catastrophic results.

Sadly, marketers love a little high-sounding jargon, as it makes what they do seem important, although its use is a great hindrance, not a help nowadays, when a grasp of plain English is at a premium.

Points to remember

- Flair and talent are overrated: you need education.
- Measurables are your best guide.
- Customers *appreciate* response devices.
- Virtually all organisations use direct marketing.
- Principles are unchanged.
- Know the rules – but don't follow them slavishly.
- Why digital? Principles are the same.
- A guarantee.

2

The Three Graces of Direct Marketing

'A Chinese sage of the distant past was once asked by his disciples what he would do first if he were given power to set right the affairs of the country. He answered "I should certainly see to it that language is used correctly." "Surely," they said, "this is a trivial matter. Why should you deem it so important?" The Master replied "If language is not used correctly then what is said is not what is meant. If what is said is not what is meant then what ought to be done remains undone. If this remains undone morals and art will be corrupted. If morals and art are corrupted justice will go astray. If justice goes astray the people will stand about in helpless confusion."'

Recounted of Confucius

'We're here, because we're here, because we're here, because we're here' ... and so on, ad nauseam.

Well-known British Army song

When I reached the august age of 51, one of my family sent me a birthday card. The front bore the legend: 'You have now reached the age where you start to ask yourself important questions like: why are we here? ... where are we going? ...' I opened the card, to see inside: '... and will the pubs be open when we get there?'

Why are you in business?

This story prompts me to inquire, dear reader, how often you ask yourself why you are here – what you are in business *for*? I have asked audiences all over the world that question. Nine times out of ten the reply is either: 'To make a profit', or 'To make money'. It seems fairly obvious, doesn't it? And it leads on quite naturally to the aim of making *more* money each year.

Yet some businesses appear to have very different aims. For instance, I was most interested a few years ago to read that an eminent Japanese businessman, when asked why *he* was in business, replied: 'To ensure the survival of my company.' I suspect this reply would not be unusual in Japan. For many years Japanese industry tended to invest a higher percentage of its profits in building for the future than the UK did. It did not feel obliged to squeeze every yen out of the annual turnover and hand it over to the shareholders.

Clearly, if you are intent upon *survival* rather than a fast buck, you are going to plan more for the long term. No doubt this attitude explains why the Japanese did better than us for a good 40 years, and still do in many areas. But whatever your aim, it will colour all you do: the way you structure your organisation, manage your staff and set their targets; everything, right down to the smallest marketing decision.

SHORT-TERM THINKING

If you look at most big marketing departments, you will be struck by one fact: the tenure of the average person in a position tends to be fairly short. I read recently that the average marketing manager stays in a job for about 18 months. Marketing directors last even less time. In that period, each person has to make his or her mark. How? Obviously, by producing quick results – and often, by change for the sake of change. That way one can be seen quite clearly to be *doing* something. (One revealing statistic a few years ago was that in 50 per cent of cases when a company changes its marketing director, that marketing director will then change advertising agencies within the next 12 months.)

This does not lead to long-term planning or even consistency within your organisation. The *urgent* is constantly taking precedence over the *important*. When you come to consider implementing direct marketing, you cannot afford to think this way. You must look long term.

Quick results – a good idea?

I am anxious to emphasise this to you because most people tend to be attracted to direct marketing for the very reason that I was: you can see what you're getting for your money. That is important; but it is only one benefit of the discipline. To explain why, let me start by asking you to try a little test. Ask a few of your colleagues to define *marketing*. I do not know you, your colleagues or your organisation, but I would be surprised if most could do so adequately. As a matter of fact, I have put the same test repeatedly to marketing people recently. Only around one in three seems able to give a good definition.

Can you define 'marketing'?

The British Chartered Institute of Marketing, which ought to know, states that marketing is '**the management process responsible for identifying, anticipating and satisfying customer requirements profitably**'.

That definition helps us place *direct* marketing within the context of marketing itself. In my experience most people think of marketing very much in relation to selling, advertising and promotion. But if you read that definition carefully, it covers just about every aspect of business, from what you pay for your raw materials right through to how you make, price, distribute, advertise and sell your product. (At this point, I feel I should beg your forgiveness: you, of course, know the answers to these simple questions, and I am just refreshing your memory. Bear with me then if, for the benefit of those who don't know what it is, I now discuss the *aim* of marketing.)

TO MAKE AND KEEP A CUSTOMER

You may have read *Management Tasks, Responsibilities and Practices*, by the American business writer Peter Drucker – a title, in my view, calculated to make anyone except the most dedicated masochist give up any idea of managing anything, ever. In this book he suggested that the aim of marketing was really to *eliminate* the need for selling. 'To know and understand the customer so well that the product or service fits him and sells itself.'

The purpose of business

Peter Drucker was one of the best thinkers in the world on business. Many years ago he suggested that the purpose of business was not simply to make money, but to create customers. This thought was developed further by Theodore Levitt of the Harvard Business School as 'to make and keep a customer'.

I think you will agree this definition makes sense whatever your objective – short term or long term. Indeed, if we simply change the word 'customer' to 'supporter', 'colleague', or 'employee', you can apply this to just about anything you want to do: run a successful charity, build a political party, or develop a hardworking, committed body of workers. However, for simplicity's sake, I am going to refer in this book mostly to 'customers' and 'business'.

If you agree with me – or rather with the experts I have quoted – on the purposes of business and marketing, then I think that once I have defined direct marketing to your satisfaction, you will quickly see the reasons for its growth, why its future looks very promising, and how it can play a valuable role within your business.

WHAT IS DIRECT MARKETING?

Since even a mature business like advertising is not clearly understood by many of its practitioners you can hardly be surprised that few understand what direct marketing is. Indeed, whilst preparing this book, I saw that, in a survey of 133 leading American direct marketers, no clear agreement on what the business is emerged.

When the phrase direct marketing comes up, most people, in my experience, immediately think of the *medium* of direct mail. Others think of direct marketing as a *method of selling*, like off-the-page selling. Others confuse it with a *channel of distribution*, like mail order.

Producing a definition as simple as 'Salesmanship in print' for advertising proved an insuperable task for the industry's pundits. So much so that (in what I can only assume was a moment of despair) *Direct Marketing* magazine – then the industry's leading American organ – summoned not one, but *three* experts to do so. The result of their labours was placed at the beginning of every issue of the magazine. It occupied two half pages, featuring one of those gloriously complicated flow charts which always throw me into a state of utter confusion.

You may consider the need for a simple definition unimportant; indeed, few people using direct marketing bother to speculate on what it really is. But I consider it crucial. Imagine spending millions of pounds without clearly understanding what you are spending them on. Not an imaginary scenario, I assure you.

Why a definition matters

In fact, not long ago, I recall a debate taking place with a leading automobile company, which we shall call Ford for the sake of argument, covering many countries and multifarious marketing problems. Was direct marketing an advertising activity? In that case the people in charge of advertising should make the decision. Was it 'below the line'? In which case that company's policy meant that a different department, usually concerned with purchasing everything down to stationery, would deal with it.

I will not go into detail, save to say that in the end different decisions were made in different countries for different reasons – most to do with these varying views of direct marketing. This is obviously stupid. And it is not likely to become any more intelligent if everybody involved has to understand and memorise a long, illustrated definition before they start work.

Moreover, the pool of understanding has been muddied further by the fact that many practitioners are not even agreed that direct marketing ought to be called direct marketing. As a result, combined with the desire to give brand names to particular companies' approaches to the business, all sorts of names have cropped up: terms such as 'curriculum marketing', 'dialogue marketing', 'personal marketing', 'database marketing' and – currently the most fashionable one – 'customer relationship marketing'. But the most common term remains direct marketing. It is certainly the one I propose to stick to.

Nevertheless, these terms do reveal important facts about the nature of the business. Certainly direct marketing revolves around the building and exploitation of a database – though there is more to it than that. Equally, building a relationship is one of our objectives – but only one. The approach *is* personal; and in the process of building a relationship, you can guide your prospect through a curriculum whereby you learn more about them and they learn more about you.

Building a relationship

But my simple definition of direct marketing is: '**any advertising activity which creates and exploits a direct relationship between you and your prospect or customer as an individual**'.

If you and I can agree that we ought to call direct marketing 'direct marketing', and you accept my simple definition, then you will immediately appreciate that a wide range of activities is encompassed.

I am sure you have been stopped by people standing on street corners with questionnaires bearing such inane queries as: 'Are you able to save as much money as you'd like?' If you are not careful, these will lead to a visit from an insurance salesman. Clearly these people are engaged in direct marketing: they are making a direct contact and trying to initiate a relationship with you as an individual.

In the same way, somebody who offers you a leaflet inviting you to go into your local hamburger joint and win a prize; or the ad for the introduction agency offering love everlasting; the note in the shop window selling a used ghetto blaster; the ad suggesting you apply for shares in British Telecom; the leaflet coming through your door in praise of your local Conservative Party candidate – they're *all* direct marketing. In fact the most popular section in many papers – the classified section – is nothing but direct marketing. And almost everything that happens on the internet involves direct marketing.

Perhaps it is worth stating here what I believe to be the differences between direct marketing and some of the other communications tools. (This is not made any easier by the fact that in the case of sales promotion, people are no more agreed about what they do than are direct marketers.)

How does direct marketing differ from other disciplines like advertising?

- *Advertising* usually speaks to people en masse, not as individuals. Although today the vast majority of ads do allow people to respond, especially by going to a website, advertising does not usually aim above all for an immediate response. It seeks to influence customers so that they choose your brand when they reach the point of decision – the shop, for instance.
- *Sales promotion* is normally designed to get action at the point of sale. Often it uses the same methods as direct marketing. It can also generate lists. But rarely is there a continuing effort to build a lasting relationship with respondents by exploiting the full possibilities of a database.
- *Public relations* employs media controlled by others to create a favourable climate of opinion. It too can create a database, for instance of replies to editorials, which are usually of very good quality.
- *Packaging* protects and draws attention to the product. It can also strengthen people's belief in your product, reassure them, make offers, and collect names cheaply for the database.
- *Experiential marketing*, a fashionable new name for what used to be called events, certainly creates opportunities for building relationships, although few are doing this with it.

How disciplines differ

Certainly practitioners in all disciplines are increasingly aware of the potential of the direct relationship, but very few appreciate its full possibilities.

Who is not a direct marketer?

Of course, it is often very hard to determine the dividing line between what is advertising and what is direct marketing; or what is sales promotion and what is direct marketing. It may even be a waste of time to try too hard, though we need definitions in business if only to decide who does what.

The guiding principle, I suppose, is: whatever you call it, is it a good idea? For example, Hewlett-Packard in Germany sent out a mailing to very senior executives. The theme was 'quotations'. There were quotations included from Goethe, Churchill, Einstein and the like – as well as from the founders of Hewlett-Packard. There was not much about products, but quite a lot about business culture. Recipients were asked to submit their favourite quotes.

Direct public relations

It was direct marketing, but also public relations; you could even call it a 'promotion'. It certainly worked: the chairman of Mercedes Benz was interested enough to send in his favourite quote. Would he have read a Hewlett-Packard ad with as much interest?

Just about every company engages in direct marketing of one sort or another. There can be hardly anyone who at some time or another doesn't make a phone call or send out a letter with the hope of making a sale. Many individual initiatives employ a direct approach. A typical example is the sales-person making telephone calls to find good prospects. If you have ever tried to control sales staff, as I have, you know this is best done in an organised way. This means you should start looking at it in an organised fashion. Looking at it as marketing – direct marketing.

The same applies in other cases. If you have a restaurant and you make the wise decision to collect the names of your customers in order to write to them with news of special gourmet evenings or you are a manufacturer of earth-moving equipment and you decide to send out a regular newsletter, then you have entered the direct marketing business whether you know it or not.

Some businesses are entirely based upon direct marketing – *Reader's Digest*, Time-Life Books, Dell Computers, Amazon and the mail order catalogue companies are specific examples. Other businesses largely depend upon direct marketing. And yet others, I believe, ought to be practising it a great deal better than they do. Let's take some obvious examples.

Credit and charge card companies

When you think about it, almost every transaction, starting with the way in which these cards are applied for, is effectively direct marketing. Take American Express. Almost every single cardmember is recruited through direct marketing. Either the prospect picks up a take-one – a little leaflet in a restaurant or retail store – and sends it in to apply, responds to a direct mail shot or advertisement, or uses the telephone to apply after watching a TV commercial.

Everything done directly

The transaction is consummated through the mail, and the relationship between cardmember and company is then conducted largely through the mail or on the telephone. Cardmembers are made offers and accept them through the means of direct mail shots and regular communications within their monthly statements. They are then persuaded to renew their membership or to switch from 'Green Card' membership to 'Gold Card' membership, perhaps to 'Platinum Card' membership, and may be persuaded to have a credit card too. All by means of direct marketing.

Short-sighted bosses

Indeed, the only time when a cardmember is likely to transact any business with American Express in any other way than via direct marketing is when perhaps booking travel or getting travellers cheques, cash or advice from a travel office. Yet even today the top brass in such organisations are usually far more interested in the latest television commercials than in the direct marketing which brings in their business and maintains it.

Banks

No personal contact wanted

A second example from the financial area. Many banks are only now realising what a valuable role direct marketing could play for them. Research repeatedly shows that most customers of UK banks have no *personal* contact with anybody at their bank (let alone their manager), nor do they wish to. The entire relationship is conducted largely through the post and cash machines.

But how many banks, I wonder, appreciate the degree to which they could benefit from direct marketing? Of course they're all *doing* it; but how well, with what conviction, and how much intellectual and financial resource are they putting behind it? Significantly, one UK bank – then the Midland, now known as HSBC – has prospered by creating one arm, First Direct, which only dealt direct and has no branches. Others have copied this. Even more significantly, customers, once they have tried this 24-hour service, prefer it by far to alternatives.

Hardly surprising. Who looks forward to visiting a bank? Or meeting a manager? Let alone asking for an overdraft.

Insurance, investment and home loans

Complex deals simplified

Almost any financial business will find direct marketing of value. A principal reason is, perhaps, that customers feel more at ease with printed material (which they can read and reread at leisure) than with relatively complex (and sometimes worrying) propositions put to them face-to-face. Far too few senior managers are sufficiently aware of the potential direct marketing offers, though all know it is important to them.

Direct Line Insurance, a subsidiary of the Royal Bank of Scotland, provided three-quarters of that bank's profits in 1992 – and their Chief Executive earned over £6 million, making him the best paid man in Britain during that year of dreadful recession. In 1993 he did even better. Eventually he was making so much it became embarrassing, and they paid him off. He then set up a series of other similar firms.

Other industries which have always depended for their success to a large extent on direct communications do not, I think, always appreciate they are really direct marketers.

Travel

The travel business is typical. In 1962 when I became a creative director, three of my biggest clients were in travel: two countries, Greece and Britain, and one tour operator. Here is another business which revolves to a very great degree around direct marketing, until the awful moment that the customer discovers that the phrase 'overlooking the sea' in the brochure has a degree of credibility that varies according to your eyesight.

For instance, millions of brochures are distributed each year through direct advertising; flights and holidays are sold through last-minute offers. But only a limited number of companies go on to establish and build a real relationship with the customer. And interestingly, those that are doing the best job are internet-based firms like Expedia and Priceline.

A longer view

Because people think very much in the short term, and very narrowly, about direct marketing, many consider it only in the context of making an immediate sale. But sound direct marketing requires you to take a longer view.

One of the many characteristics of this business which delights me is that although it is hailed on all sides as something new, so many of the activities conducted are not new at all. For instance, buttering up the customer.

In the United States over 25 years ago, Ford calculated that a customer's value to them if they could sell that customer their first car and every other car in their lives, would be $120,000. Accordingly, they became very interested in direct marketing and its possibilities.

A few years later the Lincoln Mercury Division of Ford started spending a significant budget on direct marketing activities. Their objective was to build a direct relationship with potential purchasers over a period of time so that they eventually chose Mercury, then could be 'traded-up' over a period to Lincoln. To achieve this, the first mailing sent to likely prospects simply incorporated a beautiful portfolio featuring pictures by well known photographers of the new Lincoln Mercury range. No request was made to buy anything. The mailing was, so to speak, a courtesy – a sort of commercial love letter.

The next stage was to inquire whether the prospect liked the pictures and would – as a courtesy in return – complete a questionnaire giving details of future requirements, likes and dislikes. This, of course, led to a series of mailings designed ultimately to make a sale.

The use of questionnaires

Quite clearly, if you ask somebody enough about their car-buying intentions you should be able to match their needs pretty precisely. Equally clearly, when you are talking about high-ticket items like this, if you know what the value of a customer is, you can afford to invest quite a lot of money in building up a relationship with them (or, as I put it, buttering them up) with the intention of making a long-term substantial gain.

Today no serious car manufacturer ignores direct marketing, although not all of them do a very good job. They spend for too much on flashy executions and not enough on personal, persuasive messages.

THE THREE GRACES OF DIRECT MARKETING

What is the purpose of direct marketing? In my view, it is quite simply: **to isolate your prospects and customers as individuals and build a continuing relationship with them – to their greater benefit and your greater profit**.

You can break this down into three parts, which I call the Three Graces of direct marketing.

What makes each customer different?

First of all, when you isolate someone as an *individual* this automatically implies that you discover what differentiates them from other individuals. What are their special characteristics? And by speaking to them as individuals, using the knowledge you acquire about them and their relationship with you, you will be able to make appeals which are far more relevant to them. You do this by placing that knowledge on a computer database.

The second Grace: you can build a *continuing* relationship with these people by offering them services and products which your knowledge of them tells you are likely to appeal at times you have learned they are likely to be most interested. And since in most businesses one of the biggest costs is recruiting the customer, the longer you can keep that customer, the better. That depends on building the relationship.

Build a continuing relationship

I'm not suggesting to you that in all direct marketing a continuing relationship is built up. But I am suggesting that in *almost* every case the possibility is there, if you take advantage of it. And clearly, long-term business based upon making and keeping a customer depends on building this relationship.

When first I entered the mail order business, as it was then known, I imagined that what one did was to run an advertisement, sell the goods, and retire after a few insertions. Ignorance was bliss. The truth is that hardly any business depends on one transaction. Direct marketing may have its own peculiarities, but the principles are much the same as those that operate in any other business. If you are a shopkeeper or a salesperson or a manufacturer it is very rare for profits to be made on one transaction unless yours is a short-term business, like selling London Bridge to tourists.

The first time you encounter the customer, you are learning about him or her. Likes, dislikes, peculiarities – working out what you can sell next: what other service you can render. It is with the subsequent sales that you make the gravy. You begin to know and understand your customer. You establish a relationship. That is good business.

So it is with direct marketing. Your best customer is not your unknown prospect in the street, milling around amongst others. He is the person you know, who knows you. You can offer precisely what he needs, and sell to him much more easily.

My first inkling of the fact that it was a continuing relationship that mattered in this business came nearly 40 years ago when I saw an advertisement in a newspaper. It said: 'Publisher seeks advertising agency to help in losing money.' This publisher knew he had to invest in acquiring names before he could make money.

Obviously if you understand this need for investment, this need to build a continuing relationship, you have an immense advantage over those who don't. What is more, by building this relationship you can study how your customers behave over a period of time: discover which offers which individuals respond to. In this way, you can establish the value of an individual to you over the 'lifetime' of that individual's relationship with your company.

For example, a few years ago one of my clients told me that each new name they recruit from a particular type of offer generates £12 worth of gross profit over the ensuing three years. Another company (one of the largest in Europe) is happy to wait for over two years before making a profit from a name they've recruited. These companies know there are no quick killings in direct marketing, only *suicides* by those who don't understand the vital principles that govern success.

The third Grace often has the most obvious allure to the virgin direct marketer. And that's the ability to *test*. To measure the response from particular individuals to particular messages at particular times in particular media. You can find out what works and what doesn't. Moreover, having done so you can conduct further tests and constantly improve the effectiveness of your activities. You can spend your money where it does the most good.

Test to see what works

It will not have escaped your notice that these Three Graces fit in perfectly with a couple of the expert views I gave earlier in this chapter. Direct marketing is a splendid way of making and keeping a customer, as prescribed by Theodore Levitt. And, properly conducted, it enables you to get quite close to the aim of marketing as proposed by Peter Drucker. If you have enough knowledge about somebody on your database, you can approach that wonderful situation where the product fits the customer and sells itself.

Those are important reasons why direct marketing is thriving. I would now like to explore others, to do with the nature of our society and with changes in technology.

HOW YOUR CUSTOMER IS CHANGING

Let us return to those customers you want to make and keep. Obviously, your success revolves around how well you respond to their needs and their desires. Professional marketers tend to look at customers in a way which dehumanises them. You've probably heard this sort of thing: 'The target market is B1/C2 housewives aged 24–45 in the South West, living in owner occupied properties, etc.'

Sometimes they enlist the aid of psychology to analyse their customers: 'The target market is inner-directed, upwardly mobile, tends to fantasize about her need for ... etc, etc.' These are all attempts to group people into different categories so that you can speak to them more effectively.

Such laudable efforts to group people are one reaction to the way your customers have changed over the last 30-odd years. When I first came into the advertising business, groupings didn't matter nearly as much. If you wanted to get people to come and try your baked beans, it was pleasingly simple. You ran a commercial on a Friday night and people trooped in obediently to the super-market and bought the product the next day. It's true, and the man who told me so was the founder of Tesco, Jack Cohen.

That's because in those days, the family sat around the television set watching *Coronation Street* as a group and they *all* liked baked beans. What has happened to the humble baked bean in tomato sauce since then is paralleled by what has happened to the family.

You can now get beans in chilli sauce, curry sauce, low-calorie sauce, with pork sausages, etc. And the people who eat those beans no longer sit together round the television set on a Friday night. They each have their own set. The power of the mass media is diminishing as people start to act more and more like individuals.

The waning power of mass media

A while ago, the chief executive of a large US advertising agency lamented the splintering of viewing patterns. In the early 1960s, if you wanted to reach the American public, you would find around 90 per cent watching prime-time TV on the big three networks at the weekend. By the mid-1990s, only around 60 per cent watched those same channels at the same prime time. And the percentage continued to fall as another network, Fox, emerged and cable channels grew in number.

Another striking indication of changing trends is this: the largest household category in the UK today is the single person household – a change due to higher divorce rates and young people setting up home on their own earlier.

Research a few years ago by the Henley Centre for Forecasting revealed that the family is more likely to be together when it goes *out* to a restaurant than when it stays *in* at home. The Henley Centre gave two reasons: first, the rise of central heating, which means the family doesn't have to stay huddled in one room in front of the fire keeping warm. Second, the increase in, and lower cost of, various gadgets and entertainment devices which people can use individually.

Take my own family. When everyone was at home, I might have read in my study; one child might have played a video game on television; a second might have been riding; a third practising the piano; while my wife might have been putting our household expenses on our home-computer database, if it were not so depressing.

In fact, there are many ways in which you can see people are much more individualistic. Simply study styles of dress. People were far more conformist 40 or 50 years ago than they are now. And the interesting thing to me is that wherever I go in the world – even extremely conservative societies in the East – there seems to be some trend towards individualism. In any case, no matter how conformist a society, I think you will agree your customers are not statistics: they are human beings. Thus, isolating them as individuals and approaching them as individuals is bound to make a lot of sense.

People conform less

You can take this in a historical context to arrive at the same conclusions. (And I must admit that here I am shamelessly plagiarising a speech by Lester Wunderman made many years ago.)

Two hundred years ago almost all relationships between manufacturers and customers were very simple. The manufacturer of the product also sold the product to the customer. The shoemaker made the shoes and sold them to you face to face – as did the tailor, or the carriage maker.

This form of selling enables the manufacturer to have a warm, personal, direct relationship with the buyer, and also to know a lot about the buyer's personal requirements. In some businesses this is still true. And in parts of the world where industrialisation has not yet penetrated, many relationships remain like this.

However, in the nineteenth century the second stage of marketing was developed. New technology made mass production possible. In 'advanced' countries such as those in Western Europe, the small manufacturer was lucky to survive. And the chain of distribution changed. Manufacturers sold via wholesalers and retailers, indirectly.

The impact of technology

Fortunately for the manufacturer, the same technology led to new printing machinery which made mass advertising possible. Millions of identical messages could be addressed by the manufacturer to the ultimate consumer. However, the personal relationship the individual merchant had with his customers was lost.

Direct marketing inaugurates the third stage of marketing. Its rise is due to many factors, but one major reason is the new ability to personalise messages to people – via the telephone, for example, and also through printed material. Now, thanks to the database which tells you all about your customers' needs, you can renew that direct personal link you began to lose 150 years ago. Now you can add the impact of *personal* selling to the power of *mass* communication. You have the best of both worlds. For instance, when you link your 'theme' advertising, which creates an appealing image, to specific direct offers on TV or through the mail, a powerful synergy is created.

Personal impact plus mass power

In research my agency conducted in 1985, it was discovered that where a direct mail shot featured a scene from a television commercial for an airline, awareness of that television commercial as long as four months later was 48 per cent higher amongst those who had received the mail shot than amongst a similar panel who had not received it.

**Orchestrate
your
messages**

Unfortunately companies tend to look at their marketing activities very much from an internal point of view. By some curious process they seem to relate it to their own organisation chart. This is below the line; this is above the line; this is sales promotion; this is public relations, and so on. But your customers don't see it that way. To them it is all news or information or offers from a particular company. This is a very powerful argument for making sure all these things are planned together: a process Ogilvy & Mather used to call 'orchestration' and others call integration. Yet despite its being so obvious, few agency groups or clients do it properly.

Integrate!

CONTROLLABILITY: AN IMPORTANT BENEFIT

In a world where it is increasingly hard to control anything, direct marketing makes a considerable appeal because when properly conducted it is very controllable, compared with less disciplined marketing activities.

First, the *content* and *timing* of your selling messages can be controlled. Second, the *costs* can be controlled, and the *results* predicted.

**Greater
control**

You may instantly respond: 'Well this is largely true of advertising, or sales promotion.' And, of course, it is – but I am referring here in particular to ways of talking to individuals and of predicting the results. Whether you have salesmen talking to prospects or clerks talking to customers, you are stuck with one problem: you can't control what they say, the order they say it in, the way they say it, or the way their personalities affect how the message is received. You're not really in control. With direct marketing, you *are* in control. Every message goes out as you want it to:

- using the style of language you think suits your company and your market;
- in the order you've determined is best calculated to sell;
- in the typeface you select, with the design you think reflects your image best;
- at the time you want it to ... when you've learned it will get the maximum response;
- even a phone call will be handled by your phone communicator just as your script sets down.

Your messages are uniform and go out in predetermined numbers to precisely targeted groups. They produce responses that can be measured. This leads to the second major benefit: that you can predict future responses and thus how much money you need to achieve a given result. This is rarely the case with some other methods of promotion.

Cut down the risk

All human enterprise involves risk. You're at risk from the minute you get up in the morning. The question is, how much risk do you find acceptable?

Some businesses, by their very nature, involve more risk than others. Either your likelihood of success is very remote or your volume of investment is unacceptably high; often both. But in almost all cases you have to commit yourself to a great deal before you are sure what the outcome is likely to be. Look at the retail business.

If you want to open a shop, no matter how small, you have to commit yourself to quite a lot in advance. Obviously you will think very carefully and compare what others are doing before you go ahead. But whatever you decide, you will have to find an appropriate site, rent the premises, fit them out and buy stock. Then, of course, you'll have to find staff. If the shop is at all large, that will involve advertising costs.

The risks of setting up a business

All this before you take a penny.

If you've chosen the wrong site, or the wrong merchandise, or given your shop an unappealing name, you could be in trouble. Or suppose you have decided to sell high-priced merchandise at a time or in an area where people are looking for bargains: you could equally fail.

You could find yourself with unsold stock on your hands, stock you know from bitter experience is hard to sell. You'll have a lease to dispose of, staff to pay off, bills to settle which the gross profits haven't covered.

Let's take another area: what if you want to enter manufacturing? Once again, profit margins are low, and investment high. Before you know where you are you will have laid out a great deal of money. You have to rent or buy your factory, buy machinery and raw materials and hire staff, just as the shopkeeper did. But you are, if anything, even less in control of your destiny than that shopkeeper. For between you and your eventual customer there may stand wholesaler, retailers, salesmen, or maybe manufacturer's agents. (A good reason for selling direct, by the way.)

Will all these intermediaries share your enthusiasm for your product? Will they communicate it to the consumer with the zeal you would have? Will they promote, advertise and sell it vigorously? Or will *you* have to?

If you have not chosen the right product you could fail; even supposing you have, if others do not share your belief in it the results could be just as bad. Except that in addition to the shopkeeper's problems you will have machinery to dispose of.

The point is simple. Few businesses offer much guarantee of success before you invest your money. The risk is high largely because you don't *control* the situation enough. But direct marketing allows you to *test* how people feel about your product and offer and price.

Most businesspeople get ulcers because the level of risk frightens them; they can't control what's happening. Being a devout coward, I like the idea of limiting risk. And when Peter Drucker observes that 'The first objective of marketing is to avoid making a loss', then I feel confirmed in my judgement.

Although I do not feel that the ability to test is necessarily *the* most important of the Three Graces I cited earlier, I believe the control and predictability testing can give your business activities must be one of the main justifications for direct marketing. This is true even if you only use it at the start of a venture to find out what's likely to work and what isn't.

Mythical versus real economies

Do not be misled by the belief that the chief reason for doing business this way is because it allows economies by cutting out intermediaries. You may cut out the intermediary very often. Your customers may therefore think they are getting better value – which they may be. You may as a result make greater profits.

But under many circumstances, you will *not* cut out the intermediary. Suppose you are an insurance firm trying to help your agents, or brokers, or sales people by putting together a direct marketing programme for them. Or you are a motor car company trying to help your dealers. Under those circumstances, you are not cutting out any intermediaries: what you *are* doing (which is just as important) is using a form of marketing which will make your representatives' jobs easier by giving information to these prospects and customers. You will also learn more about these customers' needs from the data you may acquire about them, either directly or from research.

Why direct marketing makes sense to customers

What I am saying is that this way of marketing does not necessarily mean lower costs of distribution. It can often simply mean that those costs are distributed differently. What it should always mean, in my experience, is that you can deliver a better service to your customer.

No: the real economies lie in the elimination of waste – what I call 'junk marketing'. In squandering money speaking to everybody, when you only need to speak to somebody. And this, of course, revolves around isolating the right individuals and speaking to them at the right times about the things you have learned interest them.

GIVING YOUR CUSTOMER A BETTER SERVICE

One of the world's most successful direct marketing companies in the world is Time-Life Books. Their founder, Jerome S Hardy, called his staff together at the outset of the business and said something which I think bears repeating a few times: 'We are going to give our customers a service better than they have any right to expect.'

This contrasts vividly with the way marketing functionaries of well known companies have started announcing – with the air of people who have just discovered the Holy Grail – that they are about to be responsive to their customers' needs. It's extraordinary, isn't it? Some of these organisations have become so fat that they forget what they are there for. Where did they think their money was coming from in the first place? Their customers, of course.

It's worth examining here some of the reasons why customers find direct marketing makes sense for them.

Perhaps the major one is that it suits them to receive information or to make purchases directly from the vendor. It's often both convenient and pleasant to sit in your own home and choose at leisure from a catalogue. You don't have to get in your car or on the bus and go into town, find the right store, and the right department, and sometimes hunt down an assistant to tell you what you want to know.

Many people also resent spending time listening to people talk about things that could be presented to them just as easily in writing. Direct mail in particular is very good at conveying complex information in a structured and easily digestible form – something people often seem unable to do. This is particularly true in business. Too often it is forgotten that business people are not a special breed: they are *consumers* when they are at home – and they don't grow second heads on their way to the office. Not surprisingly, we don't like salespeople at work any more than we do at home.

Making information easy to digest

I discovered when working for IBM Direct that if businesses were buying a typewriter, for instance, they were perfectly happy to buy it through the post. It was more convenient than wasting time talking to a salesman. Similarly, research conducted in 1986 revealed that the majority of prospects prefer to receive information about new office products not through advertising or salespeople (the most common means) but via direct mail. And they wish to inquire through the most convenient medium: the telephone.

When we were examining possible pension plans for our company, I had to spend endless hours listening to presentations from salespeople. It was time I could spare only with difficulty. And none of these salespeople had clearly written explanatory material which I could have read in order to make the right decision. Probably nobody could have closed the deal without a personal presentation. But a lead could have been solicited and the initial selling done through the post.

Even in advertisements, direct marketers can often do a better job than sales people. I recall a few years ago we ran an advertisement for a watch in a double page spread in a colour magazine. The ad was tightly packed with small type and many pictures. If you read through it, you ended up knowing more about that watch than any shop assistant could tell you – from the type of chip that was used to the ways you could use it to time sporting events.

Saying more than a shop assistant can

As goods proliferate and become more and more technologically complex it's almost impossible for one relatively untrained shop assistant to understand all about every item he or she sells. But a skilled copywriter, given sufficient time, can write an infinitely detailed description of a product. A photographer can make it look good – maybe even *better* than it is (which may put up the number of people who ask for their money back!).

Other reasons why buying or dealing direct seems to work for the customer include the fact that some products may not easily be available through any other distribution channel. For instance, specialised products such as rare coins, gourmet foods and wines, collectibles, specialised sporting goods like horseriding tackle, do well.

Satisfying shy customers

In other instances, people prefer to deal direct quite simply because of embarrassment. This could be because of the nature of the product, or the customer. One of our clients used to sell a beauty course through the post, and we noticed that a significant proportion of the customers appeared to be gay.

People often feel embarrassed, too, about money: a good reason why loans through the post and other financial propositions have done very well – apart from the ones mentioned earlier in this chapter. And, of course, most of us are quite simply shy and don't like to deal with pushy salespeople. I am sure you have sometimes been approached by an aggressive salesperson in a store and walked out.

One reason which induces both marketer and customer to deal directly is *price*. Customers very often think they are going to get a better deal by buying direct; merchants often think they'll be able to cut their selling expenses for the same reason. As I have already explained, this is not really true. Nevertheless, it seems to be a powerful motivator.

In my view, direct marketing is growing quite simply because it is a wonderful way of serving your customer better. It is quite clear that if you can understand that customer and their motivations better, you'll be able to do a better job. You'll be able to build a really good relationship with that customer.

Three steps to success

I have an exceedingly simple view of what business and direct marketing are all about. I believe the object of business is to locate a *prospect*, make that prospect a *customer* and then turn that customer into a *friend*. The secret of success is to treat people in a way which matches the nature of the relationship. If you look at it this way, you'll be surprised how many apparently knotty problems can be resolved.

Let me give you two examples, covering questions which I have been asked often.

How often should you communicate?

The first question is: how often should I communicate with my prospects or customers? This depends entirely upon how *friendly* you are with them. Would you communicate with a good friend, an established customer, just once a year? Or once every six months? I think not. On the other hand, would you communicate with somebody who was virtually a stranger, a prospect, every week? I think not.

I suggest that you would communicate with a friend as often as you had something interesting to say. Something you thought they might appreciate. Even if the person were a stranger, the same would apply, though they would be less interested in hearing from you; would be less likely to listen to what you had to say.

So the frequency of communication would depend upon the relationship. Which leads me to the second question people ask me: what should we say when we communicate?

What interests the customer?

Once again, the answer is: what would you say to a friend? Or to somebody who was just a bare acquaintance – a prospect, perhaps, whom you had only mailed once. The answer, of course, is you would spend your time thinking of things your friends, or your acquaintances, would like. You would spend your time thinking up appealing offers. News you thought they might find interesting. Things you thought would appeal to them as individuals, and you would try to talk to them at the right time.

In my view, if you did nothing else but devote your time to considering and answering those two questions, you would be a gloriously successful marketer. As an American millionaire once put it: 'Find out what people want and need, and give it to them – and you'll get rich.'

THE SPIRAL OF PROSPERITY

Of course, how often you communicate with someone and what you can offer has a lot to do with *money*. How much can you afford? To answer this question, you must ask another: how much is a customer worth? Or to put it another way: how much is it worth paying to recruit a new customer, and what will you gain from keeping that customer?

How much is a customer worth?

Each season you set a budget to mail, advertise or otherwise spend money to recruit a given number of new customers at a given cost. You are not merely trying to make sales, you are trying to make new customers, who will become friends – but only at a cost you can afford.

As you have seen, by testing you can produce more effective offers and messages. Thus you will either recruit the same number of customers for *less money* per name; or you can get a greater *number* of customers for the same investment; or, of course, your money could bring in a better *quality* of customer. You will be communicating regularly with these customers and, once again, testing will lead to better use of the database you have built up. You will be able to make it more profitable in three ways:

1 You will find ways to segment the database and thus exploit it more effectively. You will not communicate so often to those less likely to buy, which will save you money. You will communicate more frequently with those who are your friends, as it were.

Ways to greater profit

2 You will introduce new offers and new products likely to appeal to the individuals on your database – based on what you have learned about them – thus enabling you to communicate more frequently and make more profit.

3 You will also be testing new, more imaginative communications so as to get better responses to those offers you are making.

Figure 2.1   Spiral of prosperity

The magic number

You will see by looking at the little graphic above that all these activities begin and end with the individuals you recruit, and how much they are worth to you.

If you do all the things I have mentioned above, the answer to the question I posed earlier – how much is a customer worth? – will change. Customers will become more valuable to you the more carefully you consider them and cater to their needs. You will then be able to afford more money to isolate a new prospect and turn them into a customer. So, ideally, you would spend more money each year on acquiring new customers, conducting new tests, developing new offers, and so on.

Of course, the world of business is far from ideal. But only by following this logical sequence are you likely to be able to compete effectively with others. It will probably have already occurred to you that if you do so, and your competitor does not, *you* will be able to afford to put more money against customer recruitment than they will. You will ultimately succeed; they will ultimately fail. You will have a true competitive edge.

A greater competitive edge

The figure you allocate to recruiting a particular customer has been called 'the magic number'. Clearly, it is a number that can change as your marketing improves. And the different types of customer that you wish to recruit could have different magic numbers assigned to them.

So few businesses have *any* idea how much a customer is worth that this may appear to be getting overly sophisticated, but you might be surprised to see to what degree the value of a customer can vary, depending upon where that customer came from. Indeed, from a simple example you can see that unless you carefully keep track of the performance of somebody from the moment they enter into your net, you could make some serious mistakes. All prospects are by no means created equal.

Here is a series of three sets of results produced by advertisements run in America for somebody who was selling shoes direct to the public.

Table 2.1 An account of the enquiries received

Publication	Unit	Cost $	Enquiries	CPI $	Enquiry Rank
Nat Enquirer	3 × 8	2,320	3,803	0.61	1
New Woman	Page	1,495	1,241	1.20	4
Woman's Day	1/3P	5,844	8,283	0.71	2
Redbook	Page & Card	21,068	28,191	0.75	3
McCalls	1/3P	5,781	2,622	2.20	5

After six months, the marketer was able to review the original enquiries to see who had become customers. Publications performed differently.

Table 2.2 How enquiries are converted into orders

Publication	Enquiry Rank	Fulfilled Enquiries	Fulfilment Cost	Cus-tomers	% Conversion	Conversion Rank
Nat Enquirer	1	3,172	1,691	362	11.4	4
New Woman	4	1,067	547	157	14.7	1
Woman's Day	2	6,968	3,637	881	12.6	2
Redbook	3	24,538	11,953	1,446	5.9	5
McCalls	5	2,265	1,149	226	11.7	3

Finally, the marketer made the most important analysis of all, looking at how much sales revenue had been generated compared with the cost of advertising and fulfilment. This 'Efficiency Rank' is the best yardstick of all.

Table 2.3 'The full picture'

Publication	Enquiry Rank	Con-version Rank	Average Order $	Total Sales $	Total Cost %	Cost To Revenue	Efficiency Rank
Nat Enquirer	1	4	53	19,025	5,406	28.4	1
New Woman	4	1	65	10,220	2,939	28.8	2
Woman's Day	2	2	51	44,624	12,987	29.1	3
Redbook	3	5	45	65,425	45,661	69.8	4
McCalls	5	3	51	13,633	10,429	76.5	5

Measure at every stage

As you can see in the first set of figures it appears that the publications used performed in a certain order. This set of figures simply takes account of the enquiries received.

The second set of figures takes into account how those enquiries converted into orders. And the third set of figures revealed how a year later simply going on the initial results would have been extremely misleading for this advertiser.

You may say that this is obvious, which it is once somebody has shown it to you. Nevertheless, one marketer who operates in most civilised countries around the world and is widely seen as extremely sophisticated, was, until relatively recently, unable to track the performance of customers based upon where those customers had originated in *any* market; and at the time I write is still unable to do so in most markets.

The importance of tracking the performance of an enquiry was brought home to me in a way I will never forget in the mid-1970s when I elected to place virtually all the advertising money I had for a company I controlled in a particular medium which appeared, on the basis of enquiries, to be doing twice as well as any other. This was, to say the least, an unwise decision: the conversion rate was abysmal, the publication made me no money whatsoever, and eventually I had to close down what appeared to be a very promising business.

Where it fits in

Within companies people are so busy doing things the way they have always been done, or responding to head office, or engaging in the enjoyable minutiae of intramural squabbling, that – as I have already noted – they don't spend much time considering what they are in business for, or what their business is. Yet their customers seem to be very well aware of what's going on – because they're at the receiving end.

You only have to ask an audience about direct marketing, and many will immediately comment on the inserts in their monthly credit card statements. Or they will complain about the mountains of irrelevant tripe that come through their letterboxes or those maddening late night phone calls. So it may be that your customers are more aware than you are of what your business is all about. Certainly, they react in very different ways depending on the degree of care with which these messages have been prepared and targeted.

The closest thing yet to perfect marketing

I believe you are more likely to use direct marketing well by understanding its role and purpose, on which I have expressed a view in this chapter. It is in some ways, I believe, the closest thing yet to perfect marketing if the description of the aim of marketing given by Drucker is a sound one. It is also an excellent way of adhering to Levitt's description that we should make and keep customers. Finally it quite simply makes good economic sense and helps you spend your money effectively and measure the results properly.

So now that we have established what direct marketing is, why it is growing, where it fits into marketing and other related activities like advertising, let us consider more carefully where it fits into your business.

Points to remember

- Know your business aim.
- Know what marketing is.
- Think about long-term customers, not short-term profits.
- It's not a medium, method or channel of distribution but a way of marketing.
- Three stages:
  - Isolate individuals.
  - Build relationships.
  - Test to make more profit.
- Mass media waning.
- More individualism.
- Technology creates new possibilities.
- Integration essential.
- Greater control possible.
- Less risk.
- Not always a cheaper way of doing business.
- Help customers choose better by:
  - Clarifying the complex.
  - Telling more.
  - Helping the shy.
- Communicate in a way that matches the relationship.
- Establish the value of a customer.
- To increase that value follow the spiral of prosperity.
- Cheapest enquiries may not be cheapest sales.
- Cheapest sales may not be best customers.

3

Direct Marketing Can Do More Than You Think

'A wise man makes more opportunities than he finds.'

Francis Bacon

In the first chapter I told you how infallible I thought myself 40 years ago when I had my first job as a creative director. Here is another story about my unparalleled sagacity as a young man.

A humbling lesson

One day, an American came into our agency to ask us to place advertisements for what at that time seemed an unusual – indeed unique – mail order product. He wanted to sell plots of land on a more or less deserted Caribbean island called Montserrat. The advertisement he had prepared consisted almost entirely of copy, the only illustration being a small, crude drawing of some palm trees. The copy was densely set in small type.

The proposition was that people should send through the post a substantial down payment in order to secure one of these plots, which he described (rather horribly, I thought) as 'Beachettes'.

He told us that the product had previously sold very well in America. I was called in as the bright young creative director and agency expert on mail order to give my view as to whether his advertisement would work. Americans, in their naïvety, might well be persuaded to fall for his approach but I was certain that the British, with their greater sophistication, would not. Particularly because the advertisement in question was being placed in that upper-class newspaper, *The Times*.

However, our new client was adamant. He was sure the ad would succeed. Since he was willing to put up the money in advance, we were quite happy to help him place it. In fact we even allowed him to use our own agency's address for the replies. This was hardly going to strain our resources, since I was certain there would be few. My education took yet another leap forward when the advertisement proved wildly successful.

WHAT CAN YOU SELL?

Apart from being unwarrantedly cocksure in my youth, I have always been very forgetful. For in the years since that early lesson from my American client, when asked what you could *not* sell through direct marketing I nevertheless always used to reply confidently that you couldn't sell very expensive products; nor could you sell very cheap products like, for instance, baked beans or Coca-Cola.

Baked beans and Bentleys

My reasoning was simple. With an expensive product, where people were being asked to send a large sum of money to someone they had never met, words and pictures could not possibly be persuasive enough to convince respondents that they ought to take the chance. Cheap products did not have enough margin in them to justify the overheads involved in selling direct. (For many years it was universally agreed by mail order experts that you had to have 200 per cent gross profit margin to be able to sell direct – and preferably much more.)

No doubt many people went away impressed by my expert opinion, always delivered with great conviction. I owe them all an apology. For, as the story I have just recounted indicates, right at the beginning of my career I had discovered you *could* use direct marketing to sell very expensive products. I had just forgotten about it – maybe because it didn't fit in with my theory. Rather more recently I have learned that even cheap packaged goods can also benefit from direct marketing.

In 1986 one of our clients – Comp-U-Card – sent out a mailing in conjunction with the Automobile Association offering discounts on motorcars. Two of the respondents purchased £87,000 Bentley Mulsanne Turbos. In the same year, Ogilvy & Mather Direct was able to help Pepsi Cola increase distribution and sales, largely by using mailings.

These two successes were due to factors I had not considered. First, we persuaded people to buy Bentley Mulsanne Turbos through the post because they believed they would get what they were going to pay for. They were confident of the quality of the Bentley motorcar; they were also sure that the world's oldest motoring organisation would never offer something it could not deliver.

This demonstrates something general advertisers have known for many years, which direct marketers have not always appreciated: the importance of the brand name.

The importance of the brand

Of course, in this particular mailing some basic direct marketing tenets were adhered to carefully. The mailing was a very full one; there were many convincing testimonials; every question the possible purchaser might ask, we tried to answer in advance. It was a fine example of the combination of a powerful brand with effective direct marketing – a combination which is, in my view, likely to become more and more important in the future.

An intelligent contact strategy

In the case of Pepsi Cola, once again, the brand was an important characteristic. Also critical was an intelligent contact strategy. The trade in the small Italian town involved were mailed twice to stock up, since Pepsi was about to embark upon a major consumer drive. They were offered incentives, including the chance to win a competition offering a video camera. Posters were used to alert the population to the offer, which was of a one-and-a-half-litre bottle of Pepsi, free. And consumers were mailed individually with the offer. The penetration of Pepsi within that particular market surged ahead dramatically. Since that time many packaged goods marketers have tried direct marketing; elsewhere in this book you will see examples of this.

But these and other cases have shown that in laying down the law about what could and could not be sold through direct marketing, I was consigning myself to the long list of experts who have proved themselves wrong over the years. The truth is that there are very few situations in which direct marketing cannot help you. As I have already suggested, you must first understand what it is. Second, you must understand how and where it can play a role in your business. And third, you must be equipped to recognise the right opportunities and problems as they come up.

THE ROLE OF DIRECT MARKETING

An American wag once observed that the world is divided into two types of people: those who believe the world is divided into two types of people and those who don't.

I confidently predict that you, dear reader, are one of two types. Either your company sells entirely by direct marketing: it's a 'pure' direct marketing company; or you have other means of distribution and selling, and view direct marketing as just another way of improving your business.

Having made this prediction, I now realise I may be one of those who do *not* believe the world is divided into two types of people, because I have already ignored something else you could be: not a marketer, but somebody who *advises* marketers – a consultant, or agent. Even in that case, you will undoubtedly find that in addition to whatever direct marketing can do for your clients, it can probably do a great deal for your own business.

How important is direct marketing to you?

Whatever your situation, my first piece of advice is that you carefully consider the two categories I mentioned originally. Are you (or your client) really a direct marketing company or are you not? What *should* you be? Have you looked carefully enough at the kind of company you are? How important is direct marketing to you? How much direct marketing are you already conducting? You can then determine what potential you have to improve your present activities and how much importance you should attach to direct marketing itself within your business, quite apart from being able to find new areas in which it might work for you.

In short, I think you *must* establish where direct marketing does or should fit into your business. For this reason I have prepared the following list of seven points. I believe you will find it well worthwhile thinking about these when either reviewing the potential of direct marketing, or looking at the way you are using it now. Even if yours *is* a 'pure' direct marketing company you should find most of these points relevant.

1 What is your overall business objective?

Where and how can direct marketing contribute to its achievement?

Let's say you've just entered a market in which there are several well established companies doing well. Your immediate objective is not to make money, but to build volume – to recruit as many new customers as possible at an acceptable cost – rather than to make a profit quickly.

What kind of firm are you?

If this is the case, your direct marketing activities probably ought to be skewed towards generating new customers (and being quite prepared to lose money in recruiting those new customers) rather than towards profiting as much as possible from the customers you've already got.

On the other hand, suppose you are a leading company in a mature market with very little room for growth. Under those circumstances you might decide your endeavours should rather be directed at your existing customers, profiting from them as much as possible by making frequent, attractive offers which will also help to make them stay with you longer and keep the competition out. (Incidentally, one of the major sins I often see is that of concentrating too much on recruiting new customers often at very high cost when more profit is likely to come from the existing customer base.)

For that matter, your business objective could be that you wish to go public in the next three years. If this is so, you may be wondering whether direct marketing could help you influence people in the City. Or you may feel that your business should be concentrating on quality control, in which case you would be very wise to consider a direct marketing programme aimed at your own employees to motivate them further.

The point is that until you consider the context in which you use – or are planning to use – direct marketing, you cannot deploy it properly.

2 What is your positioning?

How do your customers see you? How do your competitors see you? Who do you think you are competing with?

I am going to talk more about positioning, but it's very important to understand at the outset that the way you are perceived and your position in your market will determine much of your direct marketing. For instance, the

The value of brand awareness

tone of voice you use when communicating with people, the frequency with which you communicate with them, and the types of offer you make to them. Indeed, everything – right down to the emphasis you place on your brand name in your communications.

While I was preparing this chapter, I came across two contrasting statements. One was from the marketing executive of a direct marketing insurance company called Lloyd's Life – an excellent name for anyone in a financial business. He revealed that despite repeated testing, he had never found his brand name did anything whatsoever to increase sales. This surprised me, until I looked up some research into the insurance field. Apparently consumers feel (perhaps rightly) that all insurance companies are much the same. There is very low brand awareness in this field.

On the same day, Bob Scott, founder of the Scotcade company (which introduced mail order to the more sophisticated classes in the UK in the 1970s by paying great attention to the look and tone of its advertisements) gave an opposite view. He believed heavy use of his brand name had increased his response rates by around 30 per cent. The respectability he had tried to imbue his company with, in a market where most of his competitors had rather tatty images, had obviously paid off.

An interesting point arises: if you were the insurance executive, would you not be wondering whether your communications could help give your company a good brand image in a market where nobody else has one? Would this not give you a tremendous advantage?

One UK company, Direct Line Insurance, obviously thought so. They tried very hard to build their brand in their ads and became the largest in their field in under ten years. Since then others – Churchill and Admiral in the UK and Geico in the United States – have done the same.

Apart from what you do in your advertising, what else would be possible?

Well, for a start, you could improve what you offer. Perhaps you could offer your customers a series of helpful services. If you're selling life insurance, for instance, booklets on health. If you're selling car insurance, booklets on getting more out of your motoring, and so on. Like most of the things I say in this book, these are not startlingly original ideas – unless you compare them with what is being done at the moment.

The importance of value for money

Incidentally, adding *value* is among the smartest things you can do as a marketer. A series of research studies revelling in the acronym PIMS – Profit Impact of Marketing Strategies – has revealed how important this is. Three thousand companies in Europe and the United States take part in this programme which is designed to find out what effect marketing strategies have on profits.

One dramatic finding is that those companies perceived by customers as giving more value for money tend to be infinitely more profitable. In fact, within the study, the top 20 per cent of companies judged on this basis are on average almost exactly twice as profitable as the bottom 20 per cent.

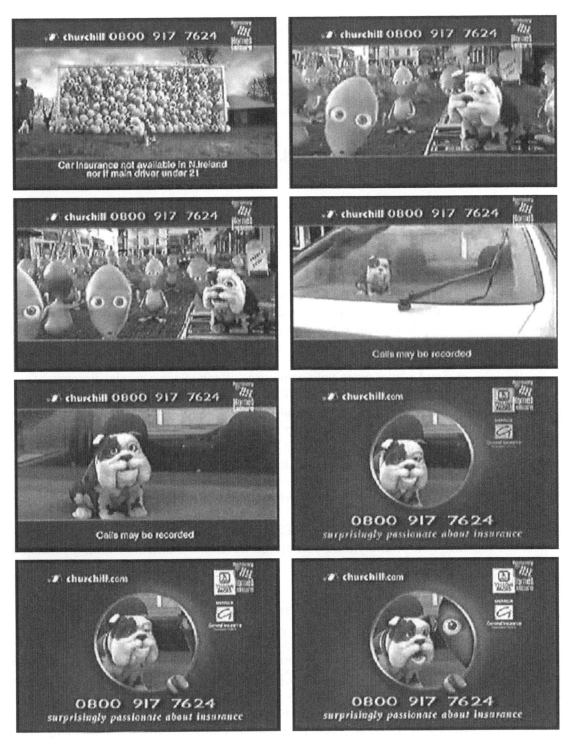

Figure 3.1 This commercial – which uses personalisation and humour extremely well – builds the brand and gets a response. I have never, for the life of me, understood why more firms don't try to. Maybe they think the two are incompatible. I can't see why.

What is one of the easiest ways to add value? Quite simply it is to *communicate*.

Communi-cation itself adds value

Communication under many circumstances is itself added value. You only have to recall waiting at an airport wondering when your flight is going to leave, without any information from the airline, to know that communication can add great value; it can sometimes be the only thing that matters.

3 What current marketing activities do you conduct?

How can direct marketing assist, complement or even replace what you already do?

Review your current business

Direct marketing is highly opportunistic – later on I will list many occasions where you can see opportunities and profit from them. But just because it is opportunistic, do not fall into the trap of simply taking advantage of opportunities as they arise. You need a plan. You need priorities. That means you must review what you are doing already.

For instance, here are three widely different opportunities you could take advantage of:

- Send a letter out to your employees offering them a special discount.
- Write to recent customers offering them the opportunity to enter a sweepstake simply by sending for a catalogue (in the knowledge that most of them will think they are more likely to win if they buy something than not, and that in any case they may be enticed by some offer you are making in the catalogue).
- If you are a manufacturer, develop a telephone and direct mail programme to introduce your products to new retail outlets, thus freeing your sales force to develop closer contacts with your existing valuable retail customers.

Each of these ideas has merit. But unless you have looked at these proposals in the light of everything you are doing on the marketing front, you cannot evaluate them properly.

4 What should be the relationship between direct marketing and your other promotional activities?

Every message matters

As I've already pointed out, you cannot look at the effect of direct marketing in isolation. Your customers don't. *Every* communication from you adds to the picture they have of you. Every message you send out, through whatever discipline or medium, contributes to their perception of your brand or company, right down to the way your people answer the phone. Moreover, in many cases they may offer new channels of direct marketing opportunity.

If you sell packaged goods then what you do on the pack can be of prodigious importance. For a start, it can build lists of names. In many markets, one neglected area is the use of on-pack material. Mattel runs a club for little girls, called the Barbie Friends Club in the UK. The cheapest source of names comes from the membership offer made on the pack. On another occasion my agency was able to build up a very useful database for a client by giving away leaflets at motor racing events.

You must consider the relationship between direct marketing and other channels of sales and distribution. For instance, should you list retail outlets, if you have them, on your mailings which sell direct? One client of mine found this was a very bad idea. People may have intended to go into the shops *or* reply directly – in the event many did neither.

If you've a sales force, unquestionably they may feel threatened by your direct marketing activities. As a consequence, many companies have given up any idea of direct marketing. The solution is to sell the concept of direct marketing to the sales force before you set out on a campaign.

In short, your concern to make sure all your activities work well together means you should review the possibilities of everything you already do and how direct marketing will affect what is already happening.

Direct marketing and other channels

5 What is the state of your database?

Your database is the storehouse of knowledge you have about one of your most valuable assets: your customers.

Who controls it: administration or marketing? How do you see its role?

It is essential that it be controlled and run by people who clearly understand the long-term objectives of the business. In the past, company databases have been set up and run by administrators or finance people, for invoicing, paying wages and so forth.

When direct marketers attempted to move in, conflict often resulted. Those controlling the database were concerned to protect their territory. More to the point, having administrative backgrounds, they tended very often to have little sympathy with the marketer. Many direct marketers have roundly condemned the computer processing specialists and administrators as people of little imagination and no awareness of the real objectives of the business. They have dismissed them as bean counters.

Who should control the database?

This actually shows a lack of imagination amongst direct marketers. Some of the brightest people I have encountered in marketing have come up via computers or finance. Here again – just as with the sales force, mentioned in my last point – the answer is *education*.

If you are in the early stages of direct marketing in your company and are encountering problems, the first thing you have to do is create a direct marketing programme to your own people. It will not reap instant rewards, but it will be a fine long-term investment. In particular, explaining to corporate people how vital their role can be in marketing is time very well spent. This leads on to my next point.

Direct marketing to your own people

6 Have you sold the concept of direct marketing within your organisation?

Is top management committed to it? If not, why not? If so, why?

When I first became involved with Ogilvy & Mather Direct, the relationship between the Ogilvy & Mather advertising agency in the UK and the direct agency was poor. The advertising people saw the direct folk as a bunch of amateurs. (I must admit, I had great sympathy with this view.) The direct people saw the generalists as people with an inflated sense of their own importance, being paid far too much money and lacking any understanding of what direct was trying to achieve. This, too, had truth in it.

My solution was to write to senior members of the general agency and ask them to attend a presentation to explain what we were doing. Most of them did, and this was the start of a fruitful relationship. The relationship can never be perfect but it became infinitely more cordial, though I fear there will always remain those unreconstructable individuals on both sides of the divide who are deaf to blandishments of any kind.

'Champions' are essential

Direct marketing, to be successfully introduced in your business, needs *champions*. Champions with power. In this respect, nothing has changed since Columbus wandered round Europe trying to find somebody to sponsor him to go and discover the riches of the Indies. He had to find his Queen Isabella. So do you if you are trying to develop a direct marketing programme in an organisation. The people at the top – or at least one person of importance at the top – must believe in what you are trying to do. Otherwise endless frustration will result.

My agency experienced this when developing proposals for a large bank. One senior manager of that institution was behind us 100 per cent. We prepared a very long report which analysed in great depth how, where and why direct marketing should be used. Just after we delivered the report this executive was promoted to glory elsewhere. The report was never properly presented to his senior colleagues. We might just as well have saved our breath. No attention was paid to what we had said; a good relationship was never built up; a great opportunity was lost.

7 Where exactly should direct marketing fit into your organisation?

To whom should it report?

The role of direct marketing

People frequently see direct marketing (and most other things, to be honest) in a tactical way. They will perhaps feel that it should report as a function to whichever part of the organisation is likely to use it most. Thus in a large organisation selling to consumers, the direct marketing function may well be required to report to whoever is in charge of consumer marketing.

Yet, as we have seen, direct marketing can play a very important role when dealing with employees, shareholders, the trade, opinion formers – just about anyone.

I do not necessarily know what the right answer to this question is; it will depend upon your organisation. One thing is certain: it should be a question which must be asked and answered – carefully.

You will notice that throughout this book I do not claim to have the answers to every problem you might have to confront. But I do believe you will do better long term by starting with the right questions. The seven points I have just covered will, I hope, start you thinking about the role of direct marketing within your organisation.

Now let us look at objectives. What are direct marketers normally trying to achieve?

FIVE MAJOR OBJECTIVES OF DIRECT MARKETERS ...

Although we've looked at many ways in which direct marketing can be applied, you can break down all the activities I know of into five simple categories. You can ask people to:

Actions, not just feelings

1 Buy through the post, over the phone, or off the TV set, either for cash or by quoting a credit card or account number. Here I include charity donations.
2 Ask for catalogues, or literature, or information which may come through the post, on the telephone or in the hands of salesmen (with or without the consumer's prior knowledge).
3 Request a demonstration either in the home, at work, or even at the seller's premises.
4 Visit a retail establishment, a film show or exhibition – or even a political or community event.
5 Take part in some action like joining a protest demonstration, or writing to an MP or some foreign power.

Notice that in all cases we are asking people to *do* something. Direct marketing is asking for action, whereas advertising is usually trying to influence thoughts and feelings. A critical distinction.

To reach your chosen objective, you can choose from a variety of routes. The possibilities and permutations are bewildering, but it is essential that you are aware of them all. A sale you could never make profitably in one step, for example, could be easily made if the product is broken down and sold in stages as a continuity product, or if the sale is made by asking for an enquiry and then following up repeatedly. Equally, a product you could not sell easily for cash might do very well if you offered it on free trial.

So let's look through the possibilities.

... AND FOUR WAYS TO ACHIEVE THEM

1 One-stage selling

When people use the words 'mail order' they usually think either of the bargain spaces in the weekend papers, glossy colour advertisements in the Sunday magazines, or those hard-sell advertisements that promise to change your life – or shape, or looks – overnight.

This kind of selling does not, in fact, represent the largest segment of the direct marketing industry. Indeed, as you've already gathered (if you didn't already know) any company that depends on this activity *alone* to make money is unlikely to prosper long. But the one-stage sell is a way you can establish the *initial* relationship with a customer (or, in the case of a political party or charity, a sympathiser).

The simplest form of direct marketing

Some one-stage selling – the least sophisticated form of direct marketing – is as simple as offering a product for sale in exchange for the full cash price, to be sent in advance of the goods being delivered. However, as you can appreciate, any way in which you can soften or delay the awful moment when the customer has to part with money tends to pay off. Nobody likes paying for anything; even less do they like sending money off to someone they have never met for something they have never actually experienced or held in their hands.

Thus one may offer:

- The Free Trial, where goods or services may be enjoyed on approval for a period before the buyer is committed.

  Response leaps when you use this offer. You must, however, have a very efficient credit-checking system since in the UK, for example, in some cases as many as 50 per cent of replies can be bad debt risks.

Possible ways to sell

- The Sale on Credit where only a down-payment is demanded.

  This is a method worth using if you have the necessary facilities. However, with the growth of charge and credit card usage it is becoming increasingly restricted to less wealthy markets.

  As I have already indicated, for years it was widely imagined that no item above £10 could be sold *without* offering credit: my client selling land was a rare exception. However, the growing acceptance of direct marketing and the decline in the value of money means that this is no longer the case.

  A high percentage – over 50 per cent of the revenue from an ad in an up-market medium like the *The Sunday Times* – may be through credit card payments.

- The Sale on Credit where no down-payment is demanded.

  This is, of course, the easiest payment option of all for the customer and thus the method which will generate your greatest response.

Once again, if you have the credit-checking facilities and the financial resources to be able to afford to wait for your money, this can be the most profitable method of selling in the long run.

Significantly, many of the most successful direct marketers often use this method; eg *Reader's Digest* and the mail order catalogues.

● The conditional free trial where you may have to send all or part of the money before getting the goods, but you are not committed to buy until a certain period has elapsed.

This method was used by Joe Karbo to sell his book *The Lazy Man's Way to Get Rich*. He said he would not cash customers' cheques for 30 days, so they could be absolutely sure they were satisfied before being committed.

There is, in addition, of course:

● The sale by credit or charge card where any of the above four options may also be offered.

This is the easiest sale of all, because it's the *least* painful way for your customer to pay.

2 The continuity relationship

Since the best direct marketing builds a continuing relationship between the buyer and the seller, many marketers establish a contract with the respondent which has a continuing arrangement built in from the start. Typical are:

Longer-term relationships

● Insurance offers, where the initial application may lead to a ten or even twenty year contract.
● Loan offers, where people may be repaying for five years or longer.
● Mortgage offers, which also end up in a relationship over a number of years.
● Charity appeals or political appeals, where the group may solicit a covenant (and in the case of many charities, this relationship may last so long that the final payment will be after death, in a bequest).
● Credit card applications, where the relationship may endure for decades.
● Membership offers – such as those made by the Consumers' Association, or the Automobile Association – which may endure until death brings a merciful release.
● Club offers, where the respondent may be offered a very low price for a selection of books or records or even a free gift to start a collection of cookery cards, for example, and have to make a positive effort to extricate himself from the relationship.
● Collector's offers, where one starts with the first of a series of collectible items, and carries on through to the end, unless one wishes to cease.

Of course, exactly the same sort of financial offers you make to encourage a one-stage sale apply to a continuity sale. Thus, insurance companies selling

**Free trial
periods**

direct often offer what they call in their quaint argot 'a deviated first premium'. For instance, the first month's premium may be free, or call for a payment of only £1. This, obviously, is a soft option for the prospect.

Equally, you can offer your prospect a free trial period of three months. Offering customers the opportunity to fill in a post-dated direct debit form in the advertisement or the order form will generally pay off. By the time it comes to cancel the mandate, the customer doesn't bother. This is really a sophisticated variation of the technique I mentioned previously, used by Joe Karbo. It is really a free trial offer with a hidden pitfall. I introduced this (for the first time in the UK, I think) in 1969 for the Business Ideas Letter.

From your point of view a continuity relationship gives you a much greater margin with which to finance the original sale. Obviously, if you are making a single sale, then the margin to pay for the promotion has to be built into that one item. But when you know that over a period of time you may sell as many as 40 or 50 items, or receive payments over a period of years, you can afford to finance the initial sale to a greater degree – or, to put it another way, you can wait for quite a while to recoup the value of that investment. To give one relevant example, I recall that a few years ago, a major marketer of book series did not recover their investment in recruiting a customer until 48 months after the first transaction.

3 Multi-stage selling

Flexibility of a different sort governs the third category we are going to consider: multi-stage selling. When you make a one-stage sale, then once the prospect has either responded or not responded, that's it. Either you've made money, or you've lost your chance to make money until the next time that reader sees your ad or mailing.

If you are merely going for an *inquiry*, then once that prospect has responded and you have his or her name on your database, you have an infinite number of opportunities to turn that inquiry into a sale. In fact, even if you don't sell the product or service you originally offered, you can try and sell an alternative.

**A flexible
selling
method**

Moreover, a one-stage sale predetermines the way in which the respondent buys: either they react in the way you suggest at the price you quoted or they don't. But multi-stage selling is much more flexible – and in one form or another is the area with the greatest potential for most businesses.

Suppose you generated an inquiry and followed it up with a letter and brochure. If those don't produce a sale, there's nothing to stop you following up with a phone call or a salesman. For that matter, if you followed up the inquiry with a salesman who did not succeed, there is no reason to believe that a letter later on may not achieve the desired effect. It's worth remembering that to get that sale you can vary terms, reduce the price, or make a free trial offer and further follow-ups. Indeed, you can keep contacting that prospect for as long as it is economically worthwhile for you.

Financially, the implications are simple. Once you have paid your entrance fee – ie paid for the inquiry – you can keep on 'milking' it until the cost of doing so exceeds the marginal profits. To take a simple example: when I was handling the marketing for the Bullworker, we used to send out up to *nine* follow-up mailings.

And like so many other simple examples in the consumer market this principle applies to the business-to-business market. If you are trying to sell an expensive piece of office equipment with a great deal of margin built in, once you have that original inquiry put onto your database, you can keep on exploiting it many times, in many different ways. The diagram entitled 'The Mill', shown on page 51, shows you how this process can take place.

Let us therefore look at some simple multi-stage operations:

Multi-stage variations

- Sales follow-ups, where information about a product is advertised, information is sent out and a salesman follows up. Common examples in the consumer field are double glazing and other home improvements; in business-to-business, computers, copying machines or laser printers would apply.
- Retail combination, where a product may be advertised in the press (or in a catalogue sent out by the store) and the respondent may go into the store rather than buy direct.
- Catalogue offers, which may be divided into those where:
  - the prospect sends for a catalogue to buy things from;
  - the prospect sends for a catalogue for which he or she may become an agent, deriving commission (savings);
  - the prospect buys and is later offered the chance of becoming an agent.
- Agent's offers, other than the ones outlined above, where the agent will represent a given line of products and may or may not have to buy the merchandise in advance, with or without a guarantee of money back if the goods are not sold successfully.
- Recruitment, where the respondent replies to an ad, gets information and then goes for an interview (as with the armed services) or may go directly to an interview.

As in so many other areas of business, some of these categories merge into each other. For instance, Avon recruits ladies who become spare time agents. The company also has a permanent sales force which 'runs' the sales ladies in given areas.

In December 1984, Avon's business in Germany was not doing very well. How could direct marketing revitalise it?

Among the major problems were insufficient new Avon ladies; lack of motivation amongst the new recruits; and not enough time and effort from the area sales force devoted to handling and motivating these ladies. The reason was that the area salespeople were so worried about trying to find new ladies. Each year, for every 12 they hired they would lose two. The solution, quite simply, was to *motivate* the new ladies. They were written letters when they joined and welcomed to the organisation. They were congratulated on their individual achievements, all of which could be monitored through the database.

How Avon recruited new staff

But how could new ladies be recruited? The answer was to run advertisements in the form of questionnaires – I have provided an example of one of these in the plates section of this book. These were based upon what was discovered through database and research about the nature of the perfect Avon lady. Depending on the answers to the questionnaires, the respondents were handled in two different ways.

Those who did *not* fit in with the profile of a good Avon lady were simply given a free gift and thanked for their interest, together with news of what had emerged from the quiz they had replied to. Those who *did* sound like perfect Avon ladies were written to and told that they would do extremely well with the company, and that they should go to their local area representative and collect a free gift. At the same time, a computer profile of the lady was sent to the local area representative who was then able to deal more effectively with her new recruit.

This project, which was devised by Ogilvy & Mather Direct's Frankfurt office, was particularly interesting to me. It used original thinking to create and utilise a database containing details of both the potential new recruit and the existing sales representative, leading to an intelligent personalised approach. A few years ago it would have been difficult to have accomplished anything like this. Technology has made the difference.

Finally, two more multi-stage operations:

- Franchise offers, where the respondent sends for details, meets the company or its representative, and may end up going into business with them.
- Sequence selling. There are many cases where you can afford to be quite patient in getting a sale. You can afford to try and mould people's opinions about your product or service before actually going in for the kill.

The simplest form of sequence probably would be where you send out an advance mailing or make a telephone call to say you are going to make a very generous offer to someone; you then make the offer; and then you may follow up with another call or mailing to remind people to take advantage of the opportunity before it lapses.

Start by influencing opinion

In some cases you may find it worthwhile to send out a series of newsletters or regular mailings which are intended to inform, educate and persuade people of the virtues of your product or service – or, for that matter, your company.

Earlier I gave an example where Ford in America send out a long series of mailings of which the earlier ones are not looking for a sale, but

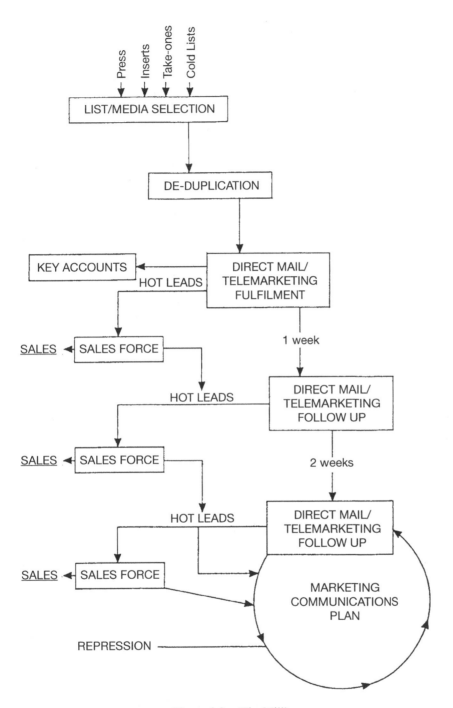

Figure 3.2 'The Mill'

My colleague Melanie Howard developed this diagram to demonstrate to Rank how leads could be managed properly. They were using sales people, but entirely the same principle would apply if you were using direct mail and the telephone.

designed to build an opinion which will lead to one. This is similar in thinking to an advertising campaign. You are building a preference over a period of time but at the same time ensuring you are ready to make a sale at the right moment. If it takes two years on average from the time when somebody buys a new car to the time when they buy another one, then you can stage a series of communications to keep them loyal to your brand, making sure that you frequently recheck when they are actually going to buy – since people's decisions are often affected by changing circumstances.

This sort of approach is also particularly appropriate for a profession like accountancy, the law or advertising. People do not wake up every morning and decide they need a new advertising agency or lawyer. You are simply trying to make sure that when they *do* have to make such a decision, they will choose in your favour.

4 Sales-promotion-linked opportunities

Many companies – perhaps most companies that are reasonably sophisticated – make offers of one kind or another which can with a little ingenuity be turned into direct marketing opportunities.

What they all have in common is that a list of names can be generated. Names can be very valuable, as I indicated when discussing the selling of Avon cosmetics. So if your company is engaged in any of the following activities, you have a direct marketing opportunity:

How to acquire names

- Competitions, where the respondent may or may not have to offer proof of purchase.
- Discounts and free offers, where a coupon may have to be redeemed at the store, or by post. These may be offered in advertisements; in the package, as with a cigarette pack; or on the back of the pack, as with sugar cartons.
- Self-liquidating offers, where a product may be offered cheaply as long as you prove you have purchased the brand.
- Direct offers of merchandise bearing the brand name, as with offers of Guinness sweaters, or Coca-Cola beachwear, or London Transport T-shirts.

In all these cases, either direct contact is involved, or it can be introduced. Thus, for instance, if you are running an advertisement which bears a redeemable coupon, then if you require that people give their name and address when redeeming that coupon you are able to capture a name and address.

My former partner, Glenmore Trenear-Harvey, worked on a number of sales promotions during his time in the advertising agency business. He often lamented, when he became a direct marketer, how it was the standard practice at that time to keep the names of promotion respondents until it was certain there would be no complaints about the offer, then throw them away. 'Like throwing money away,' he would say. 'But we never knew it.'

WHICH NAMES ARE BEST?

How can you put a value on the names you generate through the sources mentioned above?

The ideal customer

The ideal person is somebody who has bought one of your branded products through the post. This is like getting a mail order buyer's name with the additional benefit that they are favourably disposed to your brand. As we shall see when discussing mailing lists, if a person is inclined to buy direct, this is a very valuable characteristic for you.

On the other hand, somebody who is merely a competition respondent is not necessarily a mail order buyer by nature. He or she is merely someone who in exchange for an inducement will buy a particular product or brand. Whether without that inducement the purchase would be made, you don't know. This makes the quality of the name somewhat weaker when you wish to sell to them or communicate with them again.

In all the examples I have given you in this chapter, what is important is establishing a direct link between you and your prospect or customer, and the opportunity to exploit that link. How best to go about that is what our business is all about.

I hope the examples I have given you in this chapter have opened your minds somewhat to the almost limitless range of possibilities direct marketing offers. You have probably discovered though, as I have, that your mind is more often provoked by the prospect of solving some problem you face right now, or taking advantage of an opportunity you can already see. The next chapter, therefore, will deal in greater detail with particular instances where direct marketing makes good sense.

Points to remember

- Can help sell almost anything.
- Consider where it fits into your business – or could do.
- Relate to current activities.
- Look at your database – its state, its role and who controls it.
- Sell the concept to colleagues and bosses.
- Review objectives – and how direct marketing could help achieve them.
- Consider having a model to picture the entire process.

4

How to Get Started

As we've already discussed, your customers today are infinitely more demanding than they used to be. They want products and services that match their individual needs. They refuse to be categorised. They want to be in control. You have to try much harder to meet their needs.

I covered this earlier when talking about that thrilling comestible, the baked bean. But if we look at an area as different as could be – financial services – we see the same sort of thing applies.

The same principles apply everywhere

Take insurance. Where once there was just good old fashioned life insurance or life insurance with the option to invest, now special offers are made to different types of people: special terms for those who are over 50, or who don't smoke and – bizarre at first sight – death insurance, which is a policy to cover funeral expenses. Not as strange as it seems. Our English ancestors founded the old Cooperative Societies for working people to pay for funerals. And in some parts of the world today burial still represents a major expense which can cripple a family's finances.

You will certainly have noticed, also, that just as consumers are refusing to fit neatly into the categories arranged for them by marketers, those marketers are offering services which were traditionally seen as not in their province.

Once, if you wanted banking services, a bank was the place to go. On the other hand, if you wanted a mortgage, you went to a building society (or Savings & Loan in the US). If you wanted to invest in stocks and shares, you went to your broker. And if you needed insurance you went to an insurance firm or broker.

Now what has happened? Your building society provides much the same banking services as your bank – indeed, many have *become* banks. On the other hand, you can get a mortgage from your bank, or make investments through an insurance policy. And to add to the confusion, specialists have set up: some firms do nothing but offer mortgages. They have moved into the area once reserved for building societies. Some specialise by channel – on the internet, for example.

It's increasingly hard to decide what's best for you. And I haven't even considered other complications resulting from the way some financial organisations are gobbling up others. Building societies and banks have bought up chains of estate agents (and sold them again because they know less about the business than they thought). And, of course, the credit card companies will make practically any sort of financial arrangement you care to mention. They'll lend you money, help you invest, arrange insurance for you and so forth. And why not?

This makes it rather difficult for anybody trying to establish a clear position in the financial services field. Where once it may have sufficed to persuade customers you were the right bank by saying that you were 'The action bank', or 'The listening bank' – two British slogans – this is not all that persuasive when it comes to actually selling products or services. This is particularly true when you realise, as I did when looking at one British bank, that they offered over 270 different financial services of one kind or another. How on earth do you match the right service to the right customer? And how on earth do you explain the differences between all these services?

How to establish a clear position

Take a typical instance. What if you are the Birmingham Midshires Building Society, trying to persuade me to stop letting my *bank* manage my money and let *you* do it? That is going to take a great deal more than a slogan. You will have to explain to me how your new Mastercharge Account not only gives me all the benefits of a bank account, but a great deal more. That requires a long, detailed communication directed to me personally, preferably based upon what you know about me. I choose this example because this organisation did write to me personally. But they knew hardly anything about me, and consequently weren't very successful.

There is a converse side. I may see no good reason to switch my banking to a building society. But when Lloyds suggests to me that I should invest through it as opposed to a stockbroker, this makes sense to me. Stockbrokers aren't really interested in private individuals unless they have more than £100,000 to invest. And in 20 years no stockbroker ever took the trouble to find out that I was in that happy position – which, of course, brings us back to building a database.

This lengthy preamble is simply to emphasise that changes in the way we buy and sell are making direct marketing a natural choice for buyers and sellers. It doesn't just apply in the consumer field, it applies to business people with equal force.

It may have been quite easy a hundred years ago to explain to the average office manager why Watermans ink was better than Stephens ink. It was even quite easy 50 years ago to explain the difference between a Remington typewriter and an Underwood typewriter. But just you try and explain in a 30-second television commercial why an Apple computer is better than a Compaq. It's very hard, and this is one reason why such companies are turning to direct marketing, and why some of the more spectacular successes in recent years have been among companies like Dell that use nothing but direct marketing.

Make DM work for you

In this chapter, I am going to examine in greater detail how direct marketing can work for you – or do much more if you are already employing it. To do so, I shall take some typical marketing problems and opportunities. I'll be very surprised if at least one is not relevant to your own business.

DOES YOUR BUSINESS HAVE A CONTINUING RELATIONSHIP BUILT IN?

Some years ago I went to see a client to persuade them to appoint us as their direct marketing agency. I had a slight problem, which was that they were not using direct marketing and had no desire to do so. This was not surprising, because they didn't even know what direct marketing was.

However, they did have an excellent catalogue, offered to customers who came to their stores. Thinking about the possibilities this catalogue offered led to a sequence of activities which will give you some insight into the possibilities once you start thinking seriously about direct marketing.

How a retailer succeeded

- Instead of waiting for people to come to the stores so we could give them a catalogue, we started offering the catalogue in all their advertisements. The replies from the various media enabled us to discover which media were doing well for them. This confirmed what research had already suggested: their customers were better off than average. This in turn enabled us to adapt the tone of their communications and target their direct mail better.
- We ran advertisements which invited people to come in to their nearest store and take advantage of a bargain. At the store we collected their names and communicated with them later.
- Mailings to existing customers went out launching a new product. As many as 10 per cent of all customers came into a store in response to one of these mailings – and many more over time.
- By studying the kinds of areas where most customers lived around existing stores, we could target door drops surrounding prospective new stores to encourage people to come in.
- Letters went to the company's shareholders offering them special discounts on their products, thus strengthening the link between them and that important group.

- Regular letters went to employees telling them of the progress of the company, thanking them for their efforts and asking them to make greater efforts still.
- We applied our knowledge of what works in direct marketing to their recruitment advertising – the effectiveness of which determines the success of *any* business, because good people are the lifeblood of your company.
- A monthly direct mail shot went out to all the trade customers making special offers not available to the general public. A special trade card was produced to offer these customers credit and strengthen the relationship between them and the company.
- A list of people moving into new homes was acquired, and mailings went out regularly, encouraging them to come in and see the client's products.

How many of these things could you do? Obviously, with the intelligent use of the database all these various activities can be further subdivided to make them more accurate. Thus, it is wasteful to mail *all* the existing customers with every offer you make. You will find that some offers are best for people who have recently bought a certain type of product. For instance, if they've bought a kitchen from you, there is little point in mailing them with a kitchen offer. It may, however, make a lot of sense to offer them built-in bedroom furniture made from the same wood and with a similar design to the kitchen they have bought. Clearly the more you eliminate the wrong kind of customer and make the right offer to the right kind of customer, the better your results – as we discussed earlier.

Just by looking at the examples I have given of this one company, I think you'll agree that the problem is not discovering where you should apply direct marketing. It is more deciding where you should apply it *first*. Because everywhere you look, if you look thoughtfully, you will see opportunities.

SALES-FORCE HELP

Many companies immediately see they could employ direct marketing. I derived pleasure for some years by keeping track of the astronomical costs of making a sales visit. These costs go up faster than inflation, as far as I can make out. These figures used to be collected by McGraw-Hill. The last time I checked (a few years back), the figure for the United States was $230 for a visit to a senior prospect. That's a visit, let me emphasise – not a sale. If that visit was unsuccessful, you lost $230. In Europe, costs were even higher. The lowest: $128.18 in Ireland. The highest: $1,439.62 in Denmark. In England the figure was $303.82.

To put this in context, on average European salespeople complete one sale every six calls. This makes you wonder how any company in Denmark employing salespeople can *ever* make money. But it also underlines the importance of using direct marketing to make the most of that expensive asset, human beings.

I could go on – and sometimes do – about the bizarre and needlessly expensive way many firms apply their efforts. Indeed, I sometimes suspect the executives responsible can neither think nor count. It makes absolutely no sense to have salespeople going out to visit people who haven't been qualified as likely prospects. It doesn't just waste time and money; it destroys morale. Any salesperson who goes out time after time to see people who are not interested loses heart.

Many firms do something just as foolish when they use the telephone to qualify. One firm we dealt with a couple of years ago was getting between 1 and 2 per cent of their prospect list to agree to have a sales presentation (and I bet many only agreed to get someone off the phone). How would you like to sit on the phone all day being rejected that often? And how would you like to pay the bills?

Much thinking on this intelligent use of resources goes back to the observations that most of your business tends to come from very few customers, put forward as the 80/20 theory by the nineteenth-century Italian writer Pareto.

Better value from salespeople

In the United States a major drug company had the problem that their salespeople could visit all the thousands of outlets they dealt with only on a very rare basis. By segmenting the outlets, they were able to reallocate the salespeople so that they devoted most of their visits to the all-important top 10 per cent. Less profitable outlets received only occasional visits from the salespeople, but were dealt with very effectively on the telephone and through direct mail. The overwhelming majority of outlets, which were barely profitable at all, were dealt with entirely through direct mail supplemented by telephone.

In the UK my agency helped launch IBM Direct in 1981. IBM realised that some products – typewriters in particular (remember the typewriter?) – might not need personal selling at all. Their customers understood perfectly what a typewriter was, and particularly what an IBM typewriter was. They just wanted to buy them conveniently. We introduced direct mail to sell typewriters. It worked. Thus, the salespeople were free to sell more expensive products. Eventually, a complete catalogue was put together.

Pre-sell your product

Launching new products has always been very expensive. Quite a few years ago in the UK we had the challenge of helping a sales force introduce a new catering product to many thousands of outlets. We found that a simple mailing offering a free sample could get 25 per cent of the recipients to try the product. At the same time, we collected information about the outlet, numbers of meals served, what type of food sold, and so forth in order to enable the company to build a better relationship with them.

In France, the Compagnie Coloniale, who supplied top quality tea with 25 different flavours, wanted 3,000 owners of quality delicatessens and caterers to stock the product. Their problem was they only had a sales force of two. The answer was direct mail, followed up by telephone. The result? Seventy-six per cent of the prospects favourably considered the proposition on the phone. Forty-four per cent requested a salespersons's visit. All the salespeople then had to do was to go around signing people up. The proposition had been pre-sold. In the event, it cost no more to sign up a pre-sold prospect than it did originally to go in and merely visit a prospect.

SOME PERTINENT QUESTIONS

I would frankly be astonished if somewhere in your business there was not obvious direct marketing potential. You can find out where by asking the right questions.

- Do you offer after-sales service?
- Do you offer a guarantee that people have to fill in?
- Do you have a family of related products?
- Do you offer account facilities?
- Do you sell on credit, and have to invoice people regularly?
- Do you have accessories or software to sell?
- Do you have (or need) repeat purchases?

Is there already a relationship?

In all these cases you either already have a situation ideal for creating a continuing relationship, or you could easily create one. For instance, if you offer after-sales service, or have to bill people regularly, either because you sell on credit or have account customers, you have a reason to talk to them about other things they can buy. And if you haven't got a reason, it's often a good idea to create one.

I was once talking to a friend about a mail order company we were working for. I asked him how much discount they offered if, instead of paying over a period, you paid cash. 'None,' was his reply. 'They don't *want* you to pay cash. They want as many opportunities as possible to communicate via the regular invoice and sell you something more.'

The retail trade furnishes many examples of the power of the relationship with the account customer. Indeed, figures I have seen suggest that one account customer can produce more profit than *five* non-account customers.

Offering previews of sales to account customers is now very common. When it was first initiated, some years ago, I was told that Harvey Nichols, the elegant London department store, used to make more money from the one-day preview reserved for their account customers than during the entire two-week sale that followed.

How to make more money

A similar example comes from Murray Raphel, the American direct marketer who owns a retail store in Atlantic City. His five-hour sale at New Year which he promotes heavily, largely through direct mail, also produces more than the regular sale that follows.

The most extreme example I have seen of the power of a company/customer relationship was the case of a US mail order firm which sent its customers a letter apologising for the delay in shipping their order … with, on the back, an invitation to buy six more items in the meantime. It worked.

Barnardo Publications – the arm of the Barnardo's charity that sells merchandise – ran an ad to sell a machine that plays chess with you. The ad did quite well, but the returns, instead of being the usual 5 per cent, were more like 20 per cent. Jeremy Shaw, the executive at Barnardo's responsible, couldn't understand. He conducted a little telephone research and soon found out the problem. The machines were perfectly all right. They just weren't *advanced* enough. So he wrote to all those who had asked for their money back, saying: 'Here's your refund. But would you like a machine that's much more advanced, but costs three times as much?' The mailing was a simple five-page letter – no illustration – and an order form.

Twenty-five per cent bought the more expensive machine, because a relationship had been established and the company was clearly planning to behave honourably by refunding. I understand they may have made more money from the returns than they did from the original advertisement.

USE YOUR NAMES

One of the most obvious, yet frequently neglected, opportunities is that of the guarantee form – which I touched on in the last chapter. When people have bought something from you, they are usually in a pretty good mood. There will *never* be a better moment to create a strong relationship with them. Indeed, many years ago I conducted tests which proved this to be so for a company I had taken over which was going broke. Changing the timing of an offer lifted it into profitability. The quicker you sell an extra product to somebody who has just become a customer, the better you will do long term. Yet most companies never do anything with their guarantee form, though there are usually obvious opportunities for cross-selling.

The best time to start

I have already mentioned another area frequently neglected: names generated through sales promotion. These names, whilst not nearly as valuable as the names of people who bought from you by mail, can be highly responsive. In the case of a sweepstakes offer run by a cosmetics firm, we generated a 51 per cent response from a list of such names.

The importance of repeat sales

The seventh question on my list, 'Do you have (or need) repeat purchases?', is obviously one to which everybody ought to answer 'Yes'. Indeed, as you've already gathered, it is one of the three reasons why every business should be interested in direct marketing. That is why it is so important when making a sale to record the name and address of your customer – and do it accurately. After that it hardly requires genius to keep in touch. Yet how many people bother?

Many years ago, I took my children to the Earl of Bradford's restaurant, Porters, in Covent Garden. The waitress asked them the dates of their birthdays and where they lived. The next year they all got a birthday card, with an invitation to a free meal. How do you think that made me feel about the Earl of Bradford? I was amused at the shrewdness, as well as being impressed.

Far too few companies take this kind of trouble.

RETAIL PROBLEMS

Earlier I quoted examples from one of our clients in the retail business. There are many obvious ways that tactical offers of discounts, or invitations to events, can bring people into your stores.

You can help overcome such common problems as outlets that are empty on some days of the week; badly situated stores which won't attract passing trade; and, of course, stores with high rentals. Also, if a store is selling products that people buy at particular points in their lives, or consider for long periods of time before making a final decision, direct marketing techniques are ideal for keeping in touch.

For instance, when I moved into a new house some years ago, I was struck by the fact that one retailer – Wickes – used to mail me a booklet every month with do-it-yourself offers. In fact I was a peculiarly poor target for such offers: I can't change a plug without a map. But if I had been interested in DIY, I probably would have responded.

Yet what they do is not particularly remarkable. They just communicate *directly* with likely prospects. At the time I speak of, not one of their competitors did.

I have already talked about the way the car industry uses direct marketing. However, car dealers are doing very little indeed. Few take the trouble to get your name and address, inquire about your requirements and future plans, then follow up regularly. They are going to have to do so vigorously if they want to survive, as will other kinds of retailer.

Opportunities for small retailers

THE KEY TO PROFIT

Here are some other obvious situations where the direct link could be the key to profit.

Do your retailers or wholesalers dictate to you?

Why not go round them, direct to your customers? Or build an alliance with them by creating a direct marketing programme they can use? They will see you as a more desirable partner than your competitors. This works very well for anybody in the insurance business who deals with brokers or other intermediaries.

Pre-empt your competitors

Does your brand suffer from regular attempts by others to steal part of your market?

Then create a database of your customers by making attractive offers, and *keep* making them good offers so they stay with you. Such a list can be particularly valuable at a moment when you learn one of your competitors is about to launch a new product. You can steal their thunder by making attractive offers that will diminish the likelihood of your existing customers switching. This approach is being used quite a lot now for packaged and fancy goods.

Would you like to steal other people's customers?

Following the previous point, I am talking here about taking the battle to the enemy, as it were. It's perfectly possible to do so.

Some time ago in the UK, Imperial Tobacco decided to cut the number of their pipe tobacco brands by 60 per cent. Rothmans then ran an ad telling pipe smokers that if they thought they might be missing their favourite brand, all they had to do was write in to receive details of the Rothmans brand closest to it. A neat approach to database building.

Similar thinking worked very well for Compaq in America. They mailed potential customers asking them to give details of the computer they were currently using, and what they used it for. They followed up with any one of six different mailings, each incorporating information based upon what the prospect had said. It was very successful. It amazes me that more firms don't use this approach, which is over 20 years old.

When we come to talk about databases, you will see that proprietary databases enable you to attack competitors' customers extremely effectively.

Why speak to everybody when you only need to speak to somebody?

In *any* situation where you are not appealing to everybody, direct marketing makes sense. For instance, where you have patchy distribution. Why waste a fortune in national press or TV? Try direct mail, e-mail or the telephone.

This is so obvious, yet so frequently neglected, as to be quite remarkable. How many times have you seen enormously expensive national campaigns when what is being said could only be of interest to a limited number of people? Surely, direct approaches to these people would be infinitely more cost-effective than general advertising?

What percentage of people are prospects?

I shall discuss later, when covering planning, the implication of the Pareto principle. However, one calculation well worth making is very simple: what percentage of the mass market is interested in your product? Does it, for instance, make any kind of sense to spend millions on TV or on posters when making a share offering, which is what the British government did repeatedly in the 1980s? Even products with a traditional mass appeal – cigarettes, for example – only appeal to a minority. However, some products largely depend for their appeal on an enticing image. And images are generally, though not always, best built in mass media.

So although you may not want to sell to the whole world, this does not mean you only wish to speak to people who are your immediate targets.

For example, a direct marketing programme put together for a US car company, although it seemed to make eminent sense, didn't really work. The reason was that the client did virtually no general advertising. Consequently, apart from the people who were being approached directly, nobody knew about the car. It had no reputation. As a result, if anybody bought it they would not benefit from one of the great pleasures of buying cars: having other people admire your choice.

Why direct marketing is not always enough

However much sense direct marketing may make in terms of numbers, it will not always do the job on its own.

Do you recruit people?

Unless you are a one-man band, you have to recruit staff; and you certainly know how important it is to get the very best available.

Some businesses depend entirely upon a constant stream of new recruits – like firms with large sales forces working on commission only. Yet surprisingly little recruitment advertising is any good: most is abysmal, usually consisting of a heading describing the nature of the position to be filled and some extremely dull copy.

Money squandered on bad recruitment advertising

No intelligent marketer would permit such a dreary approach in ordinary advertising, yet they regularly squander enormous sums on it when recruiting people. Indeed, it may be argued that staff recruitment agencies only get their exorbitant fees because their clients don't know how to recruit people with effective advertising.

To a good direct marketing copywriter recruiting people should come as second nature. What you are doing is basic direct response advertising, except you are selling a job, rather than a product or service. In fact one of the biggest areas in direct response advertising is the recruitment of agents for mail order catalogues. When I ran Ogilvy & Mather Direct in London I made a point of writing all the recruitment advertising myself. I proved (to my own satisfaction, anyhow) that I was better than the average recruitment agency, because I *sold* the jobs rather than describing them.

Do you have a catalogue or brochure?

Few companies indeed do not have some literature. Often, large sums are paid for its design and writing, yet most languishes in showrooms or is sent out in a half-hearted fashion, usually without a persuasive covering letter, to random enquirers.

Many companies, too, have catalogues, even if they are not called that, but something like a range brochure. Planning a catalogue that works effectively is a specialised task. Even many direct marketers don't understand the subtler points that well. But it will pay you to find one who does, and listen carefully to the advice given.

Planning a catalogue – a specialised job

And, finally, can you afford to advertise as much as you'd like to?

Get a response – and find new revenue

If not, then transform your 'image-building' advertisements and see if they can't help you *sell*. Put in a response device. You will find new revenue for advertising.

If the examples above don't set you thinking about how something you're considering right now could be approached, your business probably has no connection with the subject of this book. Put it down right now and go and have a drink.

EMPLOYERS AND SHAREHOLDERS

Unless your employees are motivated to work hard, you will go broke. If your shareholders do not believe your firm is being properly run, you will prove an easy mark for the first takeover merchant to arrive on the scene. Intelligent direct marketing can do a lot for you in both cases.

Talk regularly to staff

For instance some years ago, union leftwingers had more or less gained complete control of the British Leyland Motor Company. The company solved the problem by using direct mail to the mass of employees, pointing out how their future was being threatened. They got employees to agree to policies which for years they had steadfastly rebuffed.

British Leyland were lucky. I suspect they only resorted to this direct approach because they were desperate. Wise management would regularly communicate with their workers and shareholders explaining what the company was doing and why – enlisting their support. Many companies seem to imagine regular newsletters to the employees, full of company puffery, and a near incomprehensible company report sent to shareholders once a year, will do the trick. Recent history has shown they will not.

It is a pleasure to be more-or-less right from time to time. For years, I have suggested to anyone who cared to listen – and quite a few who didn't – that £1 spent communicating with your staff is worth £10 spent on the trade or other intermediaries and £100 spent talking to your ultimate customers.

This is, of course, an estimated statistic, but a few years ago I was vastly heartened to read what follows: 'Business leaders who invest in Workplace Marketing with passion and persistence are found over 2 years to deliver 7% better return on capital than their competitors; 172% improvement in pre-tax profits and 78% more profit per employee'. (I wonder how those *without* passion and persistence do, incidentally; and how these rare qualities were defined.)

In addition, they reveal that '44% of marketing directors make little effort to share their marketing plan with their own departments and 68% fail to share them with their managerial colleagues', whilst 'less than 10% of companies with "customers", "quality", "service" and/or "people" written into their mission statements can claim a motivated workforce'. (I have long suspected any firm with any mission statement is badly run.) The statistics cited here come from Strategic Management Resources, who help you motivate your staff. They underline how important it is to communicate with those who work both for and with you.

WHO COMPLAINS?

Who replies to complaints? However fulsome their protestations of dedication to the customer, few companies like to think overmuch about them. This is not true of the really outstanding marketers, amongst whom you must number Procter & Gamble.

Quite a few years ago in the US, P&G started addressing this subject. They discovered that when customers were unhappy, only around 40 per cent could be bothered to write to the company and complain. This is not really surprising when you think about it: nobody gets into a lather of excitement over a laundry detergent (forgive the pun).

But Procter & Gamble are always excited about detergents and similar products – they are their livelihood. They wondered how they could make it easier for their customers to complain, because they had also discovered that of those who did bother to write, 90 per cent were satisfied with the company's explanation, and continued to be customers.

Make it easy for customers to complain

Accordingly, P&G decided to put an 0800 number on all their packs so that anybody who had a query could ring up free. Result? 90 per cent of potential complainants did ring up. And 90 per cent, once again, were satisfied. (Other research, incidentally, shows that a customer who has complained and been satisfied is more loyal than if they had never complained in the first place.)

Apart from retaining customers, P&G also said they learned a great deal from this. They learned which customers were using which brands. They received lots of helpful suggestions about packaging, advertising and even new product ideas. Quality control was improved and recalls avoided.

Clairol heard about this activity and formed a completely separate division – a profit centre in itself – to deal with complaints. This is a wonderful variation on the old salesperson's saying that the sale only starts when the customer says 'No'.

WHAT MAIL ORDER TEACHES

I am biased, but I believe mail order is a marvellous education. 'We sell, or else' is the motto David Ogilvy devised for his agency – one which grows directly from mail order. And although today direct marketing is employed by most firms, looking at what mail order companies have learned teaches you valuable lessons.

We sell, or else

To start with the basics, if you look today at some of the better mail order catalogues you will see they are very different to their forebears. Twenty

Mail order is now more sophisticated

years ago the average catalogue did not offer a better quality product, nor a more imaginative selection of products; it flourished because it offered credit and home delivery. The prices were rarely competitive.

No longer so. Catalogues today often offer genuine bargains, and imaginative products. Every time I fly I look at the offerings from Sharper Image and other firms. They offer imaginative products, often at very good prices.

What I am saying is that the mail order companies are reacting to meet a more sophisticated market. They're producing good products, selecting them imaginatively, presenting them well, and making good offers.

Pretty basic stuff, you will probably say. How can you succeed in marketing without offering something good? Well, oddly enough, many companies who enter direct marketing do so because they see it as a way of solving a problem – often that of getting rid of products they hadn't been able to sell any other way. There are few occasions on which this happy result eventuates, I can assure you.

THREE MAJOR ERRORS

Getting started successfully in direct marketing requires just as much hard work and application as getting started in anything else. Here are the three major errors I have noted amongst non-direct marketing companies who wish to get started.

1 Failing to espouse direct marketing thinking

Many general marketers, and especially their advertising agencies, have a disdainful attitude to direct marketing. They still see it as a junk mail, hole-in-the-wall business. I have already explained that I have sympathy with this view. But it doesn't mean you ought to approach the business casually.

A special way of thinking

Good direct marketing, as you have seen already, calls for its own special way of thinking. And those who understand it are few; there's a great shortage of talent. Accordingly, many companies employ people with *general* marketing experience. Often, just as they choose *products* that have failed, they choose *people* who have failed in general marketing. The result: disaster.

If you can't find people who have direct marketing experience, then for goodness sake try to make sure that the people you do select are really good. Then make sure they learn as much as possible about the business. There are many training programmes, hosts of seminars and conferences, and a number of excellent books. Make sure they are exposed to all these. I recommend in particular the training of the DMA in America, the Institute of Direct Marketing in Britain, and the conferences organised by groups in other countries – Spain, Belgium and Australia in particular.

If all else fails, place them for a while with a good agency.

2 Trying to do without specialist help

When General Mills in the United States went into direct marketing a few years ago, they conducted a two-year study to establish what you must do to succeed. They thought it essential to get direct marketing experts in right at the beginning and 'engage a competent direct marketing agency to help set up the operation, manage and train the people ... and maybe even run the business in the short term'.

What you must do to succeed

Whether you have to go to that much trouble, I don't know. But one thing is sure: hiring a 'below-the-line' specialist, ie somebody who knows all about sales promotion or merchandising but does not *specialise* in direct marketing, will almost certainly prove fatal. Indeed, despite the fact that many sales promotion agencies have set up direct marketing divisions, I have yet to see one of any great competence. And a general agency is almost certainly the kiss of death. I have yet to come across one that understood direct marketing at all well.

Here's a word of warning, though. To add to the perils that beset new direct marketers (and some who should know better), many of those who purport to be experts seem to have little grasp of the basics.

When this book was first written 25 years ago precious few people either understood direct marketing or could say they did with any degree of credibility. But as soon as it became widely accepted by big clients with big budgets, things changed. Flocks of persuasive jargon merchants swooped. Direct marketing agencies became big, sophisticated money-making machines in splendid offices – with some dire consequences.

To give a good example, about 18 months ago a famous insurance firm approached my agency. They had a big problem. Their agency (which had, ironically, been named Britain's best direct marketing agency by its peers) was producing results for a particular venture that were 10 to 15 times greater than they had budgeted for. They had fired the marketing director responsible, and were actually thinking of closing down the division running the business. In the event we were able to help them, and got a very nice e-mail from one of their executives thanking us for saving their bacon. But what we did was not extraordinary: it was just basic good direct marketing sense – applying basics which neither the agency nor the client seemed familiar with.

3 Trying to do it too quickly

Again, to quote the General Mills study, 'This is not an overnight success formula, but something that will take a major investment in time and funds.'

No overnight success formula

You will notice that when considering the advantages of direct marketing I have never suggested that it's a way of marketing on the cheap. You may be able to eliminate risk, but you will still have to invest. You must look at it in the same way as you would any other business. When I talk about investment, I would endorse the General Mills study with enthusiasm. In some ways the investment in time may be more critical than the investment in money. You need a lot of time to install the necessary infrastructure.

Some years ago, a major US firm came to us with the bold intention of seizing a major share of the private health insurance market. There were a number of reasons why this was a difficult thing. First, in the UK the National Health Service, though run-down, is much liked. Second, this market was and had been dominated for nearly 50 years by two firms. Third, nobody had ever heard of this American company, though it is very famous over there.

It is possible that their long-term objective might have been met, but they certainly made it harder by trying to set up everything in six months. This involved not merely marketing personnel, but people to set up a database, a telephone operation and all the considerable logistical minutiae involved in such a business. (Reflect, for instance, on the challenge of recruiting a sufficient number of private hospitals to co-operate in such a venture, and you will get some idea of what I mean.)

Valuable lessons learned, but obscured

Merely from a direct marketing point of view, the whole thing was utter chaos. In a period of 12 months, from a standing start, we produced over 700 separate pieces of direct mail and advertisements. Millions were wasted. Never was time given to stop, consider what was being learned, adapt accordingly. Many valuable lessons *were* learned, but amidst the panic-stricken gallop towards an unattainable target, these were obscured. The company did learn quite enough to realise that over a long term, approaching segments of the market, they could succeed. But it was hard for them to see this. A great opportunity was wasted when the business, after little more than 18 months, was sold off to one of the existing UK firms.

WHAT SHOULD YOU SELL?

I have just given an example of a service which was a natural for direct marketing. In fact, there are few products or services you can't sell direct as long as you give it a little thought. If you are already in business with a range of products and services, then you will probably have isolated a number of possibilities for yourself by now. However, here is some advice based largely upon my experience in the mail order business. Clearly, not all the points I am going to make will apply to you, but I would be surprised if some don't.

Firstly, the right product or service does not necessarily have to be the cheapest, or the most unusual, or have a special gimmick. Moreover, it can be something that is also available through other channels. (Some people think it has to be uniquely available direct. This is clearly not the case. For instance IBM, to whom I have referred, in some cases offered a range of different prices to the customer for certain products depending on how they bought them: from a salesperson, from a retail outlet, or direct.)

Can you make a good offer?

Generally, the thing to consider is whether the product represents good value, or is one on which you can make a good offer. Perhaps a little story will illustrate what I mean.

Some years ago, I was called in by Gerald Lipton, the chief executive of Chinacraft, an extremely successful chain of retail stores. He had heard from another client that we were hot stuff at direct marketing, and he summoned us to his rather grand office in north London.

Before talking to us, he said: 'Let me show you round my warehouse.' It was a most educational tour. I have never seen so much beautiful china in my life. Nor so much *expensive* china. There were cups and saucers there selling for nearly £100 each. I was bowled over.

Then, he said: 'Let me show you all my cheap lines.' He took us to see the crockery he sells to the big supermarket chains and catalogue houses. This was impressive in a different way. He had everything there: plates, saucers, service dishes, glasses, cutlery. I'd seen a lot of it before in various stores.

After he had shown us round, he took us back to his office, and said: 'For many years I've wanted to get into mail order. I don't know why, but I've got this itch. I've tried a few times. Sometimes I've made a little money, sometimes I've lost a little money. But I've never succeeded as I would like to.' He asked us whether we thought we could help and – eager to get the business – we said we could. He asked what we thought he should sell. With the wisdom of more experience since then, I think we should have kept our mouths shut. The selling of products is tough enough without getting into choosing them. However, we made three suggestions, all of which he tested in the press. Only one did well. It was the *least* original.

At that time, another company was running an offer of complete sets of plates, glasses, serving dishes and cutlery. Gerald Lipton knew how well they were doing; moreover, he knew exactly what they were paying because he supplied the plates. As a matter of fact he even thought they would go broke. He was right about that, too.

Our suggestion was to make the same offer, but improve on it. So he did: he offered an additional piece of crockery, and a free gift of oven gloves to go with the set. He ran that offer for years. He was able to outlive the competition because he had more margin, and he made a better offer.

CAN YOU OFFER A GOOD DEAL?

The moral is that your offer doesn't have to be original. It just has to be something you are well placed to offer a good deal on. The deal doesn't have to be outstanding: in this case the cost of an additional piece and an oven mitt was minimal. All you have to do is to come up with an offer which is sufficiently appealing to a *very small* section of the public to pay off. If only one person in a thousand amongst the readers of a national paper buys one of those sets of cutlery and crockery, then the ad is extremely profitable.

Appeal to very small segments

That leads me to my second piece of advice: remember what business you are in and who your customers are. That's a very old adage, but it's vitally important. If you are in the china business, then you understand it: the

Understand what sells and what doesn't

customers, what sells and what doesn't, how much you can charge. You are best to stick to what you know.

This cuts both ways. Thus, if you have customers who have always bought china from you, you will be ill-advised to suddenly mail them with offers of garden seeds. They are china buyers; and to them you are a company that knows about china, not gardening. Your offer must fit your position: be compatible. However, considering what is compatible with your present business in an *imaginative* way can pay off splendidly. And perhaps the company which has given one of the best demonstrations of this is the Franklin Mint.

I used to be a consultant to this company, working for a man called Ed Segal. I learned a great deal from him, at a time in my career when (not for the first time) I was sure I knew everything. He taught me a lot about writing direct mail. He also told me a very interesting story about how the Franklin Mint managed to expand its business base successfully.

The Franklin Mint was, by coincidence, founded by another Segel; no relative – as you can see, the name is spelt differently. Joe Segel was originally in the advertising speciality gifts business, where he became something of a legend. But the best idea he ever had came as a result of seeing a picture of a queue of people buying the last of the US silver dollars ever to be minted.

This made him think about how keen people are to collect rare things (or things likely to become so). He conceived the idea of *creating* things for people to collect. Items on which he would confer instant rarity, by limiting the period of the offer. He started with medals. By the age of 42, he retired with millions of dollars. (He must have got bored, because a few years later he came back into business to launch one of the first home shopping channels in America, QTV, which he sold off in 1992.)

Lessons from the Franklin Mint

However, there's a limit to the number of sets of medallions, ingots and coins you can sell. Eventually you start to run out of themes. Or alternatively, you start introducing themes which are difficult to justify.

Thus, when I was working for Franklin, one of my colleagues there spent many months fruitlessly wrestling with a series of medals called 'Heroes of the Mexican Revolution'. The problem was that most of the featured heroes had done extremely unpleasant things to each other, and most other Mexicans, too. It was difficult to bring out their heroic side with any degree of conviction. Franklin, realising that they needed to do something else, decided to find something outside their existing field to sell. But they had the sense to stay in the *collectible* area. They invented the 'Ultimate Private Library'.

This was a limited edition of magnificently produced and bound classic works. As a matter of fact, so precise was their targeting that they deliberately avoided telling buyers *which* books the series contained. They appreciated that their customers were *collectors* not *readers*. *The Times* reported that the programme was so successful it created a world shortage of second-grade goat skin.

The Franklin Mint ended up selling just about anything you want to collect. Porcelain, furniture, decorated thimbles, plates, china dolls, vases – anything you like (unless of course, you know what you want to collect already).

At the beginning of this section I was talking about offering good deals. It's important to remember that a good deal may have nothing to do with objective values. Value means different things to different people. Thus, to me a series of limited edition medals has little value; to a Franklin Mint collector they are obviously worth a lot of money. The Nespresso company, a Nestlé subsidiary, sells very high priced products to coffee lovers. They started out selling coffee by direct mail, but today they have stores. They first sell you a machine that makes excellent coffee, but you can only get the coffee in capsules which they supply. The idea is merely a variation on an old strategy used by many, many firms, such as Gillette.

Something which can certainly add a great deal of value is prestige, as American Express discovered when attempting to recruit new customers for their bank in Hong Kong. By law, they were not allowed to offer anything that their competitors did not. In fact the only thing they had was the reputation of American Express, which has high status in Hong Kong – sufficient to persuade large numbers of people to open checking accounts with the bank.

ASK YOUR CUSTOMERS

I never cease to be amazed at the things people think they can sell. On one occasion someone came to see me and wasted a great deal of my time trying to persuade me that what the world really needed was a little trolley that would carry two dustbins in it. He was absolutely obsessed with this. I asked him why this was so essential. He explained that he had two dustbins at his house, and that it made it easy to put them out for the refuse handlers to collect.

I informed him that in my country home the refuse handlers very kindly came out and collected the dustbins themselves; and my London flat was a penthouse so a trolley would be no use. He still went away convinced that humanity would be saved for ever more if somebody were to offer this product direct.

On another occasion a man came to me who had spent all his savings – and his family's savings, and everything he could borrow – putting the Bible on tape with a cast of actors. Net result: bankruptcy.

If you want to know what to sell, for goodness sake do a bit of research in advance. There are occasional inspired entrepreneurs like Joe Segel. But most of us are just fallible human beings. So don't invest in hunches; ask your customers. I cover this to some degree later on when dealing with research.

Research in advance

HOW DOES IT COMPARE?

My next point is obvious but much neglected. Compare your product with the existing competition. How is it superior? And if it isn't (even though you may be unwilling to admit it), for goodness sake apply some objectivity, and see what you can do to improve it.

The ability of marketers to delude themselves about the wonders of their products and services is almost boundless. In practice the consequence of this is simple. A client comes to you with a product and says it's superior to competition in every respect, and it's cheaper, and it's revolutionary. And so on, and so on. After a certain period of time it suddenly emerges that, 'Well, it's not *that* superior. There are in fact one or two areas where competition is better. And it isn't *that* cheap.' And so it goes. It's a process of disillusionment, which almost everybody in our business has experienced. It usually ends up when you find there is virtually no claim you can make for the product. It's just the same as everyone else's. The client had just fallen in love with it.

Be objective: can it be copied?

One point which many people ignore is: can the product or service be copied easily? If so, you may have something with such a short-lived appeal it's not worth bothering with. It's also important to check whether there are alternatives to your product – possibly from other suppliers. Products that may do the same job, even though they're not the same product.

Let me give you an example. The fax machine competed with a number of services and made them obsolete. Yet I do not think many people realised when it came out that it would represent an appealing alternative in some cases to telephone calls themselves, the mail and – one service which has almost vanished – the telex. The fax is now, in turn, becoming somewhat outmoded by e-mail.

Having chosen a product, you must also pay great attention to quality. If you are selling merchandise, get several samples to make sure the product is reliable. Will you be able to send it out quickly, properly packaged? All simple stuff; all very important. Ensure, too, that it conforms to all the relevant laws and regulations. If it has any health connotations, be *very careful indeed*.

If it's a service, then there are even more factors you must consider. Principally, they revolve around whether you are going to be able to deliver what you promise – or at any rate deliver it with the speed and efficiency required. Eg: if you're offering to give people information when they call in, have you got the necessary infrastructure set up? Will your telephone communicators, for example, have the knowledge required or easily available on a database to respond to queries?

Equally important is: have you got an alternative supplier? My hands tremble as I record this advice because 20 years ago I lost a small fortune (and many nights' sleep) because a supplier let me down when I was selling records in Scandinavia. And once we nearly lost a very large client because a supplier of personalised plastic cards let us down. On this occasion, thank goodness, we did have an alternative ready.

PAY THE RIGHT PRICE

My next piece of advice: negotiate carefully. There is the world of difference between someone who just buys or sells, and somebody who *negotiates*.

In 1981, we had occasion to look at the figures of two of our clients. In both cases, their advertising results were well above what we knew the market average to be. But neither was doing well. The reason was quite clear when we saw the figures. Neither company had enough margin to make a profit on many lines. This was not through a deliberate policy of low pricing to get names. It was just lousy negotiating. So haggle. It can mean the difference between profit and loss. You may not like talking about money, but when you go broke you'll find yourself talking about it all night. In your sleep. (For advice on negotiating, see Chapter 7.)

Linked to this last point is the need to make sure you have enough margin. How much is enough? The answer will come through testing, but as a rule, in lower-priced products (ie up to £20) you need *at least* 200 per cent gross margin on the cost to you, and preferably more. If you go below the £10 mark the margin should be even higher, assuming of course that you are hoping to make a profit, and not simply 'buying' names.

How much margin do you need?

In higher-priced products, you need less percentage margin. But don't imagine that simply by halving your price, you'll always increase your orders sufficiently to cover that loss of margin. Research by Professor Andrew Ehrenburg and others suggests you rarely will.

My next point is one to be read, marked, and inwardly digested.

DON'T OVER ORDER

When we first started working for one company years ago, the general manager showed us some of the products he was planning to sell. We were full of enthusiasm. Two products we all agreed couldn't miss were a new kind of calculator that worked by direct light so that it needed no batteries, and a dictating machine which had a calculator on its reverse. Two in one. What's more, it was to be sold at a price lower than Philips were charging for a dictating machine alone.

The client ordered these devices by the container to get a keen price. But we never realised that nobody *wanted* a calculator without batteries. Calculator batteries last a very long time indeed. They're no problem.

We did no better with the calculator/dictating machine. First, we didn't think very carefully about the market potential. How many people need a dictating machine? And what kind of people are they? The answers are: not a lot; and only business executives. Yet in order to get rid of the volume we had ordered, we had to go into mass circulation publications of general interest. There simply weren't enough executives reading these media to sell our product at a profit.

This failure may also have had something to do with the fact that a two-sided product like the one in question is almost impossible to illustrate. We had the front of the product on the left hand side of the layout and the back of the product on the right hand side of the layout. At first glance, it looked like two products. And first glance is the *only* glance you get in selling off the page.

Always order a test quantity

Moral: always order a test quantity. You may have to pay more to start with, but you could end up paying a lot less in the end.

My last suggestion is obvious, yet almost invariably ignored when people choose what they ought to sell. Talk to the people who are going to have to do the selling for you: the copywriters and art directors at your agency. As a matter of fact, even a biased creative chap like me is willing to admit that it's a good idea also to talk to the client service people – the account handlers. They have been known to come up with the odd good idea from time to time.

The message *is* the market

Remember, in the mail order business particularly, the message *is* the marketing.

You really need to convince everybody in the agency that they can create messages which will sell that product. For instance, a good copywriter and art director should be able to tell you whether something is going to be easy to demonstrate in print or broadcast. If you can't do that, your chances of success are low indeed. Notice I said a good creative person. Make sure that when you're discussing your product you talk to somebody who is really first class, not an amateur. For that matter, I would suggest you speak to more than one set of creative people, if at all possible. You will get a more rounded view of your likelihood of success.

WHERE TO LOOK

You may wonder *where* people find ideas for what to sell. I am tempted to say either you've got it or you haven't; but that's an easy way out.

Here are some suggestions:

Sources of good ideas

- Copy other people (like Chinacraft did) and improve on what they offer.
- Go to a 'syndicator' – a person who puts together mail order deals for people, in order to supply the product. But be careful that you have enough margin: it is not as easy for two to profit as one.
- Go to trade shows.
- Travel. Look at what is being sold in other countries.
- Read foreign papers and magazines. Look at the ads.
- Put together lots of items into a different combination. Like a set of motoring tools, or kitchen knives – both perennial best sellers.
- Try a successful catalogue product. A collection of sewing thread in every colour of the rainbow is one example. Many companies have done very well with exercise bicycles, in catalogues to start with and then in space advertising.

Successful catalogue products don't always do well 'solo', but they often do.

- Try to sell something connected with your own favourite hobby or interest.
    One good friend of mine lived off a business in rare coins for 30 years. It's much easier to work hard at something you know and love.

- Look at something being sold by salespeople. It could possibly be sold through the mail. And it is almost certain that you can use direct marketing one way or another to help you.

- When you've got started, don't worry. People come to you with products.

Here are some personal views on the best products to sell.

I have always believed that the very best services and products to sell are those which involve the minimum of administration and the maximum of continuity, preferably with the greatest possible mark-up. Thus, insurance is a wonderful product. There is no warehousing cost and you are merely selling pieces of paper, which you can print as you need them. And, of course, a continuity element is built in (except, perhaps, in the case of the burial expenses policy I mentioned earlier in this chapter).

My favourite example of continuity in insurance came about when I was approached to write a package to sell insurance to babies. You may imagine that the average baby is not too worried about insurance – so let me explain.

In this case, the communication was a letter to be placed in the 'Bounty Pack' given to mothers when they have just had babies in hospital. These packs contain information and samples of products the mothers will find interesting. The piece I wrote simply suggested that at this wonderful moment in the parents' lives the one thing they would obviously care about would be their baby. It was, I proposed, a very good time to consider the baby's protection and financial future.

This did very well. Certainly, if you want to build a continuing relationship with a customer I cannot see any way of starting much earlier (although I have no doubt somewhere, a wily insurance executive has already considered mailing ladies who are *expecting* babies).

For the same reason that insurance works very well, loans and other financial products are ideal for direct marketing.

Ideal for direct marketing

Any product that is simply printed paper – like a training course – allows for big mark-ups. This is particularly so if you take a book and break it up into a series of lessons. A £10 book can easily sell for several times as much when broken up in this way.

The most extreme example of taking paper and giving it high value is the collections of cards on subjects like cookery, which I mention elsewhere. The margin on that type of product is colossal. But of course the ultimate low-cost, high-margin course is one sold online. And since the latest research I have seen – in September 2005 – suggests that consumers prefer to be sold to by e-mail rather than through the post, this is probably where the future lies, for this and many other products.

Getting started – evaluating opportunities

I also believe any product for businesses has a built-in advantage. The business buyer is usually not the principal of the business so it isn't his or her money. At the same time, many business products nowadays are exceedingly complex and therefore lend themselves particularly well to the detailed explanation direct marketing can bring to bear.

My final thought on what sells and what doesn't: don't ask me – I'm always getting it wrong.

Points to remember

- Is there a continuing relationship already?
- Could you help the sales force?
- Any easy ways to create or build on a relationship?
- Do you have names and addresses lying around?
- Repeat purchases always important.
- Any problems direct might help?
- Go round intermediaries and talk directly.
- Talking direct bonds customers to you – and protects against competitor attack.
- Can you reach competitors' customers directly?
- Don't waste money to speak to everybody.
- Use direct techniques for recruitment.
- Turn your brochure or catalogue into a money-maker.

5

Positioning and Other Mysteries Explained

'This above all: to thine own self be true.'

Polonius's advice to his son Laertes,
Hamlet

'If I have seen further, it is by standing on the shoulders of giants.'

Sir Isaac Newton

Put your mind at rest: I have no intention of comparing the joys of positioning with the laws of gravity. But if Isaac Newton could learn from his predecessors, why shouldn't we?

The history of direct marketing is long. Back in the fifteenth century an Italian printer was selling books direct, almost as soon as printing itself had been introduced to Europe. He must have known something, because the company survives to this day.

As early as the eighteenth century the great writer Dr Johnson summed up in two sentences the principles that govern success in advertising – and direct marketing. 'Promise, much promise is the soul of an advertisement', he said. And when auctioning off Mrs Thrale's brewery, he told potential buyers: 'We are not here to sell off a parcel of vats and boilers; but to offer the potentiality of wealth beyond the dreams of avarice.'

Two principles of advertising

Once you study the results of tests you learn very quickly how correct he was. Firstly, advertising works best if you promise people something they want, not – as many imagine – if you are clever, original or shocking. This is not theory: in 1985 the Ogilvy Centre for Research in San Francisco set out to discover whether people buy more goods as a result of television commercials they liked. The answer, not surprisingly, was that they did. But what did they like? 'Emphatically not something original or clever, but something relevant', said the report.

Secondly, of course, people are attracted more by what something can *do* for you than by what it *is*. If every marketing director in the world, whether engaged in direct or general marketing, acted upon these two principles, I believe results would dramatically improve overnight.

Here are some other theories and principles you should find helpful, some dating back to the early days of modern advertising.

As I have already explained, today's direct marketing has come about largely as a consequence of changes which echo those that occurred in the nineteenth century during the Industrial Revolution. At that time, the technology which led to steam printing, for example, made both cheap newspapers and cheap mail order catalogues possible. Educational and economic changes created customers for the new mass-produced products – customers who were able to read the advertising that promoted them.

SOUND ADVICE ON BOASTING

Soon, advertising started to produce its own trade organs. One in particular in America was called *Printer's Ink*, published by George R Rowell, who also ran his own advertising agency. This is what he wrote over a century ago about advertising:

Be direct and simple
Come right down with the facts, boldly, firmly, unflinchingly. Say directly what it is, what it has done, what it will do.
Leave out all ifs.
Do not claim too much, but what you do claim must be without the smallest shadow of weakness.
Do not say 'We are convinced that', or 'Surpassed by none'. Say flatly 'the best' or say nothing.
Do not refer to rivals. Ignore every person, place or thing except yourself, your address, and your article.

Many people could learn a lot from that even today. Much copy ignores the facts and doesn't tell what the product is, what it will do, or how it has performed for others. Much copy overclaims. Much copy boasts. And much copy denigrates rivals – often a waste of time, because the reader ends up believing nobody.

Rowell's fame was eclipsed by that of John E Powers, who made a mint selling sewing machines in England (literally by the shipload) before going to America to write copy. Soon he was earning the astonishing sum for the time of $100 a day.

His secret weapon was the *truth*. He would have been a good soulmate for the late Charles E Brower, an American advertising man who observed: 'Honesty is not only the best policy. Nowadays it is sufficiently rare to make you pleasantly conspicuous.' Very commonly, advertisers squander prodigious sums saying what they would *like* to be the truth. In Britain, for example, the railways ran a slogan for some time: 'We're getting there'. It had to be withdrawn because it infuriated the average traveller, who knew all too well that many British trains arrived late.

Honesty is rare and priceless

But to get back to Mr Powers: his great discovery was that if you give people a *reason* why what you are saying is true, they are more likely to be swayed by your arguments. The fact is, people are suspicious – and the more seductive the offer, the more suspicious they tend to be. (On a British TV programme years ago a man offered people £5 notes in the street. Nobody would take them although they were perfectly genuine. They believed there must be a catch.)

Powers was *so* honest that one of his employers, John Wanamaker, founder of the great Chicago department store, eventually fired him in exasperation for running copy such as: 'We have a lot of rotten raincoats that we want to get rid of.' Or, '[The neckties] are not as good as they look but they are good enough – 25 cents.'

You may be asking yourself: does this advertising archaeology have any relevance today? The answer is an emphatic 'Yes'. Even today, few advertisers appreciate the importance of giving a reason. And in the last couple of years my colleagues and I have managed to improve several clients' sales markedly by using the reason technique.

Suppose you are planning a sale. Believe me, you will do much better if you give a reason for it. 'Closing Down Sale' is more convincing than just 'Sale'. People think that if you are closing down you really *do* have to sell off your stock cheaply.

Give a reason *why*

One shop in Soho had a 'Closing Down Sale' for 20 years. And some years ago the 'Closing Down Sale' of Debenhams in London did so well they decided to stay open, which they are to this day.

WOULD A SALESPERSON DO THIS?

The most valuable single statement ever made about advertising is that it is 'Salesmanship in print' – mentioned in Chapter 1. This was said originally by John E Kennedy, the first copywriter with the American advertising agency Lord & Thomas. Partly because nobody else appreciated this at that time, Lord & Thomas quickly became the world's largest advertising agency.

I advise you, every time you plan or review anything, to ask yourself: 'Is this a good sales technique?' Direct marketing is so intimately concerned with sales technique that you might imagine it is almost impossible to forget this fact. However, I must warn you that many alluring sirens lie in wait to seduce you as

Is this a good sales technique?

you make your plans or review your objectives, and they congregate particularly densely during advertising agency presentations. You will be amazed how quickly you can be persuaded you really ought to be 'building prestige' ... or 'letting people know what we are doing' ... or 'developing awareness'. The minute you hear phrases like this, start worrying. Your plans are almost certainly threatened. Sound the alarm and get back to sales technique.

I don't mean you shouldn't be letting people know what you are doing, or you shouldn't be building prestige or developing awareness – all these are very desirable. But never forget your *ultimate* aim: one way or another you want to make a sale – persuade somebody to do what you want.

Be consistent

Good sales technique has a cumulative effect. If your tone and message are consistent, you build a clear reputation. A reputation is worth a lot of money. If you go into any supermarket you can see this demonstrated quite clearly. Next to each other on the shelves are products which are as near as damn it identical save for the brand name. One, a brand which through consistent advertising has built a fine reputation, commands a higher price than another (often the unadvertised house brand of the supermarket). Research has shown that heavily advertised brands as a whole are substantially more profitable than brands that are lightly or not advertised.

Of course, reputation benefits the supermarket itself. Companies like Waitrose and Marks & Spencer sell products which themselves can command a premium. Significantly, in recent years financiers have realised that the value of a company can depend on something generally not even mentioned in the balance sheet: the value of the brand names it possesses. A value built up by years – sometimes generations – of advertising. When Philip Morris started buying other companies in their attempts to diversify, their CEO cited the value of the brands belonging to those companies as being the principal thing they were buying.

ADDED VALUE

James Webb Young, a famous creative director in the early days of J Walter Thompson, theorised that one purpose of advertising was to build a value that is not in the product itself. This added value derives from the constellation of qualities which together make up the brand image.

Brand name doubled response

One of the great names in packaged goods is Heinz. In Britain, its most famous product is baked beans. Other companies obviously make baked beans, but none is as successful as Heinz. Much of this has to do with the power of the Heinz brand. One competitor used to conduct regular taste tests to find out how their product compared with Heinz. The taste tests were 'blind', ie the brands were not revealed. Their product used to be preferred by consumers in the ratio of 2:1. The minute the brands were revealed, the very name Heinz changed consumers' perceptions. They preferred the Heinz product.

Jim Kobs, in *Profitable Direct Marketing*, tells the story of Montgomery Ward, the American catalogue company which wished to launch an automobile club. They tested the power of their brand name by doing identical communications to similar target audiences. There was only one difference: one file of prospects was told this was the Montgomery Ward Autoclub; to the others the name Montgomery Ward was not revealed. At that time the company was nearly 100 years old. It had a fine brand image. The name doubled response.

The American Express Bank example from Hong Kong given earlier shows how a brand's image alone can enable you to compete, even when you have no advantage at all.

It is because of the importance of the brand that the word 'image' has emerged from the world of advertising and become general currency. Indeed, if one were able to calculate the sum squandered as a result of that word, I suspect it would be colossal. How many times, for instance, do corporations imagine that the solution to some endemic problem like lousy products or second-rate service will be simply to have a new 'corporate image' created at vast expense by some specialist in this arcane art.

Your brand, and its image – or personality – result from what you are, what you do, far more than what you *say* about what you are and what you do. The way you deal with your customers, the products you sell, the value you offer, will do more for your brand and its image than anything else.

What is more, the consistency with which you behave and speak is of extreme importance. Wiser heads than mine have commented that one mediocre advertising campaign run consistently for 20 years will do you infinitely more good than 20 brilliant campaigns introduced at yearly intervals. This is often demonstrated in advertising research where people are asked which campaigns they remember. The answer is, campaigns that have run for a long time, in some cases despite the fact that they may not have run for many years. Once a brand image is established in the minds of the public it is very, very difficult to change the way people see that particular brand. Indeed, research shows that once you have advertised a brand heavily for a couple of years, it is almost impossible to shift consumer perceptions.

Brand names are hard to change

Some advertisers are so obsessed with the importance of the brand that they devote nearly all their efforts to promoting the brand name, to the point of not even asking people to try or buy the product or service. But the image is not the name alone.

Every communication you make affects the image your public has of you and your product. I once saw an excellent exposition of this point made by Jeremy Bullmore, a former chairman of J Walter Thompson in England. He showed a picture of a sign on a country road drawn in chalk on a rough piece of board. Scrawled capitals said: 'Fresh eggs'. The style and setting of the communication were perfect for the message and the product. An image of bucolic wholesomeness was projected.

Then he showed the sign in the same rustic setting. But the message had been changed – though not the style of the lettering – to 'Flying lessons'. The audience roared with laughter. The point was made: who would want to learn to fly from people in such a place, exhibiting such a roughly drawn sign?

UNIQUE SELLING PROPOSITION

Your brand image is primarily an emotional construct. Emotion is probably always more powerful in swaying people than reason, but people like to be able to rationalise their choices. This is where, in addition to the 'reason-why' approach, awareness of another advertising theory – the USP – can be helpful to you.

The USP, or unique selling proposition, formula was developed by Rosser Reeves, an ex-copywriter who became head of the Ted Bates agency in New York. He wrote an excellent book, largely dealing with this theory but also covering other aspects of advertising, called *Reality in Advertising*.

One feature that no one else can offer

To establish your USP, you compare your product or service with your competitor's. Then you determine one feature you have which no one else can offer. This is your unique selling proposition. It is this which you must promote singlemindedly.

A 1987 issue of *Marketing Week*, the British trade paper, gave a wonderful example of how little the average marketing executive understands the phrases he deploys with such gay inconsequence. The subject was 'Store credit cards'. A bank executive said: 'The whole point of a Marks & Spencer, Boots, Dixons or even Fortnum & Mason card is to bring people into the store – and to provide *a bit of a USP*' (my italics).

How a credit card can be a *unique* selling proposition when the same facility is offered by any number of retailers is difficult to comprehend. It reminds one of people who refer to things as being 'rather' unique, or 'fairly' unique.

Here are some typical USPs:

'Cleans your breath while it cleans your teeth.' Colgate toothpaste.
'The too good to hurry mint.' Murraymints.
'There's more for your life at Sears.' Sears Roebuck.
'It ain't fancy but it's good.' Horn & Hardarts.
'The mint with the hole.' Polo Mints.
'It takes a tough man to make a tender chicken.' Perdue Chicken.

And, finally, another gentleman in the chicken business:

'It's finger lickin' good.' Colonel Sanders.

One problem with the USP is that you sometimes have to rely upon some pretty trivial points of difference to arrive at your proposition – as you can see from the list above. And although for simple products a good USP may often supply a successful selling idea, I think it is difficult to arrive at one for complex services such as American Express or the Consumers' Association. Sometimes the secret is to say what others can say, but say it more persuasively or more fully.

However, comparing yourself against your competition to discover what USP may exist is a great aid to clear thinking. For example, I was able to improve results for Odhams' Kathie Webber Cookery Club by writing a headline which was simply a personal way of expressing a USP: 'My cookery cards mean you control your weight without giving up luscious food you love to eat.' This did well in the UK, and even in France, home of gastronomy. Moreover, subsequent approaches to selling this product revolved around this original thought.

An aid to clear thinking

POSITIONING: TODAY'S THEORY

A client once unkindly observed that advertising men go very deeply into the surface of things. I think there is truth in this. We are fickle and fairly easily impressed by new, fashionable theories.

Some of these theories reach the far shores of the ludicrous; and where better to find a ludicrous theory than an advertising agency whose very name has given pleasure to many over the years? The agency in question is BBDO – Batten, Barton, Durstine and Osborne – once described by somebody as sounding like a man falling downstairs. One of the founders, George Barton, wrote a successful book in the 1920s which put forward the proposition that Jesus Christ was the first great salesman. But I digress (because I enjoy it).

Returning to today, one currently fashionable theory is 'positioning'. An ugly word, but the thinking behind it is well worth your attention.

Synthesis of brand image and USP

You might describe positioning as a synthesis of the two ideas of brand image and USP. I think it is better than either. To try and explain what people mean by positioning, let me take you back 70-odd years and tell you a story.

What you *do* is the most important factor in success; what you *say* comes next. But sometimes, the way you say it can have great impact. This was demonstrated when, in 1919, a man called Dick Jordan decided to go into the motorcar business. He launched a car called the 'Playboy' with an advertisement which I have illustrated (see page 84).

What you *do* matters more than what you *say*

You will immediately notice two things about this advertisement. First you can't see what the car looks like; second, there are virtually no facts about how it is made, or how it performs. You may think that these considerable shortcomings would prevent the advertisement from working. But they derive from Dick Jordan's problems, and the way he overcame them.

Mr Jordan didn't have much money. In fact he couldn't even afford to make the car himself – he subcontracted the manufacture. So he could hardly afford to produce a car that was technically superior, more rugged, or cheaper than Ford or General Motors. Even the design of the car was copied on the back of an envelope from a Packard custom model and 'bumped out of aluminium' as Mr Jordan elegantly put it.

What he did was to find a unique position in the marketplace: he sold the Playboy as a *fun* car – one which would be likely to appeal in particular to women, who were for the first time beginning to attain some economic power in America. The copy reflects this clearly.

The car may not have been rugged, but in keeping with the positioning, it was lightweight, and he put into it the new Delco starting and lighting system. This enabled him to talk about the fact that: 'Any woman

Figure 5.1 'Playboy' car ad

could crank a car without breaking her arm.' Other lines include 'Everything that women want in a car ... to hell with the old mechanical chatter ... like a woman likes to look to the man who likes to look at her' (whatever that means).

From a factual perspective this is not a good advertisement; however, it reflects the positioning of the product perfectly. And this is why it succeeded, and the product was a howling success.

The Playboy was only sold for around 10 years; the company was liquidated, with a great sense of timing, in 1928; Dick Jordan and his partners made 1,900 per cent on their investment. In fact, as late as 1958, when Jordan died, everyone was still living happily on the proceeds. I do not know of a better example of the way clever positioning can overcome otherwise impossible obstacles.

Positioning is exactly what your commonsense tells you it is. Your position should reflect where you fit in the market; what differentiates you from your competitors – not merely in fact, but in the minds of your potential buyers. What they think about you is as important, possibly more important, than the truth about you.

Positioning: Where you fit in the market

The positioning statement

Positioning should be expressed through a short, simple *statement*. It should not be confused with a slogan, though if the positioning and the slogan are the same, wonderful.

The purpose of the positioning statement is to be borne in mind and conformed to in everything you say and do. And don't forget that as in everything else in life, it may be a position you aspire to, as opposed to the one you have. When you conduct research you may discover that your customers do not see you the way you would like them to. That might be described as position 'A'. Then, based upon what you have learned about your customers, your business, the future of the market, and your own plans, there will be a second position, 'B', which is where you would like to arrive.

The way you handle your customers from that point on will affect your position in their minds; as will where you advertise – up-market media or down-market media. So will the type of language you use when communicating with them, or the type of layout. Everything contributes in its own way to your positioning and to how effectively you move it from point A to point B.

Everything affects your positioning

William James, the philosopher, once quoted a carpenter who said: 'There is very little difference between one man and another; but what little there is, is very important.'

Be similar, but not identical, might be a good maxim when looking at positioning. Look at the strong points of your competitors and see if you can come up with some unique twist which will mean you have everything they have – and a little bit more.

'If everyone else does it, then I won't'

If you are a new company, you start with a blank sheet, in which case you might like to remember a phrase I once read expressing the principle of positioning very well. I saw it in the most improbable place, written in a dead language. I was travelling through France and stopped at the chateau of the former dukes of Clermont-Tonnerre. Inside the courtyard of that chateau the family's motto is inscribed. It reads: 'Si omnes, ego non', which one may roughly translate as: 'If everyone else does it, then I won't'. That is a thought well worth remembering: but do be careful. Don't be *so* different that you place yourself outside the mainstream of commerce.

Sometimes – indeed usually – your research will reveal that you have no clear position in the minds of your prospects and customers, or – even worse – you are perceived as being inferior in several respects.

Offer something better

The first thing you must do, as I have already suggested, is to offer a better product or service. That will almost invariably have a greater effect than anything else. The second thing to do is to ensure that whatever you do say about yourself is believable. You will remember my observations earlier about British Rail. In Britain in the 1970s Woolworths used to say in their commercials, 'The wonder of Woolworths'. Everyone in the country knew that the wonder of Woolworths was that anybody went in there at all – their stores were such a mess.

Poor positioning makes ads fail

This reflected poor thinking about positioning. And such poor thinking is very common. Sometimes you can look at an individual advertisement and see that poor positioning is bound to make it fail.

Some years ago a company offered two monogrammed dressing gowns at a good price in the colour supplements. I thought the ad was unlikely to succeed, partly because the creative execution was not very impressive. A good product can always overcome that, but not if the positioning casts doubt on the company's veracity. In the advertisement for these dressing gowns, the company advertising was described as 'Britain's leaders in leisure goods'. They had never advertised before. This alone would get hoarse laughs from the readers. Second, to reassure the customers, the company was described as a subsidiary of Tate & Lyle, the giant sugar combine. Why should anyone think a sugar company knew anything about mail order or leisure?

Tell the truth

The sad thing was that the company actually supplied many of the pack premiums to major advertisers. There was a good position there waiting for them if they only told the truth. They could explain that they knew all about buying good value products, that they supplied famous companies, that they had a big warehouse which could get the goods to you fast.

But they didn't bother. They used their imagination instead of telling the truth.

Research your positioning

Once you have decided on possible positionings for your product or service, research them and see which of them your target market finds credible and appealing. For instance, one of my clients used to sell a wide range of kitchens, bathrooms, bedrooms, doors, windows and the like to the public through retail outlets. We wanted to find out what the right positioning for them could be – and then reflect it in their advertising.

Accordingly, a number of lines were written, each reflecting a different position. I am going to give you these lines with a brief indication as to how consumers reacted to them. This should prove salutary if you ever feel tempted to boast or misrepresent what you offer.

1 'The best DIY store in town' – consumers appreciated that the stores were not DIY outlets, so this was seen as inaccurate.

2 'The ideal home improvement store' – consumers thought this dealt only in superlatives, which were glib and self-congratulatory.

3 'The store for top quality home improvements at value for money prices' – consumers thought this was not distinctive; it was over-used phraseology; nor did it appear credible – people expect to pay a premium price for quality.

4 'The home improvement store where service really is personal service' – the idea of service was good news, but not enough; products had to be good, too. In any case, this claim was seen as something other stores like Marks & Spencer could make better.

5 'Find out what "the trade" has always known' – people had mixed feelings about the trade. Some thought of it in association with craftsmanship; others thought of cheap workmanship and cowboy operators.

6 'The store traditionally used by the trade' – here the same negatives aroused by the previous trade line came up, though in a better sense because of the use of the word 'traditionally'.

One problem, however, is that the line implies such products need proper experience to install.

7 'Made to last by us. Sold direct to you' – this conveyed that the company was directly involved in the making of the products, not just an importer. Moreover, the line was seen as patriotic, because it clearly meant these were British goods. It also conveyed craftsmanship, durability and the good value you get by buying direct. Readers also appreciated that the line was to the point, not gimmicky. This line came out on top.

How customers judged seven approaches

Successful companies tend to have a clear positioning from which they rarely if ever deviate – and then only with great care. I make no apology for reintroducing American Express. It was positioned single-mindedly for many years as 'the world's most prestigious financial instrument for business travel or entertainment'. This positioning came out in everything American Express did. For instance, the letter sent out to solicit new members which began: 'Quite frankly, the American Express card is not for everyone ...'. This reflected the positioning so well that for many years in most countries of the world it was the most cost-effective direct mail used.

American Express in trouble

American Express got into trouble when they ignored this position, and tried to expand their base of customers to just about everyone – they ceased to be true to themselves.

Positioning important to all

Even the smallest enterprise can benefit from thought about positioning. Here is the copy for an advertisement run by a small hotel in the West Country. Almost every word reflects very accurately the positioning of this hotel.

HOT HOME-BAKED ROLLS

Wine-laced dishes with freshly picked herbs. Scrumptious puddings with thick local cream are served in the beamed restaurant of our small Georgian Hotel. Two miles Exmoor and coast. Phone owner-chef Dick or Kay Smith, WHITE HOUSE HOTEL, Williton, Somerset TA4 4QW. Tel: 01984 32306. Try a 4-day

BARGAIN BREAK
& save £30 per couple

You immediately feel the hotel is special. It is old-fashioned. You get good food. The people who run it do the cooking themselves. They even answer the phone themselves – they must *care* about their business. Their establishment is clearly positioned as opposed to a big impersonal modern hotel. (And incidentally this excellent little advertisement even contains an offer.)

One big question about positioning is whether you should position something as bought and appreciated by everybody or as something to be aspired to and enjoyed by a few. Both positionings are perfectly reasonable. One will make sceptics think that if everybody is using it, then it must be good. The other, conversely, will make prospects think that if only a few people have the taste (or money) to enjoy it, it must be good.

Take American Express. If the American Express card is not for everyone, it follows that you will not necessarily see it honoured in every retail outlet. So, when competitors attack American Express – as they do – by pointing out that their card is acceptable in more outlets, the positioning itself helps defend you against these attacks. And of course Visa do very well by going to the other extreme: 'It's everywhere you want to be.' However, as pointed out above, unless you cleave wholeheartedly to yours, you'll end up with problems.

Positioning can change with the market

The most important factor in success, after the product or service, is positioning. Positioning can vary depending upon the stage of the market. A New England stove company found that at the time of the mid-1970s' oil crisis stoves were bought as *efficient* log burning alternatives to oil. This type of stove, which had previously enjoyed less than 5 per cent, seized 50 per cent of the market for heating in rural areas.

People became more sophisticated; the stoves sought further distribution; the oil crisis receded; and the positioning of the stove was changed.

Split-run tests revealed that in this new, selective market, people were more interested in the *looks* of the stove. As the stove began to penetrate urban areas, split-run tests found that even referring to it as a stove was a mistake. It became positioned as a 'fireplace'.

Sometimes the name alone of a product or service can imply positioning. For instance, a former client of mine, North West Securities, finances companies making capital acquisitions. They called their service 'The Money Programme'. That title implies money *making* as well as money *lending*. It makes more of a promise.

Positioning in tough markets

Positioning obviously becomes extremely important where competition is fierce, especially if differences between products are minuscule. A typical example is the mail order catalogue industry.

The Next company broke into the market effectively by doing one thing: they promised to deliver goods to the customers within 48 hours, at a time when everyone else in the industry was talking about 21 days. This in itself said more about their dedication to serving the customers than anything else. At the same time they positioned themselves apart from the competition in something they said: instead of calling their catalogue a catalogue, they called it the Next Directory and gave it a distinctive visual style, and promised a 48 hour delivery. This attracted many consumers – but unfortunately they had great problems living up to that promise, which it took them some time to overcome. One of the most fatal errors you can make is to promise something you can't deliver. And the more attractive the promise, the bigger the mistake.

Don't promise if you can't deliver

In the United States the Spiegel company, a very poor fourth in the catalogue industry in 1976 – and which looked like going nowhere fast – changed everything in order to conform to a new positioning. There was nothing to recommend the position they occupied at that time: dowdy, cheap, and selling just about everything to anybody who was prepared to buy. The architect of the transformation, Henry Johnson, decided he would reposition Spiegels as the store which combined the shrewdness implicit in buying direct and thus getting good value for money, with being chic. As he put it: 'It's smart to buy from a catalogue, but chic to buy from Spiegel.'

Based upon this thinking Johnson and his team completely restructured the range of merchandise offered, getting rid of items that were dull, dowdy, widely available elsewhere, or in some cases inconvenient to handle – like cut to size carpets, floor-tiles or garden huts.

Because they wished to move to a new upscale customer who was looking for added value rather than cheapness, they dropped items which sold primarily on price – even if they were selling in considerable quantities. As Johnson put it: 'We were going to become target marketers.'

They introduced high fashion items, designer clothes by people like Kamali, Liz Claiborne, Yves St Laurent and Pierre Cardin. Everything they did matched the new positioning. They started charging for their catalogue. If it was free, how could it be desirable? As people planning to meet the individual needs of sophisticated people, they had to target more precisely. So they started breaking down their catalogue into mini catalogues aimed to meet particular needs.

It was spectacularly successful.

Talk about what you are *doing*, not what you *think* you do

In short, as I have already emphasised, what you say about yourself will never have as much impact on the way you are seen by your customers as what you *do*. Nevertheless, sometimes doing and saying can be combined very effectively. Indeed, the best advertisements and mailings generally talk about something that you are *doing*, as opposed to those which boast about what you *think* you do.

One instance of this was a campaign run by the Schwab company in Germany – a campaign which proves once and for all that the Germans have a great sense of humour.

Each of the advertisements made a free offer to readers if they conform to some unusual, sometimes even bizarre, requirements. In one the reader was offered a free washing machine if the family had more than 11 children. Ordinary people were advised in the same advertisement that they could buy the same machine from Schwab delivered, fully guaranteed and insured to their home for so many Deutschmarks. In another advertisement readers were told that if they were over a certain (very tall) height, they could have a free jogging suit with their initials on it. Those of more normal stature were advised to buy the said jogging suit from Schwab. (In this particular advertisement, incidentally, a picture of a dog was featured, wearing a jogging suit. Some wag wrote in and ordered a suit for their dog, which the company duly made for them.)

This campaign, besides generating inquiries, said something to the reader about the company: this is not just the usual inhuman catalogue company. A campaign like this will also influence *employees* a great deal. It is rarely appreciated that your customers are twice as likely to read your advertisements as other people who are not customers, and your staff are likely to do so even more. They are probably influenced more than anyone else by what you say in your advertising – and your positioning.

CHANGING THE RULES

The book-club concept

Another fiercely competitive business is the book club. The original concept developed over 70 years ago has hardly changed. Offer a very low-priced selection of three or four books for the opening order to recruit a customer, and then ask that customer to *commit* to buying a certain number of books at a higher price. Possibly the only significant development has been that of aiming certain types of book club at certain types of reader, eg a military book club, or a gardeners' book club, or a thriller book club. Attempts at positioning have been perfunctory to a large extent.

One exception which proved triumphantly successful was Quality Paperback Club in the USA, which changed the rules of the game. By offering paperbacks they were able to eliminate the long-term commitment. The offer was three books for three dollars – then buy as few or as many books as you like. This thinking led to a successful new company. One, however, which came to full bloom only when it was positioned properly. The initial advertising was relatively successful, but results improved enormously when a campaign was produced which treated the customer as an intelligent person, something implicit in the very idea of the Quality Paperback Club.

How the book-club idea changed

A series of advertisements was run featuring famous literary figures. The one featuring Vladimir Nabokov, for example, had a headline set in Russian with a picture of the writer. Underneath was the English headline: '(Translation: 3 bucks. No commitment. No kidding.)' And in the coupon the line ran: 'OK. Send me 3 books for 3 bucks. Nyet commitment. Nyet kidding.'

An advertisement featuring Hemingway had the headline: 'Tres Libros por Tres Dolares and a Farewell to Commitment. No Bull.' Another successful advertisement ran: 'QPB. The book club that doesn't put pressure on its members.' Underneath was a cartoon which showed a devil poking a man towards two doors. The signs on the doors read: 'Damned if you do. Damned if you don't.' Under this picture, once again, ran the line: '3 books. 3 bucks. No commitment. No kidding.'

This particular campaign *halved* the cost of recruiting a member. The offer was not changed; the product changed only in one respect, its lower positioning and the way it was expressed: a book club as something to appeal to intelligent people, done with verve and style did the trick. I have illustrated one of these ads in the centre section of this book.

GENERAL ADVERTISING AND POSITIONING

If you look at the kind of brief most general advertising agencies use to initiate creative work, it often has under the heading 'Objectives' two subheads. First, what the advertising is intended to make the prospect *know*. Second, what the advertising is intended to make the prospect *feel*. The thing it does not very often contain is a third heading saying what we want the prospect to *do*. Thus, much general advertising is little more than an exercise in positioning.

The difference between what we, as direct marketers, do and what the conventional advertiser does, is that we want to *inform* people, we want to make them *feel*; but above all we want them to *act*.

There is ample evidence that the relationship between the position set up by the conventional advertising and the action demanded by the direct marketing is crucial.

The relationship between general and direct marketing

In a number of cases, particularly in the United States, commercials have been run using a 'head and tail' – the direct marketing element asking for some form of action – sandwiched around a core which is the positioning commercial created by the conventional agency. This can work very well if enough time is given to the response demand.

Some points in this chapter may strike you as blinding glimpses of the obvious. All I can say is that I have seen very intelligent people make dreadful mistakes over the past 40 years because they thought they were too clever to need to master the basics of our business. For my own part, I have found that occasionally reflecting that people do need a good *reason why* before choosing your product has made my task easier. I have seen millions wasted by people who didn't appreciate that advertising is *sales technique*.

I have also found that searching for the *unique selling proposition* is particularly sensible, not only when creating a promotional piece, but when deciding whether a business is likely to be viable.

My belief in *positioning* is total. By making sure everything you say and do fits in with your positioning you start to occupy a clear place in the minds of your customers and prospects: a place from which it will be very difficult to dislodge you. In other words, you begin to enjoy something very rare in business: a feeling of security.

Yet I am constantly astonished at how few people do bother to seek the right positioning, or find out how their prospects and customers see them today, so as to improve the way they are seen tomorrow.

Just commonsense

Most of us love to make things sound more complicated than they are, just as the old mediaeval doctors had their hocus-pocus.

When I came to London to seek my fortune, having been falsely informed that the streets were paved with gold, I had to teach a trainee copywriter in my first job. A daunting task, not aided by the fact that he was undoubtedly much cleverer than me. His name was Gopal Krishna Menon, and we became good friends. He enlivened many hours telling me about his uncle, the famous Indian politician Krishna Menon.

I recall asking him on one occasion what he thought of the Indian mystics who were just then becoming prominent, it being the early 1960s. He looked at me in his portentous way, and replied: 'They are my fellow countrymen trying to make a living. I never knock another man's racket.'

Find your niche

You could simply call positioning finding your niche in the marketplace. A good old expression we all understand. But that wouldn't sound quite difficult enough – though it sounds like commonsense to me.

Commonsense also applies, I believe, to **planning** your direct marketing, which is our next subject.

Points to remember

- All about making a promise.
- Give a reason to believe.
- Just sales technique.
- Consistency builds reputations.
- Reputation – brand image – adds hidden value.
- What you do, more than what you say.
- How are you different or unique?
- Image plus USP = positioning.
- Messages must fit in with positioning.
- The truth – not what you would like it to be.
- Research to establish where you are and what is credible.
- Positioning matters whether you're big or small.
- Direct doesn't just aim to change opinions. It seeks action.
- Don't be misled by phoney theorists.

6

How to Plan Well

'If I was you I wouldn't start from here.'
Traditional rustic reply to a request for directions

*'Beware of making five-year projections, unless
you're thinking of leaving the company after
four years.'*
Stan Winston, Ogilvy & Mather Direct, New York

Once you have learned where you are now, and where you would like to be eventually, you have to determine how you get there. You have to plan.

How do people plan?

If you think the need to plan is so obvious that everybody plans, ask yourself about the advertising most companies run year after year. Why, you may wonder, is there so little consistency? Could it be because people have *no* plan? Or because their advertising is created without reference to the plan they have? Or possibly their business objectives change every year?

If you think this sounds improbable, let me tell you about the time I had to address a conference on this very subject – how to plan your marketing. The first thing I did was probably what you would do: I tried to find out what was going on. What sort of plans were people making currently? And with what objectives? How did they approach this important matter?

I was surprised at the responses I got. I had expected to discover that people's planning was perhaps less thorough than it should be; or that they set objectives which were too ambitious; or that planning gave rise to heated dispute, even discord, within their organisations.

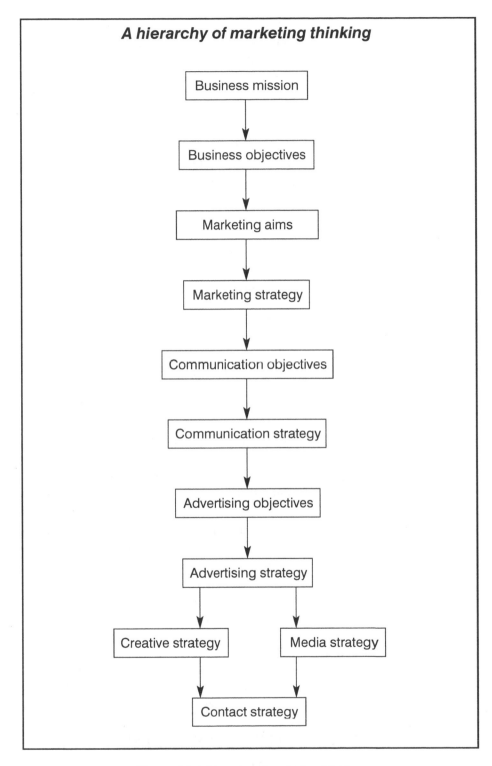

Figure 6.1 A hierarchy of marketing thinking

Nothing of the sort. Most people had no formal business plan whatever. The whole thing was done by guess and by God. This may be another facet of that English amateurism I referred to at the beginning of this book.

Most of those who *did* have plans gave two reasons for them. One was: 'We have a plan because I have always had to do one every year.' The other was: 'We have a plan because head office in America insists we have one.' Few showed any great enthusiasm for planning.

One friend, head of a major advertising agency group, said: 'I have banished these planning documents. In my last job, I spent all my time making plans. Nobody ever seriously evaluated them afterwards to see whether a plan had been successful, and if so why; or if not, why not.'

A somewhat extreme view, you might think. But one authority, the head of Porsche Cars in America, said that when he was asked to submit a plan, he naturally consulted other chief executives to learn what they thought. The general feeling was that because of the unpredictability of life nowadays, it's almost impossible to make a plan which allows for what might happen in the future. For instance, three things that had a dramatic effect upon our economy, none of which was predicted, were the Stock Exchange crashes of 1987 and 2000 and the current oil price rises.

Any plan is better than no plan

Nonetheless, I believe that with all its faults any plan is better than no plan. As circumstances change, you can adapt your plan. If you have none, you are operating in a very unsafe way. And if your plan is in your head, what if you get run over?

You need a written plan which is carefully thought through. However, clear planning is so contrary to human nature that all the endeavours in the world seem unable to enforce it. Our frivolous minds seem to prefer the erratic path, to go scampering after every enticing little thought we conceive.

What a planner does

The importance of planning is recognised to such a degree in agencies that there arose a vogue for a new type of individual: the *account planner*. A colleague of mine defined this person as being 'the customer's representative within the agency' because he or she will try to establish what the prospect or customer wants, how they think, how they should be approached, and what effect the advertising has on them.

The account planner is a hybrid. He is not an account handler, though he will spend time with both the client and the creative department. He is not a researcher, though he will often commission and evaluate research. He is a thinker: it's his job to make sure things *are* properly planned. This job used to be done (and continues to be in many agencies) by the account handlers, working in concert with the creative department, the research department and the client. To be honest, I can't think why it isn't now: but that's another matter.

ELEVEN STEPS TO SUCCESS

Winston Churchill said on writing: 'Use simple words everybody knows, then everyone will understand.'

I have a *passion* for simplicity. This is because I do not find it easy to understand new ideas quickly, but if I have simplified them enough in my own mind, I can communicate them quite well. This approach suits me, and I have found it suits most other people, too.

However, before giving you my simple recipe, let me outline the *formal* approach to planning in direct marketing. I am indebted to my former partner in London, Rod Wright, for the sequence shown on page 95.

You must start with your **business mission**. What are you trying to achieve? From this you will be able to establish what your **business objectives** should be over the period you are planning for. For example, with many hesitations along the way, Europe has almost become a single trading area. This gives companies opportunities to branch out more easily into other European markets. It also poses problems. Are other people going to come in and steal the market share you have at home?

Hierarchy of marketing thinking

When preparing a plan, no major European company can really ignore this single market. Suppose your business mission is to become the world's pre-eminent office systems company. You may have to adapt your business objectives to allow for the way you think your Italian or German competitors are going to behave. Whereas previously you might have been determined to drive them into the ground in your own home market, you might now simultaneously wish to protect your position in your own country, whilst gaining a foothold in their home markets.

From these intentions you will derive your **marketing aims**, and flowing from them your **marketing strategy**. Thus, in your own country your aims may be to protect your present customer base whilst trying to recruit as many new customers as possible. In the markets where you wish to gain a foothold, you might aim to set up a strong sales and distribution network so as to recruit new customers and serve them properly.

Your marketing strategy will depend upon your business mission. If you wish to be pre-eminent, have you decided that this will be achieved through low prices? Or should you maintain a high margin, but add value, and thus be perceived as a company that concentrates on quality, not price? Examples of these two strategies in the UK grocery retail sector are Tesco and Waitrose respectively.

Let us assume you want to focus on quality. This brings us to step five: your **communication objectives**. They might be to tell your customers and prospects that you care more about them, which is why you give them added value. Or they might be to explain how much more trouble you go to, to provide a better product.

Your **communications strategy** – step six – may be to build a database of customers and prospects, so as to initiate a long-term relationship. This relationship will centre upon communicating the added-value message mentioned to selected *individuals* (and you will notice here the emphasis we as direct marketers place upon the individual).

What do you want your advertising to achieve?

The next step, of course, will be your **advertising objectives**: what precisely do you want your advertising to achieve? What do you want your customers and prospects to *know* and *feel* about you? And what do you want them to *do*?

Because you've followed such a logical sequence, it's all fairly simple by now, isn't it? You want them to *know* you're a company that doesn't offer bargains; it offers added value for their money. This demonstrates in a practical way what you want people to *feel*: that the company cares about them, or cares about offering a better product. And, of course, what you want them to *do* is to initiate a relationship with you if they are prospects; and to cement further the relationship they have with you already if they are customers.

The **advertising strategy** would be to convey those messages through appropriate channels. You might choose television and public relations to project the image you are aiming for. Sales promotion and special offers in advertising or online could add names to your database. Then you might use direct mail, e-mail and telephone to build a stronger relationship with each individual – and, of course, make sales.

Your next step – number nine – is your **creative strategy**. How ought you to say the things you wish to say? What tone of voice are you going to adopt? What advertisements, mailings, e-mails and so on do you feel appropriate?

Your **media strategy** will be considered at the same time. Which media should you use, and in what proportions? If you're going to go on television, which channels? If you're going to use PR, which publications do you want to get coverage in? The specialist press? The national press? The same thing will apply to how you might wish to build your database. *Where* are you going to make your offers so as to reach the right individuals?

Finally – the eleventh step to success – comes your **contact strategy**. At what points in the relationship between you and your prospect and customer are you going to communicate? When and how will you use the media you have selected to reach each prospect or customer?

Emphasis on the individual

Here, once again, the emphasis you as a direct marketer place on individuals as opposed to masses is critical. Take two people you wish to sell to. From studying the database, you may discover one is much more likely to respond to a certain offer than another. Or perhaps one is more likely to influence an ultimate purchase than another. That means you can afford to spend more money to contact and communicate with that individual. This, in turn, will influence your contact strategy.

Let me give you a simple example, illustrated elsewhere, which makes the point well. In Belgium a client wished to sell a new copier to customers who had obsolescent machines. A most attractive offer was made to prospects; an offer so appealing that we felt it worth not simply mailing but telephoning these people in advance of the mailing to tell them this offer was coming. The response rate was so high – in some cases over 50 per cent – that it certainly justified a follow-up on the telephone, and even a second mailing after that.

Your contact strategy will, of course, be influenced not merely by the appeal of the offer but by other decisions you made earlier in your planning. In the case-history just mentioned it was extremely important to the client that the obsolescent copiers be replaced.

In fact, any part of planning must be viewed in the context of all other parts of that process. To take a simple instance, replacing obsolescent copiers may be a goal which flows from your business mission as much as it does from your marketing strategy. This will give it a high priority. It might even pay to lose money doing so: to put in place a very expensive programme. On the other hand, if it had low priority a much less intense contact strategy might be called for. Possibly just a single mailing.

Each point of the plan may affect the others

FIVE QUESTIONS YOU MUST ANSWER

Once you have determined your objective, to make your plan *work* you must look at things from the point of view of the people you are addressing. You should be viewing your own firm and your objectives from their perspective. It is from their perspective that communications must be planned. If it does not make sense to them, to those vital individuals, you are heading for trouble.

If you look at it with them in mind, here are five simple questions I think you should be able to answer.

1 **Who** are you talking to?
2 **What** are you trying to get them to do?
3 **Where** do you find them?
4 **When** should you speak to them?
5 **Why** should they do what you want?

What is more, on an alarming number of occasions, marketers fail to do something even more obvious: tell people precisely what they are selling.

On page 101 I have illustrated two advertisements for a marking gun, a little machine that prints price labels onto supermarket cans. They both appeared in the same publication. They are interesting because they demonstrate how easy it is to ignore some, if not all, of these important questions.

The first advertisement with the drawing at the top actually appeared in colour, so it cost more than the second, in black and white. Yet it pulled only a *fraction* of the number of inquiries.

The reasons for this are:

Be precise about what you sell

● It is not clear immediately what the product is. The art director has used a close-up drawing which makes it look like some strange ship's prow.

Why the advertisement failed

Even if the confusing illustration were removed, the headline would not tell you what the product is, because it is contrived so that it conceals the nature of the product.

● It is addressed to the wrong prospect: the **who** is wrong.

The copy makes the point that this type of gun can go round corners, thus making the job of marking easier. But the person who marks the cans – almost invariably a junior employee – does not buy the guns.

● Because it is addressed to the wrong person, the reason for buying – the **why** – is wrong.

In fact the only thing that is clear is what the advertiser wants the prospect to do – and that's because there is a coupon.

In the second advertisement, which my old colleague John Watson wrote (the one in black and white), it is instantly clear what the product is, and what it does for the prospect. This one got ten times as many replies as its predecessor. The reason, I think, is that John did a lot of research into what goes on in supermarkets as a result of bad marking. He also examined (or as he always says, 'interrogated') the product to see how it worked. And he thought carefully about the motivations of anyone who might buy such a product. Quite clearly, once you have realised who the right prospect is, money is the major issue. In addition, of course, he was able to tell a much longer and more convincing story than in the first advertisement.

Apart from the factors I have mentioned above, which revolve around the creative thinking before the job was done rather than the execution itself, I think another 'W' has been ignored in *both* ads. And that is **where** to reach the prospect. In my experience direct mail is almost invariably a more effective way of getting responses from people in the grocery and supermarket industries than is advertising in the trade press.

What is more, if I am right, then the mailings could have been *timed* to fit the journey cycles of Pitney Bowes salesmen. The **when** would have been better handled. Indeed, if a proper database had existed, the company might have known what *kind* of supermarkets would find these guns most appealing; when they were most likely to buy; and even who the relevant influencers, specifiers and makers of the ultimate buying decision were. Thus the whole exercise would have been carried out infinitely better.

The first W is the most important

You will not be in the least surprised to hear that of the five Ws, in my view the *first* is the most important. Everything else is to some degree a matter of fact; but 'Who' involves individuals, and they can never be neatly categorised. Yet thinking carefully about what makes them do the things they do is vital. And sometimes the answers are most surprising.

Figure 6.2 Pitney Bowes advertisements

Here you can't see instantly what is being sold. The benefit is aimed at the user of the marking gun – not the person who buys it. In the next ad, the message is to the profit-orientated manager.

By paying attention to the first three of the 5W's, the second ad did ten times better than the first. You can see WHAT the product is. WHY it should be bought, and it is aimed at the person WHO is the best prospect.

A few years ago I was struck by an article in a Sunday paper about a Japanese company. They had a real problem with the slipshod typing coming from their UK office. Requests, directives and exhortations had no effect. The girls in the Tokyo office decided to adopt a *personal* approach. They sent signed photographs of themselves to their counterparts in the UK. They started to make friends. And this direct, personal link did the trick.

People care about one another

People don't care about impersonal companies. They care about other people. And they make decisions for emotional rather than rational reasons. I can't implore you strongly enough to think about people and what they are like.

I spent a very frustrating day years ago driving to see a totally uninterested prospect on the south coast. But I got something out of it. Talking to the man I went with, I learned he had once worked for Sir Charles Higham, a legendary pre-war advertising figure. I asked him what this famous man was like.

'I once took him a piece of copy. He looked at it and put it down. Then he pointed to the wall of his office where there was an enormous blow-up of the FA Cup Final crowd. "Those are the people you are writing for. Now go away and do it again."'

Would you say that to someone you know?

It would seem that advertising tycoons are quite similar on both sides of the Atlantic. Fairfax Cone was one of the founders of Foote, Cone & Belding. Apparently when he saw a piece of copy he didn't like he would look over his glasses at the writer and ask: 'Would you say that to someone you know?'

It is all about *people*. From thinking about them you arrive at what will persuade them. You cannot make them do what they don't want to do, or change their beliefs: you have to go along with what they want.

When I was speaking at a conference in Monte Carlo in 1982, one of my co-panellists was the beautiful Marie Dumont. She had written (like a true Gallic intellectual) a very acute rationalisation explaining why she had been successful in selling magazines to French women. 'You must be able to sense the way women are feeling at a particular moment ... to catch that sentiment and to ride with it,' she said.

How true! We cannot *create* feelings. We must learn how the tide is running in people's minds, and float our messages on its surface. But how do you find out what your customers are thinking? One of the best ways is the most obvious, yet how many do it? Read their letters. Sometimes this will tell you more about them than any staged focus group or research project.

KEEP IN TOUCH

'Man is a gregarious animal,' said Dr Johnson. Human beings like to communicate, particularly the English. A Dutch bulb grower wrote to all his customers throughout Europe, politely saying he hoped their gardens were doing well. From most countries he got the odd reply. From England, he got letters by the thousand.

If you're starting up on your kitchen table, you will naturally read the mail. Don't stop doing that as your business prospers. Keep in touch. If you're not in the mail order business, then make a point of meeting your customers. This is something few do nearly enough.

Meet your customers

By reading correspondence, you can learn the most surprising things. I once wrote advertising for a headache relief powder. One letter we got was from a woman who used it to soak her tired feet. Whether this would have led to a whole new advertising approach I don't know – but that letter told me a lot about my customers.

Sometimes, meeting customers can be a more hair-raising experience than you might imagine. In the 1960s I worked for a fashionable advertising agency called Papert, Koenig & Lois. My Creative Director was a well known US copywriter called Joe Sacco. He was extremely keen on people going out to see the customer. I well recall arriving in a rugged part of London's East End and trying to explain to a very large man at eight o'clock at night that I had come to talk to his wife about washing machines.

From Joe I learned the importance of translating people's ordinary needs into the emotional messages that make them buy. I also acquired a deep distrust of judgements made by advertising and marketing people. Joe had been largely responsible for a detergent campaign which, universally execrated by sophisticates, was nevertheless the most successful ever: the 'White Knight' campaign for Ajax detergent. Research revealed that women hated dirt and saw their lives as a constant battle against a rising tide of filth. If only they could make it all disappear as if by magic ... if only someone would come along and do the job for them!

The most successful detergent campaign ever

In the White Knight campaign, that's just what happened. To the chant of 'stronger than dirt', a champion on a white charger dashed everywhere touching things with his lance, and turning them white. 'Abysmal! Ludicrous! Puerile! Insulting!' cried the advertising pundits. 'Stunning! All records smashed! A miracle!' said the sales figures.

The campaign transformed the balance sheet of Colgate Palmolive. For the first time ever, they suddenly became real competitors to Procter & Gamble and Unilever. It succeeded everywhere in the world, in all sorts of transmogrified versions, like the White Tornado – a sort of climatic detergent – and the Mississippi gambler – a dream-like figure wearing a white suit who waltzed round the kitchen with the housewife, obliterating dirt.

If the research on this concept had been accepted literally, the campaign would have been rejected as too fanciful and far out. If the experts had been listened to it would never have got to first base. I believe this is also true of the Marlboro cigarette advertising – probably the most successful campaign in its category ever run.

So look at the research, and listen to the experts by all means – but neither matters as much as your ability to understand your customers and their emotions – and apply that understanding imaginatively.

HOW TO UNDERSTAND YOUR CUSTOMERS BETTER

Julius Rosenwald, the great merchant who built the mighty Sears empire in America, said that he wished he could stand on both sides of the counter at once. What a wise observation; for only if you look at things from the customer's point of view as well as your own can you understand how to sell to them.

For many of us this poses a problem. The more you succeed, the greater your income becomes and the more your personal circumstances change. Thus you become more and more removed from the market. (In fact, now even the new recruits to our industry tend to come from educated middle class backgrounds – which militate against understanding ordinary people.)

I have already suggested you should read the mail from your customers, and meet them whenever possible. Here are three other intelligent things to do – particularly if you fear you may be moving in an increasingly rarefied atmosphere:

Three ways to stay in touch with your customers

1 Talk to your sales or telephone people; sit in on their sales pitches, listen to their conversations with customers.
2 Go shopping in a street market at least once a month. While you are at it go and sit in a crowded pub and listen to ordinary people.
3 Invest regularly in group discussions amongst your customers, or street interviews. Get your creative people involved in these. Even if you have no specific objective, I am sure you will be surprised at what you learn.

By doing these things you will undoubtedly find it much easier to understand all those people out there, what they want out of life, and how to talk to them in language they understand and appreciate. You will also be vastly entertained.

One thing you will certainly learn is that people very rarely devote as much time to speculating about the wonders of your advertisements and mailings as you do. Indeed, they are almost entirely indifferent to them.

For this reason, they do not spend much time trying to puzzle out what you're trying to say. So if you don't make it extremely clear what you're selling right from the start you are on a hiding to nothing.

Don't be too clever

One example which illustrated a number of other rules, like 'don't be too clever', came in the case of two advertisements for the same product. These are shown in the illustrated section on pages 216–231. It was a vacuum cleaner being sold off the page. The price was good, and the product was unique at that time in that it not only vacuumed up dirt; it could also pick up small pieces of debris and even liquids.

One advertisement for this product had the headline: 'The Jet Stream eats almost everything. Only £54.95'. And above it ran a line of captions saying: 'Devours dirt'; 'Scoffs leaves'; 'Guzzles water'; 'Gulps glass' over some very imaginative cartoon drawings. Many people in our agency thought this advertisement was so clever and creative that it would sell extremely well.

The other advertisement had as its headline: 'Now, a high-power vacuum cleaner that picks up liquids too. The Jet Stream 850 from Shelton. At only £54.95, it actually costs less than ordinary cleaners'. The copy went into great detail about the product, and a series of photographs showed the machine in action.

The straightforward – even dull – approach was astonishingly successful. The clever approach was so disastrous that the sales did not even cover the cost of the space. Why? Because the successful advertisement told you instantly what the product *was*. It also gave you a couple of good reasons for buying it in the headline. The information was presented in a way anybody could understand quickly. And it told you more.

The unsuccessful ad had a headline which was meaningless unless you knew what was being sold. In addition, an important element in the successful advertisement lacking in the unsuccessful one was that it *showed* clearly and convincingly with photographs what the headline said the product would do – I call this 'word-picture lock'. The other advertisement did *not* show clearly what the product did. It also relied on cartoons, which may have been entertaining but were not as believable as photographs.

Since these advertisements ran I have seen the results of a series of studies which show that if a picture and a headline do not reflect each other and the product, consumers find it hard to understand what is being advertised. And if they don't *understand* what is being advertised, it is very unlikely they are going to *buy* it.

In fact showing a thing and saying what it is at the same time is usually the best way of communicating. I remember years ago reading that words and pictures working together are up to five times as effective in communicating ideas as either on its own. When you plan your communications, you must devote a lot of time to creating this one compelling combination that conveys the essence of your product or service and its benefits.

You can probably think of famous examples of this yourself. The best I can recall at the moment is the famous graphic used by Hertz for many years of a man magically descending into the driving seat of a car, with the line 'Hertz puts you in the driver's seat'.

Why one advertisement beat the other

Show what the product *is*

Flop into success

A much simpler example dates back to the start of the THB&W agency in 1977. We were takers-in of other people's dirty linen. If someone had a hopeless product, we would ask them to give it to us and see what we could do in the hope of getting all that business. It was good training in a hard school. And my present business specialises in exactly the same thing – getting better results.

One company gave us a product they were about to sell off as a job lot. The product was described in the existing advertisement as a 'Regency Ensemble'. Could you tell what that is? I couldn't.

In fact it was a carved wooden case which contained a set of dials: a clock, a thermometer, a hygrometer and a barometer. All with a regency-style pediment atop. The existing headline made the bathetic statement: 'Functional things can be beautiful, too.' The writer had obviously not thought too long about the problem of how to describe it. He had simply given up.

Who is the advertisement aimed at?

Knowing the company in question, a bunch of cheapskates, I suspect he hadn't been given too much time to think about what he was doing. So he had not thought much about who he was selling to. They were relatively uneducated customers who wouldn't recognise an ensemble if it came up and kicked them in the teeth. It was a word they would never use.

Our new ad revived the product. But it was not remarkable: it simply told people what the product was. The main headline ran: 'The "Regency" 4 Instrument Clock Forecaster'. And in an overline it described each of the functions it performed. It *showed* the product and *told* you what it did. Word-picture lock.

This advertisement attracted attention as well as money. It was parodied by *Punch* magazine. This is the headline they ran:

THE CHIPPENDALE 4-MODE HOME COMPUTER

The overline ran:

Hand-worked luxury for the discerning, sophisticated few – at prices just a fraction of those you would have to pay in Hollywood, Belgravia, Paris, Honolulu or parts of Rome.

This was followed by:

Wake up to the technological miracle of an appliance lovingly fashioned by Black Forest craftsmen in solid, natural, satin-look, creamy-beige balsa – and embellished in 100% tin.

I once showed this parody to a prospective client. He gazed solemnly at it for a while, then said: 'I don't think it will ever do well.' I formed the conclusion that the man was solid balsa from the shoulders up. We got his account but he proved difficult to deal with. You don't need to add to all your other problems by dealing with people with no sense of humour.

Why such vagueness?

Why *do* people fail to describe products or services accurately? I think the reason is of one part sloth, one part cowardice and one part presumption.

Sloth being the unwillingness to spend time working out how to describe something accurately. Cowardice being a lack of faith in what is being sold, leading to the belief that if you come right out with what it is, nobody will want to buy it. And presumption because the writer *presumes* people know what you are selling simply because there is a picture of it, or a vague description.

Some may. But many won't. And if so, you have automatically lost a high percentage of your potential sales.

A very common fault is that the writer takes refuge in word-play, thinking this will substitute for information. This is rarely the case. You must work out how to describe what you're selling, and do so as precisely and briefly as possible. If it sounds boring, say it in a more interesting way, or get someone else to do the job – someone who *believes* in the product or service. At some point you *have* to tell people what you're selling. You might as well get on with it.

Describe the product precisely and briefly

The average advertisement is seen for a few seconds. If you were to start in the morning when you get up and count the number of advertising messages you're exposed to, it runs into hundreds. Every poster. Every commercial. Every newspaper ad. Every magazine ad. Every bus side. Every sign in a shop window. They're all screaming for your attention. And that's not including the mail and door drops that reach you every morning.

Accordingly, you want to know *instantly* what the product or service is. What's it all about? What's in it for you?

What's in it for you?

The last is the most important. Sometimes the most effective communication may not start by showing the product or describing it. It may start by concentrating on its benefits. In any case, until you have clearly defined and written down what it is, you will have a problem.

So you must subject the product or service to rigorous examination. Look at it. Play with it. If it's a piece of merchandise, drop it on the floor. Tear it apart. Analyse it. Think about it. If it's a service, try it out. See whether it delivers what it's supposed to. List all its characteristics, then look for the *buying* proposition. People often talk about *selling* propositions but I always prefer to look at it from the customer's angle. In terms of benefits, not attributes.

Thus, the attribute of a car may be that it will go in seven seconds from 0–60 mph. But the buying proposition – the thing that will turn you on – is the exhilarating sensation of power and speed you experience; the ability to overtake quickly; to get away from the lights faster than the next car; or accelerate out of trouble when you see someone coming towards you as you overtake.

WHO KNOWS WHERE OR WHEN?

The remaining two Ws are concerned with your choice of media, and your timing. **Where** and **When** will you meet your prospect? They are covered to some degree in the chapters on media and database. In some ways these questions are more easily answered than the other three Ws: Who, What and Why.

There is one maxim I would like to emphasise to you, because it is far too little appreciated. It is this: your customers want to buy when *they* want to buy – not just when *you* want to sell.

How company sales grew tenfold

One of the great US mail order success stories is the LL Bean company which sells outdoor clothes and tackle. In a period when they increased their number of catalogue mailings from two to thirteen per annum, their sales grew tenfold.

Many direct marketers communicate with their customers too rarely, in the fond belief that for some reason they will all be in a mood to buy exactly when the six-monthly catalogue or special offer comes out. This is arrogant. It may be true that most people are more likely to buy a number of things just before Christmas or in the springtime. But don't put *all* your faith in this.

A better way of looking at it is that if you give your buyers more opportunities, or excuses, or reasons to buy, then they will. Study of them and their characteristics will help you produce appropriate reasons. Here are a few examples.

- 'It is now a year since you first became a customer of ours. I am writing to thank you; we really appreciate your business. And there's a practical way to prove it: a very special offer.'
- 'I see it is your birthday next week. I have, therefore, taken the opportunity to review your investments with us. As a result, I have some recommendations you may find helpful based on what you have told us about your circumstances.'
- 'The budget is coming up, and the Chancellor will probably radically alter the system for tax relief. This is a good opportunity for you to ... '
- 'Although *you* are one of our best customers, we have never had the pleasure of dealing with your wife. So may I suggest ...'

Think up reasons to talk

That is not very good copy, but you probably get the idea. The more you communicate, with good reasons to communicate, the better you're likely to do.

Moral: you may easily be able when planning media to find out **where** to reach your customers, but don't underestimate the number of occasions **when** you should hit them.

WHERE YOUR MONEY WILL DO MOST GOOD

In this chapter I have looked at planning from two very different points of view. From within, as it were; starting with your own organisation's objectives; then, from outside: how what you do affects your customer.

Clearly, your customers are only affected (or not) by the communications you make. They are not interested in – or even aware of – all the effort and planning which lead to those communications. Yet if this is not carefully conducted, those communications will not do the job they should. That being the case, where should you direct your attention, your time and your money to gain the greatest benefit?

Where should you direct your attention?

The answer to that, in my experience, is almost invariably *not* where most companies do lavish most of their time and energy, which is in two areas: how much it's all going to cost; and fiddling about with the minor details of the communication which finally goes out.

Take a client who wrote lamenting the prodigious *fee* he was having to pay for a new mailing pack. You will not be surprised that despite the air of lordly impartiality I have tried to project in these pages, I was just as interested in the subject of money as he was.

My initial reaction (biased perhaps) was to point out what a splendid investment it was, and what a wonderful mailing pack it would be. This argument, based largely upon my own belief in the excellence of our work, struck me, upon reflection, as somewhat weak. Accordingly, I thought further about what the investment he was about to make could achieve, and whether it was money well spent. Let me therefore outline to you the likely effects of the actual mailing we were discussing and see what conclusions you might reasonably come to.

This mailing was planned as part of a series of tests. It was being sent out in the first place to 50,000 prospects. If it did better than the existing control mailing, it would become the new control. That meant it would then be rolled out to over a million names this year, and next year it would be used again. If, at that time, it continued to do better than any tested alternative, it would be rolled out once again.

A foolish economy

As it happens, this particular client is international. This other mailing could then be adapted for use in many other countries. In fact, quite possibly millions of pounds could be spent on this particular mailing – *if it proved good enough to beat the existing control* – ie the best mailing they were currently using.

And if it *did* prove to be that good, it would generate millions of pounds of additional profit. In the event it was a success, but initially, the argument revolved around a few hundred pounds more or less. Now I am not suggesting for a moment that you should not be concerned about getting good value for money. I think it's very important. But it is even more important that your concern should be directed properly.

A hundred extra pounds – even a few thousand extra pounds – will enable the agency to apply more resources to this particular problem, think harder, concentrate more on that mailing. That time, bought by that money, could well make all the difference between having a new control mailing or just another run-of-the-mill effort.

If the agency looks at the job and says: 'Well, there's only a limited amount of money; we can only spend a certain amount of time and effort on this', and the mailing isn't as good – and doesn't do as well as it might do – then what will happen in the end?

The answer is simple: more money will be needed to achieve the results that might have been reached. Maybe hundreds of thousands of additional names will have to be mailed. Or a new mailing will have to be created. Indeed, if you reflect upon what that mailing *did* do, and its worldwide and long-term potential, that initial saving would have been exceptionally short-sighted. The lesson is simple. Watch costs, by all means, but focus more on results.

Fight for time

Now you may be thinking I am talking about a special case applying to a firm where large sums of money are involved. Not at all: the principle we can derive applies no matter what size your business may be.

What I am talking about really is not money, but time and effort. In my view you are best advised to apply most of your time and effort *early* in the direct marketing process. Because if you don't, you will almost certainly end up spending a great deal more *later*, trying to put right the results of doing things on the cheap.

The moral is that simple. Fight for as much *time* as possible, as much *effort* as possible in the early stages of your programme. Fight for investment in research. Devote money and time into considering your positioning. Into discovering more about your prospects and what they want. Into learning about the likely reaction to your messages. And when creating and producing that creative material, look for the best, not the cheapest.

Get it right to start with

You will be astonished how much time and money you will be able to find when, in the end, the work you skimped on fails. All because you didn't give sufficient consideration to getting it right in the first place. You will be amazed how much frantic effort you have to devote into developing new offers (often in a hurry) because the one you threw together to start with, without thinking carefully (or paying enough), flops. If something fails, you will never remember how much money you saved. If it succeeds, that little extra time and money you expended will seem a wise investment.

A famous author once observed: 'That which is written without effort, is generally read without interest.' Equally, that which is *planned* without effort, generates very little interest. And very frequently that which is done on the cheap can cost extremely dear in the end. As an American colleague of mine once said to me: 'What you end up with is four monkeys in a back room churning the stuff out.'

How to plan

Points to remember

- Why you need a plan.
- Plan step by step – a hierarchy.
- Five essential questions – who, what, where, when, why.
- All about people – and feelings more than facts.
- Read letters, listen to phone calls, meet them.
- Sit in on sales pitches, go shopping, involve creative people.
- Words and pictures must work together.
- Describe fully – don't assume people know what it is.
- More frequent, relevant messages increase sales.
- Timing a good excuse to talk.

7

Media: A Different, More Flexible Approach

If you have seen a few presentations, you will be aware that shortly after the media man stands up many clients fall asleep.

A prime element of success

Media is not easy to make interesting – indeed it is not even easy to make comprehensible. But it is very important, since, after the product and its positioning, reaching people through the right media at the right time is the prime determinant of success. Even a boring message to the right people can succeed if it is timely. Even the most brilliantly conceived one will fail if poorly aimed.

Moreover, if your background is in conventional marketing it is vital that you understand the significant difference in approach to media employed by direct marketers as opposed to general advertisers. You may have to forget some things you have always taken for gospel.

WHAT IS YOUR PURPOSE?

The amount of money needlessly squandered because of poor media selection must run into billions. This is partly because some media are more familiar than others. For instance, few people really understand SMS yet (I certainly don't know enough about it). And other media are more glamorous and 'sexier'. Can you picture anyone boasting to friends about a new envelope design? But clients happily roll over like spaniels when agencies suggest television, even on very flimsy grounds, just as the idea of spending time with a celebrity persuades them that sponsorship makes sense.

Equally, creative people (who, as I have pointed out, are far more interested in their own fame than your profits) will go to great lengths to suggest you use a more visible 'public' medium. And sometimes (but not often) a very strong creative idea may emerge that relies for its success on the use of a particular medium.

So don't choose what you know or what you like when selecting media. Start, as with everything else, by looking at your aims, never forgetting the first objective in business: to avoid losing money.

Forget glamour, apply logic

You can do a lot worse than refer to the Three Graces I mentioned early in this book.

Are you trying to isolate individuals (the first Grace) so as to put them on a database? Then you must choose media which will get them to 'raise their hands' – see your message and reply – at a reasonable cost. These are often mass media like the press, television or radio, but also the internet, which is certainly a mass medium even if few people know yet how to use it very well.

Door to door may succeed if you have a product of wide appeal – and I have illustrated an example of a piece that worked very well for our client Everest. Direct mail can work too – especially if used against your own prospecting database – and in fact the piece I just mentioned was used in direct mail, the only difference being that it was addressed.

The second Grace deals with what you do with people once you have them on your database, and the database is the subject of another chapter. But even then, you must consider what medium you use to communicate and what you want to say. A postcard may work as a simple reminder; a brochure or full-scale mail pack may have an entirely different purpose, as would a phone call.

The third Grace is largely about testing so as to make more profit. Some media – e-mails, for instance – make this far easier than others. Others, like direct mail, cost a lot more and take longer.

To sum up, if I had one piece of advice to give it is: please, please, spend a lot of time thinking about what you're trying to do rather than how you plan to do it, in terms of either creative execution or a particular medium.

FIVE MAJOR DIFFERENCES

The professional direct marketer's approach to media differs in five ways to that of the general advertiser. These differences stem from the three 'Graces' of direct marketing I listed earlier.

First, you speak to individuals rather than masses; second, you test to discover what works and what doesn't – and adapt accordingly; third, you plan for a continuing series of communications.

Here are the five differences you should bear in mind:

The direct marketer's differing approach

1 The various media do not enjoy the same relative importance conventional marketers assign them.
2 Media effectiveness is often evaluated differently.
3 Schedules and budgets must be designed to allow for testing.
4 Repetition is viewed in a different way.
5 The effect of size or length of copy is regarded differently.

Let's look at these important differences one by one.

Different emphasis

The relative importance to direct marketers of each medium is almost the opposite to that given by a general advertiser.

The mailing list – a rented one or a selection of names from a database – is the medium you will rely on most. Other media, which you would scarcely mention in general advertising, are very important, too. Door-to-door drops, take-ones and inserts are typical examples.

The telephone, outbound and inbound, plays such a significant role that in terms of expenditure it may be the largest promotional medium in the United States. In some countries unsolicited outbound telephone calls are forbidden. Therefore the role of the telephone will vary according to the legal situation in your country.

Television, in many countries the chief general advertising medium, is usually a secondary medium for the direct marketer – though its use is growing fast, and most commercials now aim for, or at least allow for, a response.

The potential of television has been exploited less in most European countries, because of the relatively limited amount of commercial time available compared with the United States. There, television is a major direct marketer's medium, and its use is expanding fast in Europe, as channels proliferate. Radio enjoys even less attention than television nowadays, though in the 1940s and 50s in the United States it was described by a knowledgeable friend of mine as 'hot as a pistol'. However, it remains a powerful medium, particularly for generating leads for financial services.

In particular, a new type (well, really an old type that has re-emerged) of programme has made major inroads. This is also true on television. This is the infomercial: a programme which may last for as long as an hour dealing with such matters as how you can become inconceivably rich by following the advice of an adviser. Or how you can improve your golf beyond all recognition, or even catch monster fish with a flick of the rod.

Programmes on how to dress better, or make-up better, or even how to buy jewellery, all do well. One spectacular example of the power of this particular format occurred during the US 1992 presidential elections. Ross Perot ran a series of half-hour programmes which helped to bring him from nowhere to gaining 19 per cent of the popular vote. As a consequence he was even offered a regular television programme by one of the networks. This is a good example of something that many companies forget: consumers (electors in this case) are thirsty for useful information. They are fed up with meaningless overclaim; detailed facts often do more to convince than anything else.

Consumers' thirst for information

Posters – a big medium for general advertisers all over the world – are of relatively little interest to us.

In short, if your background is in general marketing, you must rethink your priorities when you become a direct marketer: just about the only medium general and direct see as having about the same level of importance is the press.

Individual impact versus cost

A simple way to look at the various media is to relate them to how much each costs to reach an individual. Not surprisingly, the more it costs to reach each individual, by and large the greater the impact will be on that individual.

The more cost per individual, the greater the impact

Thus, if we describe personal selling as a medium, it is certainly the most expensive. On the other hand, nothing will have greater impact on a prospect or customer than another human being talking to them face to face.

The telephone, the most expensive 'advertising' medium at our disposal, has the most impact next to personal selling.

After that, we have direct mail – not as expensive as the telephone, but still a potent communication because it reaches individuals and can, of course, be personalised and tailored to fit the information obtained from your database or rented list.

Next, we have the insert – the chameleon of the business. That's because an insert can be used in so many ways and can appear in so many guises. It can be placed in one of your regular communications. It can be sent out with some merchandise. Or it can be bound into a publication. Or it can be free-standing in a publication. It can even re-emerge as something stuck through your door, or placed as a 'take-one' at point of sale.

How to use an insert

Nearly all these types of insert will attract less attention from the individual than a direct mail shot, but usually more attention than – for instance – a full page press advertisement. Of course, when it is used as a 'take-one', it is almost impossible to predict what impact an insert might have – it depends almost entirely on where it is sited.

Nevertheless, I would say all the media I have listed so far have a greater impact in terms of reaching the individual than TV, radio and the press. On the other hand, of course, all those three media are relatively inexpensive in terms of reaching large numbers.

Obviously all the instances above are general guidelines, not universal truths. For instance, the poster is probably the medium with least individual appeal, but you have to make allowance for particular cases. A poster on a highway is almost useless to direct marketers. Most are seen under circumstances where it is very difficult to respond; they are seen fleetingly so their content has to be short and relatively unpersuasive. In addition they are relatively unselective in terms of targeting. On the other hand, a poster at a railway station, an underground stop or a pedestrian area does allow for longer reading and a more persuasive argument. And there is also the website and e-mail, covered elsewhere.

Figures not the only indication

In selecting your media you will obviously consider the demographic make-up of your prospects or customers – their location, their physical and financial characteristics – and also their psychographic characteristics: what kind of people are they?

The calculation then ought to be quite simple: how many of the right type of people can you reach for a given sum in a particular medium? This is – put very simply – the way general advertisers tend to make their media plans before proceeding to the equally important matter of how good a deal you can get from the particular medium to reach those particular people.

Some media are more responsive

Direct marketers have learned, however, that the media which appear to give the greatest number of likely prospects do not always prove as responsive as they ought. Some media appear to attract more responses than others, even though they may seem to have near identical profiles. You can take two newspapers which ought on the face of it to deliver a similar type of prospect in similar numbers for a similar cost, yet one will prove to be far more effective than another. These are facts you will learn only from experience and from studying your results. Moreover, they are constantly changing, as publications change. This means you must be unusually sensitive to what is happening day by day. You must be alert, and ready to alter your plans.

Fortunately, because you are *measuring* your results you don't have to rely on guesswork or computer analysis. But this does place unusual demands upon the direct marketing media planner. Perhaps greater in some ways than conventional media planners face.

Test budget

As a general advertiser, you may plan how to spend your budget at the beginning of the year, place the ads or commercials ... and that's more or less it. Retail is the outstanding exception, of course, where frequent swift change is called for. But in most general advertising you may, for example, have an autumn and spring campaign, but there is relatively small requirement for change. (I once spent half an hour listening to one client complaining bitterly that his advertising agency had been running the same ad, fundamentally, for 15 years ... and collecting 15 per cent every time it ran. I wish it were that easy for us.)

In our business, we know just what the results are of each mailing or ad. We are constantly trying new approaches. New sizes. New formats. New lists. New publications. For this reason, always set aside a percentage of your budget for testing. You must have loose scheduling, too. You must be ready to switch your money around dependent upon the results you are getting. Such and such a publication or television channel may suddenly stop pulling as well as it did previously. A mailing list that used to work well for you last year may suddenly flop. Another may suddenly start improving. Or for that matter the market for your particular product may suddenly turn sour. You must stand ready to change your plans instantly.

Try new approaches

In summary, the very idea of a fixed sum to be spent each financial year or season is not sensible for direct marketers. The issue is: how much can I afford to spend to acquire a prospect, or to produce a sale from a customer? And within reason, as long as you can meet that figure and you have the money, then keep spending.

Keep spending, so long as it pays

Conversely, if you suddenly find you are not getting the cost per response you want and can afford, you have to find a more effective message or medium – and pare your spending until you have done so.

Winning the battle

Marketing is a form of war. You are trying to gain and retain 'territory' in the form of market share or – as I prefer to think – individual customers. This sort of thinking led many years ago to media men thinking in terms of 'domination'. The idea was that you could dominate a particular medium either through repetition, or through big spaces.

In fact, in the 1950s the Ted Bates agency in the United States conducted a number of studies which indicated that once you had covered a certain medium to a certain degree you were better off spreading your net further and going to other media than spending more money to dominate existing ones.

Does it pay to dominate a medium?

Much earlier, some interesting research was conducted in the United States in a related area, which ought to influence your thinking. In 1912, a man called Shryer studied what happens when you repeat advertisements. He learned that if you run an ad a second time immediately after you have run it a first time, it does not get better results. It generally does worse.

Almost every direct advertiser finds this to be true. The only exceptions I have come across have been in financial advertising where the credibility of the advertiser was important. Until prospects had seen the advertisement once or twice they were worried about whether they ought to do business with that particular firm. This also applies to a series of mailings.

Prime prospects tend to reply first

Yet how many times have you heard space sellers try to persuade you to take a *series* in exchange for a discount? You probably recall the pitch: 'People may not notice it the first time. But if you keep running it, they will eventually get round to replying.' The truth is that your prime prospects, the *cream* of your market, will tend to reply to the first ad. To get the same level of response again, you'll probably have to wait a little while until more prime prospects emerge.

This does not mean you can't repeat ads. It merely means you ought to carefully consider the right interval between repetition. And what is that? Well, it depends on three factors:

Determining intervals between advertisements

- the size of the ad (the smaller it is, the more often you may repeat);
- the interest of the product (the greater the human appeal, the more frequently it will run); and
- the circulation of the medium (the larger the circulation, the more often you may repeat).

Of course, you must use your intelligence in following these guidelines. For instance, my former partner Brian Thomas (at that time marketing manager at a major catalogue company) was offered a full page in a major national newspaper – the *Sun* – one day after he had already scheduled an ad. Knowing the fall-off would be heavy he was very reluctant to run it, particularly because he had no time to alter the copy. However, the paper was desperate to fill the space and offered him a deal he could hardly refuse.

To his surprise, the second ad pulled 80 per cent of the results of the first. This was far higher than he expected. So although the response did fall as the rules say it should, by seizing his opportunity he did well.

What happens when you change the size

Beware large advertisements

The other way to dominate a medium is, of course, by buying large spaces. We have to go back to the work of a Mr Strong in New York City in 1914 to learn what a dubious idea that can be. He published a book which showed that, on average, in terms of response, if you assign a rating of 100 to a full page ad, then a half-page carrying identical copy in the same place in the same medium does not pull 50. It pulls about 68.

A quarter-page pulls about 49, whilst a double-page spread will only pull about 141. That means a quarter-page is twice as responsive as a full page.

You may wonder whether those old greybeards in the 1900s knew what they were doing. Well, the same research has been repeated since. In the 1930s by Schwab and Beatty, one of the first good direct advertising agencies; in the 1940s by Gallup; and in the 1950s by Daniel Starch & Staff. They all came up with the same result to within two percentage points.

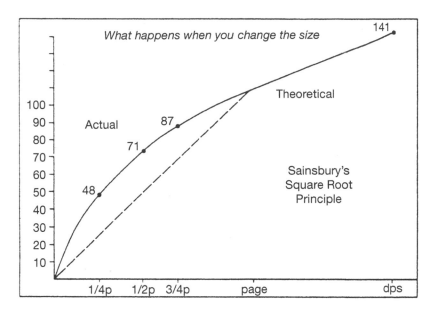

Figure 7.1 'What happens when you change the size'

This graph demonstrates what research has shown about space sizes. The important thing to remember, though, is that for a smaller space to be cost effective, the content must be exactly the same as the bigger space.

So beware the lure of large spaces unless you need a large space to tell your story fully and you make use of all the space. However, it's important to remember that long copy very often tends to outpull short. So you may need a larger space to do an effective selling job. On top of that, there have been exceptions which prove the rule: cases where simply taking an ad and making it larger has proved not only more effective in *total* numbers of responses but also *pro rata*. And if you want a better qualified lead or better quality customer, then longer copy may often pay.

Once again, only testing will discover the truth for you and your particular product, but these guidelines are generally worth following. Certainly, it's not wise to start with an unnecessarily large space to tell your story. You can develop a large ad once you have a small one that works.

Don't forget to test

Much of what I have said does not square with the way conventional marketers plan their media, particularly in respect to these last two points. But these figures are not based on opinion, they are based on results. Conventional advertisers, who don't have to measure their results, believe in 'impact' and 'prestige'. Happily, their beliefs fit their pockets. For is not the easy way the most profitable? It's much easier to take large spaces with big pictures and short copy, and repeat them frequently, than to write longer copy and change it frequently, isn't it?

THE MEDIA RECIPE

The media you choose depend on your objectives, and what you are selling. You certainly cannot divorce creative considerations from media planning. If you are selling a set of records, there is a strong argument for considering radio, which allows you to use sound. If you are selling a complex financial product, you will need room to tell your story. You'll probably be considering a flexible medium like direct mail.

But if your business is at all substantial, you will almost certainly be considering more than one medium. This is where we come to the media mix – or recipe. This is the judicious selection of the right media in combination to achieve the right effects.

The right media to achieve the right effect

Thus, a car firm might use television or posters simply to communicate awareness of a particular product and show off its looks. They might then use national press and magazines to convey more detailed information, using the local press – perhaps backed up by direct mail and radio – to encourage people to come in and test drive a car. Direct mail, e-mail and telephone can be used to stimulate loyalty and repeat sales.

From reading this book so far, you will know where direct marketing should fit into your marketing objective. And since you are looking at how you treat an individual, rather than how you reach masses of people, you ought to consider carefully the *sequence* of communications most likely to get the best results, bearing in mind how much you can afford to pay to get a lead or a sale.

Carefully consider the sequence

Suppose you were introducing an expensive new business product. You would want in the first place to make sure you were reaching the right people. You might test the telephone against a questionnaire mailing to identify the appropriate decision-makers. You might simultaneously announce to them that you are about to make a special offer which they should keep their eyes open for. You might then send out a mailing detailing this offer. And, if your response were high enough to justify it, you might send out a follow-up mailing, e-mail or phone call shortly after the mailing came out to give it greater impact. This is all part of the planning process and in particular the contact strategy mentioned in Chapter 6.

Once you have these people's names on file, you would then be thinking how quickly you ought to re-contact them, and how often, because obviously they might not be ready to buy your product when you first approach them. Other considerations might be testing the appropriate trade press to see whether couponed advertising would locate the right decision-makers as cheaply as the phone or direct mail. (In my experience it never does.)

TIMING CRITICAL

Another factor is timing, not merely in terms of what is the best time to sell a particular product or service, but how you should co-ordinate the timing between two different media. For instance, it is always a good idea to time direct mail to coincide with major general advertising pushes.

The timing and type of media you select will, of course, always be determined by the situation of the individuals you are approaching. Thus, when successfully promoting the British Automobile Association's very competitive car insurance rates, MSW Rapp & Collins in the UK faced a simple problem: in this country only a certain number of people are in the market for new car insurance at any given time. To run a national campaign over a finite period would not make sense.

The objective was to 'trawl' for prospects – to catch them at the time when they were likely to be considering their forthcoming car insurance decision. The solution was to devise 10-second television commercials which just said: 'Looking for a good deal on car insurance? Call us now.' This seemingly simple solution was one nobody had thought of before. Previously, people had been running free offers in advertisements to collect people's names and then re-contacting them at the time when they were considering car insurance.

Use short commercials to 'trawl' for prospects

Another example is that of Crown Paints. In the 1980s they were number three in the UK market. One big problem was their inability to get enough space on supermarket shelves. Unless they could get prospects to actively look for their products at point of sale, they were lost.

The strategy was arrived at first by studying the buying process. Consumers decided first to decorate, second what colour they wanted, and finally which brand. The brand was not as critical as the colour was.

Crown, therefore, tested direct response advertising and direct mail which echoed the advertising, and offered people free colour charts. The response devices asked how many rooms they were planning to decorate, and when. Crown could follow up the most lucrative opportunities at the right time and spend their money where it would do the most good.

In the event, after a very successful test, Crown underwent one of its not infrequent corporate upheavals and the opportunity was lost.

What I am trying to point out is that media planning is very much a *creative* process. The best media people know this. The worst remain chained to their sets of figures. The best work is produced when the creative people and the account planners, the media people and the client all get together and consider the problem from *every* aspect, and come up with a plan that exploits every opportunity and considers not merely where you reach people, but when, and how often. Having considered the background to the subject, what are the media available to you; what are their relative strengths and weaknesses?

Media planning: a *creative* process

THE EIGHT TRADITIONAL MEDIA AT YOUR DISPOSAL

1 Direct mail

I am constantly amazed that I made a living for many years in this business without knowing nearly as much as I should about direct mail. I was very lucky.

As I have already pointed out, direct mail is probably your principal medium. It is particularly useful for testing, and building the long-term relationship with your customers as individuals which you are aiming for.

As I have also indicated, direct mail is your most expensive medium after the telephone, per person reached. On television you can measure hundreds of impressions for every pound spent. In direct mail you can reach one or two people for a pound. But they will, if you plan properly, be the right people. People you can speak to *personally*. And with direct mail, as you will see in our chapters on testing, you can test an infinite number of variables.

Other advantages include:

The benefits of direct mail

Selectivity

You can target with great precision, using the information available on database or what you know about the list you have rented, and you can use personalised printing techniques to add impact.

Flexibility

You can, of course, choose when you mail, but more importantly, you can control what goes out. It is not a medium with only two dimensions like the press. You are not restricted to a limited space, or time as on TV or radio.

So, having a careful eye to the costs of posting, you can tell as complete a story as you wish when mailing to people, using any kind of illustrative technique or device (like a pop-up) you like. And it is also very easy to vary direct mail packages for testing purposes, in terms of the number of pieces enclosed and the messages on those pieces.

Big results

If you were lucky enough to sell one £50 product just once to one in 100 (1 per cent) of the many millions of people who read a major national newspaper, you could retire for quite a while. Even one in 1,000 readers (0.1 per cent) responding would be very satisfying.

Compared to that, direct mail produces enormous percentage results, though these don't always mean instant wealth.

What sort of results? Well, for years the magic figure of 2 per cent used to be quoted by people who didn't know this business. Where this figure came from I do not know. But let me give you some idea of the sort of results you can sometimes expect.

A major UK catalogue company could quite easily expect between 10 per cent and 15 per cent response rate when offering a new catalogue in a mailing.

What results can you expect?

Where you are simply offering the opportunity to enter a competition and win something, you can expect much higher results. 20 per cent is not at all unusual. 50 per cent is not unknown. You tend to get the lower figures appealing to businesses, and the higher when approaching consumers.

In fact, basing your thinking on some putative response rate is not good. One client in the Far East was outraged when our agency only produced a 45 per cent response rate. He felt his product was so marvellous that 80 per cent or 90 per cent should reply to it. Some optimist.

The issue to address is: how many responses do I need to reach an acceptable break-even, based upon the financial criteria I have already set up? The answer to that will depend entirely upon your own business and the tests you conduct.

The important thing to remember is that direct mail can be very profitable when approaching relatively small numbers of people compared with the press. And the big percentages make it an obvious test medium. Above all, it is the way you normally reach your most important group of people: your own customers.

Reach the most important people

The one-piece mailer

Some years ago, changes in printing technology led to the design of machinery which can, with one pass, create pieces which, after folding, act as complete mailings in themselves. In effect, you have a very low-cost mailing all made from one piece of paper.

A one-piece mailer can be used as an insert or as a pure mailing piece. Its variety of applications makes it a potentially very powerful weapon.

One-piece mailers have many uses

However, the principal advantage of this kind of format (which includes the ability to *personalise*) is that you can incorporate a letter, order form, brochure ... even a catalogue if you wish. All printed at once, from one sheet of paper. When you tear open the outside envelope, out they all tumble. What's more, it is possible to personalise these mailers. Very involving.

We have tested these mailers in various ways. They rarely (in my experience) work as well as the conventional mailing in an envelope in terms of percentage response. But because they cost so little, they can be more effective, particularly when you are going for inquiries or sales requiring a relatively low commitment.

Use the most cost-effective format

The answer, again, is to work out how much a sale is worth to you, and use the most cost-effective format. You could be pleasantly surprised.

The co-operative mailing

This medium is so far relatively underdeveloped in most countries. But I think, with the postal costs we have to pay, it is bound to develop much more.

Incidentally, postal rates in some countries are so high that it can pay to mail in bulk from elsewhere. The unusual origin often attracts more attention. On more than one occasion it has paid to mail from abroad to customers in this country. In Italy, Pepsi Cola once sent a mailing to retailers from the US which was highly effective. Some people mail from Hong Kong, finding it both cheap and efficient.

The co-operative mailer can take the form of a 'card deck': a number of cards of a particular size all put in one envelope which goes out to a specified list. This is particularly effective for selling business books. People love to pore through these cards and make a selection.

A good way to generate enquiries

Another form of co-operative mailing is a long strip divided into spaces and folded into a concertina to get it into an envelope. This too is a very cheap way to reach a well targeted group of customers and has proved very effective for business-to-business, particularly for getting inquiries.

This medium is now being well targeted so that you can, for instance, buy space in mailings only aimed at specific groups such as personal computer owners.

If you do have the opportunity to go into a co-operative mailing like this, make sure the offer you are making does not conflict with one that someone else is making. Unless, of course, yours is a better offer; in which case you will do even better than if you were out on your own.

2 Door-to-door drops

Door-to-door has many of the virtues of direct mail, but in less degree. By definition, it is less selective, since the logistics of delivering to a particular list using door-to-door would normally make it uneconomic.

Obviously, this medium is suitable if you are in a door-to-door selling business: double-glazing, swimming-pool installations, home improvements, for instance. You can arrange your canvassers or salespeople to follow up immediately after a drop has been made.

What are the advantages and disadvantages of door-to-door?

May be half the cost

Door-to-door is obviously cheaper than direct mail since you have no postage to worry about and no list to buy. It could cost as little as half as much. It is becoming increasingly popular, and research suggests this will continue. For instance in 2004 figures showed that:

The pros and cons of door-to-door

- up to 79 per cent keep, pass on or glance at door drops, exactly the same as direct mail;
- 38 per cent keep them a few days, 13 per cent for a week or more;
- 71 per cent find free samples delivered via letterbox useful, 66 per cent say that of supermarket offers, 62 per cent of money-off coupons and 47 per cent of new product trials;
- 48 per cent either visited a shop, sent for information or bought after getting promotional door drops, versus 47 per cent for direct marketing, 47 per cent for television and 60 per cent for newspaper ads.

MASSIVE SUMMER SALE

UP TO

40% OFF*

PLUS 10% CASHBACK**

CALL **0800 010 123** NOW
AND QUOTE OFFER CODE *JL0703*

TO THE HOME-OWNER

July 2007

Now with one free phone call:

✓ Make your home infinitely *safer* - and *warmer*
✓ Keep infuriating outside noise out - for good
✓ Never worry about painting and maintenance again

Dear Home-Owner,

And get up to 40% off* just for reading this

OK, you've guessed: I'm talking about home improvements.

But please keep reading, because if you need anything doing, this letter will make it well worth your while. To the tune of £500 or £1,500 - maybe even £3,000. Just call 0800 010 123 free and quote the offer reference at the top of this page.

How can we afford it?

It's simple. Our Massive Summer Sale is now on, so if you want to improve your home - or its security in any way you can get an astounding discount of up to 40%* - and an extra 10%** cashback. But you must reply by 3rd August.

But the discount alone is not what makes this offer special. It's what you get for your money. We may not be the cheapest but we do genuinely "fit the best". Perhaps you even recall the old TV ads that said so - we recently proved to an independent assessor† that, 20 years later, we still do.

From the outside most firms' products look quite alike. We think ours are more elegant - but that's a matter of taste. More important, we think, are the things you can't see and what they do for you.

Our PVC windows, entrance doors and conservatories are so rugged that it's nigh-on impossible to break-in through them. That's because they are reinforced in steel - the only ones you can buy that are 50%

† With specific reference to windows and doors, conservatories, roofline products and garage doors.

Please read on...

---

more secure than BSI standards call for.

We also offer different degrees of insulation to keep every level of outside noise outside - from faint sounds to hue and cry. We even created a unique sealed unit for one of the noisiest areas in Britain that reduces noise by up to 39 decibels.

Quiet - or *very* quiet? Which do you need?

Your area probably isn't that noisy. But a Building Research Establishment study says *"more than two thirds of British households are experiencing nocturnal noise levels higher than international health guidelines"*(45 decibels). Source: The Sunday Times, 28th November 2004.

Councils are very picky. They are legally bound to abide by strict criteria when giving out contracts. We were chosen to fit double-glazing in London's Euston Tower and the Blackpool Tower, to name just two.

Small "details" make a vast difference

You get the best combination of heat and sound insulation because we leave a 20mm gap between the two panes of glass.

These things are quite technical - but they make a huge difference. And they really matter when you make what may be a once-in-a-lifetime investment.

Our PVC-U products: windows, entrance and patio doors, and conservatories insulate far more than ordinary ones. That's because our frames have four chambers; many others have only three (those four chambers also give added strength).

Unique "Heatlok plus" technology keeps cold out better - retaining 5 times more warmth than a standard window and one and half times more than ordinary double-glazing.

If you take advantage of our up to 40% off Summer Sale, your reward could be as much as £500 or £1,500 - maybe even £3,000. You won't get a better deal - so why not act now?

And let me stress one more thing.

Your entire installation is guaranteed 10 years. In addition you get a *lifetime* guarantee against fog or condensation in the sealed units of our PVC-U windows and doors. Nobody else gives you such a guarantee.

Your taste matters as much as our workmanship. So we give you more choice of material: wood grain windows with mahogany or golden oak finishes. You can also choose different styles for conservatories, from ultra modern to traditional Victorian and Edwardian.

But whatever you choose, they never flake, rot, peel or rust. They never need painting, and wipe clean quickly and easily. You can often get cheaper elsewhere. But not better. You cannot get products with the

Please read on...

---

same specifications for the same money - anywhere.

In fact, if you find *exactly* the same product at a lower price, we refund the difference. We can only make you this promise for one reason: no other firm can offer you what we do. No matter how much you pay.

So if you accept this offer you get, quite literally, the best for less. It may be a conservatory, some windows, a security system, or even a new patio, our latest product. You can't find better quality or performance.

Why not act now? Call us free on 0800 010 123 and quote the offer code at the beginning of the letter whether you're interested or not. If you are, you can get a terrific deal. And if you're not, I promise we won't pester you. All you have to do is reply.

✓ Say *"Yes, I'm interested"* and one of our surveyors will visit you, discuss what you want - no hard sell - and give you a price. Plus up to 40% discount* if you wish to buy whilst our Summer Sale is on.

If, after hearing what he or she has to say you don't think this is the best deal you'll ever get, just say so. That will be the end of it.

✓ Say *"Not now, but maybe later"*, and we'll make a note to keep in touch - but we won't pester you.

Please reply no matter what you decide. And if you'd like a quieter, safer, more insulated home and up to 40% discount*, call 0800 010 123 and quote the offer code at the beginning of the letter now. Why not make it the next thing you do?

Yours sincerely,

Paul Mitchel

Paul Mitchel
Head of Home Improvements

P.S. You'll see more products in the leaflet I've enclosed. They're all different, but have one thing in common: *quality*. And *all* of them have up to 40% off* and an extra 10% cashback**. But to get these savings you must reply by 3rd August. So why not call now?

P.P.S. New - offered nationally for the first time ever! Our new 'A' rated energy efficient windows save up to one third on your heating bills.

*Off list price. Dependent on order value and product.
Offer open only at time of quotation. Not to be used in conjunction with any other offer.
** Payment by Everest Homeaccount finance. Subject to status. Terms and conditions apply. Written details on request.

We would like to tell you from time to time about other products and services, from ourselves and other companies, which may be of interest to you.
If you prefer not to receive such information please tick the box on the right and return this letter to Everest Limited at the address overleaf ☐

Less control

Unfortunately you can't always be sure what people who are supposed to stick literature through doors actually do with it. There are many hair-raising stories of vast quantities of leaflets being furtively slipped down drains. For this reason, the more reputable companies have inspectors who monitor the activities of those who do the job. Moreover, the Royal Mail offers this service.

Therefore, make sure you are dealing with a good company. I recall a while ago having a drop scheduled for a client which was supposed to go to the financial area in the City of London. He was somewhat surprised – and we were embarrassed – when one leaflet arrived in Berkeley Square, Mayfair, several miles away from the City.

Quality controllable – but ...

Of course, the *quality* and *content* of a door-to-door piece can be controlled. You have the same flexibility in that respect as with direct mail. But the results will be much, much lower.

Ernest Palfrey, an alumnus of *Reader's Digest*, conducted several tests a few years ago which directly compared door-to-door with direct mail. He sent out identical packages using the two alternative means of delivery.

... Less effective

Door-to-door got 52 per cent fewer responses than direct mail. This, of course, does not even take into account another important factor: direct mail can usually be addressed to the specific name of the recipient; door-to-door can't. And, of course, you can find appropriate lists of people with a special interest in your offer which, of course, would enhance response significantly.

My advice is only to use door-to-door for products of pretty universal appeal, or because you have need for large numbers of leads regardless of cost. An interesting sidelight, by the way, is that in some countries the postal service is so appalling that door-to-door becomes extremely attractive.

When to use door-to-door

Dr Alberto Foglietti in Italy discovered a few years ago that door-to-door in one city was *more* effective than the post. Another puzzling piece of information is that the Italians seem to like receiving direct mail more than any other European country according to recent statistics. My Italian partner tells me this is attributable to the inefficiency of the Italian postal service. They are delighted, even surprised, to receive anything through the post.

Door-to-door magazines

One door-to-door activity of great interest is where a magazine (usually full of offers) is dropped through household doors.

It has been used in this country to some degree, and can work very well. In the United States and Scandinavia it is one of the most popular media of all.

Postcode classifications

In many countries you can target both direct mail and door-to-door drops pretty accurately as a result of databases developed from information available in the first place from census statistics.

These statistics enable a particular list or a particular locality to be broken down into relatively small groups of households which are *likely* – but not certain – to have characteristics in common.

Use available information

The principle is quite simple. First, demographic information is extracted from the electoral register. This provides information on household composition by size, sex, age, mobility, and the length of time a particular household has lived at an address.

In addition, it is possible to identify the likely type of building presented by the address: an apartment, a detached house or a farm, for example. Other significant information can be overlaid, such as the result of financial searches conducted by the courts.

To give you an idea of the sort of thing I mean, let us take one particular database of this type. This is the Mosaic Database developed by Experian in the UK. On this database you will get the address, postcode (and the number of other houses sharing that postcode) as well as demographic data such as the composition of the household, type of address and any information available from the 300 census variables which tell you something about this type of address.

Things that only *your* database can tell you

The only thing this sort of database will not tell you is information you can only obtain from your own dealings with a particular household. For instance, if you are a credit card company you can take a particular postcode and calculate the likelihood of the people in that particular area being amongst your card carriers. In this way, you need only mail those areas you are interested in – be it the ones where people are more likely to accept your card and are therefore better prospects, or contrarily, those where you have poor penetration and wish to improve it. (The former will be more profitable.)

This subject is complex and constantly developing. I advise you to look very carefully into this sort of database which is a very valuable tool – particularly when planning proposed outlets for retail chains, such as banks. You can, for instance, very quickly estimate where you are best advised to site branches for maximum penetration of an area without over-lapping other branches. Similarly, if you are a car dealer, you can work out where your competitors are strongest, and choose a site where your business will flourish.

3 Newspapers

Newspaper readership varies widely throughout the world. For this reason newspapers can be more effective as a medium in some countries than in others. For instance, in the UK and Japan – both small countries – newspaper readership is very high, and national newspapers are very powerful, so the newspaper is a very valuable medium indeed.

In America, on the other hand, until recently there has not been anything you could really call a popular national press with comprehensive coverage, though *USA Today* now offers something very similar. I have no doubt new technology is going to make it possible to produce a much more genuine national press in that and other large countries.

Project fast

The press is powerful, pervasive, and quick to pay out. In a business based on testing, this last is a characteristic hard to overemphasise. You can, if you are in a hurry, prepare and test a new approach within a week, and two weeks later you can proceed to roll out a successful advertisement based upon your results. Only the internet is quicker.

Prepare and test – quickly

Test availability

There is quite a lot of availability for testing, both in terms of A/B splits (see page 339) and geographical breakdowns.

Uncertain quality, not enough colour

You do not control the quality of the print in the press, so for certain products you may find it far from suitable. Until recently colour facilities were very limited in the press in many countries, but colour availability is now increasing as a result of new technology.

The press has one additional benefit: it is usually less costly to test than direct mail, TV or inserts. And the ability to project fast enables you to make swift and profitable decisions.

4 Magazines

Magazines, in which I include the colour supplements many newspapers incorporate, are another important medium with significant advantages which counterbalance the problems of the press – but with one major disadvantage. This disadvantage is so important that I shall give it first.

Reasons to be wary

Long copy dates may invalidate test

You may have a lead time of weeks before you can place an advertisement in a magazine. Add to this the time it takes you to conceive, plan and prepare the advertisement and you can have a major problem with a magazine.

Sometimes a product which looks very good now can be quite out of date by the time you run your ad, particularly when we are talking about technological products.

I recall, for instance, a camera offer made by one of our clients which was unusually good value when we prepared the ad. Between the time the ad went to the publication and the day it appeared, prices for this type of product had dropped so fast the offer turned out to be no more than average in price terms, and the ad lost money. This is not unusual at all in fast-developing product categories like that.

Better reproduction

Magazines usually give you better colour facilities than the national press. Because you don't control the production of the magazine you can (and should) make sure somebody goes down to look at the work on the presses. You are about to invest quite a lot of money. And if you don't do that, you certainly ought to keep a very sharp eye on the proofs.

The importance of reproduction is overstated

I aim this advice particularly at agencies. Clients tend to get very, very excitable indeed about the reproduction of their products. I imagine this is probably because it is one subject which anybody can be an expert on, assuming they have good eyesight. In reality you don't have to worry too much because I have found time after time that appalling reproduction has had very little effect whatsoever on results, even for products where you would think looks are very important. Indeed, I have come to the conclusion that the public is purblind.

Pulls over long period

Magazines keep pulling in responses for months, and even years. I remember preparing an advertisement to sell swimming pools for my late brother. Two years after it ran in a publication with only about 50,000 circulation it was still producing replies.

Often a good test medium

Magazines tend to offer a fair range of test facilities in terms of both regional and A/B splits. Some offer outstanding opportunities in this area.

Let me quote for you what was offered by the *US TV Guide* – the largest publication of its type in the world – the last time I checked.

- 106 separate geographic editions you can buy individually, ranging from 58,000 to 2,500,000 in circulation.
- A guaranteed weekly audience (2006) of 26,300,000 copies.
- Because it prints two-up, you can get perfect A/B splits of black and white ads in 74 editions.
- The four-colour sections in the front and back allow for perfect A/B splits in eight major markets.

So, it is difficult to imagine a more perfect medium for testing. Nor one which at one fell swoop, once you have tested, you can roll-out to such an extraordinarily large number of people at the same time.

Inserts for tests

The magazine insert is – as I point out in my chapter on testing – a very valuable format. It gets high responses, so you don't need so many to get a valid, reliable result. And it offers almost unlimited test opportunities. You could test ten different inserts in one publication if you wished.

Total control

Because you control the quality and content, you can use any creative technique you like, without fear that the publication will screw the reproduction up.

I regard the insert as peculiarly valuable for another reason. This is that the insert, by its nature, is something of a chameleon. It isn't an ad; it isn't a mailing – it has characteristics in common with the two. Once you have found an insert that works effectively, it is not difficult to develop it into a mailing or into an ad, whichever you prefer.

The insert as a chameleon

Use many ways

The magazine insert can easily be used in other ways. As a bounce-back in your own merchandise when it is sent out; as a billing stuffer; as a 'take-one' in retail outlets; or to go out in other people's mailings or fulfilment packages.

Many very successful direct marketers use inserts as their number one medium. And they seem to work whether you are dealing with a relatively up-market clientele, like American Express, or with a relatively down-market clientele, like my former clients Odhams Mail Order, who sold cookery cards and the like.

Many formats

The insert is not only an effective medium; it is growing and developing fast.

Different formats, sizes and shapes will produce very different results. For instance, stitched-in or bound-in inserts get higher responses than loose inserts. Some formats can incorporate rub-off sections to reveal prizes, or have a built-in envelope. These formats tend to overcome inertia and do better than the standard format.

One form of insert which is very popular, particularly in the United States, is the multi-page free-standing insert. These look rather like small magazines. They are delivered inside your Sunday newspaper, and at the time of writing offer advertisers something like a 50 million circulation.

They work very well for packaged goods firms making money-off offers, self-liquidators and premium offers. They are also used by mail order companies for making direct offers, and catalogue companies to obtain leads. Because they offer a wide range of regional editions, they are valuable to firms wishing to reach particular demographic targets.

They have something in common with the door-to-door magazines and co-operative mailings I mentioned elsewhere. Indeed, the same sort of companies find that they work.

5 The broadcast media

The importance of the broadcast media varies depending upon the country and the stage of development reached in radio and television.

For instance, radio is a highly developed medium in the United States and Australia. In the UK, radio stations vary in quality greatly. Some offer very good coverage; some do not. Some attract great loyalty from their listeners; some don't seem to. But the development of digital radio will make them increasingly important.

Great opportunities for negotiating keen rates

Television is a popular medium in every country but the regulations governing the availability of commercials vary widely. For instance, in the United States and UK you can watch television around the clock and there is a wide range of channels to choose from. This gives great opportunities for negotiating keen rates.

For many years in the UK, there were only four channels – of which only two were commercial. And only one of these channels broadcast 24 hours a day. The result was a shortage of TV time; and that which was available was over-priced as compared with other markets. Now this has changed completely.

Linking TV with the press and other media

My experience of television as a direct marketing medium dates back to the 1960s, when I worked for CPV, the agency which handled the British Army recruitment campaign. The army considered TV would be ideal for its prospects. It inaugurated something which has been used a great deal since:

linking TV with the press. This was not a predetermined decision: it was stumbled on by accident.

In the first place we used the standard TV format of that time – the 30-second commercial. Our client soon found out, as many others have since, that 30 seconds is not long enough to *sell* anything. The reason is simple. In 30 seconds you don't have time to convince anyone of anything important, let alone give them the time to get a paper and pencil and take down the response details.

What could have been done at that time – but was never thought of – was to run very long commercials. What was done was to feature the press ads in the commercials, asking people to look for the ads and respond to them. This proved highly effective. In the UK this form of TV back-up to advertising, mailings or door-to-door drops still works very well.

In one case where a very heavy door-to-door drop activity took place in the North, a 30-second back-up television commercial apparently increased response by 50 per cent. In my own experience, television campaigns backing up direct mail activities and door-to-door drops have increased response by between 20 per cent and 40 per cent for different clients selling different products.

Big increases in response

To create such a commercial you do not need to be elaborate or clever. Just draw people's attention to the fact that an offer is coming through their door and make it quite clear what the offer is, so that it is recognised immediately. Spots as short as 20 seconds and 10 seconds have been found effective in achieving this.

The secrets of success on TV were well covered in a book by Al Eicoff of the Chicago agency Eicoff & Company in his book *Or Your Money Back*. Much of the information I give here is contained in much greater length in this book – Eicoff conducted research which confirmed many facts I already knew, but which he was the first to explain. For example:

You need time to sell

The technique I have described, developed in the 1960s, was using TV as a secondary medium. I have mentioned the use of TV to get inquiries.

Short spots get enquiries

You can, of course, do the same thing with radio. But whichever of the two media you wish to use, if you want to sell then you have to remember you need at least 15 seconds to tell people how to reply.

Eicoff found that you need two minutes to create an effective *selling* commercial. On the other hand, others have conducted tests which have proved (to their satisfaction at any rate) that a good job can be done in one minute. And to get enquiries you don't need long spots, as I have already mentioned.

Demonstrate, repeat

A product that requires demonstrating, visually or in sound, is ideal. Records, books and household gadgets have done well in these media. Financial services firms – especially those offering loans – find TV ideal for generating enquiries.

These media are fleeting. You cannot (unless you have a video tape recorder) turn back and see or hear the commercial again: and who listens or watches for the commercials?

You need to repeat the commercials a number of times to make them work. Typically you would run a burst of commercials over a six-week period, then rest for four weeks before trying again. But, once more, this depends on *your* experience with *your* product.

Off-peak works

In dealing with TV and radio, many people have found that *off-peak* spots do very well as compared with the same money invested at peak time.

> Viewers are more inclined to respond during the morning, and ads shown between 9.30 am and midday get twice as many calls as any other time of the schedule.
> *CIA Multimedia Research, 1995*

I have three theories about this. I was very pleased that Eicoff's research confirmed that two of them at any rate appear correct.

Why off-peak works

- At off-peak you are not competing with the all-dancing, all-singing £50,000 extravaganzas put out by the big packaged goods companies. You're up against the dull efforts of the local department store. And, often, old rerun shows. People are happy to stop watching a programme and start buying a product.
- Late at night or early in the morning many people are at their lowest ebb: less able to resist your blandishments.
- Many people listening to radio or watching at two in the morning may have little else to do with their time save reply to your offer. (I have no research to back this up, just my own belief.)

Shop around ... extensively

TV and radio reach a huge audience; in terms of cost per thousand impressions they are the cheapest media of all.

Beware of high costs: shop around

But on TV, production costs are staggering if you are not careful. If you shop around carefully though – I suggest more carefully than with any other medium – you will be surprised what you can achieve in cost savings.

There is, hardly surprisingly, constant complaint in the UK and the United States about the astonishing costs of producing television commercials. I am not surprised. I suspect advertising agencies (and clients, too, for that matter) are somewhat gullible when it comes to costs.

This was brought home to me when in 1987 I had to make a training video for our agency. The video was produced to a high standard by a reputable production company and when completed lasted 52 minutes. It wasn't a particularly complicated video – basically me sitting at a desk talking, with lots of cut-away shots to demonstrate various points I was making.

I asked an experienced creative head who had done a lot of TV how much she thought this video must have cost. 'I suppose you could have got it done for as little as £20,000,' she replied.

The actual cost was £4,000. Having made quite a few commercials over the years, I find that if you really want to it is usually possible to make them for a lot less than many people might imagine. Eicoff found that cheap films did far better than expensive ones.

In radio, production costs are very low. Even the most gullible can see that sticking someone in front of a microphone and recording them cannot cost all that much money. Moreover, radio offers great opportunities. It is a medium in which you have to create word pictures. It has been much under-utilised, but is really taking off now, growing in the UK at a significantly faster rate than direct response advertising generally.

6 The telephone

This medium arouses such strong feelings that in some countries unsolicited telephone calls have been banned.

However, it is extraordinarily potent. In 1980 *The Times* was moved to refer to it with what (by their standards) might be described as hysterical enthusiasm. 'The most cost-effective marketing tool invented lies unused on desks up and down the country.'

It has the value of immediacy, with all that that implies in terms of reading results fast. It is *interactive*: apart from face to face selling, it's the only medium where objections can be stated – and overcome. By the same token, you can establish what the best appeals are for your product.

The value of immediacy

It is therefore a good research medium, especially when, for instance, you are following up unconverted leads for a product. You will not only find out how people feel: you will also sell. Indeed, I have lost count of the number of times I have said to people who have been asking me why I thought a particular mailing did not work: 'Why don't you ring a few of the people and *ask*?'

A chief benefit of the telephone is that customers like it. The average catalogue company used to have 70 per cent or more of their sales coming in on the phone. Research into businesspeople's inclinations shows that almost

A useful research medium

exactly the same percentage said they would prefer to enquire about new products on the telephone. The fact that people like to phone and call you gives you additional possibilities. The same applies to e-mail with its immediacy.

Now the internet is changing all this fast. (In 2006 research it emerged that 26 per cent of people preferred to get news of products via e-mail rather than through the post.)

Create more sales

When a call comes in, you have an opportunity. Be it an enquiry, an order or even a complaint, it is often a chance to create more sales. (It is not often sufficiently realised that someone who cares enough to complain does so because they have a real *need* for the product. They can be sold to far more easily than someone who has no interest at all, as long as you are polite and helpful.)

In conjunction with the intelligent use of database information the telephone can be extraordinarily powerful.

Let me give you an example. Supposing somebody rings in who has bought maternity clothes from you. When they ring up you can pull up their details on a video display unit, discover what they bought last and talk to them about the possibility of selling them baby clothes, cot, and all the other paraphernalia associated with a new birth. The same technique can be applied in almost any product area.

The telephone is very expensive, of course. It might cost you £10 to reach a decision-maker in a company. First to find out *who* you should be talking to; second to find out whether they are *there*; and third to ring them later when they *are* there.

Very expensive, but very effective

But cost is relative. Although a phone call is expensive, it can get five or six times as many sales as a mailing selling the same product or service. Indeed, a phone call can get several times as many sales as a mailing, even if it is directed to a list of people who have been previously *unsuccessfully* mailed.

Let's face it, paying £10 to talk to somebody on the phone may seem dear. But how about spending lots on a sales call to the same person?

Many, many times a phone campaign will pay where salespeople can't. Indeed, there are cases where customers *don't want* to see a salesperson. They are too busy. They will often answer the phone and do business with you as long as you're polite.

In the case of one bank it was discovered that for a particular loan service the customers not only preferred to deal with telephone salespeople, but the actual *sales result per call* was greater than that of a personal call. For that reason, don't ignore the potential of the telephone.

Builds loyalty

Unsolicited outbound calls to people who have no previous relationship with you will, unless carefully timed and scripted, cause considerable irritation. However, calls to people with whom you do have a relationship are often welcomed as a sign of interest and a kind of service. In the UK it was learned that one call to recent customers simply thanking them for buying increased the number of purchases by 13 per cent over the subsequent six months, with an increase in order value of 16 per cent. And why not? We all like to be thanked, but few merchants bother.

Saying 'thank you' pays

Gets attention

The telephone has unique attention value. It *demands* a response.

I quoted earlier the remarkable amount of money spent in the United States on telephone marketing. I was surprised when I read that figure, until I remembered a heading I wrote in an advertisement: 'It uses no petrol. It gets decisions from 4, 6, even 12–15 people every hour. It's never sick. It says exactly what you want. It works.'

The telephone *demands* a response

The late Robert Leiderman of Leiderman and Roncoroni, had a beguiling way of describing why the telephone works. 'When did you last leap out of the bath and run downstairs to look at a television commercial?' he asks. Yet we all do that sort of thing when the telephone rings.

I am also indebted to Robert for his way of describing the fundamental difference between just making telephone calls and telemarketing.

You've already got phones and some people who are under-utilised. So you test it by using what I call the Linda method. That's L-I-N-D-A, LINDA. This is usually the first step in starting a telemarketing campaign. You take a sample of about 50 names, put them on your secretary's desk, and say, 'Linda, I've got a job for you. Call these people in the next three days and sell them our widgets.'

The difference between telemarketing and telephoning

Now Linda, who has worked for you for the last 15 years, knows the product backwards, forwards, inside out, and upside down, and she's helped you look at your direct mail and space, so you know Linda is not going to say something wrong. Three days later, she comes back and tells you the results – she actually spoke to 30 of the 50 people, and got 20 to say 'yes'.

'Incredible,' you reply, 'a 67 per cent response! That's a lot better than 2 per cent by mail.' Linda, though, being a realistic and helpful person, says: 'Well, it is a 67 per cent response of the people I spoke to, but since there were 50 people, I'd really have to say it's only 20 out of 50.'

'I can live with 40 per cent. What a gem you are, Linda. Not only have you proved how successful the telephone is, you've found a way for us to hit our targets, and saved me from making a mistake on my projections.' Then, you give her a fiver, to show your thanks.

Based on this little test, you decide to contact 30,000 consumers in the next month, before rolling out to your 150,000 customers. So, you do some quick calculations: 30,000 × 40 per cent or 12,000 orders on your test.

Then you look at the list and see that there are no telephone numbers on your file, so you send them to someone for looking up and you find that only 50 per cent have a phone. Well, 6,000 orders ain't bad either. So, you have 15,000 names.

Linda goes crazy. She is not about to call 15,000 people.

So, back to the numbers. Fifteen thousand names at about 12 completed every hour is 1,250 hours. The calls can be made, say, for six hours a day, so you need 208.03 man-days. Or, on a five-day week, 41.67 man-weeks. Now, since your full plan needs to be approved within three months, you need numbers quickly, and you want the test completed within one month or 4.3 weeks.

That means you have to find 10 people to do the job. So, you find the 10 people – who are willing to work for a month – have Linda tell them how to do it, and wait for the orders to roll in.

Unfortunately, they don't. The whole thing falls flat on its face.

Tempting as it may be, don't fire Linda. She was good. The problem is that you didn't test the telephone. You tested Linda. And to get the same results with other people, you would need people with the same skills, the same gift of the gab, the same product knowledge, and very often, the same high salary that goes with all that.

A properly designed telephone marketing programme does not rely on Linda or a whole room of Lindas. It relies on a system which incorporates the best elements of the person who knows the product, the person who knows the communications channel, the person who actually delivers the message, and the person who is asked to buy.

By putting these different elements into a telephone campaign, you limit your variables – as you do in other direct marketing methods – and have projectability. Surely, you wouldn't ask your postman, who talks to many of the people on his round, to write a special letter to each one – you'd never know why you got the results you got. How can you project it? How can you be sure the right message is delivered? Certainly the same is true by phone, when it is used as a 'verbal letter'.

A neat little story, I think you'll agree, which makes the point beautifully.

7 Posters

Where posters work

The only time we used outdoor posters for one of our clients was when we were offered them free. But as a secondary medium, I believe they have their place. If you were planning a huge door-to-door drop, you could schedule posters in that area. Or, if you were a charity, you could run posters when you were doing your annual door-to-door collection.

For that matter, if political parties were clever enough with raising funds by direct mail, they could schedule posters to coincide with their efforts in areas they thought particularly favourable to their views.

The perfect poster

The problem is that the perfect outdoor poster has about five words on it, plus the brand name (or, even better, *including* the brand name).

They are designed to attract the fleeting attention of drivers – and as such, are a menace, apart from being a blot on the landscape. But five words are hardly enough to deploy a meaningful argument. So a poster cannot be expected to do more than attract an enquiry, on its own. This is how, for example, La Redoute, the big French mail order firm, uses them to generate catalogue enquiries.

Some kinds of poster work very well: those that people have time to read, like underground posters. We find them very effective in attracting enquiries on the telephone.

8 Customer magazines

Customer magazines: people like them

Twenty years ago, the editor of the British advertising magazine *Campaign* asked my advice. Did I think it a good idea for him to go into business publishing customer magazines, his first client being American Express.

I told him I thought it an excellent idea and he went ahead. He tells me my advice had a lot to do with his decision, though no doubt he consulted other, wiser heads. He ended up running the largest firm of its kind in the UK.

The arguments for this medium are so compelling that the top three UK customer magazine publishers – including his, Redwood – have been bought by leading ad agencies.

I had nothing to do with his subsequent success, but more recently I got involved in helping promote the idea of customer magazines. To do so, I had to do some research. I was quite amazed.

If you are a copywriter – which is one of the things I do – your job is like that of a defence lawyer: dwell on the good things whilst suppressing, or certainly not talking much about the bad ones.

This was what I planned to do in this case. But when I looked more into the idea of customer magazines, I learned that I didn't have to be a clever lawyer to come up with good arguments. I began to understand why the idea is growing so fast and why my old associate is so much richer than me.

Clearly commercial

Currently 13 of the top 20 magazines by circulation are customer magazines. In fact the top 10 bar one are all customer publications. *Sky Magazine*, which has the highest circulation, reaches nearly 7 million people. These figures are sourced from the latest ABC data, correct at 5 December 2006 (www.abc.org.uk).

By 'customer magazine' I mean something produced with the clear, undisguised intention of promoting a firm's products or services. I don't mean an airline in-flight magazine, which masquerades as ordinary reading material; I mean something unmistakably commercial. Thus, the Marks & Spencer offering is simply called *M&S Magazine*.

You might imagine customers would reject such unashamed commercialism; but they don't. And the results can be remarkable.

One firm wanted to get some of their account customers back into the habit of buying – people who hadn't used their cards for six months. Apparently, their magazine managed to get 25 per cent to start spending again. In another case, 60 per cent of the people who read the magazine were impelled to buy something in the store that produced it.

When I first drafted this (in 1999), customer magazines were perhaps the UK's fastest-growing promotional medium, with the industry growing by 12 per cent a year over the previous five years. Seventy-seven per cent of the population reads or receives one of these magazines, and they are read by one in five of all 'ABC1' women. (ABC1 is a demographic classification that defines people with most money to spend.)

What is really surprising is that it can cost less to send these magazines to a customer than a piece of direct mail. One reason is that they can be subsidised by other advertisers – some titles are subsidised by up to 50 per cent.

More appealing than direct mail

Nobody sane wakes up in the morning wanting to read direct mail, let alone passes it on to their friends, but the best of these magazines are read, enjoyed and passed on.

These magazines are no longer low-quality freebies. There is a considerable emphasis placed on editorial integrity – more than with some news-stand magazines – as anything misleading will backfire on the client, and the company will lose customers.

Some titles are already exploring methods initiated by direct-mail marketers, like segmentation. They are also producing online versions.

You might ask, if this medium is so powerful, why use direct mail or other media? The reason is that if you want to sell a single proposition forcefully, direct mail, advertising or the phone remain irreplaceable. The customer magazine is less direct, but well worth your attention.

The main drawback of customer magazines is that firms often turn to them as a sort of all-purpose panacea. Bad magazines – like bad advertisements – are more about the firm and less about the customer.

What about newsletters?

A related medium, the newsletter, is often tried for the same reasons. Bad ones suffer from the same vices, plus an additional one: companies often try to make them look like magazines. I discovered what a bad idea this is when I published a newsletter many years ago.

A newsletter should always have a private, personal, almost secret feel to it – as though it has been produced for a limited number of readers. This is what gives the newsletter its value; you are supposed to be giving people valuable inside information. This is why newsletter publishers are able to charge more for a few cheap-looking sheets than others can for a glossy magazine.

Benefits of newsletters

It should (though hardly any do) have the style and tone of a letter, not a magazine.

OTHER MEDIA

Many years ago, somebody who travelled to California commented: 'I have seen the future and it works.' The same applies to some new media.

It is fearfully difficult to predict what is or is not likely to happen in our business because so much depends upon technology. And if the future can be gauged from the past, then only one thing is sure: the developments I imagine will prove crucial won't; those I never dreamed of will.

However, here are examples of developments I consider already represent serious new media.

The fax machine

It is a surprising irony that some people find the fax works better for them than the telephone, even though it has less humanity. Certainly it works – to the degree that there are quite a few complaints now about 'junk fax'.

Fax has advantages often worth paying for. When you can actually see something on paper, it can be conveyed much more precisely – it doesn't take as much time to transmit information which in speech you might waffle on about. When something reaches you through your fax machine it tends to attract your attention more than a mailing would. Because it is in writing, if it involves some kind of contractual obligation it can be legally binding. And finally, of course, you can use fax off-peak, giving you a very low rate per communication.

When a fax is ideal

I believe that fax should ideally only be used where the content has an element of urgency. Of course, e-mail is now a useful alternative to the fax, which is becoming increasingly sidelined.

Videos and DVDs in mailings

Some years ago Ogilvy & Mather encouraged Winifred Hirschle of Middlesex Business School to conduct a study into whether videos in marketing worked. At the time, something like this coming through the post was not an everyday event. However, now that these things are common or garden, many recipients simply never get round to viewing them. However, for certain types of product, the ability to demonstrate means videos and DVDs make sense.

The study concluded that where the product in question was something people were very *familiar* with visually – eg a car that had been heavily promoted on television – the impact of this sort of communication does not necessarily pay off. People are already familiar with what they are seeing and, in the end, it all comes down to 'do you like the car when you drive it?'

Works better for unfamiliar products

On the other hand, where a product is little known, or entirely new, or is of a highly technical nature, then this obviously makes a lot of sense. In addition, as I have pointed out previously, US experience shows that videos designed to appeal to specific groups are heavily viewed and pay off.

INTERACTIVE, PERSONALISED MEDIA

There are some words that marketers seem to love, as they suggest novelty. Digital is one. Interactive is another. I'm not sure why, as any reply is 'interactive'.

I find it almost impossible to understand how some of the media now emerging work. However, their potential is quite clear. Here's a good example of what I am talking about. Some years ago I read that in the United States ACTV were about to offer a remarkable new service on cable television.

What interactive TV can do

Some of the experiences subscribers were about to have struck me as less than breathtaking: for instance, they'd be able to play Black Jack with on-screen opponents, or challenge them to trivia tests. They could even confide the details of their love lives to an expert and receive advice on relationships. Much more interesting from a marketer's point of view is the fact that during the station breaks they'd see commercials specifically targeted at them as individuals.

In effect, interactive TV allows the viewer to talk to the television through a remote control device. For instance, when an expert asks you: 'Where did you meet the person you're dating?', four choices appear on the screen:

1 Through friends
2 At work
3 At school
4 At a singles bar.

Should the viewer press No 4 on the remote control, an expert appears on the screen shaking his head sadly: 'Unfortunately,' he says, 'studies show that relationships that begin that way may not work out. I am worried.'

On the other hand, if the viewer taps 1, 2 or 3 the announcer rejoices and predicts a more rosy outcome.

Here's another example showing how an advertiser could use specific data to determine who sees which commercial. If a host on a show asks, 'Do you own a dog?', only those who say 'Yes' will see a dog food commercial. If the host asks, 'Do you make over $100,000 a year and live in Manhattan and own a dog?', only those who reply 'Yes', 'Yes' and 'Yes' will receive a commercial for an expensive kennel. Fascinating, isn't it?

I am not going to go much further into this, and I should like to acknowledge that the information I have just given you is lifted shamelessly from an article in *Advertising Age* by Lenore Skenazy. I should add, too, that the whole area of interactivity is changing so fast that hardly anyone really knows what will happen next.

But I think you are beginning to get the idea. Through this sort of medium (which is still in its infancy), people can not only interact with the programme on television: the entire selling process can be matched to them, including the ability literally to order directly off the screen. This ability to have a truly interactive medium whereby the customer can respond to a range of alternatives and select a product fitted to him or herself represents the future.

Add to this the range of different alternative media – mobile telephone, i-pod and so on – and you have a splendid recipe for confusion and lots of bright ideas that won't work.

The creative challenges all this is going to summon up are such that I find it difficult to envisage them, but a good example came from Spain a few years back. There a project was run whereby viewers could join in television quiz programmes as they were being broadcast, or request discount vouchers for products being advertised on the commercials, with the vouchers being printed by means of a small box on top of the television set. Like many such experiments around the world, it flopped.

Of course, any means of communication is a medium. You can put direct response ads on matchbox covers, bus tickets, for that matter camel sides. Some have more merit than others. I am not entirely convinced of the merits of the camel side, but unquestionably matchbox covers work extremely well for advertisers trying to generate low-interest enquiries for products or services of general interest: for instance, Join the Army. Putting advertisements inside taxis must work under certain circumstances, but I have never seen any research on this.

Other media opportunities

The medium that has unquestionably generated the most excitement since the advent of television is the internet. It has proved to be such a phenomenon and is so intimately a part of the future of direct marketing that it deserves its own chapter, which follows. Much of it was written by my partner Marta Caricato, who has ruthlessly taken my original draft, trampled all over it, added a great deal to it and removed a fair bit, too. She is certainly qualified to do so, having spent most of her career working in one of the fastest-moving of all internet businesses, gaming.

SUCCESSFUL MEDIA SELECTION

Don't be a pioneer

In our sales formula on pages 99–100, the last two Ws are: *where* are my prospects, and *when* should I reach them? These are media questions.

Turn to past precedent

To aid you in determining the answers, you must turn to past precedent. You'll temper this with commonsense, naturally, and look carefully for any factors which may have affected your results. You must also refer to the many statistics available in print. Plus, of course, any research you have available.

In most countries there are extensive readership surveys in addition to the figures that the media print to prove (to their own satisfaction, anyhow) that you should put every penny you've got with them. All these will act as a gloss on your own past results and aim at helping you to make the right decisions.

Observe and copy

But what if you are a newcomer? Then you must *observe*, and *copy*. You must get on as many mailing lists in similar product areas as possible. Get copies of all publications you think may be relevant. (How do you get on a mailing list? Buy a product or make an enquiry using a name or address variation so that you recognise where subsequent mailings come from.)

There is no substitute for spending a great deal of time sifting through publications to see where and when your competitors (or, if it's a new product, similar products aimed at similar people) spend their money.

In the UK, for instance, MEAL is a service which tells you, in exchange for a subscription, where and when companies are spending their money. Such information tends to be very partial though. For instance, it often does not cover the local press properly. One of my clients was consistently misrepresented for years as spending far less than they actually did because of this.

So you have to read these statistics with great care. They are in some ways not as valuable as seeing the actual publications. Apart from anything else, you see not only *where* people are placing their money but what precisely they are *doing* with it. What sort of advertisements they are running.

Evaluating the use of mailing lists is much more speculative. But you can build up an overall picture. If a soundly based company runs ads *consistently* in a certain publication, or *repeatedly* mails a certain list, then you can assume it works for them.

Rule of three

What do we mean by 'consistently'? Well the old rule is: one insertion is a trial. Two is to confirm the first result. And three means it worked, so you should try it. The same applies to repeated mailings.

But beware of one thing. That big, well-established organisation may have more money than you. They may be able to pay more money for each initial order, in order to make money long term. So judge your results with that in mind. And for goodness sake, adopt a sceptical view. Lots of smaller companies (and even the occasional large one) aren't reading their results as carefully as they might. They could be living on their fat – and you can't afford to do that.

An instructive story on this subject (and a very sad one) was told to me by an old colleague in New York. I asked him why a big company that had been in business for many years in the US had suddenly gone broke. They had always seemed exceptionally professional in everything they did.

Be sceptical

The answer was that the founder had contracted a terminal disease. He didn't care any more, poor man, and the company went into bankruptcy.

So, follow, but with caution. And whatever you do, never pioneer unless you have to. The best place to put *your* market stall is where all the others are.

Where you will do best

I gained my education in space planning and buying when I was running the marketing of the Bullworker. It was a valuable education because I learned everything bit by bit.

I discovered that the best media were, not unnaturally, publications with a heavy sport or health orientation. They would produce inquiries for the product five times more cost-effectively than the second most effective type of media, which were general-interest weekly magazines. These in turn tended to do about 50 per cent better than the daily newspapers.

What I learned about the media

Since I was working on share of profits based on reaching a lot of sales, I could not rely upon the relatively small numbers of health magazines enquiries. Although they were very cheap, and highly profitable, these publications had small readerships and tended to 'tire' very quickly. Nor could I even reach my targets by advertising in addition in the general interest magazines. I had to make the national press work.

This proved difficult. To start with I found the only spaces that would pay out for me were little bargain spaces in the pages which run every Saturday in the British national press offering lots of gimmicky items. Even this was not bringing in enough sales.

I then tried running advertisements in the body of the paper. They did not pay for me. I finally got the breakthrough I wanted when I started testing ads on the sports pages. I found my ads would pay if I could get a position on the back page – the most prominent of all the sports pages. Elsewhere they did not do well.

As time went by, I refined my planning. I realised that where small ads did exceptionally well – in the health and general interest magazines – I could afford bigger spaces. Indeed, in the former I ran full pages, whilst in the latter I built up a big editorial-style ad.

So apart from the publication, position is vital. An ad that does well on the sports page may flop on the leader page. An ad that succeeds amongst the earlier pages of a magazine, may fail through not being noticed when placed four pages from the back. Indeed, that is what we found out for one of our clients. Eighty per cent of their successful ads were near the front of the publication. Their unsuccessful ones tended to be towards the end.

Always remember that if a small ad is working exceptionally well for you, try a bigger one – and conversely, in a publication where your big ad is not working, try a smaller one.

Here are some guidelines on what works and what doesn't.

The best advertising spaces

- As a whole the front half of a publication is better than the back. The front page is best (if available) followed by the back. Then the inside-front right. Then the inside-front left. Then the inside-back right. Then the back left. After that it tends to be in order going from front to back.
- Right hand pages do slightly better than left. And it is generally agreed that pages facing editorial do better than otherwise – though one piece of research I saw a few years ago suggested this was not the case. I have to say, however, that it was for a particular magazine, and I suppose once again the answer is *test* and find out what does best for you.
- Any ad in magazines or newspapers which is next to the letters pages, TV programme pages, or horoscopes does well.
- Gutter positions do worse than outside positions. The gutter is the fold that runs down the middle of the paper when you open it out. You want your advertisements to be on the outside edges of the newspaper, not the gutter.
- Any ad surrounded by matter (so you can't cut the coupon out easily) will do worse than otherwise. This will not matter if you are just displaying a phone number or web address.
- Special positions are usually worth paying extra for.
- If there is a feature directly relating to your product, then a medium that is not normally worth going into may prove profitable. Thus, if you are lending money, a home improvements feature might do well for you.

Once again, as in every other aspect of our business, these are only general rules. Results may vary according to many other factors. And a good position won't save your lousy ad.

In mailings, one thing is obvious, and it's almost all you need to remember. If your mailing hits a prospect just after someone else offering a similar product, it can't help. Unless, of course, you are offering a better deal. But such clashes are to be avoided.

When you will do best

'When should I run my offer?' is the final question to ask.

My experience is based upon the western hemisphere. For this reason the monthly listings I am going to give below apply to our climate. However, whatever the country, here are two accepted facts: the first is that you will generally do better in winter than in summer; and you will *not* generally do well during public holidays. (Obviously, there are exceptions, like seasonal products which appeal in the summer months.)

Thus, here and in America, for most advertisers the best month is January, and then February. The sequence after that is difficult to place exactly, but September would probably be next, then March, October, April, November, August, May, and – the poor months – June and July.

The best months and days

Then, death on skates: December. Research has suggested that the greater the volume of direct mail, the lower your response should be. So far, I have seen no proof of this.

Equally, the days of the week vary, as I have noted in the chapter on testing. Tuesday seems to be best for many people.

Sometimes, because you can get a very good price from the media, bad months can become good months. And the same applies to public holidays, with the exception of Christmas (only holiday advertisers seem to do well at that time). I recall negotiating for Bullworker a very good deal on Easter Saturday and Easter Monday with the *Daily Express*. We got our best-ever results in a national paper. And one of our clients put nearly *all* his money into August, because he got good deals.

Experience – and chance

I don't think I can repeat too often that it all depends on your experience ... and on *chance*.

Some years ago I had an interest in a company. What happened is a cautionary tale. The company was importing its product from Germany. We tested, with enormous success, the *Sun* newspaper. Indeed, the results were so outstanding that I made that paper our main medium.

A cautionary tale

In April/May of the year in question, three things happened. First: the pound dropped 20 per cent against the Deutschmark. Second: results that year (for everyone I spoke to) dropped dramatically at the end of April. Third (and I should have waited to find this out): the conversion rate to sales from enquiries in the *Sun* turned out to be much lower than in other media we had been using, which was exacerbated by the overall slump in results.

You can imagine the combined effect. Utter disaster all round. We went broke.

So as you see, timing in media selection can be of inordinate importance. All media planning should be conducted on the basis of pessimism, moderated by gloom, with a healthy dash of caution.

However, there is another important lesson I learned from that experience: the quality of sales or enquiries can vary enormously from one publication to another. Indeed, I have since learned that this principle applies much more broadly. A customer recruited through direct mail can be of greater or lesser long-term value than one recruited on the phone, or through the press.

All customers are not created equal

You have to study the behaviour of particular groups over the time carefully: all customers are *definitely* not created equal.

PROVEN PRINCIPLES OF NEGOTIATION

This leads me to the very special area of *negotiating*, which can make nonsense of everything I've just said.

There is one overriding principle of negotiation. A principle which was proved, in controlled tests, by Dr Chester Karrass of the Californian Centre for Effective Negotiating to hold true: **The person who asks for least (or offers least) will always come out best in a negotiation … assuming his offer is not so ludicrous as to make it insulting**.

As long as you are pleasant and not too aggressive, never be afraid to make an outrageous offer. This is so important not only in media buying, but in buying or selling anything, including your product or services. I will give you one or two examples from my own experience.

Many years ago, I became involved in a series of negotiations to obtain the rights to a central heating system which converted an ordinary coal fire into a most effective heating method. My partner (and mentor) in this negotiation was a man called Fox, who had worked all his life in the toughest business on earth: the rag trade.

The system had been developed by a big engineering company who had no idea of how to sell it. They had lost a fortune trying. It had cost £50,000 to create. Fox and I went to see them.

He said he wanted to make an offer. They asked how much. He said: 'I'd rather not tell you, because you might laugh and end our discussions. You tell me how much you want.' People hate to make the first offer, as well he knew, and he had already made them realise he was not going to pay a lot. They then insisted on him telling them the figure. Once again he demurred. They realised this really *was* going to be a low offer. They insisted. He said: 'Are you sure you won't just end the discussions when you hear what it is?' They then reassured him. He said: '£2,000.' They were stunned: 'But this thing cost £50,000 to develop.' Nevertheless, their expectations had been brought right down.

Offer the least

He said: 'What are you going to do with it? You might as well dig a big hole in the ground and bury it, for all the good it is to you.' This brings out another important principle: always study your opponent to establish what his own position is. Fox knew they didn't know how to sell the unit.

In the end we got it for £5,000, but never made any money, so even a low price can be too much.

Don't worry about refusal

My late brother worked in another tough business, property, and used to operate the same sort of system, but in a more systematic fashion. I asked him how he managed to make such a profit on taking a property and doing it up to sell it.

'Very simple,' he replied. 'I look at about ten or twelve houses that seem suitable every month. On each of them I put in a very low offer that's bound to give me room for a profit. Nine out of ten will say no. Sometimes they will *all* say no. But I find there's usually somebody who has good reason to sell. The right price is what people will take. The big mistake most people make is to fear being turned down.'

So another rule of negotiating is that if you don't ask, you won't get.

You will be surprised, if you approach the media with an eye to their position as much as your own, what good deals you can get. You may be sitting worrying about making an offer that will be refused. At the other end the man may be praying for *any* kind of offer. What have you got to lose? Only a good deal!

Remember, a newspaper is like a railway train. Each day, it runs whether the seats (or advertising pages) are full or not. So if you make it easier for them, they will often make it cheaper for you. In this way, everybody is happy. And that is the *best* form of negotiation, because you are not just negotiating: you are establishing a relationship.

If you don't ask, you won't get

TEN GOOD DEALS

Here's how you can help yourself, and help the media. The obvious opportunities come first.

1 Volume discount

You'll usually get a better rate if you promise to spend at a certain level.

Help the media – and yourself

2 Series discount

Almost every medium offers a discount for taking a series of ads.

3 Run of week discount

You may prefer to go in on a certain day of the week. But the publication may like to have an ad ready to slot in on *any* day and give you a discount for the privilege.

4 Standby discount

If you have an ad standing by with the publication which they can drop in whenever they've got a problem, you should get a big discount.

5 Distress discount

This is the miser's favourite. Have an ad ready so that when they call you (and you let them know you are always interested if the price is right) you can negotiate a rate just short of daylight robbery.

6 Rate protection guarantee

Rates go up, but rarely, if ever, down. When negotiating, try to get the publication to guarantee you the rate at the time for a given period. It could be a big saving.

7 Special position free

If you have a good enough relationship with a medium, you may be able to get a special position (or time) with no premium. It's got to be worth it. And there's no harm in trying.

8 Specified day free

You can do the same with the specific day you want.

9 No payment for solus

A solus position on the page is usually worth paying for. Try to get it free, if you can.

10 Soft period discount

When space is hard to sell, and easy to buy, that's known as a soft period. You should make hay then.

The perfect deal

Finally, there's the *perfect* deal. The PE or per enquiry deal. There are few times in life when you can get something for nothing, but this is the next best thing.

You know how much you want to pay for an order or enquiry. The publication (or list owner) knows how much he wants for the use of his medium. If you can agree with him that you will pay so much per sale or enquiry, and he'll take it, then what could be more perfect?

Several TV stations in the UK were trying this method with direct advertisers for a period until an outcry from other advertisers forced them to stop. However, in most areas you will find somebody willing to have a go.

PE is the perfect way to *test* a new medium. The sales rep will tell you what a marvellous medium he is offering you. You will wonder. The best way to find out is to do a PE deal. In the end it will be to the interest of both parties. If only all media would do it, media buying would be so simple!

But one word of advice. No matter how well you negotiate people down, don't boast about it. Keep quiet, and protect your deal.

Media – very different thinking

Points to remember

- Let your aim not the appeal of a medium guide you.
- Five differences from general advertising approach:
  - media rank differently in importance;
  - effectiveness evaluated differently;
  - allow for testing;
  - repetition viewed differently;
  - space size and copy length viewed differently.
- The greater the impact, the higher the cost.
- Figures mislead: some media more responsive.
- Nothing fixed: spend on what works – and vice versa.
- Beware repetition – results fall off fast.
- Small sizes often pay better.
- Think in terms of sequences.
- The medium should fit the objective.
- Timing critical:
  - when using media together;
  - when messages relate to events (eg renewals or prospects' buying plans).
- Things to consider:
  - acquisition or retention;
  - cost;
  - targeting – how selective;
  - how much you can say;
  - likely responses;
  - quality of reproduction;
  - controllability;
  - testing possibilities;
  - lead times;
  - flexibility – can it be used in other ways?
  - attention value.
  - ease of add-on sales.
  - likeability.
- Interactive: not new; just faster and more personal.
- Planning: start by copying.

- The rule of three.
- Look for easy wins.
- Importance of position and month.
- Negotiation: winners offer least – or ask for most.
- Ten good deals to remember.

8

Digital Marketing: The Internet and E-mail

I wrote the sentence above some years ago, and felt quite pleased with myself. Then I realised that Confucius, quoted at the start of this book, said it a lot earlier and better. But it is important to define what we are talking about. Indeed this book came about because 25 years ago, as far as I could see, nobody had defined direct marketing simply.

And guess what? History repeats itself. As far as I can see, nobody has defined digital marketing simply now. Even 'digital' has quite a few definitions – six, says the *American Heritage Dictionary,* or eight, say the people who contribute to Wikipedia. It doesn't matter, because in truth once again marketers have fallen in love with a fancy phrase that makes them feel that what they do is complex and important. And why not, if it makes them happy?

So before we go further, digital marketing logically should mean marketing in which messages are sent using a medium that depends on digital transmission. Text messaging, for instance – which could become far more loathed than junk mail or spam, as it intrudes on such a personal device. Equally logically digital marketing *should* include digital TV and radio, but I've never seen anyone claim it does. Anyhow I cover these elsewhere, so I shall just point out the only thing you need to know. **Whatever fancy name you like, to succeed online or digitally you must simply practise accelerated direct marketing**.

That's because the internet, by far the most significant digital medium, is not just an advertising medium, which many saw it as originally – and some still do. It is a near-perfect direct marketing medium because it involves a two-way exchange between user and provider of a service or a product. In that respect it is like the telephone, a powerful direct medium, whether fixed or mobile.

But no matter what science makes possible, digital or otherwise, I predict one thing confidently: marketers will misunderstand and misuse it extensively and expensively. That's because no technology will confer commonsense and imagination – both essential to understanding people and business.

Three very powerful benefits

If you think about it, any easier, cheaper or quicker way to communicate always does well. This is precisely what digital is, whether we are talking about texting or the internet: easier, cheaper and quicker, hence its uniqueness. But the internet is 'more' unique than other digital media, if that were possible, and it is what I propose to focus on here.

All other media depend upon you, the user, being for whatever reason where advertisers display their messages, or where they can reach you. You read a newspaper – you see advertisements. You watch television – you see commercials. You walk down the street – you see posters. When you get your mail, you find direct advertisements. And sometimes when you pick up the phone, someone tries to sell you something.

Some messages will be timely and relevant – but very few. Most will be money down the drain for the marketer. Because unless it's Saturday night, your pipes have frozen, the house is flooding and you go through the pile of door drops looking for a plumber's leaflet, you don't necessarily want to be exposed to advertising messages. You are a passive recipient. Advertisers have to work to reach you. And they often have to make costly, ill-informed assumptions on whether you are in the market, when you will respond, or what will persuade you to respond.

The *uniqueness* of the internet

With the internet things can be different. You can minimise risk and wastage by making decisions based on not what you assume but what you know. Your prospects are doing something online – looking for something. They are telling you they are in the market; they are raising their hands. They are probably there only because they want to get something – and it could be your products, services or the information you offer.

What's more you can talk to them at that very moment. You can get them to respond almost immediately. You can act, test, learn, improve – all in the space of a day, not a month or two. It is hard to conceive of a more propitious situation.

With other media, how often can you know you are talking to people who have actively searched for what you offer? You also normally have to appeal to those who *may* want what you offer. And the more people you try to appeal to, the greater the cost, risk and waste, and the less the power.

The *sameness* of the internet

Yes, the internet, whether you see it as a distribution channel or as a medium, is unique because the relationship people have with it is unique. But is it so different that managing it calls for a totally new set of skills? Is the internet the realm of the internet experts – so they should deal with it?

I have my opinion – and a very strong one, come to that. I won't tell you what it is till the end of this chapter, but keep those questions at the back of your mind while you read these pages, because I am sure you will form your opinion and guess what mine is.

GETTING IT RIGHT FROM THE START – SEVEN THINGS YOU MUST ASK YOURSELF ABOUT YOUR SITE

Do you have a website? Or if you are starting a new business, are you planning to have one? I bet the answer is yes. If you already have a site, you may find it useful to ask yourself the following questions and see how your site scores against them. Even better, if you are about to build a site, use them to guide your planning.

1 Why a website?

Ask yourself scrupulously why you are doing this. For personal reasons? They will probably turn out to be wrong. For corporate reasons? What are they?

The internet reminds me, as I have already noted, of what happened when the database first came in. Dim marketers feared being left behind, spent squillions building databases which were far too often unsuited to their needs, and then sat around wondering what to do with them. Most did very little – still true to this day.

Just as many are mesmerised by the idea of advertising on television so as to boast about their new commercials at the golf club, others like to prattle about their website. They pile in because it's the thing to be done; everybody else is doing it: why not us?

2 Who are your customers, and who do you want to attract to your site?

Everything starts with one question: who do you want to talk to? Define your customers and prospects demographically and psychographically, never forgetting that the prospects are likely to be very similar to your customers. By demographically, I mean what kind of people they are, socially and from an economic point of view; by psychographically, I mean what motivates them, and how they think and feel.

So how much do you know about your customers? Do you have a database that tracks their behaviour? Your answers will determine everything from the content of your site to the reciprocal links you set up with other sites.

Even better, how much do you talk to customers? One of our clients is marketing director of the UK's most successful firm of independent financial advisers (IFAs). He bases most of his articles for their in-house magazine on conversations he has with customers. Hardly surprisingly, they always find his articles relevant and interesting – and often say so.

It doesn't take a lot of effort – just the occasional visit to your customer services department and a little curiosity – but it pays off for a simple reason: you can decide on facts, not assumptions.

3 What do you want your site to do for you?

For example, do you want to redefine or reinforce your positioning? To increase sales by 5 per cent through e-commerce in the next year? To free space or resources for other things? Write it down – with precise figures and time limits.

Five critical objectives

To succeed you must focus on these five objectives:

- get people to your site;
- keep them for as long as possible, or certainly long enough to convince or sell to them;
- persuade them you are one of their natural options – preferably their ideal one;
- get them to respond; or, failing that, decide to revisit for more information;
- get permission to talk to them.

Your site can help position you as an authority – and you should aim for that. Since most people seek information on the web, those who seem better informed are seen as better.

Your site can generate sales – though not perhaps as quickly as you hope. Few people buy the first time they visit your site. This is no surprise. McGraw-Hill discovered years ago that on average a salesperson does not make a sale until the fifth call. But your site can do four other things:

Four practical benefits

Some benefits are to:

- help identify your customers' buying patterns;
- enable you to provide more and better services;
- deliver free, valuable and relevant information to keep them coming back, attract fresh prospects, and build trust;

- help with one of your most important jobs: attracting new employees, and thus slashing normal recruitment costs.

4 What draws people to a site?

Since people go on the internet to find something – a product, service or information – the more you give them what they want, the more they will be drawn to your site. For instance, if your main aim is to sell, make your products easily available, make offers and use incentives, and sell the benefits strongly, repeatedly and extensively.

Never underestimate the power of information. Guides, white papers, free reports, glossaries, lists of specifications, comparison guides, FAQs, press, experts' and customers' quotes to name a few, are always good, especially if what you sell is complicated, technical, expensive or an important buy.

And remember: when people are online, they expect to get everything quickly. When you go to a supermarket, you expect to waste time: you will walk down different aisles looking patiently for what you want. You may even enjoy it. You'll probably wait for the shop assistant if you need to ask something: you'll almost certainly join a queue at the till. But you'd be hopping mad if it took too long to get through the front door. A website is similar in some ways, though not all. People expect to find everything straight away, not to have to go on a treasure hunt – though once they've started they will happily waste lots of time.

Be quick: people are impatient

If you are unhappy about the service you get at a supermarket, you're unlikely to just dump your trolley and go to another store. But if you are unhappy about a site, it only takes half a second to leave it and go to another. You have very little time to grab and retain your visitor's attention. To put this in context, on average people only spend 44 seconds on a webpage, says the Nielsen/Netratings Global Index Chart (month of November 2006, Panel Type: Home, at www.nielsen-netratings.com/resources.jsp?section= pr_netv&nav=1). Do you think that's very little? Well, that average allows for all the half-hours people spend on pages that do interest them.

What's more, the same research reveals that each person visits an average of 43 pages per surfing session. Admittedly they could be 43 different pages of your site, but they could also be pages on your competitors' sites. So it makes sense to tip the odds in your favour. Make sure you 'signpost' things clearly, so visitors can easily find what they are looking for. Perhaps the best example is Amazon (see Figure 8.1). No matter what you are looking for, I bet you will find it in seconds – by clicking on the tabs at the top, the text links on the left, or by running a keyword search in the whole Amazon database or one of its sections.

By the way, is there anything else you notice on that screenshot? Offers, discounts and new products are really hard to miss! Amazon strikes the perfect balance between making it easy for you to find what you want to buy –

Amazon: the perfect balance

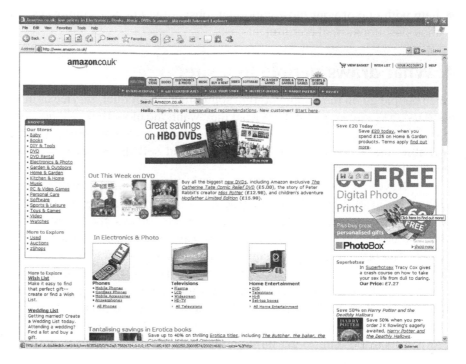

Figure 8.1 Amazon's website

if you have something specific in mind – and at the same time tempting you with what they want to sell.

5 What keeps people on a site, and what persuades them while they are there?

Again, the answer is simple – and it's pretty similar to what attracts them. Not clever technique, but better content, and more of it, that gives customers what they want: useful information and greater benefits. My firm's site has somewhere over 420 pages (it keeps growing). We answer common marketing questions; we give case histories; we offer advice.

The second most important thing is how the content is organised. Is it easy to move from one page to another? Is it easy to search for things? Is it easy to read the content? It may be tricky to answer these questions yourself: when things are familiar, it is very common to become 'blind', failing to miss even the obvious.

If you already have a website, speak to your customer service people. They will know what your customers' complaints are about the usability of the site. If you are building a site, ask one or two people to look at it with a fresh eye. Observe what they do when they get there and then ask them how easy to use they found it.

6 What makes people return to a site – and reply?

Quite simply, if they like what they get, they will come back. But you have to remind them. Just think: how many times do you go to a restaurant, have a wonderful meal and tell yourself, 'Oh, we'll definitely get back here!' – then never go again? Now imagine: suppose after a couple of weeks that restaurant sent you a message, maybe telling you about their new menu and offering you a free glass of wine with your next meal? Wouldn't you be more likely to go back? At the very least, I bet you will think of that restaurant when deciding where to go. So keep in touch. Do what you'd do in normal direct marketing.

7 You give people something – what can you get in return?

The most important thing you can get from your visitors is permission to talk to them. Yet a surprisingly high number of companies don't do so – or at least don't succeed. So suggests the *National Client E-mail Marketing Survey* report, published by the UK DMA in December 2006, and containing the information shown in Figures 8.2 and 8.3.

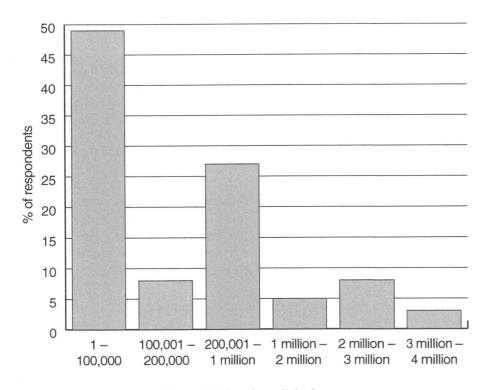

Figure 8.2 Size of e-mail database

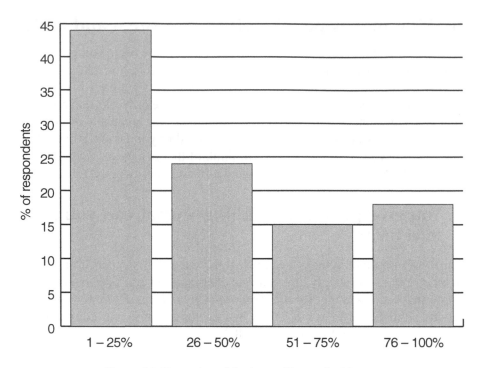

Figure 8.3 Proportion of database with e-mail addresses

The greatest proportion (44%) of respondents said they only have e-mail addresses for up to 25% of their entire database, and only 18% have 78–100%. Within this section, however, a significant proportion did have e-mail addresses for their entire database, which suggests that e-mail marketing is vital for their marketing and that they collected these addresses online. This in turn suggests these companies do all their business online: they are e-commerce organisations. (Direct Marketing Association (UK))

You must ask your visitors for their e-mail address whenever you reasonably can – and offer them something in exchange. People increasingly realise the value of their contact details. They don't give them out light-heartedly; they need a good reason. So ask as much as possible, ideally on every page, with each order, with each new account, and every time someone asks for information.

Here are just some things you could offer in exchange:

● contact-us buttons;
● polls;
● ask the expert features;
● ask a colleague features;
● forums;
● free catalogue;

- free quote;
- a free 'white paper' (a report on a subject of interest);
- customer quizzes;
- competitions;
- members-only areas;
- newsletter sign-up.

You should definitely try to get your visitors to complete an online questionnaire for you to learn as much as you can about who they are, what they want and what they think of your offerings – anything you can use later to talk to them more relevantly.

As with any other kind of direct marketing, incentives are important: prizes, discounts, extra services. If you're a wine merchant you can offer meal-planning wine lists, or regular half-bottles of new labels with a purchase. If you sell or service cars, offer daily-updated tables of the best deals for customers' marques online.

Whatever you do, use the data you acquire sensibly and deliver what you have promised. When you collect the data, reassure people: spell out how you are going to use it, and stress that if at any point they don't want to hear from you any more, they only have to say so. And do so in plain English, avoiding copying and pasting straight from the Data Protection Act.

But let me stress this: no incentive, no matter how valuable, will work if your website fails to give people what they want and make them trust you.

How you 'give people what they want'

There is a 'convenience paradox' on the web: people use it to save time, and to waste time. Make it easy for them to do both.

Once you've got visitors to your home page, you must persuade them to explore. Map out your flow of information following how one of your salespeople would handle a customer. As with normal direct marketing, tell your prospects all about the benefits you offer – descriptions, pictures, and demonstrations if possible. Give them valuable information. Quote reviews, testimonials; show satisfied customers; explain how easy it is doing business with you. Ask for their comments. 'E-mail us. We'd love to hear from you' is a message that works for us.

Inform, amuse and benefit your visitors

The nature of traditional sales material is often governed by cost – how big is the mailer going to be? Four pages? Eight pages? Online you have all the space in the world to do a thorough selling job. You can get people to explore your content by making sure every angle that may interest them is covered – not something you can do with a two-page glossy leaflet. And if you can think of something entertaining, involving and relevant, put it in. It could be something that requires them to join in – but isn't too demanding – and offers a prize. They will then tell you about themselves. (Does this sound like a sweepstake to you? Quite so.)

The perfect place for selling

What your site must deliver

Here are seven things I believe you should demand of your website, and one suggestion. Does your site meet these desiderata?

- Is it a pleasure to visit – with easy-to-read script?
- Are transactions easy?
- Does it feature benefits, or just product names?
- Does it involve – or confuse?
- Does it try to learn about customers?
- Does it work hard to get replies?
- Is it quick?

I've already mentioned this earlier, but it is so important I'll repeat it in a different way:

Ask 10 customers who are not familiar with your site to try it – without any help.

If you are selling from your site, use your own credit card and buy something. See what happens when your customers buy from you. In short, as with everything else, only the customer knows for sure. Far too many marketers forget this.

Shelley Taylor, author of *Click-Here Commerce*, surveyed 50 sites, including CDNow and Blockbuster Video. Only two would work with older computers, 24 per cent offered no pre-sale assistance, 32 per cent didn't tell you how to buy, only 12 per cent offered third-party reviews of products and only 30 per cent told you whether products were available. I doubt much has changed.

Another relevant example is AOL, a leading service provider which suffers from the slight shortcoming of providing an abysmal service. They ask me to report problems – and do nothing about them. They ask me to fill in surveys – and don't react. And they charge money to call for service. The nadir was perhaps reached when I was in the United States recently and had a problem. I spent 20 costly minutes on my mobile phone just getting through to them – only to be told that as I am a UK customer, they wouldn't help. What kind of rubbish is that from an 'international' firm? And with what glee I cancelled my account – which of course they made as hard as possible, just to ensure I never want to rejoin. A lot of these people are going to find out the hard way if they don't learn the basics – fast.

A–Z OF BUILDING AND MANAGING A WEBSITE

Your **A**udience must like what they see. Design with your visitors' browsers in mind, as well as their demographic taste.

Your website can become a **B**usiness in its own right.

Commitment is vital. The internet is a fast-changing environment. Many new sites don't stay on the World Wide Web for long because maintenance, publicity and ongoing programming and design costs are sometimes underestimated and often under-quoted.

Design information for your customers' preferences, not yours. Information your customer is lured by should only be a mouse-click away. Think Excite, not Yahoo!

Engage your visitors with content that's irresistible, involving and packed with information and benefits.

Fancy graphics can lose you business. First impressions are made in 6 to 10 seconds – so if a graphic takes longer than that to download, ditch it.

Make sure your visitors can **G**et in touch with you easily and quickly. Make sure all contact information is not more than a mouse-click away. Provide names for visitors to contact personally.

HTML, Java, Flash, Oracle: you can teach yourself these; you can scan every image on your site yourself. But you'll probably build a better site if you find a programmer and designer you can trust, who'll make sure everything on your site will actually work, whilst you concentrate on the most vital aspect – content.

Like arresting creative work, each web page should contain one **I**dea. Decide which idea you want visitors to remember from each screen.

Join the online community yourself. Lurk at newsgroups, and then start contributing. Register with information services, review competitors' e-mailings and spend time browsing their sites.

Keep on going. Expect criticism, be brave with new technologies (if your customers' browsers or connections support them) and be prepared to change content 'on the fly'.

Less is more. Once you've built your site, cut out what you can until only value and intrigue remain.

Magnetism. You've either got it, or you haven't. What can you build on your site that will keep visitors coming back, time after time, to participate? An industry market-share index? A regular quiz? A game? A round-the-clock commodity monitor? A buzzing message board full of favours and contacts?

Network. Our service provider has a diesel generator in their basement, so our sites will be online even if the power in San Francisco and London fails. You must have confidence in your network service provider and ensure you have an adequate back-up plan should things go wrong, especially if you're building e-commerce applications. Watch the league tables in internet business magazines or ask a forum.

Offer fresh content each time visitors return. A dynamic, database-driven website that builds content 'on the fly' for individual visitors may be a distant strategy for you, but you can give visitors a reason to return to your site by offering fresh industry news, research in PDF files, interviews/ transcripts/articles, and limited offers.

Permission marketing is easy – and essential. One of the internet's best advantages is that it allows marketers to send frequent personalised e-mail messages extremely cheaply. Learn what your customers want. Ask their permission to send them more news about what they rely on you for. And deliver it on your site.

Be **Q**uick to improve your content, which dates a couple of months after launch.

You must regularly refresh your site to guarantee **R**epeat visits. Frequency will build familiarity and trust, and your visitors will buy from you when they need your products. Understand that this is not a one-off cost. It takes constant improving to breathe life into your sales. Updates must be made; imaginative online marketing has to happen.

Build a **S**earch engine on your site, so visitors can find what they're looking for quickly.

Use a **T**heme to draw your content together, as you would when making a presentation, or writing a proposal.

URL – your address online, eg www.rollingstones.com. It's vital. Take time getting it right. Print it on everything offline – letterheads, business cards, invoices, press ads.

Brilliant advice I read online: all graphical content must add **V**alue to what you're communicating. Explain your ideas to someone who doesn't flatter you. Discard anything that doesn't add value for your audience.

Watch what your competitors are up to online, and who they're attracting. Look at the portals for navigation and flow ideas; at games and internet technology sites for the latest in design capabilities. Watch what's coming through and choose the technologies likely to provide your customers with the best service. The coming of Wireless Application Protocol (WAP), or wireless technology, means more of your customers will be accessing your site from their mobile phones.

Constantly re-e**X**amine your objectives and your reasons for doing business online. Ask the same group of people for their feedback every few months. Make sure the group includes the sort of person who looks for the pitfalls.

Pick the browsers you support, software, servers, networking and hosting based on **Y**our needs, not your internet consultant's.

A website could place you at the **Z**enith of your sector, whatever your company's size.

YOU HAVE A FANTASTIC SITE – WHAT NEXT?

Imagine this: you spend a lot of time and money creating and printing a superb brochure. Then you don't send it to anyone. Nobody sane would do that, would they? Yet a great many firms, especially selling to businesses, do just that with their sites. They spend an awful lot of time and money creating them and then tell nobody about them.

Of course, getting people to do anything – in this case visiting a site – can be expensive. So, as with everything else in direct marketing, the challenge is to strike the right balance between cost and results. The cheapest way to promote your website is to include your URL and preferably an incentive to visit the site in all your literature, from stationery to every marketing message that goes out in any medium. It won't cost you anything to print an extra paragraph or add this to all your commercials. But that alone won't be enough, especially if you have a serious e-commerce operation and need a critical mass of visitors/customers on your site to make it profitable. How do you go about it?

A surprising – but luckily decreasing – number of firms, mostly those that only operate online, think that just because their website is on the web, they should only promote it there. It's rather like saying that as movies are shown at the cinema, you should only promote them with cinema commercials. Your visitors 'do things' when they are not online: they read newspapers, watch television, listen to the radio. Don't underestimate the power of offline media to drive traffic to your site.

The most common mistake

Look at Expedia, perhaps the most successful online travel agent. They launched in 1998 and at the beginning of 2000, they were the first online UK agent to advertise offline, with an integrated campaign of press and online ads, television commercials and PR activity. They keep using all these media, with the latest campaign being launched in September 2005 and still running at the time of writing. I don't know the results, but unless Expedia are working towards a fast tax loss, I bet offline media are working for them.

Depending on what you sell – and who you want to talk to – different media make sense. The principles on which you should base your choice are those described in Chapter 7, so I won't repeat them here (I will however dedicate the following section to using online channels to drive traffic to a site). Only two things are worth highlighting here, because they are specific to using those media to promote a website:

- Make sure you promote a URL that is easy to remember and unlikely to be misspelled. People won't go online as soon as they have seen your television commercial. If your URL does not satisfy these two criteria, then consider promoting a different URL that points automatically to your website and maybe relates to your advertising.

  Think of Norwich Union: in all their offline communications they ask people to go and visit www.quotemehappy.com ('Quote me happy' is the strapline they've used in the last few years.)
- Make sure everything is in place so you can track as precisely as possible what communication generates how much traffic. If you are making an offer to drive people to your site, ask them to quote a reference code to get that offer. Even better, advertise a special URL, pointing to a customised splash page. (A splash page is a specially created welcome page for people

who've seen your message – it can even be personalised to improve the response.)

So, for instance, if you are advertising in the *Sun*, ask people to go to www.yoursite.com/sun and then customise the splash page so that it welcomes *Sun* readers and gives them access to the offer advertised in the paper. Your webmaster can tell you very easily how many people responded to the ad, because nobody would have known to type www.yoursite.com/sun in their browser unless they'd seen the ad.

DON'T BE BAMBOOZLED: COMMONSENSE ONLINE TECHNIQUES

Let's say you have the best possible website and you are driving traffic there using all your existing communications – and perhaps even running a dedicated offline campaign. The next step is using online tools.

Isn't that the responsibility of online marketers? Don't you need some kind of online expert to manage that? I won't reply to this here, but again, please keep the question at the back of your mind while you read this brief and simple practical analysis of all the online techniques you can use to drive traffic to your site. When I looked at each of them, I asked myself why I should choose one rather than the other, trying to understand individual advantages and disadvantages according to two criteria: how many people you reach and how precise your targeting is (that is, how likely they are to respond to you).

Driving visitors to your site: the online effectiveness hierarchy

Unless what you sell only appeals to a very limited number of people – and you know exactly who they are – you will find this little pyramid extremely useful. It evaluates the different ways you can promote yourself online. At the top is the most relevant, targeted – hence least risky – way, and at the bottom the one with greatest reach, but most wastage.

1 RSS

What it is: RSS stands for 'Really Simple Syndication'. If like me you are still no wiser, think of it as a subscription based distributable 'What's New' for your site. Subscribers need special software – now largely available free.

How it works: RSS feeds were originally used to broadcast news updates. You download a piece of software and you receive the BBC news on your Yahoo page, for instance. More recently, commercial organisations have started to make clever use of this technology. If you have an RSS reader try and go to www.toptable.co.uk: you're prompted to subcribe to a number of restaurant's feeds. You'll receive news and offers from them on your Yahoo

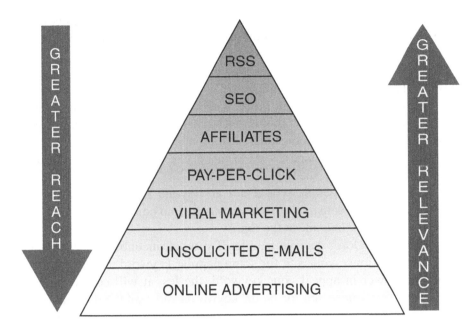

Figure 8.4 The online effectiveness hierarchy

page – hard to ignore. Messages can be made even more intrusive. For instance, if you are a Manchester United fan, you can receive news about your team – straight to your desktop, whether you are online or not. Of course, you will also be prompted to buy the latest strip, and maybe a Manchester United season ticket.

Pros: If people take the trouble to download a piece of software to hear from you, it means they are more than warm prospects – they are as hot as they come.

Cons: You only communicate with a small percentage of your universe of prospects – those who have downloaded the software. What's more, tracking could be tricky.

Caveat: Strike the right balance between information and promotion. If you just use the medium to sell to people, they will soon lose interest and you will have alienated your best prospects.

2 SEO

What it is: At least everyone agrees what SEO stands for (Search Engine Optimisation). The more optimised your site is, the more likely it is to come up in the first pages of a search on a search engine.

How it works: When you search for 'SEO' on Google, 176,000,000 pages come up. Most of the entries are from people who promise you the perfect recipe to make your site shoot up the natural listings. Broadly speaking, the position is determined by the combination of two factors: your site's content and the number of quality sites that link to it. However no formula is guaranteed to deliver a number 1 ranking. The most you can do is try to influence the most important variable under your control: your site content. As Google puts it, 'Give visitors the information they're looking for.' To which I only add, 'the more, the better'.

(If you want to know more, you can read several pages in the 'Webmaster Help Center' on Google – it's a very comprehensive guide, most written in English, not techno-gibberish.)

Pros: It's the cheapest way to make your prospects find you at the very moment when they need you.

Cons: Most people would not go beyond the second page of the search results. And realistically, unless you have no competition at all, it will be hard work to get your site at the top.

Caveat: Don't deceive people. If you sell incontinence pants, don't cheat: don't optimise your site for some popular keyword. (In fact the more precise, narrower in appeal your keyword, the less it will cost you.) I also recommend that you search for 'your' keywords and read the description that comes up. Make sure it makes sense and does justice to what you sell. For instance, as I write if you search for 'weekend getaway', one of the results that comes up is shown below

3   Affiliates

What they are: They are websites offering related but non-competing products or services that link to your site.

How it works: You may exchange links or you could offer to pay the affiliate. You can either pay a 'bounty', a fixed amount per each sale or customer they refer, or a percentage of the sale. If you are really confident in the quality of the traffic, you could also agree to pay a commission based on the number of clicks you receive. You only need to supply the affiliate with information about your product or service, and a unique tracking link.

Figure 8.5 Search for 'weekend getaway' and …

Spend half an hour every day thinking of products or services related to what you sell – and find any relevant comparison sites. If you are short of ideas, check what sites link to your competitors' sites (just type in Google: link to:www.yourcompetitorsite.com). The best candidate to be an affiliate is a medium-sized site with relevant content.

Pros: You talk to the people you need to talk to – and only pay if they do something, so the financial risk is minimal.

Cons: It takes a lot of time and effort to get and retain affiliates. Unless you completely misjudge them, the quality of the traffic they send you should be good, but check constantly that they send you enough traffic to make your efforts worthwhile.

Caveat: Treat your affiliates like a sales force. Give them all the tools they need to work properly – fresh ideas, creative, support. Monitor their performance and concentrate on the best.

4 Pay-per-click

What it is: It is any kind of agreement whereby you pay every time a visitor clicks on a link redirecting to your site. The expression is however commonly used as synonym of 'Adwords', the paid-for search advertisements in Google.

How it works: You choose the keywords and keyphrases that you want to advertise. Then you write a headline and a small ad that will appear when someone searches for that keyword. You only pay when people click on your ad. The starting price of a click in Google is $0.15; however the more the competition, the higher the price. What's more, paying the top price does not guarantee your ad will be shown first, as the position depends also on how relevant your ad is considered.

Pros: You talk to the people who are looking for what you sell. It's rather like having a stall that sells drinks and that magically appears next to someone when they are thirsty.

Cons: Unless you have no competition, all your competitors will be playing the same game. This means each click will become increasingly expensive. And don't forget: it's just a click, not a sale. Constantly monitor your conversion rate and your cost per sale to make sure your pay-per-click campaign is cost-effective.

Caveat: Think not only about keywords but also about key phrases. If you sell curtains, buy not only the keyword 'curtains' but also 'velvet damask curtains', if this is what you sell. You won't get as many clicks, but it will be cheaper and the clicks should convert better. It's the same thinking that makes a precise headline do better than a vague one. Lastly, give a lot of thought to your ad. You are talking to people who are interested, but you only have a couple of seconds to persuade them to come and visit you. Give them your best pitch.

5 Viral marketing

What it is: Quite simply, whenever you ask your customers – or your website visitors – to forward the link to their friends, you are practising 'viral marketing'. It is the online version of word of mouth and referral schemes like member-get-a-member.

How it works: You can track how many people accept your invitation to forward the link and in some cases, even who forwarded it – and to whom. Depending on what you seek to achieve, whether getting traffic to your site, getting new names or making a sale, you may test different formats.

Games, video or any involving content tend to work well – if they are fresh and well made. Last Christmas one of our clients published on their site a flash animation, where the user had to kill a number of turkeys appearing in quick succession. It was fun. I played it a couple of times and forwarded it to a couple of friends. Would they start investing with our client? Let's say I cannot exclude the possibility.

If you don't want just to drive traffic to the site – but also to get names or make sales – it always pays to offer incentives: one for the person who is referred and one for the person who refers them.

Pros: As the old saying goes, 'birds of a feather flock together'. The people your customers know are likely to be similar to them and fit your target profile. But the big advantage of this tool is that if you use simple messages, it can be relatively cheap and lets you talk to cold prospects who have been warmed up by their friend's recommendation.

Cons: The cons are the same as with any targeting based on profiling: you are assuming people will be interested in what you offer because of their demographics and lifestyle (assuming they are similar to those of the customers who referred them). However you have no idea whether they are in the market when you contact them – or at all. Quite frankly this doesn't matter much if your format is cheap and you ask your prospects to take action (give you their details or buy something). But it becomes rather less sensible if you go for a more expensive solution, like a specially created game, hosted by a dedicated viral portal.

Interestingly, says the American Marketing Association online, as reported by Bruce Horovitz on *USA Today* in November 2006, 'there has been a huge increase in viral advertising spend over the last 24 months, a large part of which can be put down to the huge increase in the costs the dedicated viral portal and websites are commanding to host virals'. When you consider that such viral campaigns do not usually offer accurate tracking, paying for this seems unduly risky.

One way to minimise that risk is to try as hard as you can to capture details when running an expensive, hosted viral campaign. If you are using a game, for instance, league tables and message boards are the best options to get people to leave their details.

Caveat: If you want your customers to effectively become your advocates (this is what viral marketing is, in the end), you have to give them a compelling reason to do so. An offer so good, or creative idea so much fun they want to share it with their friends – and/or a good incentive to do so.

6 Affiliate networks

What they are: Quite simply, they are firms that manage your affiliates for you. They work with a number of websites that are willing to publish advertisements.

How it works: If you are an advertiser and join one of these networks, you must decide which categories of websites you would like to advertise on and what you will offer them. You then decide how much you want to be involved in the daily management of your affiliates (most affiliate networks offer the option of a fully managed solution). You only pay the network a small set-up fee and then a commission on top of what you pay the actual affiliates.

Pros: It's the perfect solution to get relevant sites linked to you if you don't have the time or the resources to build your own affiliate network. Or you could even use it alongside your own affiliate network to build up the traffic quantity. Ideally, you should manage yourself the top affiliates and let the network manage the less profitable ones.

Cons: As there is virtually no personal relationship between you and your affiliates, they tend to be less committed. You may end up with thousands of affiliates who only refer a handful of customers every month. But then again, you only pay for those customers, so you have nothing to lose.

Caveat: Even if you decide to let the network manage your affiliates, give them good promotional tools and check on their performance. Give bonuses to the best ones and maybe even negotiate a special deal with them.

7 E-mail marketing

What it is: Needless to say, e-mail marketing is any message delivered via e-mail to a group of recipients, who have given you permission to contact them via this medium.

How it works: Depending on the broadcasting system you use, you will be able to see instantly how many people opened the e-mail, how many clicked on each link you included and how many replied (if you included such a call for action).

The good news is that you can target e-mail campaigns based on what people have been looking at on your website, where they have gone next, how long they spent in each place, what they have bought before, how much they spent in the past, when they bought from you and previous campaigns they responded to. On top of this, most list servers can now detect the e-mail programme used by recipients, and deliver the message in the most appropriate format: for example, containing images.

Pros: It is a very low-cost and intrusive medium

Cons: Because of its low cost and intrusiveness, it is widely used. On the basis of the data provided by the latest 'National e-mail benchmarking report' published by the DMA in December 2006, it appears that each e-mail service provider (ESP) sent an average of 16 million e-mails during the first two quarters of 2006. Multiply this figure by the number of ESPs, then add all the e-mails that are sent from some obscure ESP in a remote island in the Caribbean – scary, isn't it? Because of this, people are getting increasingly annoyed with the amount of spam they receive, and it is therefore far harder for advertisers to get their message through.

Caveat: Don't be discouraged. The same observation is made at regular intervals about direct mail. Yet advertisers still use it – and, more importantly, people still respond. The truth is that if a message is timely, relevant, well targeted and includes a good offer, it will be read and acted upon. But more on this in the session about e-mail creative later on.

8 Online advertising

What it is: It's every banner, video, flash animation, button displayed on somebody else's website, in a space that you have 'rented' at a rate based on number of impressions.

How it works: Quite simply, you supply the creative to the publisher site – although the technicalities of it are indeed more complicated and vary depending on the publisher. You also supply the unique tracking link that lets you measure how many people clicked through.

Pros: Depending on the popularity of the publisher's site, you can get your message in front of literally millions of web users.

Cons: It is quite costly – even more than television ads in some cases. What's more, people are so used to seeing advertisements that it is easy for them to just ignore them, especially as most are not really targeted. The only good news about targeting is that opportunities are starting to emerge, with the increasing popularity of social networking sites like Bebo and Myspace (see section below on this subject). For instance Bebo has recently announced that it wants to give users the power to select areas they're interested in, so they only see ads relevant to them.

The next step, which we won't see till the cost of the technology to implement it drops, is to use behavioural data to target messages. Just as offline, people pay less and less attention to advertising when all they see is the same ads again and again, whether they've already responded or not.

Caveat: While we wait for decent targeting at an acceptable cost, the only way to ensure you have a reasonable click-through rate is to make your ads really stand out. This calls for highly intrusive formats – hence the popularity of rich media and oversized, expanding ads – or interactive formats (a flash game, for instance). Perhaps even better is relevant content – maybe supplied via a live feed (if you sell investments, you could have a banner that displays share value in real time).

Measuring results can also be tricky. Of course you know how many people clicked through, but it is more difficult to be really sure how many subsequently converted. However there are quite a few specialist pieces of software that can do the job.

HOW YOUR TRAFFIC HELPS IMPROVE YOUR AIM

At the risk of boring you by relentless repetition, a chief advantage of direct marketing is that it makes it easy for you to test different things, measure and compare results, so you can aim better next time. It all goes back to the spiral of prosperity I mentioned early in this book. The internet is no different. Indeed, it's better because, as I've also pointed out, the process is accelerated to an extraordinary degree – and you can learn far more. If you want to test two headlines in direct mail, you have to wait a week or more to know which was doing better. If the headline is online, say in an e-mail, you'll know almost instantly which attracts more clicks.

But the advantages of the internet go much further – it really gives you 'big brother' power. Suppose you send out a direct mail pack with a brochure. What if you could tell exactly how many people opened the envelope, how many acted, and which of the many calls for action prompted them to do so? Then, what if you could see also how many looked at the brochure, whether they looked at the front or back first; how long they spent on each page, and which page they looked at last? Wouldn't that give you an unfair advantage next time you plan and design your mail pack? Well, that's what the internet gives you.

Your unfair advantage

You can have records of absolutely everything that happens on your website: how many people visit it, when, for how long, where they come from, whether they are visiting for the first time or not, on which page they land, on which page they spend most time, on which page they spend least time, on which page they leave the site and so on. You can have a record of every click for each of your visitors – it's now even possible to see how people moved their mouse around.

All this means the amount of data is *huge*. You must transform it into information that ultimately leads to useful action. Luckily there are now many programmes and pieces of software – free and paid-for – that translate the data recorded on the weblogs into information that's easy to digest, usually in the form of graphs and charts. But even then, the sheer volume can be over-whelming, so it is paramount that you define clearly what is really important to you. And let me stress: this is a business decision, not to be left under any circumstances to the IT department.

Beware of too much information

As with all kinds of research, the quality of the answers you get depends largely on the quality of the questions you ask or, in the graphic phrase, 'garbage in, garbage out'. It is crucial to define exactly what you want

The curse of GIGO

to learn – and this largely depends on the nature of your business and its aims. However I believe there are things any business should keep an eye on – and act upon:

'If you can't measure it, you can't manage it'

- Follow visitors' 'click route' – and where they came from. This tells you which campaign/source works better for you – where to invest more and where less. And if you sell something on your site, remember, the conversion rate, not the click-through rate matters. It's like the way one press ad may get more replies, but fewer sales.
- Do many visitors leave your site on a particular page? Try to understand why, and test different things to see whether they make any difference.
- Is there a particularly popular link? Maybe a download? Make it prominent on every single page – maybe even advertise it.
- Is there a pattern in the navigation? Do visitors tend to visit certain pages in succession? You could make the navigation between those easier. For instance, suppose you have a page for worldwide holidays and a lot of people who land there go on to UK holidays. Have a special button that takes you there, bypassing the worldwide section. Or you could have a special reference and link in your copy.
- If you sell something, pay great attention to the click route on the buying pages – from the 'add to basket' button to the information collection through to the order confirmation page. What percentage drop out after they have started the process? At what stage? Again, test changes and measure their impact.
- Is there a page that is especially popular or where people stay longer? Try to give them more of that kind of information.
- Check your busy times – it will tell you the best time to do promotional campaigns and when is best to perform maintenance.

Whatever you look at – whatever action you take – the most important thing is to record and measure accurately before and after results, both in response and conversion.

JUST A REMINDER: IT'S ACCELERATED DIRECT MARKETING

Remember the two questions I mentioned earlier that I suggested you kept at the back of your mind? They were both about whether the internet is something new, to be dealt with by internet experts, or not. The internet is indeed a new distribution channel and medium – but the principles that should govern your thinking are just good, old-fashioned direct marketing principles. The only difference is the speed at which things happen.

But don't take my word for this. I shall prove it to you, first with an experiment, then with an example.

A little experiment: new versus old

When something new emerges, so does a new vocabulary. But does that mean that we have 'new things' or are we simply giving a new name to 'old' things? Let's examine all the 'new things' that have emerged with the internet and see whether there is something more to them than technological novelty.

Old friends in disguise

Your website = your catalogue

Start with your website: the technology behind it is new, but the purpose it serves and the principles governing it are the same as the oldest direct marketing medium, a mail order catalogue. Can't see it? Let's look at all the things a good catalogue does – and see whether they apply to the internet.

1 Give people what they want

The success of a mail order catalogue is largely based on making it convenient for people to get what they want: a selection of products they may prefer to buy this way, for whatever reason. Catalogues can be less threatening than going into a shop and give you a greater feeling of being in control. They can remove confusion, allowing you time to study anything that puzzles you. This is exactly what websites do, except that technology can simplify and speed up the process – just press a few buttons, and the machine does what you want.

Online services are not only quicker; they may be even better because of the ability to link a vast amount of knowledge held on a database to customers' needs. The economics of the internet are such that some firms like Amazon only offer their services via this medium.

What online can do better

New ideas always create new problems – and they can create new business for older media. Telephone call centres – expected to suffer from this new competition – are attracting a lot of new business handling complaints from customers. So a touch of scepticism is not inappropriate.

2 Lure people in with enticing offers

How do catalogue companies build their database? They do so by making very appealing offers, usually via advertising. And they keep making offers, to keep people's attention. Look at any good catalogue. One thing you will always find at least in two places – the front cover and the order form – is a special offer, a discount or incentive. Again, this attracts people to a website. But online you have the advantage of speed I keep mentioning. And just as you can offline, you can make relevant offers to customers, based on their past behaviour – which you know a lot more about.

For instance, if I send out an e-mail offering our services, and I see that person has gone on to our website I can (and sometimes do) get on to that person and offer a special deal as a first-time client.

3 Make browsing a pleasure

The more you browse through a catalogue, the more likely you are to buy. The same applies to a website: involvement devices on a site can engage people in a pleasurable way. They are the online equivalent of all the stamps and scratch-cards that work so well in print. I mentioned earlier the turkey shoot one of our clients offered.

Technology should be a tool, not a barrier. Your site can be very confusing if you're not careful. So don't show off with too many flashy tricks – and beware of baffling jargon. 'The devil is in the detail', so make sure everything on the site works. Not for designers with fancy Macs, but for people sitting at home using their kids' PCs. For both large and small screens, and different browsers. The advanced technology available to your designers will not be in many people's homes. Smart record producers used to play their potential hits on cheap radios to see how they would sound to their customers. The same principle applies.

4 Signpost things clearly

Is it easy for customers to find what they want – and go there quickly? Are the verbal descriptions clear, even to an idiot? Look at the Argos catalogue, perhaps the UK's largest. No matter whether you are looking for a light pull or a digital camera, you'll find it in seconds (and probably buy a few more things in the process).

My partner, Alastair Lee, once created a website for a lighting company. It had thousands of pages. Before the MD signed it off, he grabbed one of the cleaners, set her down in front of the computer and asked her to find a particular kind of light. To Alastair's relief, she did so immediately: he would not have got his cheque otherwise.

You will find an amazing number of sites where nobody bothers to tell you a) what to click, b) what will happen next, or c) what the benefits of the site are. Imagine if the beautiful Prada shop on London's Sloane Street had a front door your couldn't see. How would you get in? Now look at the home page of this fashion website. What do you click? I tried the picture, the logo, even the white space – I haven't managed to find my way in yet.

5 Sell more while they're browsing

Again, I'm talking about basic direct marketing principles: the 'instant bounce-back'. All good mail order traders know the best time to sell is when

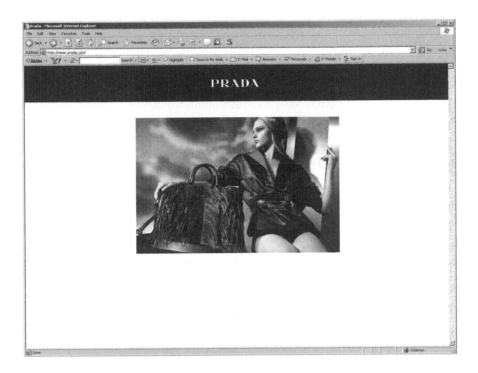

Figure 8.6 Prada's baffling home page

people have just bought. That's why in catalogues you'll always find offers bundled together. And what happens when you receive your order? You'll find more offers.

Amazon has got this trick down to a fine art. Whenever you look at a book, they tell you:

- Buy this together with another one from the same author and save even more.
- People who bought this, also bought this other item.
- People who had this in their wish list also listed this other item.

(They even tell you how you can make money by selling the book you've bought and read, but that's another subject.) And when you receive the book, what do you find in the box? At least a couple of leaflets trying to sell you more things. They actually use an offline medium called paper. Simple, right? But now they call it 'integrated marketing'. Yet many people ignore this principle, even some very good people.

I recently ordered my food shopping from Ocado, a year since the first time I visited the site – I'm a slow converter, because I enjoy buying groceries from supermarkets, and little speciality stores, too. I was impressed by

Ocado's impeccable service, but I was really surprised that they missed something utterly basic. They left with me a full-colour, nicely designed receipt. But that's all. It would have cost them nothing to print an offer on it. Even something as simple as 'Would you like the same delivery at the same time next week? Confirm this now and get £10 off.' They ignored one of the most basic rules in mail order. Why sell one item when you can sell three? This process is infinitely faster on the internet.

6 Keep in touch

Everybody knows that once you order once from a mail order company you'll never stop receiving mailings from them – and possibly from similar companies. Remember the rules of direct marketing. Build a good database – and exploit it. Communicate more, rather than less, because if you bought once, you will buy again or, at any rate are twice as likely to buy as somebody who has never bought before.

     The same applies to websites. Your visitors are like your responders to an ad, so miss no opportunity to capture your visitors' data. Then follow them up remorselessly. If people have visited your site and have liked what you offer enough to leave their details or buy from you, they are likely to visit or buy again. Yet if there is one area where I find internet marketers weak, this is it. When you order on the internet, firms ask for your e-mail address so they can reach you, but then do nothing. That is a missed opportunity, although like all things it shouldn't be over-exploited.

7 Do a thorough selling job

A good catalogue always comes with a persuasive letter. That's the job your home page should do. Most don't. They are usually all about the company – a huge mistake, as nobody goes on the web to learn all about you. They want to know what you can do for them. So tell them.

     Among the direst offenders are the big ad agencies and – funnily enough – firms that purport to be internet experts. They often use the opening to boast or talk pretentious drivel – just go online and look at a few and you'll see what I mean.

Your weblogs = your transactional database

Weblogs are like an almost instant transactional database. Just as in mail order the history of each customer and prospect is recorded, on your weblogs the history of each visitor is recorded. It's just that more information is available more quickly. So you should study what people do on the site and use that information intelligently – to communicate more relevantly and give them more of what they want.

Your affiliates = your agents or resellers

Your affiliates are like agents or resellers. And their quality can be gauged just as you would gauge that of any agents or customers. Some send you many visitors (but only a few buy) and others only send you a few (but most buy), and so on. There's no harm in using both, provided you only pay a commission on what gets sold.

And just as you would give your agents any possible tool to make it easier for them to sell, give your affiliates all your support. Share with them what works for you – it will work for them too. Teach them all you know, and tell them what you know about your customers: they don't have that information.

Pay per click = classified ads

Pay per click is like classified ads, except you know exactly how many people see them. They call for few, but powerful, words – a headline that offers a clear benefit, with preferably an incentive. You must ask forcefully for a response – and make it easy (a click-through).

Banner ads = direct response ads

Banners are like direct response ads – or Yellow Pages ads. Would your banners work as press ads? Make sure they would – and exploit technology like 'expanding' banners. For the British Horseracing Board we created a very successful ad years ago which featured a horse galloping across the screen.

Search engines = directories

Search engines are like a huge telephone directory, with the only difference that people can make their search much more precise.

Viral marketing = refer a friend

The oldest trick in the book practised by the savvy catalogue companies: 'Would any of your friends be interested in this catalogue?' Viral marketing is just accelerated member-get-member. Do you offer an incentive for forwarding your message? You would in direct mail. Why not now?

WHOSE WEBSITE IS IT ANYWAY?

The internet has been dominated by 'techies'. It was the same when television came in. Advertising agencies hired a lot of out-of-work actors and failed directors because they thought film technique was what mattered. Eventually, they realised commercials were just advertising, and those who would do best were probably advertising people. A similar principle applies to the internet, but even more so, as it is not so completely an entertainment medium as television.

So if, as I've just demonstrated, the internet is just accelerated direct marketing, why should anyone other than someone with a direct marketing background be in charge? Here are two comments, one from my former partner, and one from someone in publishing. Although the first seems a little intemperate, both, I think, have validity:

> As someone who has to 'hand-hold' and talk non-internet savvy companies through the hype and bullshit of the new generation snake-oil salesmen – the internet chipheads who tend to know little, if anything, about the fundamentals of direct response… some should step out of the 'virtual' world into the 'real' world of generating profit.
> Glenmore Trenear-Harvey

And here's Rupert Goodwins of Ziff-Davis:

> Your marketing department won't understand how technical projects are managed and implemented, but they'll try to define what they should do… Commercial enterprises should be marketing-led, but without an awareness of the implications on corporate resources, this approach can lead to projects from hell. And if the technical departments get the upper hand? Well, let's be honest. Websites designed by engineers often lack that certain sparkle.

True, direct marketers very rarely understand the technicalities of the internet. But then again, they don't understand the technicalities of printing. Yet nobody ever suggested that printers should dictate what goes into a catalogue or direct mail pack. So why should IT people rule what goes on your website, or what your e-mails look like?

Take what happened when we set up www.draytonbird.com. It underlines this problem of the technician versus the marketer. The programmers wanted to show off the technology; I wanted to communicate effectively. Their proposed format was hard to read, much of it in either caps or sans serif type with ragged setting on both margins, all reversed out on a light background. When I protested, I was given all sorts of gobbledegook to convince me there was no other way, which being translated meant, 'We don't want to change because it's too much work, and we're very busy.' It took a lot of time and effort – and money – to get it right.

The same applied to one of their pet projects, which was to put video extracts from some of my speeches onto the site. These never worked properly, making me look like a particularly moronic marionette. I took a year to get rid of them – although now that most people's computers boast more advanced technology they would make sense.

Mind you, I am not suggesting that you ignore what techies say – just as you wouldn't ignore what your printers say. Often they can come up with solutions you would have never thought of. And anyway, you need them. The solution, as in any relationship, is more, better communication. It will pay if you spend some time with them explaining what you want to achieve – and why it matters to you, the firm and them. Don't treat them like uncooperative suppliers or skilled workers – they are your partners. But nor should you take for granted what they tell you. The reason is simple – and you will see it for yourself by comparing what the experts tell you and what test results prove about e-mails.

A difficult marriage

I cannot count how many times I've heard from this or that e-mail expert – although it's getting more uncommon with time – that e-mails should be short and eye-catching. Quite frankly I could never believe this to be true, probably because so many times over the odd 50 years I've been in this business I have heard similar claims about direct mail, press ads, television – you name it. And time and time again, whenever a client has been willing to test a short message, perhaps with a very eye-catching graphic – against a long, relevant and interesting message, the latter has performed better. Would this apply to e-mails too?

E-mails: who gets it right?

Statistics show people are interested enough to open most mailings. But while they may not lose sleep over how much direct mail they get, they resent bad direct mail more than other forms of bad advertising. Because it is so intrusive, they hate unsolicited phone calls. I don't know how much spam infuriates them – but it may be even more. Yet we send out an e-mail newsletter and e-mails selling our services once or twice a month – in fact whenever I think of something people might like to know. It is pretty much the only marketing we do. We always give people the opportunity to have their names taken off the list. Less than 1 per cent do. The key is to make the content of interest, not just to sell. You can see two of our e-mails below – both did well.

What people hate – and what they like

Do you notice anything about them? The basic rules for e-mail are pretty much the same as for direct mail and direct response advertising (an e-mail can look like an advertisement or a letter). Here are some guidelines, which sound very familiar to me:

- Don't worry about being too long – worry whether you are interesting enough.
- Try to cut copy as much as you can.
- You should write for scan-ability with short paragraphs, subheads, and bulleted lists. Again, very familiar.
- People don't see the whole of your copy at once – they only see the top. So concentrate the most important promises there – don't waste that precious space for images that could be placed anywhere else in the e-mail.
- Focus on the subject line, just as you would focus on the headline in any printed communication.

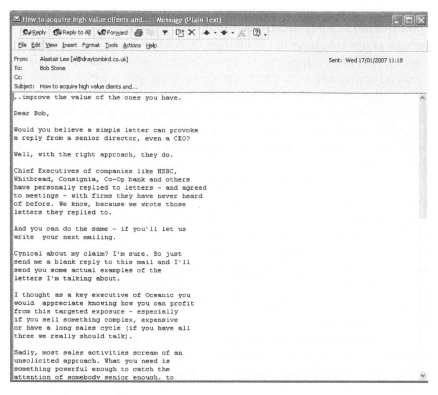

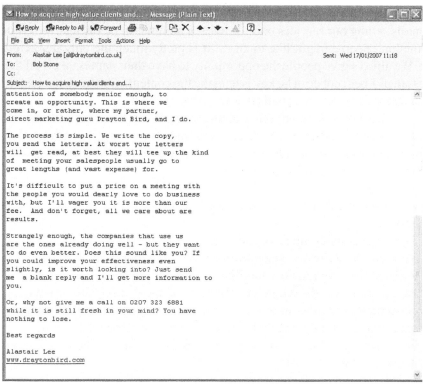

From:	Alastair Lee [al@draytonbird.co.uk]	Sent: Wed 27/09/2006	15.46
To:	Denise		
Cc:			
Subject:	Thanks for looking at our site		

...now improve your results by avoiding these seven deadly sins.

Hi Denise

The easiest way to improve your ads, emails and mailing is not to consider what makes for good work, but why most work stinks. Until you banish the bad, how can you hope to do well?

I bet if you look through your ads and mailings you will find some - if not all - the following seven common sins appear regularly.

1. Being slow to get to the point.

Weak beginnings kill sales. Signs of a weak beginning are being slow to mention the main benefits and incentive. (You don't offer an incentive? Shame on you. They always, if they are relevant, increase sales by more than they cost.)

Unless you have good reason to do otherwise, the incentive should be impossible to ignore. The purpose is not merely to persuade people to reply, it is to encourage them to read.

Some research I once read showed that if you can get people to read the first 250 words of your copy, 90% will read all of it. So a weak beginning looses your readers when it matters most.

Copywriters seem to have minds like old car engines, which need to be warmed up for a few minutes. They often put in a couple of paragraphs of waffle before they get to the point. Maybe it's fear of being rejected when they do.

You will often find you can edit the first three paragraphs down to two without loosing any meaning, but gaining in "attack". On a surprising number of occassions you will also find the best place to begin is round about paragraph three.

If copywriters are slow to get to the point, art directors often want to use clever pictures rather than ones that are instantly understood. Maybe they fear being direct and obvious won't work.

Our job is to communicate as fast as possible what we are talking about. Customers don't have time to work out out clever ideas or subtle approaches. Remember, they only have one thought in their minds: "what's in it for me!"

2. Forgetting there must be something for your prospect at every point in the message.

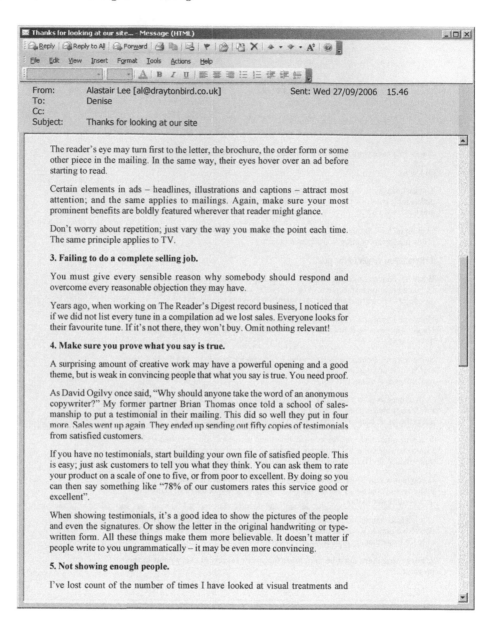

The reader's eye may turn first to the letter, the brochure, the order form or some other piece in the mailing. In the same way, their eyes hover over an ad before starting to read.

Certain elements in ads – headlines, illustrations and captions – attract most attention; and the same applies to mailings. Again, make sure your most prominent benefits are boldly featured wherever that reader might glance.

Don't worry about repetition; just vary the way you make the point each time. The same principle applies to TV.

3. Failing to do a complete selling job.

You must give every sensible reason why somebody should respond and overcome every reasonable objection they may have.

Years ago, when working on The Reader's Digest record business, I noticed that if we did not list every tune in a compilation ad we lost sales. Everyone looks for their favourite tune. If it's not there, they won't buy. Omit nothing relevant!

4. Make sure you prove what you say is true.

A surprising amount of creative work may have a powerful opening and a good theme, but is weak in convincing people that what you say is true. You need proof.

As David Ogilvy once said, "Why should anyone take the word of an anonymous copywriter?" My former partner Brian Thomas once told a school of sales-manship to put a testimonial in their mailing. This did so well they put in four more. Sales went up again. They ended up sending out fifty copies of testimonials from satisfied customers.

If you have no testimonials, start building your own file of satisfied people. This is easy; just ask customers to tell you what they think. You can ask them to rate your product on a scale of one to five, or from poor to excellent. By doing so you can then say something like "78% of our customers rates this service good or excellent".

When showing testimonials, it's a good idea to show the pictures of the people and even the signatures. Or show the letter in the original handwriting or type-written form. All these things make them more believable. It doesn't matter if people write to you ungrammatically – it may be even more convincing.

5. Not showing enough people.

I've lost count of the number of times I have looked at visual treatments and

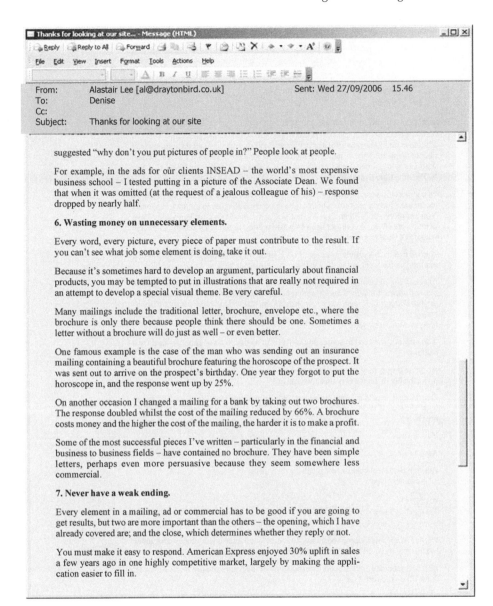

suggested "why don't you put pictures of people in?" People look at people.

For example, in the ads for our clients INSEAD – the world's most expensive business school – I tested putting in a picture of the Associate Dean. We found that when it was omitted (at the request of a jealous colleague of his) – response dropped by nearly half.

6. Wasting money on unnecessary elements.

Every word, every picture, every piece of paper must contribute to the result. If you can't see what job some element is doing, take it out.

Because it's sometimes hard to develop an argument, particularly about financial products, you may be tempted to put in illustrations that are really not required in an attempt to develop a special visual theme. Be very careful.

Many mailings include the traditional letter, brochure, envelope etc., where the brochure is only there because people think there should be one. Sometimes a letter without a brochure will do just as well – or even better.

One famous example is the case of the man who was sending out an insurance mailing containing a beautiful brochure featuring the horoscope of the prospect. It was sent out to arrive on the prospect's birthday. One year they forgot to put the horoscope in, and the response went up by 25%.

On another occasion I changed a mailing for a bank by taking out two brochures. The response doubled whilst the cost of the mailing reduced by 66%. A brochure costs money and the higher the cost of the mailing, the harder it is to make a profit.

Some of the most successful pieces I've written – particularly in the financial and business to business fields – have contained no brochure. They have been simple letters, perhaps even more persuasive because they seem somewhere less commercial.

7. Never have a weak ending.

Every element in a mailing, ad or commercial has to be good if you are going to get results, but two are more important than the others – the opening, which I have already covered are; and the close, which determines whether they reply or not.

You must make it easy to respond. American Express enjoyed 30% uplift in sales a few years ago in one highly competitive market, largely by making the application easier to fill in.

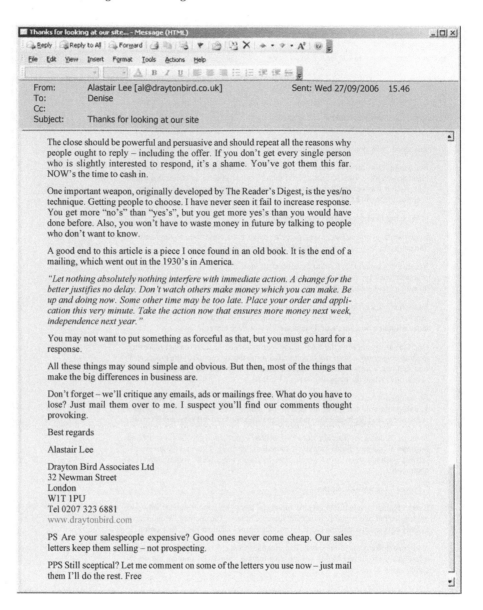

The close should be powerful and persuasive and should repeat all the reasons why people ought to reply – including the offer. If you don't get every single person who is slightly interested to respond, it's a shame. You've got them this far. NOW's the time to cash in.

One important weapon, originally developed by The Reader's Digest, is the yes/no technique. Getting people to choose. I have never seen it fail to increase response. You get more "no's" than "yes's", but you get more yes's than you would have done before. Also, you won't have to waste money in future by talking to people who don't want to know.

A good end to this article is a piece I once found in an old book. It is the end of a mailing, which went out in the 1930's in America.

"Let nothing absolutely nothing interfere with immediate action. A change for the better justifies no delay. Don't watch others make money which you can make. Be up and doing now. Some other time may be too late. Place your order and application this very minute. Take the action now that ensures more money next week, independence next year."

You may not want to put something as forceful as that, but you must go hard for a response.

All these things may sound simple and obvious. But then, most of the things that make the big differences in business are.

Don't forget – we'll critique any emails, ads or mailings free. What do you have to lose? Just mail them over to me. I suspect you'll find our comments thought provoking.

Best regards

Alastair Lee

Drayton Bird Associates Ltd
32 Newman Street
London
W1T 1PU
Tel 0207 323 6881
www.draytonbird.com

PS Are your salespeople expensive? Good ones never come cheap. Our sales letters keep them selling – not prospecting.

PPS Still sceptical? Let me comment on some of the letters you use now – just mail them I'll do the rest. Free

- Make sure it looks as though it has been sent by a 'real person' – just like the signature in a letter – so don't use obscure sender names. You wouldn't sign a letter 'postmaster' or 'info', would you?
- Exploit fully the medium potential. Use personalisation – it's free!

A firm called Sun.com had some research conducted into how people read on the web. All I can say is that it sounded extraordinarily like the way they read normally. In truth, the only difference is that when you read on a computer screen the light is reflected, which makes it a bit more tiring.

The research revealed that the *subject field* is critical. No wonder: it is the first thing people see, like the headline. It explained that benefits are important and that you should use plain language – no puns, humour or playing with words. You should be careful about teasers – busy people dislike surprises.

Other important points were that you must make it easy for people to unsubscribe. Why build ill-will by pestering people who don't want to listen? You should define the relationship early on. People forget who you are and want to know why you're writing. This pays in direct mail, and perhaps even more so in the e-mail due to the huge volume.

For obvious reasons, make a point of your privacy policy. This is so important in this intimate medium. And remind people who they are: 'You are subscribed as jbloggs@e-mail.com'. This may sound crazy, but it's the equivalent of the 'do we have your details right?' in direct mail. People often join things and forget. And with e-mail it's even more essential, as many people have several addresses.

Whenever we have tried to apply these principles to our clients' e-mail campaigns, they worked too. Here is the second of a three-e-mail campaign we created for DHL. We offered recipients a free white paper, in exchange for some information. Responses were overwhelming and although it was clear that the e-mail was part of an e-mail broadcast, the conversational tone, the sender's name and the personalisation created an illusion of sincerity, to the point that some of the recipients actually replied asking Mark (a real DHL employee) about his family.

Tried and tested

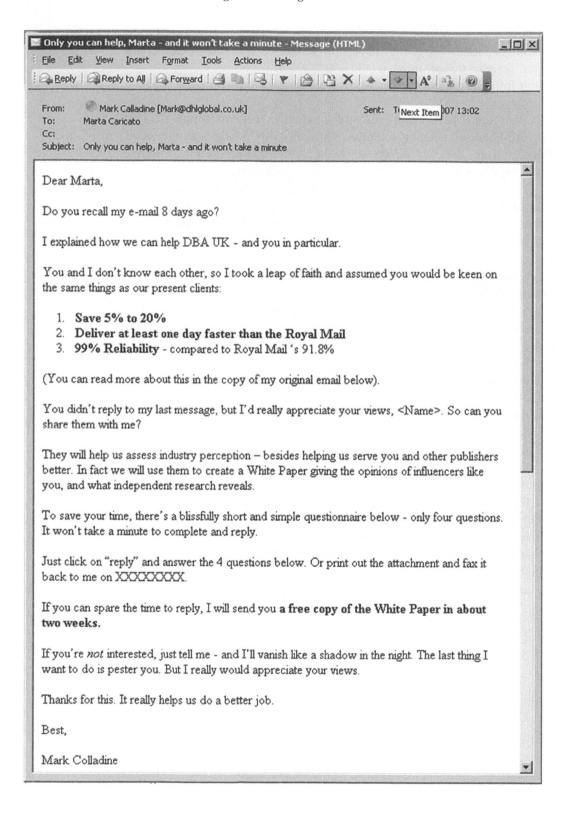

Only you can help, Marta - and it won't take a minute - Message (HTML)

File   Edit   View   Insert   Format   Tools   Actions   Help

Reply | Reply to All | Forward | | | | | | X | | | | A |

From: Mark Calladine [Mark@dhlglobal.co.uk]   Sent: T| Next Item |007 13:02
To: Marta Caricato
Cc:
Subject: Only you can help, Marta - and it won't take a minute

Dear Marta,

Do you recall my e-mail 8 days ago?

I explained how we can help DBA UK - and you in particular.

You and I don't know each other, so I took a leap of faith and assumed you would be keen on the same things as our present clients:

1. **Save 5% to 20%**
2. **Deliver at least one day faster than the Royal Mail**
3. **99% Reliability** - compared to Royal Mail 's 91.8%

(You can read more about this in the copy of my original email below).

You didn't reply to my last message, but I'd really appreciate your views, <Name>. So can you share them with me?

They will help us assess industry perception – besides helping us serve you and other publishers better. In fact we will use them to create a White Paper giving the opinions of influencers like you, and what independent research reveals.

To save your time, there's a blissfully short and simple questionnaire below - only four questions. It won't take a minute to complete and reply.

Just click on "reply" and answer the 4 questions below. Or print out the attachment and fax it back to me on XXXXXXXX.

If you can spare the time to reply, I will send you **a free copy of the White Paper in about two weeks.**

If you're *not* interested, just tell me - and I'll vanish like a shadow in the night. The last thing I want to do is pester you. But I really would appreciate your views.

Thanks for this. It really helps us do a better job.

Best,

Mark Colladine

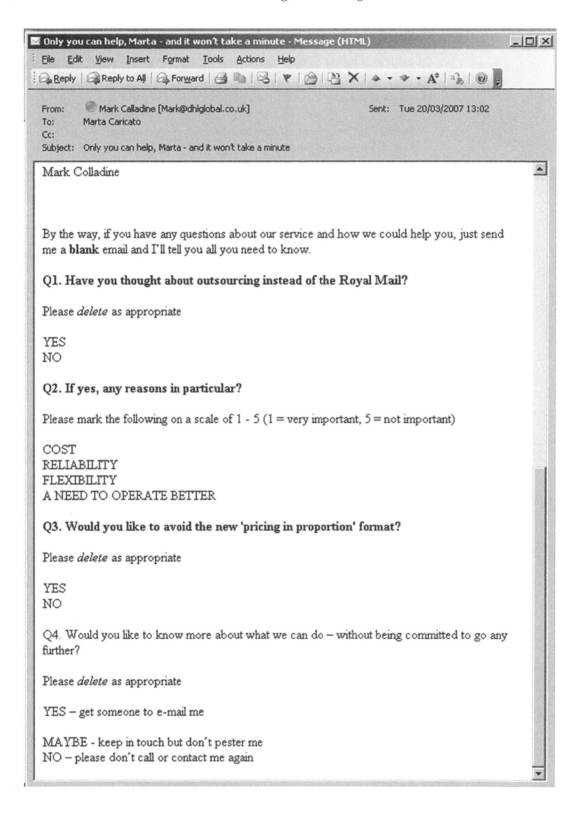

Only you can help, Marta - and it won't take a minute - Message (HTML)

File   Edit   View   Insert   Format   Tools   Actions   Help

Reply | Reply to All | Forward

From: Mark Calladine [Mark@dhlglobal.co.uk]   Sent: Tue 20/03/2007 13:02
To: Marta Caricato
Cc:
Subject: Only you can help, Marta - and it won't take a minute

Mark Colladine

By the way, if you have any questions about our service and how we could help you, just send me a **blank** email and I'll tell you all you need to know.

Q1. Have you thought about outsourcing instead of the Royal Mail?

Please *delete* as appropriate

YES
NO

Q2. If yes, any reasons in particular?

Please mark the following on a scale of 1 - 5 (1 = very important, 5 = not important)

COST
RELIABILITY
FLEXIBILITY
A NEED TO OPERATE BETTER

Q3. Would you like to avoid the new 'pricing in proportion' format?

Please *delete* as appropriate

YES
NO

Q4. Would you like to know more about what we can do – without being committed to go any further?

Please *delete* as appropriate

YES – get someone to e-mail me

MAYBE - keep in touch but don't pester me
NO – please don't call or contact me again

It works just as well for small businesses

Of course it helps if your recipients recognise your name, but the same principles work even for small businesses, targeting recipients who have never heard of them:

From: CityServant [mailto:request@thecityservant.co.uk]
Sent: 05 July 2006 09:01
To: Angela Denny
Subject: Liverpool city centre post office queues get worse

Angela,

The queues for the post office in Liverpool city centre can now take up a huge chunk of your lunch hour. Or for businesses, having staff queue up is costing you.

Don't you just hate it? Braving the elements, standing around waiting, and all for just a stamp.

We're a little strange though, we love standing in queues. It's our job. So why not try us out?

If you want 2 or 200 first class stamps, give me a call and I'll deliver them to your office. There's no charge bar the cost of the stamps.

That's just one of the hundreds of things we do for busy city centre workers to give them back their lunch hour or save valuable staff time.

THIS IS VERY IMPORTANT. Every single business in the city centre can try us out free of charge. So to get a free 'errand', please click reply and I'll send you a voucher together with our usual charges should you wish to try us out again.

Want your dry cleaning dropped off or picked up?

Want the ingredients for a Chinese meal you're cooking picked up from Chinatown?

Need to buy a card and CD from HMV on Church Street for your partner's birthday?

Need some documents delivering by hand to another company in the city centre?

Why not reply now? It will take you a couple of seconds, but it will save you upwards of 20 minutes next time you have an errand to run anywhere in the city centre.

P.S. We're giving away 'City Servant' branded suit carriers to the first 10 people to reply and try us out.

Regards
Dean Scrutton
The CityServant
Making your life simple

WHAT'S MAKING MONEY – AND WHY

The final test of whether what I am saying is right it is to look at the businesses that, more than any others, are making money out of the internet. I'm afraid human weaknesses are a great source of revenue. You can get all sorts of information on the internet, but what many people like most is look at pornography: 70 per cent of browsing is done on sex sites. Don't be shocked: anyone in the hotel business will tell you the videos most looked at in their rooms are the sexy ones. Whatever else happens, new technology is not going to stop sex being the most important thing to most people once they've filled their stomachs.

Many of these sites are so sophisticated technically that 'legitimate' marketers often study and copy their ideas. And of course, they all use traditional direct marketing techniques – especially incentives and discounts. I won't show examples from this market for obvious reasons, but it is interesting to look at examples for the other two very profitable markets on the internet: gambling and self-improvement/get-rich-quick.

If you look at the list of 'website musts' I described earlier on, you will see these guys do not miss a trick (despite the heavy regulations, in the case of gambling). OK, so you're not a pornographer or a gaming expert and you don't want to promise people they will become millionaires in their sleep. How much money can you make on the internet?

There are hundreds of examples of very profitable online operations even in more 'traditional' markets. Firms like Ryanair and easyJet rely almost entirely on internet sales. And in the past few years, Ryanair was one of the few airlines to show a profit.

In England, Tesco overtook their great rivals, Sainsbury, some time ago to become the number one UK supermarket chain, partly, as I have noted, by using their database when others didn't. They also set up a good website. Then they went one step further: they offered their own internet access, becoming an ISP – internet service provider – and giving that access free. This move was judged so clever by the investment community that the day it was announced, Tesco's shares leapt up. At the moment they are probably the largest online retailer.

Many traditional retailers pursue what is called a 'Clicks 'n' mortar' strategy. John Lewis, the best-managed department store group in the UK, saw a 70 per cent increase in online sales in the years 2005–06, and their online

sales will soon overtake those in their flagship store in London's Oxford Street.

The truth is that digital will never entirely replace traditional media, but if you're *not* using these media, your competitors probably are – and stealing a march on you. This applies to almost any product or service you care to mention. For example, I met a man on a plane not long ago who sells hardwood flooring. He told me his business had been in deep trouble for the last two years, but he had only just discovered why. His competitors were using online and he wasn't.

Some services – like online grocery ordering – appeal to some, but not to others. Just as some don't like buying through the post, so others won't like the internet. They will prefer to touch and feel before they buy. And sometimes people will use either method depending on how they feel.

Dell Computers, which sell directly, became, partly because of this, the world's biggest computer firm. Dell turn over many millions a day via the internet. I must say, though, having bought from them, that their service – like that of many others in the field – does not match their claims, which is one reason why their growth has faltered. And the phrase 'via the internet' is deliberate. Dell get enquiries on the internet, but not all sales are actually consummated that way. (Additionally, they have a hidden advantage: Intel heavily subsidises their advertising.)

Look online, buy off – or vice versa

The truth is that although people search for what they want online they may buy offline. Not long ago we bought a brass bed. We found what we wanted online, but the best deal by far was a long way away. Nevertheless we drove 220 miles to choose, examine and buy the bed from Heavenly Beds in Wales. (I recommend them, by the way. If you want to know what constitutes good service, visit them: they are superb marketers.) By the same token, when deciding which television to get, we visited some of the shops on Tottenham Court Road, to actually check image and sound quality – but we bought the set online, for the simple reason that it was a much better deal.

Beware: nothing fails like success

Much of Dell's success was due not just to selling directly, but to giving customers what they wanted – a computer configured to suit them, delivered quickly at a low price. Then they forgot what made them successful.

As I pointed out earlier, a better product or service is – by far – what matters most in marketing. But as I also pointed out, what happens after the sale counts even more. Dell delivered the product, then forgot the customers. Both they and AOL are in trouble as I write because they do an unsatisfactory job of handling customers. (Incidentally, if you want to know more about how much this matters, read *Simply Better: Winning and keeping customers by delivering what matters most* by Patrick Barwise and Sean Meehan.)

Details that enrage customers

Dell and AOL – plus quite a few others – fail in one simple respect which could easily be remedied. They conduct what I call inhuman direct marketing. Sure, you can buy from then directly. Sure, you will get messages from them. But if you want to talk to a human being, you can't. When it matters they prefer a one-way relationship: you can't talk back. But talking back is what people want. They want control. What's more, the internet gives it to a greater degree than ever before. If you have a bad experience with a firm, you can tell the world. And people love to do so.

The other side of the coin

Amazon sit instead at the other end of the spectrum. They are not perfect – who is? – but they work hard towards perfection. Here's a simple example that tells a long story. Some months ago, my colleague Alastair Lee bought a book from them for £8. He never received it, so he contacted Amazon and explained what happened. Mind you, he didn't have anything to prove his story, as Amazon orders are not sent with registered delivery and the online tracking system showed the book as 'delivered'. Yet he was sent another copy of the book free. What's more, he received his £8 back, as an apology. Where do you think Al did all his Christmas shopping this year?

But then again, Amazon's daring strategy was to reinvest all their potential profits in improving their offering, so as to build their brand and get in more customers in the hope that they could make them loyal – or at any rate profitable – before their competitors got hold of them. Offering service that exceeds expectations was apparently part of the strategy. After a great many nerve-racking moments, it paid off, even despite the great internet bubble of 2000.

We are talking here about the value of a customer – a critical subject discussed earlier when looking at the economics of direct marketing. A few years ago Amazon were apparently paying £50 to get a customer. I have no idea how long it took them to generate that much profit per customer – but that's the key calculation, and they obviously had the nerve to wait for the magic moment and the determination to implement their vision at every level.

Beware the power of the user

So far, many companies have been able to thrive despite not making any efforts to please their customers. I predict things are going to change quickly, for two reasons. First, as happens in every market reaching its maturity, product and price will no longer be enough to guarantee a competitive edge. Service has to enter into the equation. The second is because of the growth in popularity of users' exchanges over the net. Think of the huge communities created by MySpace, Bebo and Facebook. Think of how easily people can share opinions, videos, and any kind of files on those and other sites, like Flickr and YouTube. Or think about blog-related sites such as LiveJournal, also extremely popular and with a slightly higher age demographic than MySpace.

Sites like Yahoo! Answers are taking advantage of this collective contribution: they use users to provide answers to thousands of questions free. Wikipedia meanwhile uses collective contributions to provide one of the most comprehensive online encyclopedias available. What all these sites have in common is that the content is being managed by other users – not a firm.

Traditionally the only relationship that mattered was the one between the company and its customers and employees. Outside of this triangle, there are the brand advocates who not only have a relationship with the brand but also with other customers. Although marketers have long realised the power of word of mouth, they generally haven't taken full account of the influence of brand advocates with other customers or offered them a forum to communicate.

Just think: if Amazon hadn't sent Al another book, he would have been disappointed and upset. A couple of years ago, he would have probably told his story to his friends. Now, he could just post an entry on his Myspace page – and potentially reach hundreds of thousands of people. Is this a risk worth taking?

AN EXTRAORDINARY, RARE OPPORTUNITY

For 30-odd years I have slogged around the world preaching the gospel of direct marketing. Looking back, I am amazed at my persistence, since so few people wanted to listen most of the time. I never lost hope, because it seemed to me inevitable that this form of marketing would triumph, as it is now doing. A change in the climate has occurred. Direct marketing, from being beneath contempt, is now fashionable.

This isn't for some inchoate reason: it is because all the factors I mentioned earlier in this book suddenly became so relevant that nobody could ignore them any longer. Technology was one – and the internet is a product of new technology. Lots of firms rushed into direct marketing. Most still do it wrong. The same applies to the internet. Many new entrants remind me of the old joke about the man who jumped on his horse and galloped off in all directions. Their enthusiasm has outrun their intelligence.

But more importantly, you can divide direct marketers – whether they use digital or more traditional media – into two kinds: amateurs and professionals. Those who know what they doing – and those who don't.

The professionals did not necessarily get that way because they were cleverer, nor are the amateurs hopeless because they are stupid. The difference between the two is simple, and I explained it when looking at two types of advertiser right at the start of this book. The professionals are those firms that have no choice, because they rely entirely, or predominantly on this medium. They *have* to make it work, or go broke. The amateurs are those who do it because they think they should, or because it seems fun, or fashionable, or whatever.

In fact, just as most firms are useless at marketing, even more are useless at *this* kind of marketing. And the biggest culprits are often those with the most money – because they have more to waste.

Most firms are more enthusiastic than competent

Here is a cautionary statistic for you: most websites are never visited by anyone – ever. And even when they are, things don't always go very well. I was also not surprised to hear recently that a significant number of requests for information – free brochures and such – from websites were not replied to. It's just the same as in the world of print.

Strategy and planning are important in this as in all else. You must consider what you are trying to achieve, why you are doing it, how you plan to set about it – and all the other little obstacles that may occur along the way. It will probably cost much more than you think. If you don't know what you're doing, this is a pretty good way to waste money, much more money than you would imagine. Despite technological advances and more trained people, the average cost of setting up and running a site has soared. That trifling sum mentioned initially by the people who create it for you may bear no relation to what it eventually costs.

So here is a series of questions to help you to get on the right lines. Think about them carefully, answer honestly – and you're far less likely to squander valuable time and money.

Twenty suggestions for you to consider

- WWW – why??? Ask yourself why you have a website. You may recall that right at the beginning of this book I quote the old army song – 'We're here because we're here.' Well I've asked audiences all over the world why they have a website. And many admitted it was because they (or their bosses) thought they should – often because their competitors had one.
- Make it pay for itself.
- Use every road to reach it.
- Make it work with other media.
- Beware of experts. 'One thing long experience has taught me: beware of experts' (Lord Salisbury).

- Realise the medium may have changed; the customers haven't.
- Compare it to what you know.
- Every page is the first page to someone.
- Make offers.
- Don't talk about yourself.
- Go for action on every page. 'The most essential gift for a good writer is a built-in, shock-proof, bullshit detector' (Ernest Hemingway).
- Test.
- Measure.
- Act.
- Gain knowledge about customers.
- Make it easy: signpost clearly.
- Copy good sites.
- Keep in touch.
- Be personal.
- Make it easy to reply.

And remember, it costs you nothing to test – and the results may astound you. One of our clients hit their yearly sales target with just three e-mails. Goodness knows how much it would have cost through other media. Another increased loan applications from 0.48 per cent to 2.2 per cent with one small, easy-to-miss change on one of the many pages of their website. Another got a 5 per cent response from their e-mail where previously they got 0.2 per cent. What could you achieve? With intelligence, understanding and commitment, who knows?

Going digital: the basics

Points to remember

- The internet is 'more' unique than other media.
- Ask yourself what you want from your website.
- Five critical objectives for your website:
  - get people to it;
  - keep them there;
  - come across as an ideal option;
  - get people to respond;
  - get permission to talk to them.

- Four practical benefits of your website:
  - help identify customers' buying patterns;
  - provide more and better services;
  - deliver information;
  - attract new employees.
- Be quick: people are impatient.
- Ask for e-mail addresses, but offer something in return.
- A successful site should be a pleasure to use.
- Promote your site offline to attract browsers.
- Use online techniques to attract browsers.
- Ensure marketers and not techies are in charge of the process.
- Plan e-mail communications with care.
- Integrate online and offline marketing.

9

Your Greatest Asset

'Father, Mother and Me,
Sister and Auntie say
All the people like us are We
And everyone else is They.'

Rudyard Kipling

'The one thing our industry does not lack
is computer people with the personal characteristics
of a Messiah plus a willingness to dress up a
perfectly ordinary mailing list maintenance system
and call it a "marketing database".'

Ian Goodman
Acxiom UK Ltd

The word direct marketers probably use more than any other was hardly mentioned in the first edition of this book 25 years ago. That word is *database*.

In those days, people talked about *lists* – as they had done for many years. Now, the simple (and inexpensive) list has been cast into outer darkness and replaced by the sophisticated (and sometimes very expensive) database. In fact, one of the leading UK experts on this subject once asked me: 'At what point, Drayton, do you think a list becomes a database? What *is* the difference?'

Lists were relatively inexpensive because everyone understood what they were, and thus what they were paying for when they compiled or rented one. 'Database' is a word many do not entirely understand. A very profitable industry has evolved to cater for this ignorance, with predictable results: many people spend prodigious sums, even millions, without gaining a great deal of satisfaction.

It is easy to waste money

But, I have good news for you. If you start by thinking about lists, you will end by understanding databases and what they can do rather well. Indeed, I hope to reassure you: you probably understand a great deal more than you may have thought.

THE VALUE OF A NAME

I refer elsewhere to Jerry della Femina, who once said he thought advertising 'the most fun you can have with your clothes on'. This displays a worrying ignorance of good music and fine claret, but I know what he meant.

Working in our business is not as worthwhile as being a conservationist or a surgeon, but it is fun, and you get involved in some interesting areas of life. For example, I once wrote copy for a racing tipster service. It all came about through a couple of friends, one of whom gambled professionally, and the other of whom already ran a tipster service.

This taught me a number of things, especially that the average professional gambler is not too hot at running any kind of service, let alone one which requires you to be at the office first thing in the morning to give people tips.

But the most interesting fact I learned was that the name of one regular purchaser of racing tips was worth £1, making the value of a list of 1,000 such names £1,000. To put this in context, at that time the pound sterling was worth four times more than it is now and in those days even a list of extremely wealthy people would have cost you no more than £50 per 1,000 to rent once.

Talk to the right people I tell you this to emphasise that with the right people to talk to you can hardly fail. The most wonderful mailing on earth will die the death if sent to the wrong names. The worst mailing on earth can succeed if it goes to the right ones. I shudder to think how much money has been thrown away because insufficient thought has been given to the people who are being spoken to. If you don't know who you're talking to, you're highly unlikely to make the right offer, let alone gauge why they should want to buy whatever it is you're selling.

This is true even of the broadest appeal – like a sweepstake. Almost everybody likes the idea of winning something for nothing. But some people are put off by this sort of approach. One company which operates in almost every civilised country on earth has hardly ever been able to make a sweepstake pay. Their type of customer simply isn't interested; or to be more exact, does not find that sort of approach from them appropriate – an important distinction, obviously derived from their positioning.

The problem is that, particularly for people accustomed to general advertising, it's easy to think of a list as a *medium* like a newspaper. Yet in fact, of course, direct mail is the medium; the list is the equivalent of the readership of a newspaper. More importantly, a mailing list, if carefully compiled and properly analysed, will reveal far more variables than you could discover about the readers of a particular publication, or the viewers of a TV programme.

List experts sometimes utter a rather dull, but very relevant expression to recall us to the most important truth about lists. They say 'Lists are people'. And – you might reasonably reply – so are the readers of a newspaper or the viewers of a TV show. But direct marketing is all about how people can all be approached as individuals – to return to the besetting theme of this book. And the point about individuals, as I indicated earlier, is that if you can learn enough about them and their needs, you can meet those needs better, and get closer to perfect marketing.

Get closer to perfect marketing

THE RELATIVE IMPORTANCE OF THE LIST

The role of the list as compared with the other factors in a mailing is well illustrated by the results of some tests we conducted a few years ago for one of our clients.

Mailings were sent to 12 lists we thought likely to succeed. We also tested three prices, two ways to pay, different times for mailing, alternative ways of responding and several creative approaches. The best combination of all these factors produced a result 58 times as good as the worst combination. By far the most important factor in these tests was the choice of list – as you can see from the following abbreviated figures.

Lists: the most important factor

Typical mailing test results

Factor	Difference between best and worst
List	× 6.0
Offer	× 3.0
Timing	× 2.0
Creative	× 1.35
Response	× 1.2

Let me emphasise that we had no clear idea in advance which of the 12 lists would work best. In fact, the winner was something of a surprise to me.

This book is not the place (nor am I the person, for I have little sympathy with the subject) to go into the fine and dreary detail of list buying, holding and maintenance, though I hope to give you some helpful advice. But you will have gathered simply from looking at the test results above that the role of the list is critical in this business. Let me now transfer your attention from the list to the database.

Nowadays, people generally hold their lists on computer. It's easier. And the computer is getting infinitely less expensive to buy and run. In 1985, *Direct Marketing* magazine stated that 'Since 1960 the cost of computer mainframe storage has plummeted roughly 20,000 times – whilst speed of operation has increased by a factor of about one million. There is now a 50 per cent gain in efficiency per annum.' This has continued at the same pace.

**Build a
database**

This enables you to build (increasingly cheaply) a more detailed kind of list: a database.

There is a lot of talk about databases, not all necessarily well-informed. Indeed some time ago, one expert asked a group of his colleagues to *define* 'database marketing'. They all gave different answers.

This gives you some insight into the confusion surrounding this word. Yet, in my view, a database is only a list of customers or prospects incorporating relevant information about them. This enables you to target your messages in a way which is much more interesting to your recipient – and therefore likely to be far more profitable to you.

One publication remarked a few years ago that the importance of the database is such that it believes the *primary duty* of a direct marketing agency is to build its client's database. I think this a sweeping and inaccurate assertion. After all, the agency must also be able to help the client exploit that database in an imaginative and profitable way. And if an agency cannot help the client acquire customers and keep them profitably, there will be no money for database building. The business will go broke.

A database is a tool, nothing more. It is your skill at building the database, analysing the information it holds and using your knowledge to construct more effective communications that will determine your success.

Be that as it may, once you understand the principles of list evaluation, you are a fair way to understanding all about databases. In fact, the idea of building a database – of acquiring information about your customers or prospects which you can note down in conjunction with their names and addresses – is not new at all. I am indebted to my friend Roger Millington, a keen historical sleuth, for an example of database-building which dates back quite a while.

It is the case of a company with a medical product asking respondents to give details of their injuries or illnesses as a result of their war experiences. Obviously, this would enable them to target those people better: to offer them the right products.

It was not particularly difficult for the company in question because they made Dr Williams' Pink Pills for Pale People, which had the uncanny facility of being able to cure everything from the common cold to cancer. Probably they merely adapted the messages – based upon the information their respondents supplied – without adapting the product.

**Nothing new
in the
database**

What is most interesting about this example is that it dates back over 130 years, to the period of the American Civil War. Not only is there nothing new under the sun, there is not very much new in a database: simply greater technological proficiency as a result of the computer.

Let us now return to the fundamentals of the mailing list.

Three simple facts to start with

All understanding of mailing lists starts from three simple facts.

1 Lists may be conveniently divided into two kinds: your own, and other people's.
2 Your own list should always give you better results than anyone else's.
3 The best lists to rent or buy are those which are most similar to your own.

Which lists work the best?

I think this is fairly simple. But in case you have any doubt, let me explain that by 'your own' list I mean any list of people who have transacted business with you or had a contact with you, and thus know you.

In business, people prefer to deal with people they know. This is particularly so in the mail order business where customers have to have confidence in the vendor. To send you money for a product they don't have in their hands they have to believe you are reputable. If they've done business with you before, they are going to be that much more confident.

But you will be interested to know that the same thinking applies whether you're talking about mail order or any other form of marketing. For instance, one of my clients uses salespeople. They have discovered that it is four times easier to sell to existing customers than it is to sell to similar prospects who have not done business with them before.

So the important thing to remember is: if people have done business with you or had contact with you previously, their names and addresses are valuable.

In the mail order business, it is reckoned that a mailing to your own list will be about three times as effective than if it were sent to someone else's list on which the names had similar characteristics.

The customers you want are like the ones you have

You will, I am sure, have nodded in agreement at all this. It makes sense, doesn't it? The customers you wish to get are likely to be very similar to those you already have.

Predicting success

Gordon Grossman, a former marketing director of *Reader's Digest* in the US, wrote an article in December 1982, 'Foreshadowing response: the muscle in your merge', which demonstrated in the most startling way how important it is to remember the fact that new customers' responses can be predicted from old.

Grossman noted that if you compare the lists that are working for you currently with ones you are thinking of testing, you can predict with a high degree of certainty which lists are likely to work.

Predict which lists will work

When people rent lists, they have to complete a computer run to eliminate duplication – known in the trade as 'merge and purge'. Having removed this wasteful duplication the average mailer carries on. Not Grossman, because he takes a look to see how *similar* the lists are. He points out that in his experience: (1) if the duplication factor between the two lists is 25 per cent, your mailing has about an 86 per cent chance of succeeding; (2) if it is under 10 per cent, the likelihood of success is about 3 per cent.

Not long ago, a direct marketer attending a seminar I was conducting told me that her company had discovered the same figures applied to within 2 per cent.

Your ability to place on a database relevant information about the people you are interested in, to analyse what you have learned and then exploit it, determines your success in direct marketing. Here's a simple example which shows how *little* the thinking has developed since Dr Williams' Pink Pills were saving lives (or not, as the case may be) 100-odd years ago.

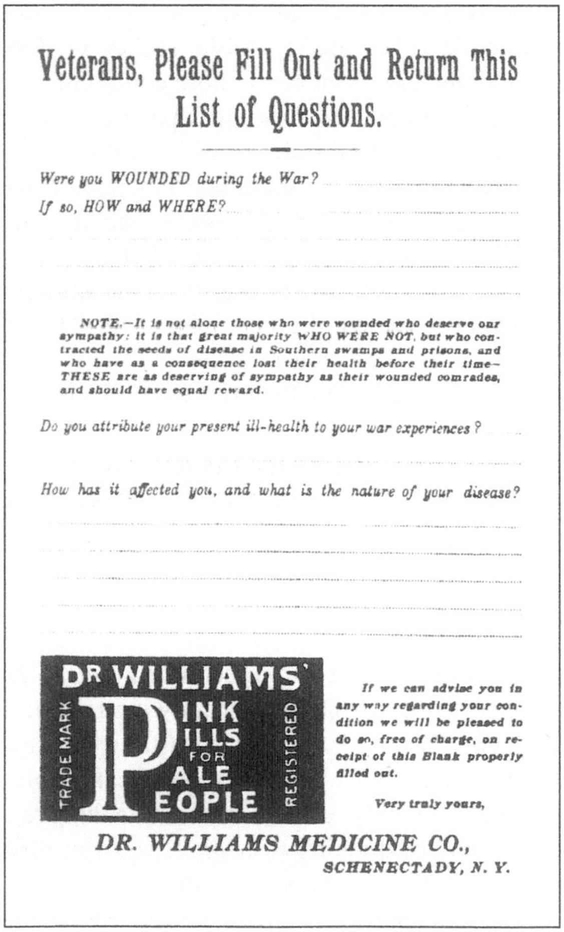

Veterans, Please Fill Out and Return This List of Questions.

Were you WOUNDED during the War?

If so, HOW and WHERE?

NOTE.—It is not alone those who were wounded who deserve our sympathy: it is that great majority WHO WERE NOT, but who contracted the seeds of disease in Southern swamps and prisons, and who have as a consequence lost their health before their time—THESE are as deserving of sympathy as their wounded comrades, and should have equal reward.

Do you attribute your present ill-health to your war experiences?

How has it affected you, and what is the nature of your disease?

DR WILLIAMS' PINK PILLS FOR PALE PEOPLE

TRADE MARK

REGISTERED

If we can advise you in any way regarding your condition we will be pleased to do so, free of charge, on receipt of this Blank properly filled out.

Very truly yours,

DR. WILLIAMS MEDICINE CO.,

SCHENECTADY, N. Y.

Figure 9.1 Dr Williams' Pink Pills. This example of database-building goes back to 1868: there's nothing new under the sun

In the chapter on positioning I mentioned North West Securities and a mailing they sent out to prospects asking them to reply to a simple questionnaire. The questionnaire answers revealed what assets prospects planned to acquire over the next 12 months, how much they thought they would cost, what makes and models they were considering, when they intended to buy and the best time to talk to them on the phone.

This is all enormously valuable ammunition for the company. It also makes sense to the prospect. He (or she) knows that he is only going to be approached by the company *at the right time* to talk about something *he is already interested in* in a way which is *relevant*. In this way the company can offer a better service than it could without that information.

The importance of analysis

Every relevant piece of information can help you build up a picture of your best prospects or customers and enable you to do a better job for those people. This principle applies whether you are talking about business-to-business or consumer marketing. The information you use to enrich your database can come from many sources, internal or external. And you can acquire it in many ways.

One way is to look at who has responded to your previous communications, and discern the characteristics they share with other respondents. The converse is equally true: you can see who does *not* respond. In this way, you can target your communications to those most likely to respond and eliminate those least likely.

This means that you can take a list of people which as a whole would not be profitable to mail and, by eliminating the least responsive names, cut down the size of that list and make it profitable to mail the remaining names. In effect, you transform failure into success. Alternatively, you can make a list which is *already* profitable *more* profitable.

You can use generally available information to enrich your knowledge of the people on your database. For instance, in the public domain there is often information about particular residential areas: what sort of people live in them, what sort of accommodation they inhabit. This is usually available through postal or census statistics.

You can also acquire information from your order forms; often simple but valuable data, by asking whether people have telephones, how old they are, how many children they have and of what sex and age. By comparing this information with the responses you have received from other customers you can predict likely responses from those people. Every shred of information helps build up a picture of the people you are talking to and their probable behaviour.

If you like to blind your colleagues with science, the phrase 'regression analysis' can be used to fine effect when discussing this.

And if you like to impress your colleagues with good profit and loss statements, I should state that generally this technique – though it costs money – tends to generate more profit than it costs: indeed, you can *double* your profitability.

Of course, unless you have your list properly organised, with every possible factor about your buyers incorporated into the database, such analysis is very difficult.

What is your best prospect?

For instance, we once learned for a client that our best prospect tended to have an 'ethnic' surname – that is, not English, and that included Scots and Irish. If English, they were likely to have more initials than average, to be a professional person inhabiting a house rather than a flat, and a house with a name rather than a house with a number. Information like this can, as I said, enable you to transform unprofitable mailing lists into profitable ones simply by eliminating the names less likely to respond.

For a large business, developing your own prospecting database can save millions. One of my clients, American Express, used to be amongst the largest renters of mailing lists in Britain. They employed a considerable staff to do the job, and spent enormous sums both renting and deduplicating the lists. In the end they decided to build their own database from the electoral register, and used the information they already possessed about their best prospects and customers to target the best names on that file. It took time and money, but the final result enabled them to mail that database for no more than their rental method used to cost them – but with no rental charges.

Develop your own database

Most businesses of any size can apply the same sort of thinking. If you are not a large, sophisticated company with its own database, the good old-fashioned mailing list will be critical to you.

TWELVE CRITERIA FOR EVALUATING LISTS

Here are 12 points to consider when assessing a list's value, in *rough* order of priority – based on what the traditional direct marketers have learned.

1 Are they your customers, or someone else's?

If they are someone else's, one way you can get a better response is by persuading the list owner to write an endorsement of your product to go out with your mailing.

2 How much money did they spend per transaction?

Obviously, the £1,000 buyer is likely to prove a more lucrative prospect than the £10 buyer. Equally, when you come to communicate with him or her you will use a very different tone of voice.

3 Have they bought recently?

Recent buyers will always do better than others. In the US they are sold as 'hot-line' buyers. Often, when other names will not work on a list, people who have bought recently will work. In one company I was involved in at one point, whereas we were failing to convert customers by mailing them after six weeks, we were wildly successful by mailing them immediately after a purchase.

4 Have they bought frequently?

Recency, frequency, monetary value

In the same way that recency is important, so is frequency. In fact the three factors that often make the most difference in a list of database selection (apart from accuracy) are recency, frequency and monetary value.

5 How up-to-date is the list?

People sometimes move home. They move jobs more frequently. Unless the list has been mailed recently and the 'gone-aways' have been cleaned out, it could be full of out-of-date names. Business-to-business lists can be particularly poor. I recall a list which we discovered was 50 per cent inaccurate although it came from a very reputable source.

6 Are they mail order buyers or not?

Some people like to buy through the mail. Some don't. So a list of retail buyers or competition entrants will not be nearly as good as mail order buyers – though a list of your own competition entrants will almost certainly do better than a list of somebody else's buyers. The same principle applies to online buyers

7 Were the sales for cash or for credit? What sort of credit?

A cash buyer would be better than a hire purchase buyer. But a credit card buyer should be better than a cash buyer. And a charge card buyer should be better than a credit card buyer. They generally have a higher socio-economic rating.

8 Are they buyers, or just enquirers?

Normally buyers will be better for you than enquirers. Sometimes, though, when renting outside lists, you may find enquirers work better.

9 Is it a list of people who have established a business relationship with someone?

Or is it a compiled list, taken from printed records of some kind, like the telephone directory? Compiled lists are not nearly as good. Moreover, if they have dealt with someone, that enables you to approach them by referring to that relationship. This establishes a reason for writing – very valuable.

10 If it is someone else's list, how similar to your own are the people on it?

By age. By socio-economic background or, if this is business-to-business, by type of company. This is, of course, quite apart from whether they have bought the same kind of product. The best list for you is a list of people who have bought an identical product to yours. (You may find this hard to understand, but, as Shakespeare said, 'The appetite grows by what it feeds upon'.)

11 How often is the list mailed?

You may be surprised to learn that the best lists are those which are mailed often. The people have got into the habit of responding to offers. If a list has only been mailed once in the last six months, the people on it seem to languish.

12 Is the name as well as the title of the person on the list, if it's a business list?

Some lists may only have the company name on them. Make sure you're getting the detail you think necessary. In my experience, rather than settle for what are likely to be inaccurate personal names, you are better off going for the title.

Apply criteria intelligently

If you take all these criteria and apply them intelligently, you should find assessing the likely responsiveness of a list much easier. Indeed, by looking at a list or database and thinking about it attentively, you will frequently come up with the offers and even the products you should be marketing. After all, what you sell, the offers you make, and how you make those offers all start with studying the customer or prospect.

Take two examples from the same field. People who paid £145 cash through the post for an exercise bicycle might read your new £12 a year publication on fitness. On the other hand, subscribers to your publication on fitness are not proven mail order buyers who spent good money recently: they might not be at all prepared to pay £145 for an exercise bicycle – let alone through the post. You would approach your test with fewer expectations.

Your business revolves around your knowledge of individuals

But let me repeat: your entire business should revolve around considering the individuals on your database or the people you wish to recruit as new customers and thus enrich your existing database. Considering those individuals will not merely help you formulate the right offers and the right products to offer; it will enable you to *communicate* your message more effectively. As a copywriter, I always find information about the people I am about to write to and how they have behaved in the past – and indeed *anything* I can find out about them – is immensely valuable in helping me do a better job.

Even scrutinising the names and addresses on a list can sometimes tell you a lot. People with upper class names and smart addresses are different, clearly, from those with working class names living in cheap neighbourhoods. It is *particularly* worth your while to read customer correspondence, as I suggested earlier.

Know how people behave

Perhaps a little story will illustrate how it can pay to think carefully about the people on a list.

Some years ago some enterprising folk opened offices in Manchester and printed a lavish catalogue full of attractive consumer durable goods. They mailed the catalogue to a large list of people who had bad debt records. All the goods offered were available on low deposit.

People behave as they are accustomed

Because they had thought about the nature of the list, the mailing was extremely successful, pulling some £60,000 in deposits, so my informant told me. A few weeks after the mailing had gone out, the entrepreneurs vanished with the money.

This is quite the most successful approach to the problem of bad debt I have heard of. It also illustrates one of Francis Bacon's maxims: men behave as they are accustomed.

You should never forget this when making fresh offers to customers you have recruited, for generally speaking they will respond well to the kind of appeal that attracted them in the first place. Thus, to take a simple example, people who were recruited via a sweepstake offer will respond to that sort of offer later, and so on.

YOUR DATABASE AND HOW TO BUILD IT

A list can belong to anybody; but your database only belongs to you, designed to meet your particular needs. It is simply a list of names and addresses to which are appended all the things you think might be relevant; the information you can discover that will help you deal better with these people: talk to them about the right things at the right time.

One point to remember: don't waste time and money acquiring information about people and placing it on your database – which costs money – when that information is, however interesting, of no real value. This is a mistake often made.

Ways to acquire names

There are only two ways in which you get people on to your database. You may know enough about them to identify them as prospects for what you're offering. You therefore place them on your database and start communicating with them until you find it is no longer worthwhile, because they are clearly not going to respond. Or they identify themselves by replying to communications of one kind or another – advertisements, commercials, take-ones, or syndicated questionnaires (more about this in a moment).

At conferences, people often say to me: 'We don't have a database; how do you build one?' Being a bit of a smart Alec, I always reply: 'Surely you must have a list of customers? Even if it's only to send out bills? Surely you must have a list of your staff? This is your database. All you have to do now is enrich it by adding information about these people on to it.'

Although this is a bit of a simplification, it is true. Most people actually have important lists under their noses which will form the basis for their database and either fail to see their value or don't realise the names are there just for the compiling.

Some years ago, somebody in the very competitive business of photographic developing came to see us. He spent most of the meeting telling us what a hot shot company he had. At the end, we asked him what he did with his database. 'What database?' he asked. 'The list of all the hundreds and thousands of people who send in for free films,' we replied.

'Oh, those. We take their coupons and use them to send the film back – it saves money,' he replied. 'Making a list would be far too expensive.'

Always take customers' names

Anyone who thinks that a list of satisfied customers is not worth the expense of compiling is being very shortsighted indeed. And when you are in a highly competitive – even cut-throat – business like the one this gentleman was in, you should be particularly anxious to communicate regularly with the customers to retain them.

So the first place to look for lists which can build you a database is in your own backyard. Some of the sources are so obvious it's easy to overlook them.

Trapping customer names

Gordon Grossman, whom I have already quoted, once wrote an article with the pleasing title: 'If your customers won't make you rich, then who will?'

It's vitally important that you trap the name of every customer you have, or have had in the past. They will come in from your direct advertising and mailing, obviously. But what if you're just starting out on direct communications? Then you must look elsewhere.

Ways to acquire more names

- Get everyone who deals with customers to record their names and addresses. Your telephonists. Your receptionists in the showroom. Your complaints department. Your service people. Your sales people. Your marketing people.
- If you have retail outlets or agents or a chain of dealers, get them all to do the same.
- Do you offer a guarantee? Get those names and addresses on file.
- What about your past records? Invoices you have sent out, old customers (a lapsed customer is one of your very *best* prospects), past enquiries.

- Do you attend exhibitions or shows? Collect names there.
- How about competitions? Always capture the names of entrants. They should be useful, too.

A little chart overleaf shows you how names come on to a database. I can understand it, unlike most business charts, so I hope you will.

What should go on a database?

Building a database requires careful planning. Sometimes costly errors can be made. For instance, a few years ago the Automobile Association discovered that when planning its database it had neglected to include information about the makes of cars members had, and how long they had had them.

Your database is only as good as the information you hold on it. The more information, the better the database; but the information must be relevant.

Information must be relevant

You need to know as much as possible about what kind of people they are; where they live; how many people live in the household; how old they are; what sort of home they live in. Depending on what you sell, you may want to acquire other information.

For instance, one of my favourite campaigns a few years ago was a series of pages for Fancy Feast cat food, with the engaging headline: 'The richest cats in the world and how they live'. The reply section asked for such information as: 'How many cats do you have, how old are they, what are their names, what cat food do you buy, and how much?' Information like this is obviously of critical importance to that company.

Indeed, *everything* relevant you can learn is likely to make your endeavours more successful. Suppose you wish to sell home improvements. You will obviously be better off appealing to certain types of people living in a certain type of property. If you wish to sell children's toys, you want to find households with children of the right age, and so on.

Equally, as you have already learned, if these people have either bought from you or received communications from you in the past, that must go into the database. *If* they have bought, *when* they bought, *how recently* they bought, *how much* they paid and *how* they paid – all valuable ammunition to help you build a dialogue and create a relationship with your prospects.

Build a dialogue

The same thing applies when you are dealing with business-to-business. Let's examine the type of information you might want to hold. It will probably fall into the following categories:

- purchase history;
  value/date of last sale/frequency of purchase/product range;
- company profile;
  business type/size/credit rating history;

Valuable information

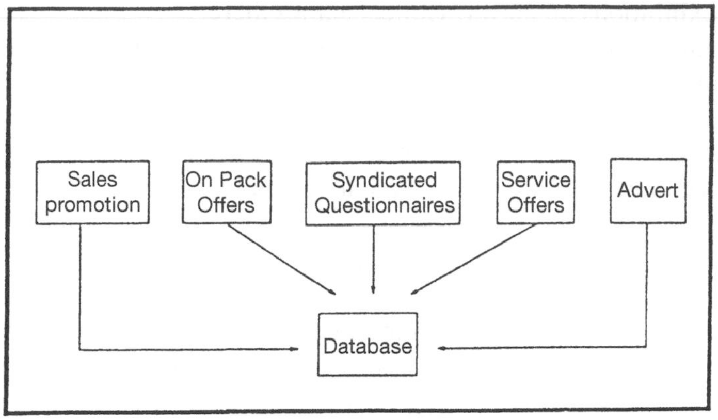

Figure 9.2 Identify individuals

- marketing data;
  source of name/promotion history;
  (i.e. mailings/telephone calls/sales visits)
  expressed interest in other products or services.
- You need to know who the influencers, specifiers and purchasers within a company are, so you can address each individually, addressing his or her motivations. That's because most buying decisions are made by more than one individual.

The potential of cross-selling

If you know what interest a customer might have in other products or services you offer, it helps you to cross-sell. This is obviously desirable, but few people do it as well as they might, simply because they lack this information. But what happens when you do have it? Some years ago, the Trustee Savings Bank announced unusually good results. The reason given by informed observers was that they had developed unusual skills at cross-selling. 'Around the world the bank has been held up as an example of what you can do when you know your customer base', said one leading analyst.

If your business relies on personal selling, a rich database enables you to manage your sales force leads in a sophisticated manner, helping you monitor and control all your sales activities far more efficiently. Because you are constantly acquiring more knowledge about people as individuals, you can manage your database to identify your best prospects.

Identify best prospects

As we have already learned, those prospects will be those whose characteristics most nearly match those of your existing customers. Thus, retailers can examine regional distribution and identify the best areas for potential new outlets by analysing what they know about their existing customers.

We suggested to one of our clients, for instance, that by analysing the geographical distribution of their best customers and prospects, they could convince retailers that a market existed in their area. In this way they could persuade them to join a preferred supplier scheme.

Markets where there are 'no databases'

Some of my colleagues in less developed markets say to me: 'There are no proper databases in my market. In fact there are hardly any decent lists. Nobody knows how to put databases on computer.'

Is this an insurmountable problem? Of course not. As I have already pointed out, people were using forms of database over a hundred years ago. Marketers like *Reader's Digest* were using the database principle before the introduction of the computer. The computer is just technology which enables you to create a database more easily. Moreover, if your clients don't have databases, then start creating them. If you're a client, start creating your own.

The computer is not such an awesome mystery after all. You might be encouraged, when contemplating possible mistakes, to realise that the big companies are *constantly* screwing it up gloriously. It may be that you have little to lose and much to gain by attacking the problem yourself.

But you will need specialist help. That is precisely what I sought when writing this chapter. I went to a leading expert, Ian Goodman. Ian gave the following examples of computer problems during deduplication.

Simple overkill

Where things go wrong

Mrs J Smith
Janet Smith
The computer compares these two names at the same address and decides they are duplicates. In fact they refer to mother and daughter. What if Mrs Smith is a bad credit risk, but her daughter isn't?

Invalid marketing information

The computer discards Janet Smith after crediting her history of purchases to Mrs Smith, who now appears to be a splendid customer.

False name creation

The computer creates a non-existent person by amalgamating the names into Mrs Janet Smith.

Sequence-dependent overkill

A Mr John Smith, Motoring Ltd
B Motoring Ltd
C Mr John Brown, Motoring Ltd

The computer compares A with B and decides that A=B. It marks B for suppression. The computer then compares B with C and decides to mark C for suppression. Thus only A will be mailed.

Same name, different companies

Mr Smith, Motoring Ltd
Mr J Smith, Cars Ltd
Suppose both records refer to the same address. Either they refer to the same person who works for a group of associated companies, or they refer to two different people whose companies share the same business premises. How does your computer cope?

Synonymous titles

Mr John Smith, Managing Director, Health Care Ltd
Mr David Jones, MD, Health Care Ltd
Perhaps the company has joint managing directors. Perhaps one of these records is quite old, referring to a person who has retired. What does your computer make of this?

False title creation

Mr David Jones, MD, Health Care Ltd
Does your computer 'improve' MD to managing director? Or does it realise that Mr Jones may be a doctor?

Sequence straitjacket

Computers rarely demonstrate any flexibility about the way they sort names and addresses into geographic sequence before deduplication. The tiniest spelling variation in two otherwise identical names and addresses can play havoc with a computer sort, forcing the records so far apart that the computer cannot spot the duplicates.

Suppose the computer is sorting by street name. Consider Alder Road and Older Road. Imagine the number of other street names which may be sequenced alphabetically in between!

Tie-breakers and heart-breakers

Suppose the computer resolves its sorting problems and notices the two addresses for Alder Road and Older Road. How far will the computer go to test if one of these names has been incorrectly spelt? Consider the possibilities.

- Alder Road exists, but Older Road does not;
- Older Road exists, but Alder Road does not;
- Both Alder Road and Older Road exist;
- Neither Alder Road nor Older Road exist;
- It is possible to match either street name with another street in the locality, after allowing for a different kind of spelling error. For example, Alder Street.

The computer might resolve these conundrums by referring to a gazetteer of all known streets in the locality, using any given postcode as a tie-breaker. But it does not take too much imagination to see that the rules required to break the tie are extremely complex, being variably dependent upon both the given names and addresses and the particular mix of real street names recorded in the gazetteer in the given locality.

How far does your computer go in resolving these problems? What protections exist against incorrect address correction?

Do you know what you are doing?

Ian ended with a sobering thought you might like to consider. If 99 per cent of direct mail managers do not know the answers to the above questions, and 99 per cent of computer people are equally uncertain, then only 0.001 per cent of all computer deduplication work involves people who know what they are doing – all the more important to make sure you get the right people working for you. If this sounds somewhat cynical, then consider this: some years ago one famous advertiser in Britain managed, I am told, to spend over £50 million without creating a workable database.

WHERE TO FIND THE BEST NEW CUSTOMERS

Just as your own customers are the best people to make you money, they are the best source of new customers. Always spend time and thought on ways of encouraging them to give you the names of possible new recruits. This activity – known variously as 'Member-get-Member' or MGM, and 'Friend-get-a-Friend' – tends to be the most cost-effective of all ways of getting new customers.

Get your customers' help

In fact in the United States, some research into why people buy cars revealed that the chief influencer for choosing a model was not television ads, which is where car firms spend most of their money. It was word of mouth. The second biggest influence was looking on the internet, and direct mail from dealers came third. It follows logically that any direct mail based on personal recommendation is likely to work very well, and it does.

It will normally pay you to offer incentives in exchange for the names of customers' friends. (The incentives only being received when the new name buys.) Usually it pays to offer the new recruits a gift, too. That way they do not feel exploited.

This activity of stimulating your own people to give you names is surprisingly neglected. I think it is so obvious that people tend to dismiss it as

It looked like a set up to me.

Mail Order Mansion

It's only 6 million dollars and comes complete with swimming pool, tennis court and a breathtaking view.

By Joseph Sugarman

Have I got a deal. And even if you don't buy this home you'll love the story.

It all started with an invitation. I was invited by one of the top real estate developers in the country to attend a party at his home in Malibu, California. I didn't know why. All the developer would say is, "Just come."

The jet was waiting for me at O'Hare airport in Chicago and his chauffeur driven limousine met me at Los Angeles for the drive to Malibu. It was class all the way.

When I drove up to the home there was a party going on. Rolls Royces were lined up everywhere and the noise and music from the house made it clear that something special was going on.

VERY FAMOUS GUESTS

After I entered and was introduced to the host and his wife, they took me around and introduced me to some of their guests. "This is Joe Sugarman, that famous mail order copy writer who writes all those interesting mail order ads."

I met a famous movie star, a nationally famous sports broadcaster, a soap opera TV star, a few famous baseball players, the most famous quarterback in football, another famous movie star and two famous California politicians. I recognized everybody and a few even knew who I was. In fact, some of them were my customers. But why was I there? I still didn't know.

I had a chance to look around the house. Now, I've seen beautiful homes in my life but this one had to be the most impressive I've ever seen. First, it was on top of a 90 foot bluff overlooking a sandy beach and the Pacific Ocean. Secondly, it was night and I could see the entire shore line of Los Angeles. It was like I was on a cruise ship at sea and I could look over the Pacific and back at the city.

Then I recognized the cliff. Was this the site of the most publicized wedding in show business where seven helicopters hovered above taking pictures? I found out later that it was.

The home took complete advantage of the view. Practically every room faced the ocean. And the sliding glass doors completely opened so you had an unobstructed view of the Ocean—no partitions, no supporting beams.

The sound that filled the house with music first appeared to be live. But later I found that the home had the best acoustics ever designed into a personal residence with a sound system that rivaled a recording studio. And what a personal residence.

There was a sunken tennis court, a swimming pool, whirlpool bath and solid state electronic lighting system that was controlled from any place in the house. The ceilings were 25 feet high and the interior decor was so tastefully done that I could easily understand why it won all sorts of awards. But why was I here? Why were all my expenses paid for? Then I found out.

The developer and his wife set me up in one of the five bedrooms and after the guests had left invited me into the living room. "Joe, the reason we've invited you here is that we want you to write an advertisement to sell our house. You're one of the nation's top copywriters, and since this house is an award-winning world-class residence, we wanted a world-class copywriter to do it justice."

Now I'll admit, I was flattered. "But I'm a mail order copywriter. How could I possibly sell a house this expensive?"

VERY SPECIAL

"Easy," replied the developer. "By its value. This property is very special. It's on a peninsula that sticks out of the curved part that faces Los Angeles. When you look from the cliff you see Los Angeles as if it was rising out of the ocean. And because we are on a point, we do not get the harsh winds off the ocean but rather gentle breezes all year long. The property itself is so valuable that our next door neighbor paid close to 9 million dollars for his one bedroom house."

I was starting to feel uneasy. "I'm sorry, but there's no way I can sell your home. I refuse to write anything except under my own company name. And I'm not in the real estate business." But the developer persisted.

"Joe, you really can be. This house is an investment. There's a lot of foreign money out there. And all it takes is that special person looking for a celebrity-status world-class home on one of the best sites in America and presto, it's sold."

FINAL REFUSAL

I refused and it was my final refusal. "I'm sorry. I cannot sell anything without a 30 day return privilege. My customers all have the opportunity to return anything we sell them for a prompt and courteous refund. And then there's the credit card issue. We make it easy for them to purchase with either Master-Card, Visa or American Express."

Well, the rest is history. I am indeed offering the house for sale. Please call me at (312) 564-7000 and arrange for a personal showing. Then I urge you to buy it. We accept Visa, MasterCard, American Express, American dollars, Japanese Yen or any negotiable hard currency.

After you buy the home, live in it for 30 days. Enjoy the spectacular view, walk on the beautiful beaches, experience the spacious living. If, after 30 days, you aren't completely satisfied, return the home to the original owner for a prompt and courteous refund.

The developer and his wife are thrilled that I am selling their home. They realize that the mail order business is a lot different than the real estate business and are willing to compromise. But don't you compromise. If you truly are one of those rare people in search of a spectacular home on the best location in America, call me personally at no obligation, today.

PS: If you don't have time for the showing, please order a video tape of the home. (Please refer to product number 7077YE). Send $20 plus $3 postage and handling to the address below or credit card buyers call our toll-free number below.

Malibu Mansion $6,000,000

One JS&A Plaza, Northbrook, Illinois 60062
CALL TOLL FREE 800 228-5000
IL residents add 7% sales tax. ©JS&A Group, Inc. 1987

A thoroughly modern mail-order man.

Joe Sugarman started out in the way pioneer mail order entrepreneurs did: on his kitchen table. He writes all his own ads. This is a typical example, but I must admit the product seems a little expensive. Note the long copy. Joe believes as long as you make sure people want to read *the next sentence*, that's all you have to worry about. Sounds much easier than it is. Note also, no coupon. His readers all have phones and credit cards.

A good example of how advertising and direct marketing work together.
The advertisement positions the product and describes it, but does not ask for any action. That is done most effectively by the tipped-on card on the right, which had a coupon and questionnaire on the reverse. Renault see direct marketing as an extremely important weapon, not merely a tactical add-on, in their battle against competitors. Incidentally, a tip-on card in a prominent position like that gets as many as five times more replies as an ordinary coupon.

These two advertisements appear identical. In fact there's one piece of copy different in the ad on the right: underneath the offer of a free ABBA record, there is a line limiting the period of that offer to seven days. This single change increased response significantly. Good to remember if you ever wonder whether people read long copy; also a powerful demonstration of the way limiting offers increases responses.

This advertisement seeking an enquiry does not need a lot of copy. The headline does a good job. First, it attracts attention by promising a benefit; second, it quantifies that benefit. It would have been even more effective if they had made the figure not £50 but £50.75.

This traditional mail order advertiser recruits individuals by making free offers like this with the aim of building a continuing relationship by selling first one series of self improvement cards, then other products.

They also test a lot to maximise profits. The ad on the right did well because the product is a good idea. But it featured the product itself rather than its benefits.

The ad on the left was three times as successful. It featured the benefits of the product and also exploited the endorser better. Her signature adds credibility.

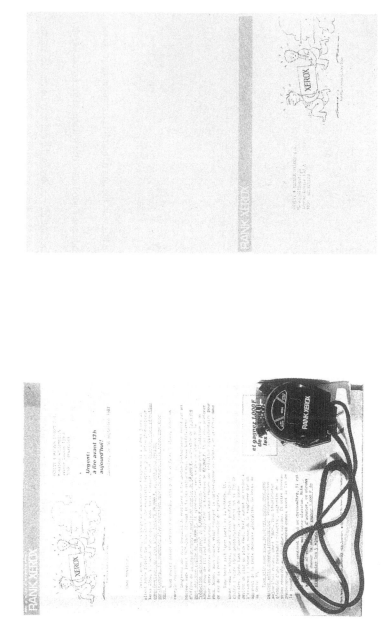

This box containing a stopwatch was sent out to companies in Belgium which had obsolescent Xerox machines. They were telephoned in advance to tell them a pleasant surprise was on its way – though the nature of the surprise was not revealed. When this mailing was first sent out, over 50 per cent of recipients bought new machines.

The offer was good: a big trade-in allowance on your old machine if you bought a new one. The stopwatch drew attention in a relevant way – you had to order your machine before 1 o'clock and start the stopwatch. The company guaranteed to deliver the machine before 6 o'clock that evening, and pay 1000 francs for every five minutes they were late.

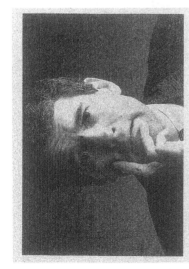

Without the free Guide to Network Servers,
you could be a couple of gigabytes short
of a 128-bit interleaved memory bus.

The Compaq Guide to PC Networks.
It's the difference between an educated guess
and an executive decision.

Which of these two advertisements would you have expected to do better? The answer is: the one on the left. The other one is merely competent. The winner uses jargon which computer people would find amusing – one of the rare occasions when jargon is appropriate, because you are talking to a technical audience. Another important element is the person staring out of the page at you: this always boosts readership

This American Express mailing worked spectacularly well when sent out to a group of people who had previously refused to respond to invitations to apply for the Gold Card. It simply asked them why, and gave them the opportunity to refuse further mailings, or indicate to what degree the Gold Card interested them.

OEH! DAT VALT NIET MEE

DE NEDERLANDSE KAT KRIJGT DE FELIXSMAAK TE PAKKEN.

Een Felix kat is nu eenmaal ondernemend. Zozeer zelfs dat je in af en toe een dansje ziet maken voor 't eten.

En hoe langer hoe meer katten in Nederland krijgen de smaak van Felix te pakken, sorry de vijf smaken. Overal in Nederland hoor je 't gerommel van het Felix pak.

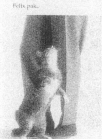

Tja, dat wil natuurlijk ook wel eens katten trekken die 't thuis niet krijgen. Maar ach, u neemt toch ook wel eens iets mee?

MAAR DAT DANSJE, DAAR HEBBEN SOMMIGE NOG MOEITE MEE.

Daarom heeft Felix de originele passen voor uw kat begrijpelijk uiteengezet op een fraaie katten place-mat, met plaats voor zijn bakjes. Kan-ie telkens voor 't eten even oefenen en naar hartelust met zijn eten stoeien.

Maar wel één goede raad: gaat u er niet bij kijken als-ie oefent. Een Felix kat durft veel aan, maar hij heeft ook zijn trots.

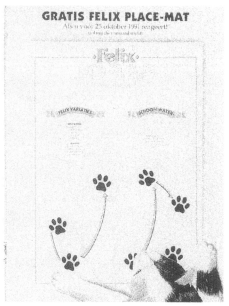

GRATIS FELIX PLACE-MAT
Als u vóór 25 oktober 1991 reageert!

In recent years packaged goods advertisers have become increasingly interested in direct marketing. As one American executive commented in 1992: 'A year ago I would have scoffed at direct marketing no wow'.

The above mailings are part of a campaign running in Holland, linked to TV advertising. The commercials featured a cat owner dancing in samba-like fashion in its kitchen, whilst shaking a package of dried catfood and coming out with the ludicrous phrase: 'ooh, that tastes terrific'.

The owner's cat dances in sympathy.

The mailing offers a placement with dance steps on it so that your cat can learn to dance. It is 'signed' by the cat who appears in the commercial.

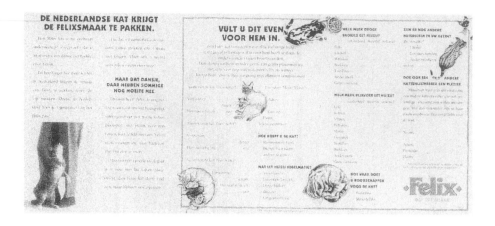

Dear Mr Echo

This letter is really meant for your cat, but
since I don't know his name, I am addressing it to
you.

Perhaps you know me, the name is Felix. I am the
cat that made dancing a favourite sport amongst
Dutch cats. You know, from television, from 'Ooh,
that tastes terrific!'

And nowadays it appears that a lot of cats try
to dance too, but not all of them manage to do
very well. That is why I have prepared a cat
place-mat, on which the proper steps are
explained.

It is a very nice place-mat, if I may say so. And
handy because not every cat has the finest of
table manners (but never mention that to him, we
have our pride too).

*Your cat is getting it free, if, before 31
October 1991, you tell us his name and answer a
few questions.*

And who knows, maybe I will send him something
else. Since I became a TV-celebrity, those guys
from Felix tend to listen to what I say, you know.

So if you answer a few questions, you can simply
close the leaflet and mail it. You don't even need
a stamp. Ain't that easy?

Felix

P. S. Don't forget to fill in your cat's name, so I
can write to him or her in person, from one cat to
another.

The questionnaire in the mailing asks such questions as the name and birthday of the cat or cats. Then there is a follow-up birthday mailing.

Birthday mailings are very successful. One sent out in Hong Kong for BMW on the anniversary of owners purchasing their cars pleased one recipient so much he bought a second car.

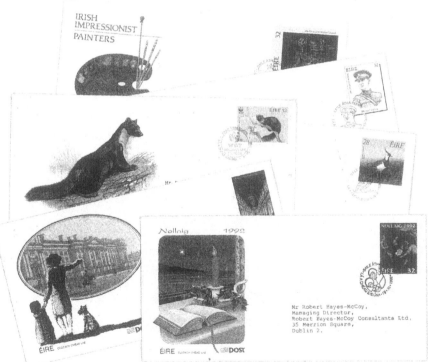

If you want to do business-to-business direct mail, Robert Hayes-McCoy, an Irish direct marketing consultant is a good man to copy. His monthly mailings illustrate five important principles. First, they constitute a *campaign*: they all have a similar look and tone. Second, he is persistent: he's been sending me these mailings for three years now. Third, the mailings are impossible to ignore. Indeed, you want to collect them, because they come in first day covers featuring new Irish stamps, which are in themselves valuable. Fourth, each mailing *demonstrates* what he is selling – his skills. Fifth, the writing style has charm.

I have shown these ads to audiences all over the world. The vast majority think the 'clever' ad was more successful than the other. In fact, the reverse was the case. The clever ad never even covered its cost. The other advertisement – written by my former partner John Watson – was tremendously effective. Mainly because it got to the point, told a complete story as a salesperson would and – incidentally – contained in the headline not one but *two* unique selling propositions: one based on price; the other on function

Figures I saw a few years ago suggested that more money was spent on telemarketing than any other medium in America. This was one of the most successful ads ever run for British Telecom's telemarketing business. I recall it particularly because I was spurred to produce it by a previous advertisement I had written, of which I was exceedingly proud, but which produced hardly any response.

Note the heavy use of testimonials: at that time people simply didn't believe the telephone could work for them.

Regular inserts like this go out in communications from most credit and charge card companies. As a rule the more transactions a customer has with you the more loyal he or she will be. Research a few years ago showed a bank customer with four different types of account was 100 times less likely to leave that bank than a customer with only one type of account.

Ogilvy & Mather Direct, Frankfurt, created this ad for Avon. They started by analysing the characteristics of successful Avon ladies, then set out to attract more of the same.

A cardinal rule on database is that the customer you want is likely to be very similar to the customer you've got.

A series of ads like this ran, each featuring a quiz. Readers were asked to fill in the answers, and respond with the promise that they would be told what kind of person they were, and receive a free gift.

If their replies indicated that they would make good Avon ladies they were directed to their nearest Avon supervisor. The details stored on the database were printed out and sent to the supervisor, who was thus motivated and encouraged. Those who didn't fit into the right category were simply sent the free gift.

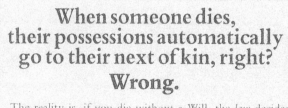

Really outstanding creative is relevant, with a touch of the unexpected. An idea that works can be applied to more than one situation. The ad above was prepared for a charity who never ran it (which I think was a shame). The writer Randy Haunfelder, then adapted the idea to sell pensions, very effectively. The headline ran: At 26 you're too young to be thinking about a pension, right? Wrong.

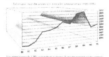

'Promise, large promise is the soul of an advertisement' said Dr Johnson. The promise in the headline of this Portuguese advertisement for an international investment fund runs: 'How to gain access to 99.87% of the investment opportunities in the entire world'.

I wondered how such a claim could be justified. The answer is in the first paragraph which simply states 'Did you know that all the investments in Portugal only represent at most .13% of global investments?'

One of the most bitterly competitive fields on earth is the Book Club business. QPB came up with a new idea, paperbacks instead of hardbacks. This enabled them to change the offer. When you join QPB you aren't obliged to buy a number of books a year, as is the case with hardback Book Clubs.

Here are examples from three campaigns for this book club, created by Ogilvy & Mather Direct in New York. The first campaign featuring famous writers like Ernest Hemingway did remarkably well. In tests, the campaign featuring Larsen cartoons did even better, and the ones with Groening cartoons better still. Cartoons are the most effective illustrative device for attracting attention. They do better than conventional illustrations or photographs. On the other hand, photographs are more credible. I've always found photographs outpull illustrations when selling merchandise.

something they will get round to when they've solved their big problems, such as the design of the new corporate logo. Apart from collecting and exploiting testimonials, it may be the most neglected marketing ploy I can think of. Yet I can imagine few circumstances, save perhaps recommendations to a clinic for unsociable diseases, where it would not work, and I know of no easier way of increasing your profits.

Referrals: neglected, but hugely profitable

It's normally a licence to print money, because the message that solicits the new names goes out as part of your regular commerce with existing customers. It rarely requires more than a simple leaflet, sometimes less. Unlike a mailing or an ad soliciting new members, you have no need to spend much time persuading people your product is good; your satisfied customer is already convinced. In fact, the most cost-effective example I have ever seen (which I mention in another chapter) consisted of a simple one-line request on an envelope flap, offering no incentive at all. *Nothing* could be less expensive; I have never heard of *anything* as cost-effective.

So, write it in letters of fire over your desk: 'I need an MGM programme because it's money for old rope'.

Pass on the message

While I am on the subject, what about the converse: what can you do with people who won't buy? Your customers will help you recruit new customers; what about those who aren't your customers? It is by scavenging around in piles of what appear to be otherwise useless commercial debris – like non-customers – that you can sometimes find little nuggets of gold.

Therefore, put a line in your communications suggesting to recipients that if they are not interested themselves, will they pass the message on to someone they think may be. A good place is behind the window on an envelope in a mailing so the message appears when the contents are removed. Another is in the PS to the letter.

In business-to-business mailings it's particularly important to do this sort of thing. That's because although it generally pays you to mail people by name, this is not always true: sometimes the additional cost is too great to justify the additional response. Often people move positions within organisations, or from one company to another, so that you may be better off mailing to a title. This is not always the case, but it generally is because of the large

Beware of out-of-date names

number of executives who change their jobs – or lose them – each year. One respected UK list broker stated a few years ago that 30–40 per cent of all names on the average business list at any time were likely to be inaccurate.

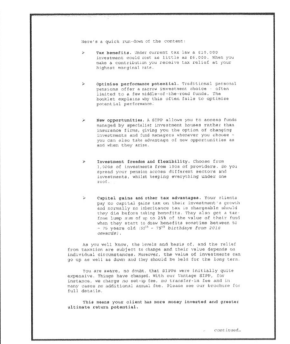

The same principles apply whether you are selling to consumers or businesses. This letter to accountants got the highest response the firm had ever had.

Often, it may not be at all clear who the real decision-maker is in the case of your product or service. That makes it particularly important that if you mail the wrong person they pass the message on to the right one.

Never assume that people will do it automatically. But if you point out to them that the better a job of informing their colleagues you can do, the more it will benefit their company, they may be more than happy to help you. I have illustrated one way of getting these names below.

LIFESTYLE DATABASES

The syndicated questionnaire, and the database developed from it can help you build your own database. Such databases can contain much or all of the information you need to target people accurately. I am only familiar with this form of database building in the consumer area, though clearly it would apply for business-to-business as well.

How syndicated questionnaires work

This is how it works. Consumers are offered incentives – often free or discounted samples – in exchange for completing a questionnaire. The questionnaire may be in the form of a door-to-door leaflet, an insert in a newspaper or magazine, an insert with a product delivery, or even part of a product guarantee form. The questions cover the characteristics of the household, and the individuals within it, in considerable detail. What they buy, what brands, when they buy, how often they buy, what their hobbies and interests and habits are – almost everything you need to know. With the aid of this information you can target more accurately.

For instance, suppose you are selling Brand A coffee, you can then offer households who buy Brand B free samples of your brand and thus attempt to convert them. To households already using your brand, you can make a different offer. Perhaps one which encourages them to buy a greater quantity.

The firms running these questionnaires generally offer marketers the opportunity to sponsor questions – which they can help formulate – in areas that interest them. A car manufacturer can sponsor a section on car ownership. What car do you own? How long have you owned it? When do you plan to replace it? Obviously the firms pay for this privilege, which offsets the cost of sending out the questionnaires.

This offers you what is potentially a *guided missile* for your marketing. You are able to target your competitors' customers and make them compelling offers. And it works. In the case of a pain reliever in the United States, one brand was able to persuade between 50 per cent and 75 per cent of the customers of a competitor to try their product.

Like most new ideas, this can give rise to vain hopes, if not considered carefully. The truth is that most sophisticated marketers are aware that just to get your prospect to sample your product once is only the first step on the way to brand loyalty – that nirvana of the sophisticated marketer. Nonetheless, it is

The 1999 Silk Cut Leisure and Lifestyle Survey

What makes you tick? Would the chance of winning £10,000?

Start ticking, send us your completed, signed Survey and your name will be entered in our special Free Prize Draw. Win and we'll give you £10,000 to spend as you wish. Blow it all on a holiday that you and all your family will remember forever. Or save some and spend the rest on a new runabout - it's up to you.

Please answer the following questions so we can tailor any future offers we may make to suit you. Anything you tell us will be treated confidentially in accordance with the Data Protection Act. Thank you for your help and good luck with the Draw.

We've tried to make this Survey easy to complete, by using tick boxes where possible, so it should only take you a few minutes. If there are any questions you'd prefer not answering or that aren't applicable, please feel free to leave them blank. We would much rather have your Survey returned to us without these facts, than not receive your Survey at all. Once completed and signed, please return the Survey in the reply-paid envelope provided, or send to: The 1999 Silk Cut Leisure and Lifestyle Survey, FREEPOST SEA7364, Eastbourne BN20 8BR. Your name will then be entered automatically in the Free Prize Draw.

Don't forget to sign the box to confirm you're a smoker aged 18 or over, or your entry in the Prize Draw cannot be accepted.
CLOSING DATE FOR RECEIPT OF ENTRIES IS 31 DECEMBER 1999.

Start ticking now for that big prize!

SECTION A - YOU AND YOUR PARTNER

1. Mr A Sample
   1 Sample Street
   Any Town
   Anywhere
   AB1 2CD

   9999999999   B1
   (If any of the above details are incorrect, please cross through and write your corrections clearly alongside in block capitals.)

2. Why keep a good thing to yourself? If you give us your partner's name and get them to sign at the end, they can hear of offers too.

   · Mr ☐   Mrs ☐   Ms ☐   Miss ☐   Other ☐

   Forename ☐☐☐☐☐☐☐☐☐☐☐☐

   Surname ☐☐☐☐☐☐☐☐☐☐☐☐

SECTION B - SPORTS AND LEISURE

Knowing more about you helps us to send you stuff which you'll appreciate. Please answer as many questions as you can, but do feel free to leave out any which are not relevant.

1. Do you or your partner REGULARLY enjoy any of these leisure activities and interests? *(Please tick all that apply.)*

	You	Ptnr		You	Ptnr
National Trust	01	02	Current affairs	03	04
Theatre/Cultural/Arts events	05	06	Gourmet food/Fine wines	07	08
Gardening	09	10	Book reading	11	12
Photography	13	14	Crossword puzzles	15	16
Fine art/Antiques	17	18	Hiking/Walking	19	20
Collectibles/Collecting	21	22	Home computing	23	24
Eating out	25	26	Sewing/Needlework/Knitting	27	28
Further education	29	30	Shopping	31	32
Self improvement	33	34	Health foods	35	36
Do it yourself	37	38	Fashion/Clothes	39	40
Household pets	41	42	Orienteering	43	44
Nightclubbing	45	46	Doing the pools	47	48
Shopping by catalogue	49	50	Going to bingo	51	52
Going to the pub	53	54	Watching video films	55	56
Going to the cinema	57	58	Camping	59	60
Betting	61	62	Competitions	63	64

2. And if you're the sporty type, which of these activities do you enjoy REGULARLY? *(Please tick all that apply.)*

	Watch	Play		Watch	Play
Cricket	01	02	Golf	03	04
Snooker	05	06	Ice hockey	07	08
Motor Racing/Formula 1	09	10	Ten-pin bowling	11	12
Cycling	13	14	Snow-skiing/boarding	15	16
Sailing/Wind surfing	17	18	Fishing	19	20
Jogging/Exercise	21	22	Rugby	23	24
Football	25	26	Racquet sports	27	28

3. Do you support a premier league football team, or another?

Arsenal	01	Aston Villa	02	Blackburn Rovers	03
Charlton Athletic	04	Chelsea	05	Coventry	06
Derby	07	Everton	08	Leeds	09
Leicester City	10	Liverpool	11	Manchester United	12
Middlesbrough	13	Newcastle United	14	Nottingham Forest	15
Sheff. Wednesday	16	Southampton	17	Tottenham Hotspur	18
West Ham United	19	Wimbledon	20		

Other ☐☐☐☐☐☐☐☐☐☐☐☐ 21

4. Do you or your partner have a flutter on any of the following? *(Please tick all that apply.)*

	You	Ptnr		You	Ptnr
National Lottery	01	02	Littlewoods Pools	03	04
Vernons Pools	05	06	Other Pools	07	08

SECTION C - YOUR SHOPPING

In this section, we'd like to find out a bit about your shopping habits. It all goes to helping us to send you offers you'll appreciate.

1. Where do you generally shop for food and groceries? *(Please tick all that apply.)*

	Main	Secondary		Main	Secondary
Aldi	01	02	Alldays/Circle K	03	04
Asda	05	06	Budgen	07	08
Co-op	09	10	Farmfood	11	12
Gateway/Solo	13	14	Iceland	15	16
Lidl	17	18	Mace/Spar/VG	19	20
Marks & Spencer	21	22	Netto	23	24
Kwiksave	25	26	Safeway	27	28
Sainsbury	29	30	Savacentre	31	32
Somerfield	33	34	Tesco/Tesco Metro	35	36
Waitrose	37	38	Petrol Station	39	40
Corner shop/Other	41	42	7-Eleven	43	44

S6

Figure 9.5 The first page of a four-page syndicated questionnaire

a very important first step. (One of my clients reckoned it took seven purchases to 'hook' a prospect on the brand.)

If you offer customers a series of incentives which persuade them to keep using the product, then you are getting somewhere. However, always make sure that you tell people why you are offering these incentives – as a spur to loyalty, or as thanks for their custom.

COMPILED LISTS

Evaluating whether people are likely customers or not is something I have covered already to some degree, but I have not dealt with the tedious business of *compiling* lists of names of likely prospects.

How to proceed

Generally speaking, you should only do this if you have a subject for which there is no list available from a broker to suit your purpose. Even then, though, it may pay you to go to one and get them to compile it for you. They may do it cheaply in exchange for the right to hold the list and make money by renting it out to other users. You obviously make sure you retain the right to restrict rental to people you approve of, ie non-competitors.

But if you have a pool of fairly intelligent people willing to pore through business directories and put lists of names on to word processors for a pittance, then by all means compile your own lists. Your sources for this heart-breaking task will be some (even all) of the following: telephone directories, trade directories, membership lists of relevant associations or clubs and any private lists you can beg, borrow or otherwise lay your hands on.

It is frequently worthwhile compiling your own list in business-to-business. Business products are becoming ever more sophisticated, and inside businesses there are functionaries who did not even exist a few years ago. Like a data processing manager.

Sometimes the value to you of reaching a named executive can be great enough for it to pay you to *telephone* companies to find out the right people to talk to. You might also pick up valuable information on how buying decisions are made. We have someone in my office who does nothing else.

The list industry

When I first became involved in this industry, there were many occasions when one had to compile one's own lists. There was no other option. Now, happily, this is less frequently needed.

A history of lists

In those early days, too, the industry was infested with jolly pirates offering to sell (or even *steal*) lists for you. Some left the business; others went 'straight' and became pillars of the industry.

So today, although the list business worldwide is not as highly developed as in America, it is becoming fairly well-organised. As long as you take sensible precautions you can normally rely on getting what you have paid for.

Some of the rogues I knew in the 1960s whose pockets were stuffed with ill-gotten cash would have been stunned to see that there is a List Brokers and Managers Association in the UK. They must have felt rather like aged gunfighters did when the law came to the Old West. In their day, the business was often conducted over bars, with the unit of exchange purloined postal dockets. These would be filled in with fanciful numbers and shown to gullible clients as proof that their mailings had gone out.

Nowadays, if the thrills and spills have diminished, there are still quite enough things that can go awry to keep the adrenalin flowing.

Lists today

Broadly speaking the list industry is divided between list managers and list brokers. A manager will look after lists on your behalf, whilst a broker is a middleman. In many countries such fine distinctions have not really caught hold. Most brokers will manage; most managers will broke.

Any broker can normally get hold of most available lists, so it really comes down to finding a broker you think is efficient. In a nascent industry, this comes down to trial and error, and consulting your friends.

You can go direct to the owners of the lists, too. In Britain people who buy data regularly are most likely to use Listlink, but with the changing marketplace, online resources are also becoming more widely used. In the US there are many such sources. In less developed markets, none.

Use an expert

Although you will end up paying one way or another for his services, I think it's worth going to a broker.

So many things can go wrong with the way names are held (eg what kind of computer program is it held on?) and with whether you get what you paid for (eg the number of names on the list, or the number actually still alive and kicking) that you should make sure you have someone else to worry about it. And of course to *blame* when things do go wrong.

I will only give you two words of advice on this subject. First, make sure you are not paying *two* sets of commission rather than one. Sometimes the broker you are dealing with may be charging a commission and the one who is managing the list may be, too. Let them split their earnings, not double them.

Second, take the time to go into every conceivable detail about the lists; or to make sure that the broker has done so. Other, more technical books deal with this at great length. They are worth studying if you can't afford an in-house expert. It is a good idea to arrange to phone some of the names as a check.

All I would urge you to bear in mind is that this is a world on its own, with more possibilities for foul-ups than you can imagine. All the criteria I listed earlier in this chapter apply, plus questions such as whether the computer can provide an *nth* selection for testing? ... Are the names in postcode order or in alpha sequence? ... On what kind of labels will they appear? ... Does the owner insist on mailing himself? ... How recently were they mailed? ... How soon can *you* mail them?

A world of foul-ups

Every question contains the seeds of a sleepless night if it hasn't been asked and answered, I promise you.

The cheapest way to rent is: pay nothing

Many direct marketers believe list rental is good for three reasons:

The pros...

1 Having your list mailed regularly keeps it 'clean' by taking out the gone-away names, as well as making it more responsive.
2 Mailing list rental income is easy money, for the overheads are minimal, and the revenue almost entirely profit.
3 The activity nourishes the industry generally by giving everyone another source of sales.

...and cons of list rental

But there are also good reasons for *not* renting out your names. Some companies use their lists so much they are worried that additional use by outsiders would kill the goose that lays the golden eggs. Others are just naturally cautious: they fear they will have their names stolen. Personally, I would take the money and take the precautions.

One way to overcome this problem (particularly with a competitor, who may be worried about his precious customers) is to exchange names – possibly names of lapsed customers. That way, you pay no rental, and everyone feels secure. Another is to mail the list yourself.

Renting out your own names

It is perfectly possible for list rental to make the difference between profit and loss in a modest business. The average rental today in the UK is about £130 per 1,000 names. If you only have a small list of 100,000 names and you rent it out once a month, the pickings are quite toothsome. This being so, only good reasons of corporate policy (or reactionary masochism) can impel one to non-rental.

Seed your list

But you must take precautions. You must seed your list with trap names – the names of people who work for you, or are associated with you, to monitor what goes out. And, of course, you must let those who rent the list know that your list is so protected. Equally, before letting anyone use your list, make sure they show you what they are sending out.

Other sensible precautions include storing a copy of your list elsewhere, in case of fire or theft – indeed, anything you would normally do with something of value. Simply think about the list not just as some *names*, but as a precious business asset and act accordingly. Maybe just by calling it your *database* you will treat it with appropriate respect.

Incidentally, one consequence of renting out your list is that you get to see other people's packages and learn how they are doing.

The most crucial element

Mailing lists, or even databases, may seem at first sight rather dull. But please give the subject great priority. This is possibly because, as I have already admitted, I suffered for many years through knowing far too little about it. More important, these are *people* we are talking about.

Thinking deeply about the people you mail or telephone is vital. For example, if by analysis you can make unprofitable lists profitable, and profitable lists *more* profitable, this affects your business right down the line.

You can, for example, afford to mail a greater number of outside lists, thus enlarging your business base. You can also make more money from your own database. First by segmentation, secondly by communicating more often, and thirdly by delivering more potent messages.

In testing, it is the *people* – the lists – that make the biggest difference. In creative, the same: how well you speak to them will determine your results. In choosing the correct position for your business, once again, your knowledge of people is critical.

The database, or list, is your treasury. What you do with that treasury will determine the future of your enterprise. And how well you manage that treasury will be determined by how well you understand those people.

The list is your treasury

JON EPSTEIN'S 11 DESIDERATA

I am no database expert. So I went to one of the best people I know, Jon Epstein of r-cubed. Jon's refreshingly down-to-earth approach – 'it's all about return on investment' – has worked with clients as varied as Coca-Cola and American Express.

I asked him how he would tell a client what, in terms of data analysis, would most benefit them. I was reassured to see that what he said fitted in very neatly with how I see direct marketing.

- Define the ends exactly – only then talk data.
- Find the 20 per cent of effort that delivers 80 per cent of results.
- Never talk about the average customer.
- Deselect your worst customers.
- Contact your best customers more often.
- Spend more on new customers and new prospects.
- Ask your best enquirers and lapsers to come back.
- Sell when your customer is ready to buy.
- Keep and use your contact history with individuals.
- Use silent controls to prove real incremental impact.
- Ruthlessly keep demanding 'why did they do that?'

I asked him to explain why those 11 points matter, and here is what I learned.

Define the ends exactly – only then talk data

- Quantify 'success' exactly, or you won't know when you achieve it. Most marketers aim to do 'better', but too few define how much better.
- Nail your colours to the mast! Have the guts to tell everyone how you define success.
- Will you be able to see that you have achieved success when and if it occurs?
- Supposing it doesn't, will you be able to learn from failure – and if so, what?

If you say no to any of the above, Jon thinks you should start all over again. Most of the money spent on creating, analysing and exploiting data is lost at this first stage.

Find the 20 per cent of effort that delivers 80 per cent of results

- The Pareto principle to which I've already referred applies here.
- It has strong financial implications which you ignore at your peril as this is not an academic exercise.
- It's not about response but about money.
- Only invest in data if you can see it's likely to produce more money than it costs.
- If you think it makes sense as a loss leader, can you point to and measure where else the profit will be made?
- Watch out for weasel words about strategy or brand building. This must pay off sometime, somewhere.

Jon talks about your investment as 'data-money', and asks: how will you and your data-money make more than it would at the bank?

Never talk about the average customer

- There is no such beast. We are talking about individuals. Don't treat them all the same.
- While drafting this we were working with Jon on a client's problems. He found that 10 per cent of one file of customers provided over 90 per cent of the results. The same principle will apply to you.
- You must vary your investment by individual, not list or segment. In every cell there are better and worse customers.
- Don't be average: it only leads to average results.

Jon, like all good people, is enraged by the second rate. 'Why do so many people still base their targeting on segmentation, the land of the average consumer?' he asks.

Deselect your worst customers

- Direct marketing is about spending your money where it does most good.
- So what's better, £80 sales for £20 cost, or £100 for £50? The answer should be obvious – but it isn't to many marketers.
- Finding the worst is far easier than finding the best.
- It's far easier to predict the many *least likely* than the few *most likely* to respond – and you need far less data.
- You lose very few sales by dropping the worst but you save lots of money.
- You can reinvest that money in talking to the best or testing.
- You *must* find the 20 per cent that delivers the 80 per cent.
- Then you must quickly apply the principle everywhere: data, systems, data preparation, selection, analysis.
- Speed and flexibility make money, not completeness.

Data, targeting, analysis and so on can *never* be perfect! Trying to make them so is very, very expensive. As Voltaire noted, 'the best is the enemy of the good'.

Contact your best customers more often

- First you must define what you mean by 'best'. It is what achieves your objectives.
- Usually that is the greatest return for the least cost – the most possible ROI.
- Nearly always, your most recent, most frequent and highest-spending customers deliver that, and it's not hard to see.
- This is actually the oldest, simplest list-rule: *RFM – Recency, Frequency, Monetary value*.

As Jon puts it, 'It's as old as the hills – it's easy – it works – *use it.*'

Spend more on new customers and new prospects

- When you are new to people, they are more interested: the ROI of first-time contact is always dramatically higher.
- Marketers talk about the 'afterglow' – that rather agreeable feeling when we have just bought something.
- That is when customers are at their most receptive, but they cool quickly.
- As customers, they become bored or dissatisfied. As prospects, they will be ruthlessly courted by others.
- 'New' gives us a clean slate for communications. Some marketers ring fence and protect their new customers – they're mad.

I have pointed this out already: when they're new they are far more hot to trot. Neglect this opportunity and you throw away a fortune.

Ask your best enquirers and lapsers to come back

- 'Once they've dropped off, it's not worth trying.' *False.*
- They may leave or not convert for temporary reasons. We may be still relevant, even loved, but it's not the right time.
- There is usually data to differentiate the best prospects among enquirers and lapsers from the worst. These are the ones to resolicit.
- Remember, if you don't ask, you don't get.

I have talked elsewhere about the extraordinary impact and memorability of a simple 'thank you'. Customers love to be remembered and acknowledged.

Sell when your customer is ready to buy

- People buy when it suits them – not you.
- Who would you target? The customers with the right profile, or the ones ready to buy?
- *When* is more powerful than *who*.
- 80 per cent of non-response is down to the wrong time.
- Work out *when* they buy, don't imagine your messages will change them.
- Look for 'hot data' that could trigger activity.
- An unexpected contact may be a buying signal – say an enquiry about something you haven't offered, an insurance claim, or a change of address.
- Make sure staff are listening!

Jon is particularly keen on this. When the right time is glimpsed, he says ROI can be multiplied.

Keep and use your contact history with individuals

- What's it worth spending on an individual or a household?
- You can't say if you don't know how much you spent in the past – and what it produced.
- One big sin is comparing customers by past sales, without looking at past investment.
- If you know what you spent on each person, and what it produced, how do you use that knowledge?
- You may find that repeat purchasers have had masses spent on them.
- Does it affect future investment? When do you cut off spending?
- Do you use that knowledge by segment, or by individual?
- Do you use mailings, phone, e-mail, friend get a friend, inbound and outbound?
- If so what are the key moments when it pays off? Is data recorded? Is it usable?

Jon has found that smart use of contact history can outperform all other data. But, he laments, some clients still look at buying third-party data first.

Use silent controls to prove real incremental impact

- 'The mailing did well – 20 per cent response!' 'Yes, but how many would have bought *anyway*?'
- The real response cannot be known without a controlled test. No technology or technique can overcome this.
- This is a basic rule of targeting – it's worth many millions of pounds.
- Yet amazingly, few companies measure real results.
- No measurement – no comment.

As Jon points out, good marketing generates incremental sales, not ones you would have got anyway. And for that you must follows the basic rule of testing: compared with what? He elaborates on this in his last point.

Ruthlessly keep demanding 'why did they do that?'

- You've had a good idea – how will you know it works?
- Test it against doing something different, or nothing at all.
- A properly tested result = learning = repeatability = gains.
- This is the beauty of DM – it is easily measurable – but you have to want to learn.
- Untested activity implies a 'we can't improve it' attitude, but there is always a better way to get more ROI.
- *But* poor (or, even worse, no) testing = wrong insight = waste and loss.
- *And* good analysis is driven by good questions, not data or statistics.

I couldn't have put it better myself – actually, not nearly as well. But Jon's points show how universal principles apply in this business.

To give you an idea of what this sort of thing means when it comes to money, I spoke to one of Jon's colleagues, Kate Williams. Take the largest direct marketing category – financial services. Suppose you start with something pretty basic. Say you analyse your customer base, looking at things I've already mentioned like recency, frequency of buying and how much they have spent as a result of other offers. This alone could increase your sales by 25–30 per cent, and your profits by 200–250 per cent, since you make these extra sales with no extra budget. This very simple analysis is not advanced metaphysics – it's been around for at least 50 years. Yet an astounding number of allegedly sophisticated firms don't apply it.

Then suppose you do a test mailing and look at the response and conversion results so as to target better. Again, not magic: just good sense.

This could increase your sales by 70–75 per cent and your profits by 400–450 per cent since, once again, you make these extra sales without spending any more money.

If firms applied themselves more to such analysis than frittering away time, money and executive energy on navel-gazing about their new slogan, mission statement or sexy TV commercial they would post infinitely better profits. But I have to tell you that there is little sign of any such dawning consciousness.

Database: the heart of your business

Points to remember

The right people matter more than better messages.

- Not new thinking – new technology.
- Building a database – collecting every name possible – essential.
- Your names best; names most like yours next best.
- Duplication not just needed but indicative.
- Recency, frequency, monetary value usually matter most.
- Names worth money: ensure they are always collected.
- Keep a keen eye on where things can go wrong.
- MGM (viral) highly effective.
- Not interested? Pass it on.
- Compiling lists often pays.
- Brokers – don't pay commission twice.
- Should you rent? A matter of policy.
- Exchanging names often pays.
- Eleven practical suggestions from an expert.

10

Where Ideas Come From and How to Express Them Persuasively

> *'Genius is one percent inspiration and ninety-nine percent perspiration.'*
> Thomas Edison

> *'Everything that is written merely to please the author is worthless.'*
> Blaise Pascal

THE BIRTH OF AN IDEA

You only have to look at your children's drawings or listen to the odd little phrases they coin to know that humanity is born with a creative urge. Yet sadly, most people lose this urge as they grow older.

Many 'primitive' societies seem far wiser than us in the way they nurture this quality. For example, I have in my home some masks and statues from New Guinea, tapa cloths from Samoa and aboriginal paintings. Artists like Picasso learned much from this kind of art, and the artistic impulse – seen in acts like body painting and tattooing – seems more widespread in their communities.

But we 'civilised' folk in pursuit of such worthy ends as direct marketing allow this inherent ability to atrophy. We have come to think only a special, gifted few can be 'creative': you have to be a specialist. Yet, who has not used the phrase: 'I've just had an idea'? The question is: was it a good idea or a bad one?

What is a good idea?

Those who don't do it for a living tend to imagine having good ideas is a matter of flair; of letting the mind wander where it will. This is a myth. Your imagination flourishes best when guided. You are more likely to have good ideas if you go about it in the right way. I am not saying everyone can be a great writer or painter. But when someone asked Johann Sebastian Bach the secret of his genius, he responded: 'Anyone can be a genius if they work as hard as I do.' But work hard in what way?

I have already mentioned James Webb Young, the American copy-writer. He became a successful mail order operator after he retired from J Walter Thompson, so he would seem better qualified than most to advise you on how to get ideas in this business.

How do great artists, writers and musicians find and develop their ideas, he wondered. He did a lot of research and found out their methods were often very similar. From them came a book, *A Technique for Getting Ideas*. Much of what he learned is encapsulated in the following three steps.

1 Master your subject

You must be thoroughly familiar with the subject. David Ogilvy once said that before he set about writing any advertisement he looked at all the advertising that had been done for the category of product for the previous 20 years. You may not have the time or resource to go to such lengths, but the point he was making is important.

Steep yourself in knowledge

Suppose you have to write about something pleasant like a tourist desti-nation. First, steep yourself in knowledge about it. From this knowledge will come your raw material. Learn all you can about the people, the places, the amenities, the local customs, the beauty spots. Compare it with alternative desti-nations. See what its strengths arc. Takc note of its shortcomings, too.

It is from the *truth* that you will create good work. Your imagination can never dream up anything to beat the truth. This process of learning is vital. It will determine your positioning.

Think about your prospects. Read any market research there is available. Speculate about those wishing to visit the country. What kind of people are they? Why would they wish to go there? Make lots of notes. What would *you* like about going there? What would disappoint you? Talk to your colleagues and ask their views. Jot down any ideas you may have (no matter how odd).

I chose this example – a tourist destination – because I spent years working on such accounts. Two examples show how taking the facts and posi-tioning the destination carefully on that basis can prove very successful.

About 40 years ago, when the Greek National Tourist Office set about selling Greece, four benefits stood out:

Note your benefits

- There were miles and miles of unspoilt beaches.
- The weather was exceptionally pleasant.
- The people were unusually hospitable.
- There were outstanding historical sites.

Comparing these facts with other destinations and with what tourists liked, it emerged, for instance, that prospects were not interested in learning about antiquities – though they appreciated beauty. So the advertisements showed famous sites, but did not talk much about them.

This, of course, was an English advertising campaign. I believe that had we been selling to the French or Germans, research would have revealed different inclinations.

However, to return to my story: we learned that our prospects loved sunshine and beaches. What is more, at that time French hoteliers were building a reputation for rapacity; the Italians were becoming known for a very imaginative approach to preparing their bills; and Spain was full of half-built hotels, with – in those that *had* been built – waiters who often got jobs in exchange for helping to build the hotels.

Accordingly, a campaign was devised based upon the positioning (and the slogan): 'Greece greets you warmly'. Every ad also ran the line: 'Summer in Greece lasts from April to October'. And every ad mentioned the hundreds of miles of unspoilt beaches in Greece.

The campaign rightly won many awards. More importantly, it produced an astonishing number of enquiries and sales. Somebody at head office must have got bored, because they stopped running it after a few years. They were foolish. I do not know who first thought it up, but it was a brilliant solution to the problem. In the years since, Greece has become one of the most popular of all European tourist destinations, but the advertising has never been as good.

I also worked for some time on the British Travel Association account. The only thing I learned from that was that if you put a very large FREE next to a picture of the brochure, you get a lot of replies. Mind you, this is well worth knowing.

Another tourist destination which has been promoted brilliantly is Singapore. Singapore is very small, unbearably humid, and there are no real beaches. On the face of it, the only good reason to go there is for shopping or business. However, if you are travelling between Australasia and Europe, Singapore is as good a place to stop off as any.

The city is inhabited by four different races: the Chinese, the Malays, the Sri Lankans and the Indians. Each has retained its own culture. So it has been sold as a place where, in a few square miles, you can experience all those four cultures, whilst having a break from your trip across the world.

The cleverness of it is that the advertising does not try to sell a two-week holiday in Singapore. It points out that you can see it all in a few days. It is based on the truth, and is thus wildly successful.

Campaigns like this can only be created because somebody has started by mastering the facts, which leads us to the second step in getting good ideas.

What I learned about tourism

2 The inner game

I once read that your brain is a computer with so many connections that by comparison even the mightiest man-built computer is the size of a pea. With the rapid development in the capabilities of computers in recent years, this may no longer be true, but no computer can yet do what a brain can do. Your brain is perfectly able to do all the analysis and synthesis you need to get ideas – if you have faith in it.

Let your subconscious take control

You must have heard people say: 'I have no idea where that idea came from.' Well, a lot of what we achieve comes from the subconscious. Indeed, in a totally different field, many top sporting coaches have come to believe that if you just let your brain and body run on 'auto-pilot' and stop concentrating consciously, you will do better. One of my former colleagues who is a pinball fanatic told me this works for him.

It seems that in getting ideas the same principles apply. At a certain point you must let your subconscious take over.

Once you have stored up all the facts about your problem in your brain, and talked to other people about it, and written down any ideas that occur to you – even ones that seem crazy or irrelevant – just relax. Move on to another job. Don't struggle, just forget that particular problem. But set a mental 'alarm clock'. Tell yourself you need to look again at the problem on Tuesday morning. Then let your subconscious worry about it. On Tuesday morning, sit down and see what ideas come to mind. Start writing! You could be pleasantly surprised.

This method does not guarantee success. No method can. But many people find it works. The secret seems to be relaxation. I find that going for long walks seems to help. (So did Beethoven, which makes me feel good.) Mozart played billiards. Some like lying in the bath, or having a drink. Apparently the philosopher Descartes conceived his maxim, 'I think, therefore I am', whilst sitting in an oven in Poland. I suggest you do whatever you find most relaxing to help your brain get to work.

3 Use sounding boards

A chief benefit of working with others is that you can talk to them about your ideas. When you have an idea or some alternatives, discuss them with your colleagues, your secretary or – always a good idea – potential customers. They always see the benefits or drawbacks more clearly than you.

Many people hate doing this. We identify strongly with our ideas. They are our creatures. It is hard to expose them to the bitter wind of criticism. However, you are not creating for yourself, but for others.

A word of warning, though. Make sure when asking for others' reactions that you don't ask leading questions. I used to provide a lot of innocent amusement to my colleagues by the way I phrased my requests for comment. I'm so delighted with getting *any* idea that I tended to say something like: 'I've just had this fantastic idea. What do you think?'

Only close friends (or unfeeling wretches like my associates) are willing to tell me the truth – that my brilliant idea has about as much chance as a snowball in hell ... that nobody would understand it ... or, more than once, that I hadn't even made clear what the product was.

So phrase your questions carefully. Don't incorporate the desired response in the question. 'Can you understand this?' Or: 'Would you buy this product?' Or: 'Is this credible?' Or: 'Do you think this is worth the money I'm asking?' Particularly valuable is: 'Have I missed anything out?'

Have I missed anything out?

Of course, some kinds of people seem to get better ideas than others. They are better prepared. If you have what is known as a 'well furnished mind' you are likely to do better. Read a lot (anything and everything). Watch TV. Go to the cinema. Visit art galleries, shows, exhibitions. Travel. Don't just think about marketing, or you will end up very dull indeed.

Above all, be *curious*. 'Questioning is not the mode of conversation amongst gentlemen,' said Dr Johnson. But it is amongst good copywriters.

I am also inspired by example. Watching any supreme performer in any field fills me with greater keenness for my own endeavours. It doesn't matter what they are good at, I find it makes me want to go out and do better myself. Anyone who excels, from those doing simple things to those with great gifts – from street traders to virtuoso cellists: they all inspire me if they are really good.

The secret is *awareness*. Don't be dull. Be alive!

Having ideas is only part of the process of persuading people to want to do what you want. You have to marshal your ideas and put them on paper.

Marshal your ideas

Writing is not an airy-fairy pursuit. It is just hard graft. Forty years ago I wrote a novel. When people asked me what it was like, I remember answering that it was very hard on the fingers (I am a two-fingered typist, and didn't have an electric typewriter). It is also hard on the nerves. Especially when you are confronted with that first blank sheet of paper.

I recall working in one agency where one writer just couldn't come up with ideas. Day by day he came in later and left earlier. Finally he disappeared. Some years later I met him in Regent's Park. He was working as a telephone operator. His case is not unusual. People talk, for instance, of 'writer's block'. Even great authors fear it. F Scott Fitzgerald was terrified by the thought that he had within him a well of inspiration that would one day dry up.

Nearly every good creative person I know has this awful feeling when first facing a problem that *this* time they won't be able to cope. I certainly do. Times without number I have smiled confidently at a client, promised I could handle the task – and gone away full of despair, wondering if I was up to it.

If you are not a writer or an art director, you may imagine that this is confined to 'uncreative' people like you. Well, now you know it isn't.

GETTING ORGANISED

I have given you a sequence based on how other people get ideas. But you may rightly ask: how *do* you marshal your ideas? How do you start?

The great appeal of working creatively is that it is not like working in a factory, producing so many car panels a day, or so many mouldings. But the drawback is that what you do is hard to measure or evaluate. Nobody can look at the number of words you have produced and say: 'Ah, that's 20 per cent above target, have a bonus.' And you can't just switch a machine on and get on with it each morning. You have to start your *own* little machine, and discipline yourself. It's hard.

Be disciplined

To create good selling messages, you *need* discipline. Anthony Trollope used to get up every morning and write for three and a half hours before going to work in the Post Office. Sir Walter Scott was driven by the need to pay off massive debts. Dickens succeeded by writing to the demanding formula of a monthly serial. You shouldn't feel too proud to work in a disciplined way.

Throughout history, great creators have been confined and thus forced to exercise ingenuity, either by convention or by self-imposed guidelines. In mediaeval times writers, musicians and artists were obliged to work on religious themes. Otherwise, they could not eat, for the church was the major source of patronage. The great composers of the classical period wrote within rigid structures: the symphonic form is quite a straitjacket. Chinese and Japanese poetry for thousands of years was produced to very precise rules.

I am not suggesting that producing advertisements and mailings is great art. But I can tell you that, having written just about every kind of communication, commercial or otherwise, over the past 30 years, they *all* demand some kind of discipline. They all benefit from a proper structure.

Form a proper structure

There are a number of formulae you can follow if you want to ensure that your work follows a logical sequence. However, the most famous is also the best in my view. It is certainly one that has stood the test of time. Here is how a book called *The Inner Side of Advertising*, written in 1920 by a former advertisement manager of the *Daily Mail* called Cyril Freer, put it:

Steps to create a good message

Here are the component parts of a good sales letter:

The *opening*, which should attract the reader's attention and induce him to read.

The *description and explanation* should hold his interest by causing him to picture the proposition in his mind.

The *argument* should create the desire for the article offered for sale.

Persuasion should bring the reader around to your way of thinking by seeing how the article is adapted to his needs. This is followed by:

Inducement, which gives him an extra reason for buying, and in conclusion you have –

The *climax*, which makes it easy for the reader to order, and assures that action by causing him to act at once.

This formula is variously known as AIDA or AIDCA. If you want to remember it, recall the name of the Verdi opera. AIDCA stands for Attention, Interest, Desire, Conviction, Action.

AIDCA

Clearly in order to deliver your message, you must first attract *attention*. Having done so, you must *interest* people in what you have to say. But this is useless if they do not *desire* what you are offering. And even if they desire it, they must be *convinced* what you say is true. You will also notice that in Mr Freer's recipe there is the inducement. This can be the incentive or the penalty, ie 'We'll give you something if you reply now; and if you don't reply within a certain time, the offer will lapse'. As we saw in the *Reader's Digest* split run example shown elsewhere, this approach, even though buried in a very large advertisement, can make a big difference.

All this is wasted if you do not then get them to *act*. The inducement or incentive has two purposes. First to get people to pay attention; second, to get them to act. More on that later.

CONTEXT IS EVERYTHING

'Circumstances alter cases' is a legal maxim you should bear in mind. That which is relevant today can be supremely irrelevant a year from now, or even a week from now. Poor creative people fail to adapt to circumstance.

The most obvious example of considering the circumstance is that of adapting the *tone* to match the advertiser and the audience.

Adapt tone to fit the circumstances

Equally obvious are cases where the whole communication is based upon the circumstance: eg a mailing on someone's birthday, a new year, or the anniversary of their first doing business with you.

When considering how somebody will react to your message, simply think about what makes sense. Thus, I once received a letter from my optician. It had a very good opening: 'It hardly seems a year since I saw you last!' They wanted me to come in and have my eyes tested again.

This excellent opening, however, was far less effective because:

1 I didn't actually *know* anybody at that optician's – yet they were writing to me as though I did.
2 The thing wasn't properly signed by anyone – there was just a meaningless squiggle at the bottom. A good idea ruined by lack of attention to details.

Considering the situation carefully can make for breakthroughs – either because you come up with a new incentive or a new way of presenting the product to a particular audience.

Consider the situation carefully

A few years ago American Express introduced the Gold Card. It was a radical concept; saying to cardmembers that there was now a Gold Card for those who were rather more important than Green cardmembers was sufficient to get sales. In the UK the appeal of the Gold Card was bolstered by giving cardmembers access to a line of credit. This worked extremely well – but not everyone responded, obviously.

Here is the opening to a successful follow-up letter which I wrote to offer the card.

> You may recall my writing to you some while ago inviting you to apply for The Gold Card – which gives you access to benefits greater than those available to Personal Cardmembers.
>
> You will, I believe, find these well worthwhile: particularly the £10,000 unsecured overdraft facility, which many Cardmembers certainly find invaluable. This overdraft, which is available through American Express Bank Ltd, can be yours *in addition* to your present banking arrangements.

Of course, it didn't take long for the banks to come up with their own gold cards. What could we do then?

The answer was to make a more competitive statement. Here is the opening to the letter I wrote with that in mind:

A more competitive statement

> You may recall that I invited you a while ago to apply for Gold Card membership.
>
> As you are aware, there are now other 'gold cards' – indeed you may possibly have been offered one; so you may well ask: 'Why the *American Express* Gold Card?' It's a good question.
>
> The Gold Card is designed to give certain Cardmembers a complete *range* of privileges; exclusive privileges which will make your life easier and more pleasant. Indeed, we have recently introduced several *new* benefits, which is why I am writing to you now.

Both these mailings were successful but, as you can see, they depended on what was happening at the time.

What do you know about the people?

Let's look at using what you know about your customer to communicate more accurately. I once had to write copy for a firm, Ace Gifts & Cards, which recruits agents who sell to other people – usually friends and neighbours.

The only thing clear to me was that the prospects wanted to make extra money – or save money for themselves and their family. And the best prospects were likely to be sociable.

The best prospects

The list mailed was one of people who had recently moved home. The audience was not very sophisticated, so we made the personalisation very overt – each personalised section was marked in yellow. We found this simple device lifted response.

Here's the opening of the copy:

How to make money as you shop –
and make new friends around Chalk Lane.

Dear Ms Berger,

Hello! How are you enjoying life at No. 18? Let me tell you about a new idea that could make (or save) you money as you shop … help relatives and your family with their gift problems … and even make friends amongst your new neighbours.

You may say that such personalised 'tricks' are too obvious to work. But as I was drafting this I saw a case – in Australia, in fact – where heavy personalisation raised response from under 5 per cent to over 22.5 per cent. It was linked to a personalised website.

My colleague Malcom Auld developed a campaign for a print company to launch their new digital colour print service to the marketing team at Qantas – like most airline marketers they are inundated with gimmicks and offers to advertise in every media around town and are not easily impressed.

The invitation was a tent car. The front was printed black and white with a personalised message '<name> you already know we're big in black and white'. The inside message was a colour version of the same black and white image but with the recipient's name tattooed on the 'bloke's arm' - 'now we're also big in colour personalisation'.

The recipient was invited to link to their own personal URL (known as PURL) and enter some data as part of their RSVP process. All people attending were to be collected by bus from their office and driven to the launch event.

On the site they indicated their favourite colour, the food and drink they'd like to have on the short bus trip, the type of wine (red or white) they'd like to take home and the colour of the iPod they'd like to win. So if a respondent picked green as their favourite colour and an apple and juice to

Green spread

Front of invitation

<Ian>, we're expanding our dependable black & white printing
capabilities to include a revolutionary new colour service.

PMG Solutions and the i2media team would like to invite you to join us for refreshments,
as we introduce the new digital colour printing service that will enable you to personalise your corporate communications
in exciting new ways. We feel it will provide you with a more direct medium to target key customers;
literally transforming your direct marketing and corporate communications.

Two noted industry speakers will talk about marketing trends and the potential of this new printing technology:
MD of Fuji Xerox Australia, Phil Chambers and DM specialist Malcolm Auld.

Phil Chambers will show how PMG Solutions
can help you maximise the benefits of this
groundbreaking new system.

Best-selling author Malcolm Auld will
suggest creative ways to dramatically
increase your response rates.

The comfortable minibus trip will only last a few minutes, and we estimate the event itself will take about an hour.
Afterwards, we'll arrange the minibus to pick you up and return you to the Qantas Centre at Mascot.

RSVP: <www.pmgsolutions.com.au/launch/ian.crute>

P.S. You could win an iPod mini on the day. **Visit your personal website now to tell us your favourite colour.**

Location: i2media, Rosebery
Date: Thursday 8 September
Time: 4pm - 6pm
RSVP by: Thursday 1 September

Inside invite

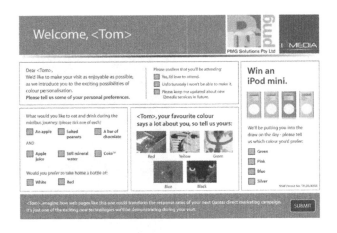

PURL

Name tag

Personal travel label

Black spread

have on the bus, their travel bag label was printed in green with an image of an apple and a juice bottle. If they picked black, chocolate and coca cola then their label was printed in black with those images. Each travel pack label was created from the data entered on the PURL.

Those who attended also received an A4 book explaining the benefits of the new variable colour print service. But the front cover and first spread were personalised and printed in the colour the recipient nominated on their

Green lover

Black lover

PURL. Each book was manufactured on the printer according to the PURL data provided. All delegates had name tages written in the tattoo font used in the invitation.

One of the things I discovered was that most sales were made not from a desire to make money, but from a desire to save the agent's commission. Another was that good agents were very sociable. They liked meeting new people.

Calculating the message

Let me give you another instance. I was asked by the Save the Children Fund if we could persuade people to leave them legacies. This struck me as difficult. The same problem had been attacked quite simply by other charities offering a free booklet in advertisements on how to make your will. This seemed to me a good idea, but to succeed it depended upon people actively responding to an advertisement dealing with a very delicate subject – death. I found the idea of writing a mailing with the same objective daunting.

I spent a lot of time considering my target audience – elderly people – and their circumstances. I thought about elderly people I know. After reflection I realised that elderly people think about death quite a lot. I also considered that elderly people are slightly more religious than the mass of the population.

I determined to try fundamentally the same approach, but with two different openings. I wrote two envelope messages. One read: 'Do you believe in life after death?' The other read: 'For everyone over 55. Inside: an important question that cannot wait ... and some *free* advice.'

Both the mailings attempted to empathise with the prospects. Let me give you the opening of one of them:

> A free 12-page booklet, with our compliments, which may prove *of priceless value* to those you love.
>
> Dear Reader,

Do you believe in life after death?
This is one of the questions which people talk about less nowadays than when we were young. Yet if you – like me – are over 55, I would be surprised if you are not more concerned than you used to be about what will happen when you pass away.

You will notice that, in accordance with my own rules, I open with the offer – although I do not make it clear what that offer is.

Both approaches proved successful, one more than the other: I wonder if you can guess which? The answer is: Life after Death did about 25 per cent better than the other message. Nevertheless, the client felt that that message was too insensitive for our target audience, and we pursued the less successful one. (Incidentally, the mailing also raised a record amount of money for Save the Children, apart from a lot of requests for booklets.)

Again, with this subject as with others, we derive the same moral: considering the people you are about to address, what they want, and what situation they are in is invariably the key to success – rather than the key most people try, an ingenious or clever approach.

> **Consider who you want to address**

NATIONALITIES AND SOCIAL GROUPS

Direct marketing works in every country I have worked in – 41 so far – to most social groups, in both business and leisure contexts. **'People are more united by their similarities than divided by their differences'**.

> **United by their similarities**

Time after time I listen to self-important businesspeople who tell me that of course businesspeople are far too busy to read those long, boring letters, or play with those little stamps on mailings. Or particular nationalities claim that direct marketing won't work with their compatriots.

Happily, I have had the opportunity to see my copy run in many countries, and appeal to many groups of people over the years since I first got into international direct marketing with the Bullworker. People everywhere respond to the same motivations. For the most part they respond to the same copy.

My last job at the Franklin Mint was to write a mailing package for a product (to do with baseball, incidentally) to be sold in Japan. Prior to that I wrote for Italy, Belgium, France, Australia, Holland and, of course, the UK. The same appeals worked everywhere.

> **The same appeals work everywhere**

There are clearly products and services likely only to work in particular countries, because of national peculiarities. For instance, one of the biggest sellers in Japan for some time now has been a cooker which will prepare your rice for you while you are out at work. In Britain and the United States, the general population do not eat rice every day. Such a product would not be appropriate. In China or India it would.

Other products clearly have appeal no matter what the country. Coca-Cola is perhaps the most famous example. Credit and charge cards seem to have a pretty universal appeal, too.

> **Does the product have universal appeal?**

The moral is to allow for national differences, but profit from similarities. Often you don't have to reinvent the wheel by creating entirely new copy for a market you are about to enter. A lot of people will tell you otherwise. Almost all nationalities hate to admit they are in fact similar to other races. My advice is, if it seems to make sense, *test* the creative work that succeeded for you in another country, even though you may simultaneously wish to try a different approach for the country you are moving into. And don't make *any* changes unless they are clearly necessary because of national peculiarities. *Reader's Digest* have found that where an approach transferred from one country to another fails, it is often because some element was needlessly altered.

Another canard is that businesspeople become different animals when they get in their cars to go to the office. Of course they don't. They are human beings first, and businesspeople second. If you write to them about some way of doubling their profits, they don't say: 'I'm too busy to read this ten-page letter.' They say: 'Do we need extra profit. I wonder if they've got something here.' After that, it depends on how cleverly you tell your story.

This point about businesspeople is not something I have just dreamed up. Both research and experience indicate clearly that businesspeople respond extremely well to gimmicks; particularly things they can play with – and they are *always* happy to read news they think is relevant.

All you have to do when addressing people is to bear in mind who they are. Don't be put off by their desire to imagine they are either superior to, or different from, others. Their motives are what matter. If you have the right message, it will overcome even the most crass of approaches. On countless occasions, even the most aggressive, insensitive US mail order blockbuster has succeeded because it offered what people wanted. And if people want something, they want to believe they can have it.

Motives matter

Once again, it comes down to commonsense. If the product makes sense, and the motivation is there, you can usually find a way of presenting that product to the appropriate audience and selling it.

Of course, sometimes it isn't always clear whether there is a market for the product you have in mind. Xerox, for instance, had great expectations years ago of a copier that could reproduce in colour. It seemed a brilliant idea. It *was* a brilliant idea. Unfortunately, as one of their top executives observed wryly afterwards: 'You have to have something to copy from.' And there simply wasn't a great deal of full colour material people wanted to copy. So the product was not the success they thought it would be. They are still busy barking up that particular tree.

However good the idea, whatever the nationality, whatever the social group, you'll find that the principles you apply always hold true. Curiously enough, the same thing applies when considering another question: how do you approach working in different forms or media; how do you translate ideas from one to another?

WebCast
live internet broadcasting

13th November 1996

Dear Mr. Bird,

Now, at last, the Internet is delivering what it promised...

"Through the remarkable technology of live Webcasting, **half a million people** around the world took part in Apple's **Live** Worldwide Developer's Conference last May - though **only 2,000 were actually there** in San José."

All business involves risk, but I think you'll agree that some things can keep you awake at nights a whole lot more than others.

For instance, launching a new product or service, giving a live demonstration or holding an important conference.

Your company's future - and sometimes yours - may depend on it. You must convince many audiences it will be a winner. Your customers. Retailers and distributors. Suppliers. Financial institutions. Journalists. Opinion formers. Your salesforce. The rest of your staff. Maybe even your colleagues. Not to mention your competitors!

And you must convince them fast. Because in those first few critical days and weeks, they will form views - good or bad - which you won't shift easily.

I'm sure you can think of other examples of events that must succeed - or else. Your annual conference. A major exhibition you're showing at. A shareholder's meeting. At all of them, you have to get as many people as possible together to explain, persuade and enthuse. The more you can get on your side simultaneously, the better you'll do.

This letter is about a form of technology which has been proven not only to increase but **transform** your likelihood of success.

WebCasting enables you to **multiply** the audience for a range of messages and events which are utterly time critical to your business.

And all for a **fraction** of the cost of previous technology, like satellite transmission.

128 Cleveland Street . London . W1P 5BR . Tel: 0171 388 4100 . Fax: 0171 388 3300 . e-mail: mail @ webcst.co.uk
WebCast Limited . Registered No: 3220067

Here's a simple example. A couple of years ago an interactive learning system connected by satellite helped Mercedes Benz familiarise 4,000 employees in Germany with its new model in just 20 days. The cost was pretty huge, as you can imagine. **We could well have cut that cost by 75%.**

Essentially, WebCasting is live broadcasting over the Internet. In addition to "real" attendees, it gives you a much larger number of "virtual" delegates. In effect you can have the whole world attending your next important event. Or you can talk to select groups that matter to you.

They experience what those on site do - as it happens. **Sound, pictures, movement: everything.** But in addition, your WebCast can do some things that aren't even possible at an ordinary conference or exhibition. You'll appreciate some of those possibilities.

- Your WebCast participants can **direct questions to experts** at a conference. So you know what concerns them; what they understand and don't; what turns them on; what they have doubts about. And they enjoy the involvement.

- You can **track** which parts of your event attract most interest, and how individual delegates make their way round the WebCast. (Haven't you often wondered whether attendees were really as keen as they said - or were just being polite?)

- You learn as much, and maybe more about delegates as if you met them in person. You can **link demographic profiles with "interest paths'**, to see what attracts particular types, or even individual delegates. Just like following them around.

- **How about instant market research?** They can **vote** on particular ideas or issues -- so you know how they feel about your concepts or products. You learn what your audience thinks, as they think it. You don't have to undergo that familiar nail-biting exercise after most events: "how did we do?"

- You can learn an extraordinary amount about **who** "attends" your event. You can call up demographic data at any time on how many people have logged on, and their Internet addresses.

- "Virtual" delegates can **talk to each other** over the Web during the event - just as if they were there. Very important because as you know delegates love to exchange ideas and gossip with each other.

- And delegates themselves can get further information or **expert advice** on any product or service of yours that interests them.

I don't want to get too technical because buzzwords confuse more than they illuminate. But frankly, this **is** a breakthrough. You don't have to know the jargon to appreciate the rewards.

Now you can get thousands, tens of thousands, or even like Apple, hundreds of thousands of extra participants at your next event. Moreover, compared to previous technologies the costs are very modest. And many major firms are exploiting this approach to communication.

A recent business school advertisement noted that this type of technology helped **Andersen Consulting** reduce staff training time by 50% whilst saving $2 million on payroll and $8.5 million on delivery a year. Rupert Murdoch's **Fox TV** in the US uses the Internet to learn what viewers want - it even led to the name of a hot new TV programme, "Models, Inc."

Today approximately 30 million people have direct access to the World Wide Web. And they are special people. In the UK there are over 2.7 million, with average salaries of over £35,000 a year and over 50% educated to degree level. Many companies now use the Internet as an indispensable business tool.

A letter - even a fairly detailed one like this simply cannot reveal all the possibilities WebCasting offers, **whether communicating within or outside your business.** I'd like the chance to show you. If you have an event large or small that matters to you coming up in the next 12 months, we should talk.

A demonstration only takes an hour. You'll find it intriguing - and fun. There's no cost or obligation. But that hour could make a remarkable difference to the results of your next event - and the future of your business.

I have only written to a small number of companies, including yours, who I thought would have the vision to appreciate this. I don't expect you to say right now "let's do it." But I am suggesting this is something you can't ignore. You really should be getting in on it before the competition.

You're busy, I'm sure. But I hope not too busy to look at something with such huge possibilities for your business. I think you'll be pretty staggered by the potential. Why not return the enclosed reply-paid card today? Better still, why not call me now? I look forward to hearing from you.

Yours sincerely,

Moira Thomson
Business Development Director

P.S.   If what you have read has whetted your appetite, I should tell you the lead time for planning a WebCast is six weeks. Don't hesitate to let me know if you are not interested, in the space provided on the card. I don't want to waste your time in future.

MEDIA VARY; PRINCIPLES DON'T

Most of the principles which govern success in creative work tend to apply to *all* media.

By that I mean they apply to advertisements, door-to-door leaflets, direct mail letters, complete mailing packs, inserts, television and radio commercials, posters, websites, e-mails – everything.

Start with what works

This is hard to realise when you start as a writer or art director. When asked to prepare a direct mail pack for a product which has already been sold successfully through advertisements, the novice will commonly scratch his or her head and wonder how to set about it. The answer, of course, is to *start with what has worked already* and see whether you can adapt it to the new medium. Some approaches do not always translate easily into another medium, but with a little ingenuity they often will.

If you start with the simplest format – an advertisement – and look at the elements, you can then build up from there to other more complex formats.

The elements of an advertisement (also true of a single-sided leaflet) are usually a headline and a picture which together attract attention; subsidiary headings and pictures supported by copy and captions do most of the selling job; and then the coupon or, if it's a very small advertisement, the request to write in or ring up gets action. This is also true of any page on a website.

Building a good opening sequence in a simple mailing pack – envelope message, opening to letter, opening to brochure and heading to order form – is not that unlike starting an advertisement. The first difference is that the envelope message need not necessarily reveal the full benefit or offer: it could be a tease, designed simply to get you inside the envelope. The second difference is that once inside the mailing pack the reader can choose to turn anywhere – the letter or the brochure or the order form. (Some research suggests they turn first to the order form to find out what the commitment is and what the price is.) With websites too, each page must be an 'ad' in itself since people can land on any page.

Nevertheless, in all media, you must first get the prospect to start reading, and to start reading in the right frame of mind. Or to start paying attention to the broadcast message – once again, in the right frame of mind.

Let's return to the AIDCA formula. The sequence is not rigid. Sometimes, the urge to action can come at the very beginning of the message. There are often other good reasons why it should. It may of itself compel a degree of attention. Sometimes the interest, the conviction and the desire are inter-mingled. But *whatever* you do you certainly have to attract attention somehow.

What gets attention

The only figures I have seen suggested only 20 per cent of the readers of a newspaper even notice the headline of the average one-eighth page advertisement – and a far smaller proportion carry on and read it.

In the case of a direct mail shot, the most recent research I have seen – from the Royal Mail – contrary to the suggestion that people don't read direct mail – suggested only 15 per cent of mail from financial services firms is never opened, and the industry average is 22 per cent. According to the Direct Mail Information Service, direct mail volumes were down by 5.3 per cent in 2005 to 5.1 billion items, little more than one item per person per week. The reduction is down to better targeting and a lot of clients turning to e-mail.

Again, when it comes to online selling people can land on any page, so each page must be an 'ad' in itself.

Virtually every telephone call is listened to, but this is the nature of the medium. And most catalogues are obviously opened, because they are either requested or, at the very least, seen as a pleasant read.

The situation is different with a television commercial: most viewers will probably notice your commercial and sit through it. The problem is, will it motivate them to *do* anything? In fact TV and radio have their own special requirements which I shall touch upon, but for much of this chapter we are talking about your major direct marketing media, and especially how to get people to *start* reading your ads, mailings, e-mails, web pages and inserts. And *keep* reading them.

Happily, we do not have to guess what most often attracts attention, because the famous copywriter and research pioneer John Caples spent many decades testing to find out.

Headlines that gain attention

In advertisements, the attention-getter is almost always the headline/picture combination. It is vitally important. Yet over eight out of ten advertisements are never read beyond the headline. So most headlines are not good enough to make people want to read on. Ergo, not enough work was put into them.

Headlines and pictures are critical

Most people think (especially consumers, when asked their views on ads) that unusual, shocking or funny headlines work best. This is not so. The best attention-getters are headlines promising *benefits* to the consumer. (If people want to be entertained they will watch TV or go to the movies, or read a book. If *you* want to entertain people, get a job in the entertainment business, and get out of direct marketing.)

The second best headlines give *news*. People like to know new things. The third best headlines are *curiosity* headlines.

Note that I say 'headlines'. Some may say a picture is worth a thousand words. Not so in our business. A picture should complement the words or lead you into them – certainly never conflict with them. But it is almost impossible for a picture *alone* to express a buying proposition, or benefit. You need words. On the other hand, words *can* very often explain your proposition, unillustrated.

Words are more essential than pictures

Some of the very best headlines combine the elements of news, benefit and curiosity. Thus, several fortunes were made in the 1950s and 60s from a mailing and ad for a special kind of spark plug. The headline was: 'Now, run your car without spark plugs'.

It was a startling way of implying a benefit. I tried to write a better headline for some months, featuring the big fuel savings that the product could deliver, but my headlines never beat that unusual opening, which in any case was followed by the main benefit in a bold subhead.

Don't rely upon curious headlines

We all like to be clever or original. All too often one comes out with a striking phrase and says: 'How can anyone ignore this?' I have lost count of the number of times *I* have said that. For example, some time back one of my partners wrote an ad for Dr Barnardo's with the memorable headline: 'The frightening truth about Barnardo's new adoption shop'.

I thought this brilliant. So did the writer. The frightening truth was, of course, that without enough money, the establishment would have to close down. The public was unmoved, and sent hardly any money in. Our faith in their curiosity was not justified.

When curiosity works

Clever curiosity lines rarely work in ads. But they often do well as envelope messages. Sometimes, a curiosity line can be very powerful.

The 'Damn' envelope I have illustrated is such an example. (Though it also says 'I want to stop cussin' and start crowing' – a pleasing, if vague benefit.)

In the broadcast media, which are entertainment more than news-orientated, you will often find relevant and amusing curiosity is very good in attracting attention. Thus, in the 1950s, for a commercial selling hair-restorer, the opening line was: 'Did you ever see a bald sheep?'

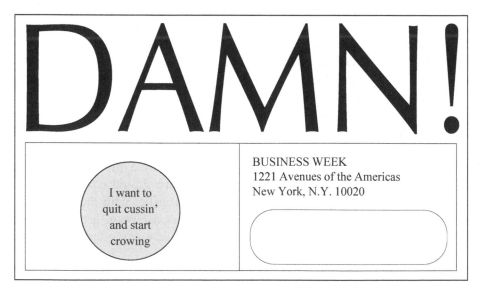

Figure 10.1 This is from the team of Bill Jayme and Heikke Ratalahti. They specialised in magazine subscriptions, and probably did it better than anyone else.

The problem with using curiosity appeals is the same as the problem with humour. What some people find funny, others don't. The great Claude Hopkins (more about him later) used to say flatly: 'No man buys from a clown.'

In fact humour can work if it does not overshadow the message. The idea of a bald sheep is not only curious: it is funny.

Humour can work

If you think you have a clever opening, it's a good idea to put in a benefit by way of an insurance policy. For example, Courtney Ferguson, formerly a colleague of mine, has a bizarre sense of humour which results in some pretty striking lines. Being a professional restrains her wilder excesses.

Walking past her desk one day I saw two lines she had written to go on the envelope in a mailing to sell dried minced beef to caterers. One said: 'You can't send cottage pie by post'. The other said: 'How to get 2lbs of minced beef, free'. She had rejected the first as too far out. We discussed it, and ran them both, the first very large, the second quite small beneath it. The results were very gratifying. There was a clear benefit. And caterers were naturally interested in cottage pie anyhow, which is a rather dull but very popular British dish composed of mashed potato, minced beef, onion and stock.

You can't lay down hard-and-fast rules about which headlines will work and which won't – only for which are *likely* to. You could probably write a book on the subject. But since nobody has done so, the next best thing is to get a copy of a marvellous opus by Vic Schwab called *How to Write a Good Advertisement*, which contains a list of 100 effective headlines. For 40 years I've kept a copy in my desk. Every time I'm really desperate, I look at this list and see if it doesn't start me thinking. It usually does.

Which headlines will work

When I first came into this business, people used to talk about 'stoppers' – headlines that would 'stop' the reader. But it's no use stopping them if you don't immediately start them, too.

A charity ran the headline during the Biafran war, 'Fresh food is flying into Biafra daily'. It showed a giant picture of a locust. It garnered hatfuls of awards, and made the writer's reputation. What a stopper. But it produced hardly any money, I was told by a member of the governing body of that charity. Who likes looking at locusts? A picture that stops you dead may not make you want to read on.

Often the best headlines are not originally conceived as headlines. They are *buried* in the copy. That's because writers and art directors tend to be like car engines: they take some time to warm up. Often the first ideas they come up with are by way of revving up; the first few paragraphs of copy are just a series of circles around a problem. You will often find diamonds in your own back yard by looking through the body copy for a good headline. (For the same reason, when editing copy you will often find it pays to cut out the first two or three paragraphs almost entirely.)

Look to copy for headlines

Sometimes the opening to the letter in a direct mail package is really the attention-getter. The envelope may have no message on it at all. Often the quietest openings, which merely *single out* the prospect, work best.

One famous letter opening is: 'Dear Mr Bird: If the list upon which I found your name is any indication ...'. It works because people often wonder where you got their name from.

Here is the soft, but very effective beginning of a letter I wrote for an insurance policy aimed at teachers: 'Were you aware that there is an insurance company which offers preferential terms exclusively to teachers and their families?'

The most *boring*, unimaginative way to single out a prospect is to say: 'As a teacher, you ...'. Poor stuff – very common amongst second-rate writers – but it works because it is relevant.

Once you have gained people's attention – what next?

Each medium may have its special demands when it comes to attracting attention, but it is when you try to create *interest in* and *desire for* your product that professionalism often shows most clearly.

Above all you must keep your reader with you.

Joe Sugarman, the US mail order wizard I mentioned at the beginning of this book, has likened good copy to a 'greased chute'. All you have to do is make sure the reader will read the next sentence after the one you have just written. True, but easier said than done.

You must look back at what you have *already* said, and see what the person would next like to know. And – just as important – what you can assume about them simply because they read the previous copy.

The only thing you know about the person who starts to read the body copy is that they have probably already read the headline. Thus, the opening should amplify or explain what the headline has said; *enlarge* upon it.

That's why so many proven ads begin with something like: 'Yes, it's true, you can (do whatever has been promised).'

Picture your reader

One measure of good copy is what I call the *nod factor*. You must picture your reader, and see how many times you can get him to nod in agreement. People like to have their prejudices confirmed. It keeps them reading happily.

Let's follow the sequence in the teachers' insurance package I mentioned when discussing how to open the letter copy. After the first sentence, the copy goes on to say: 'Although we choose not to spend large sums of money advertising the fact, we have been helping teachers with their investment and insurance plans for over a century now.'

Thus, the reader knows more about you, realises why he has never heard of you before and the mention of the century in business shades into *conviction*, another of our key objectives. The sentence also implies a saving, and capitalises on many teachers' dislike of advertising: it gets a nod.

In the next paragraph of our letter we go on to say: 'Over the years, we've helped many thousands of NUT members,' and so on.

As you see, nothing in this sequence is unclear or tricky. Each point logically follows the one before.

The assumption is simply that if the reader found the last thing you said relevant and interesting, all you have to do is follow with something that explains or elaborates (without wasted words) and carries your argument forward.

You need an ability to get inside the skin of your prospect which few possess. You need to be able to write the telling phrase which only comes from deep thought and understanding of both product and market. The phrase may even come from something you have heard your prospects say themselves.

Be straight-forward

Yet, difficult as this talent may appear, many people have it, if they will but bring it out. We have to communicate every day. So imagine that's what you're doing. Don't be 'literary'; be straightforward. Imagine you are sitting across the table from your prospect, and speak in his language. Here is the kind of expression I've found helps:

- 'When we obtained the rights to a remarkable new product from Canada I thought of you immediately.'
- 'I think that the perfect chest of drawers should have six special qualities. I wonder if my checklist agrees with what yours would be?'
- 'I'd like to tell you about a remarkable breakthrough we have just achieved, which you as one of our customers are the first to hear about and benefit from.

    'If you're interested, then I can tell you you're in excellent company, because already three of Britain's leading direct marketers have decided they can't pass this opportunity up.'

Some good openings

- 'I am sure that you, like me, are often assailed by people making "limited" offers of "unique" experiences; which is why I had quite a problem when I sat down to compose this letter to you.

    'You see, I *do* have a unique experience to propose ... one which indeed will be limited to very few people. In fact only 700 will be able to join us on our World Cruise.'

I have already referred once to sloth. Once they've had the bright idea that got people into the copy, writers tend to be lazy when it comes to the 'nuts and bolts'. But it is in the detailed explanation, the piling-on of facts, that people become convinced that what you say is true. You must work on this. Otherwise the sale will slip away. Tell people what it is you're offering in clear and unambiguous terms. Explain why it is better than alternatives (if any). Go into detail. Use all your persuasive powers, quietly and reasonably. *Not* with the hysterical enthusiasm so often found in copy.

Go into detail

Here's how I started to describe a bio-feedback device which was sold extremely successfully to previous buyers by one of our clients:

This remarkable monitor actually 'teaches' your body to relax. You're familiar no doubt with the saying 'a healthy mind in a healthy body'. But only in recent years have doctors and psychologists learned how true this saying is.

Now it is possible, by measuring the stress your body is undergoing from minute-to-minute, to *train* yourself to relax.

> And this unique device does it all for you, measuring how your system is physically reacting to surrounding pressures, and then enabling you to adjust your emotional reactions so as to relax easily.

And so on ...

Let me emphasise that *every* product – whether it is an insurance policy or furniture – needs to be explained fully. You must consider and explain every possible advantage and forestall every possible objection.

Thus, in the letter quoted above, I went on after the passage quoted to reassure people, for I knew the claim was hard to believe.

> *Impossible*? I myself thought so until I actually placed this monitor in the palm of my hand and used it.

Desire – or want

I have used the word 'desire' in our formula, but you could just as easily talk about encouraging people to *want* what you are selling.

Explain fully

By this I do not mean the old canard put about by half-baked sociologists that we can 'create' wants that didn't exist before. There has to be an underlying need for what you offer, otherwise it will never sell. But the way you remind your prospects about that need, or amplify it, is very important. It's usually done by the use of example, imagery and 'word pictures'.

Better perhaps even than painting, word pictures is getting people to try the product for themselves: this can be done if you send a sample.

Here is the start of a letter I wrote many years ago to sell a fireproofing treatment. I'd got the client to soak the paper on which the letter was to be printed with the treatment and then stand it up and run a blowtorch along the top of the letterhead. The copy ran as follows:

> Could a little arson improve your sales, your margins and your profits?
>
> As you can see, the top of this letter has been burnt. Now I would like you to set fire to one of the bottom corners. As you can see, the paper chars but does not flame.

I went on to explain that timber merchants (to whom I was aiming the letter) would improve the value of what they sold and become more competitive if they treated their timber in this way. To build conviction I simply obtained from current newspapers examples of horrifying fires which had been taking place, and gave information about the wave of new legislation which had just come in encouraging people to fireproof their timber. Here is what I wrote:

Paint 'word pictures'

> As you know – no matter what politicians say – the world's economy is in a bad way. And looks like getting no better. People like yourself, whose businesses depend to some extent on the construction industry, are well placed to see this, because the construction industry is very sensitive to economic change.

Yet curiously, amidst this depression, some people in the wood and paper business are doing much better than others.

I travel all over Europe, viewing factories such as yours. Outside some there are huge piles of unsold stock. Outside others this stock situation is less depressing. And even in these difficult times they are making headway.

I am happy to say that many of these companies which continue to thrive are my customers. Which brings me to the reasons why I asked you to practise a little arson.

This letter has been treated with 'Fyreprufe' paper fire retardant to prevent it flaming. We also make a wood-fire retardant which will prevent wood burning.

And so on ...

Your reader can appreciate this. It talks about something he wants: he would like to be one of the timber merchants who are doing well. This copy incorporates both a word picture and relevant examples.

Here are some extracts from letters written for The Royal Viking Line, to sell extremely expensive sea cruises:

> From the very moment you step on board one of our ships, you're pampered. A steward shows you to your Stateroom. We give you time to settle in ... order Room Service ... and relax, before inviting you to join your fellow passengers on deck for a big send off from port:
>
> > Champagne and a live jazz band spur on
> > the jubilant atmosphere. Waving crowds on the
> > quayside are showered with confetti and streamers
> > as the mighty ship pulls away.
>
> There's no more exhilarating start to a holiday. And as you lean on the railing, feel the quickening sea breeze ...

Expensive sea cruises

Here's more for the same client, selling a cruise to the Orient. We start creating desire on the envelope, with the line: '"Like jasmine blossom carried away by the stream ... sail to a world of which you cannot dream." – Chinese poet Li T'ai-po.'

When we get inside, the overline to the letter runs: 'Mist-shrouded hills ... sampans silhouetted on silver rivers ... proud pavilions of red and gold ... rice paper screens dappled with sunlight ... incense drifting softly through temple courtyards ... quiet gardens of graceful willows and bubbling streams.'

For a product such as this, the ability to create images which build desire is critical.

Create images that build desire

Incidentally, in this pack we placed a sachet of jasmine tea which showed through the envelope, and certainly helped attract attention. People imagine gimmicks like this do not work with sophisticated clientele. They certainly do: 8 per cent of those on The Royal Viking Line prospect list had titles – Sir this; Lord that; and so on.

Perhaps one of the greatest examples ever of creating desire for something comes from a famous advertisement written by John Caples 80 years ago – 'They laughed when I sat down at the piano'.

Here are two extracts from that ad.

Then I Started to Play

Instantly a tense silence fell on the guests. The laughter died on their lips as if by magic. I played through the first few bars of Beethoven's immortal Moonlight Sonata. I heard gasps of amazement – spellbound!

As the last notes of the Moonlight Sonata died away, the room resounded with a sudden roar of applause. I found myself surrounded by excited faces. How my friends carried on! Men shook my hand – wildly congratulated me – pounded me on the back in their enthusiasm! Everybody was exclaiming with delight – plying me with rapid questions ... 'Jack! Why didn't you tell us you could play like that?' ... 'Where *did* you learn?' ... 'How long have you studied?' ... 'Who *was* your teacher?'

Remember the copy for the hotel advertisement I picked out earlier (see page 88)? As I pointed out, this advertisement positions the product very well, but it also creates interest, builds desire, instils conviction and asks for action through the offer very effectively – as well as using phrases which enable you to picture the hotel in your mind.

Demonstrate the product

Fairfax Cone, whom I quote elsewhere, once said, 'Advertising is what you do when you can't be there in person'; and of course if you were there you would *demonstrate* the product. That is why copy which paints word pictures is good. Here is another old example. It asks the reader to compare the paper that they are using with a new, improved type. I think you will agree that after reading it you almost feel as though you have tried this product.

You can prove the excellence of our goods in a second; just tear off a corner of this sheet; now get a magnifying glass and examine both torn edges. You find long fibres – linen threads – on ours, while on yours the fibres are short, woody.

HOW TO BUILD CONVICTION

Writing copy to sell direct is the literary equivalent of having the kind of face that nobody trusts.

Readers are suspicious

Readers know you're trying to sell them something. That alone arouses suspicion. And because you are not selling face-to-face, people are often even *more* suspicious. So this section is very important. It's an area much neglected by lazy writers. Here are ways to be more convincing.

1 Make sure the tone is appropriate; and don't overstate

I once received a letter from a company talking about 'an exciting range of loans'. Ridiculous. I am intensely irritated by this sort of thing – copy in which everything is superb, high quality, tremendous and fantastic. It belongs in a never-never land only inhabited by poor copywriters. Therefore, eschew superlatives. Don't bullshit people. Talking loudly does not make people listen: it just annoys them.

Equally, this sort of copy is rarely appropriate either to communicator or audience, and thus lacks credibility. The copy must always reflect the source. Eg, if you are a bank, talk like a banker; if you are selling health products, talk like a health enthusiast. The only area I can think of where copy-writers' superlatives are appropriate is that of the used-car dealer.

And the copy must not only be appropriate to the source; it must also be appropriate to the audience. What is the right way to address your prospect? Once again, most writers behave as though they're addressing a group of subnormal teenagers.

2 Be specific

It reassures people that you know what you are talking about and that they will get exactly what you have promised.

So spell out your offer (and everything else) fully. Eg don't say: 'I will send you lots of lovely knitting ideas for an incredibly low price.' Rather, say: 'I'll send you 73 knitting patterns, plus 12 free books of hints for 49p a week.'

3 If the product is at all technical, give the specifications

Ways to convince readers

Some people will want to know, and those who don't will be impressed anyhow. Always include exact dimensions and weights of products.

4 If it is a compilation, like a record album or anthology, give every title

Thus you convince people that they are getting a lot for their money. And, of course, somebody, somewhere will be looking for the one you miss out, and you'll lose a sale. The one that would have made the ad a success.

5 Write in the present tense as far as possible

The words 'will' and 'can' and 'could' imply less certainty of benefit than the word 'is'.

As soon as you can after opening the copy, you must move into the present tense. Thus, you say: this product *does* this; you *feel* this; not it *will* do; or you *will* feel.

6 Make it sound easy

Don't talk about the buyer having to do anything – talk about the product doing it for them.

Thus, you do not *learn* to type – our course *has you* typing. (And, being *specific*, it has you typing in 30 days … and being *convincing* … your money back without quibble if it doesn't.)

7 Re-state your benefits before closing

This is 'make your mind up time' – so bolster their enthusiasm just before you ask for the money. Remind them what they get by replying, and what they lose if they don't.

The power of emotion

About 20 years ago, I was hired by a friend to work as a consultant to his agency. He introduced me to his staff as 'Drayton Bird – but you can call him Mummy.' The joke centred around a job I had done some years previously for the old Pritchard Wood agency. They had gained the Chambers' Encyclopedia account, but knew little about direct response advertising.

However, they put their top team to work on the job. One became a well known TV commercials director. The other became probably the best advertising creative director in Britain.

They laboured long and hard, and created a beautiful full-page ad, which ran in the *Sunday Times* colour magazine. It had the headline: 'Do you have a bright child?' The picture showed a child looking out of the page.

The thinking was bang on target. The product was positioned as an educational aid. And they addressed their prospects directly in a flattering way. But the headline was too cold. The ad only attracted literally a handful of replies. This sort of thing comes every now and then to remind us we are but frail mortals.

Emotion versus reason

The agency called in Bird, the man who specialised in the grubby business of mail order. (Our business really *was* the poor relation in those days.) I decided the previous ad was far too *rational*. I wrote an ad with the headline: 'Mummy, Mummy, I've passed.' The picture showed a child running up a garden path, obviously having just passed an exam, with the mother waiting to embrace him. The subhead said: 'What can you do to make sure this magic moment comes true for *your* child?'

This little gem appeared in a little eight-inch double column space. It got so many replies the salespeople couldn't cope. There is little doubt that the secret of this headline was that it *dramatised* the emotional moment when the benefit was realised; then it said something which made the reader want to go on.

I never got the chance to find out what would have happened to my other headline: 'Daddy, what's a hormone?' However on a trip to Australia I saw somebody in Melbourne running the 'Mummy' headline to advertise prizes for children who had excelled at school. You can see the common appeal.

Most outstanding business thinkers realise how important emotion is. Once I spent a day with Dr Ernest Dichter, the celebrated proponent of motivational research. How he conducted his research I do not recall, but he seemed to have an intuitive understanding of people's real motivations.

'A convertible is like a mistress,' he said. And: 'People buy a car for that first 20 minutes when they drive around in it.'

A good story to remember when thinking about those inner emotional benefits is the one about the businessman who saw his friend stepping out of a brand new Rolls, looking as miserable as sin. 'What's the matter?' he asked. 'That's a beautiful car.' 'I know,' the man replied. 'But I can't *see* myself in it.'

Outstanding campaigns always find a way to exploit emotional reactions. Years ago I saw a presentation made by Leo Burnett in Chicago to the Harris Bank, an extremely conservative organisation. The team proposed the use of a cartoon lion called Hubert.

At the time this must have seemed the idea of a group of demented visionaries. In those days bank ads looked like mausoleums. In a brilliant dramatised presentation the Leo Burnett team made the point that nobody cares about a stuffy old bank – but everyone would like a trustworthy, courageous, lovable lion. The appeal was almost entirely emotional.

Hubert is still around, I believe. And another lion worked hard for Credit Lyonnais in France. Lloyds Bank has a black horse, and in the US again, a highly successful financial animal was called Wally the Walrus. For the Marine Bank, he helped to pull in $80 million in deposits in two brief direct campaigns in the early 1980s. Emotional, irrational appeals for the world's most rational business, banking.

In creating attention-getting combinations of words and pictures, try to answer the single question: 'How can I dramatise the *emotional* benefit of this product or service?'

THE NUTS AND BOLTS OF GOOD CREATIVE COPY

I'd like to turn to some of the issues that come up again and again when people are discussing what makes good and bad creative work. Starting with headlines.

Short headlines or long?

In the 1950s, one famous English advertising agency had a Hungarian creative director as an art director. He would produce a layout, go to a writer and say: 'I vant three vitty vords for the headline.' Beware the three-vitty-vords system. Research shows that long headlines usually do better than short. Wit is often wasted on busy prospects.

Long headlines often work better

Here's a headline I wrote for Bullworker which ran unchanged for 14 years:

Britain's heavyweight weight-lifting champion 1962/3/4 shows *how these 7 exercises will build you a power-packed body in exactly 49 seconds a day* or all your money back instantly.

It showed a picture of my mighty friend Dave Prowse (later better known as Star Wars' Darth Vader) demonstrating the exerciser. It constantly proved a 'banker' ad, until they produced a new model of the product. Even Muhammad Ali, who was used in some ads, never did better except when he had a big fight on – context, again, being the reason.

Here are some other successful headlines, none less than seven words long.

Some successful headlines

Here's an extra $50, Grace. I'm making real money now.
We travelled 2,000 miles just to save 2c.
To men who want to quit work some day.
At 60 miles an hour, the loudest noise in this new Rolls-Royce is the ticking of the electric clock.
You can laugh at money worries if you follow this simple plan. (This one, over fifty years old, was adapted a few years ago by a UK finance house. It worked.)
The amazing facelift in a jar. Used by Hollywood stars who don't want plastic surgery.
How to burn off body fat hour by hour.
The lazy man's way to get rich.
17 ingenious (but perfectly legal) ways to avoid paying your debts.
How to double your power to learn.

Research shows that readership of a headline drops from 100 per cent who may read the first two or three words, down to about 70 per cent who will read seven words. After that the drop is insignificant.

But we do not want 100 per cent or even 70 per cent of our readers to reply. No product can appeal to all those people at one time. We want a *small* percentage to whom we can make a *precise* offer. Precision is not often achieved briefly.

Persuasion is our goal

Of course, art directors love short headlines. It makes their layouts stark and dramatic. But drama is rarely what we want. Persuasion is our goal; and that takes words, not pyrotechnics.

Envelope messages

Perhaps the most common points of debate about *direct mail* are: what – if anything – should you put on the envelope? how many pieces should be in the package? how important are personalisation and gimmicks?

The purpose of the envelope message – if any – is not merely to get somebody to open the envelope. Most will probably do that anyhow. Human beings are generally too curious not to. The question is, will they be *eager* to open the envelope: will they open that envelope before the other envelopes? In other words, will the envelope message *set them up*?

How to single out your message

The brilliant man who set the pattern for much of *Reader's Digest* activities in the United States, Walter Weintz, wrote an excellent book called *The Solid Gold Mailbox*. In it he states that what you do with the envelope will have more effect on success or failure than anything else, because it will single out that message from the many others you receive that day.

Others believe there is no need to put any message on the envelope because that tells the reader that a commercial message is inside, and this tempts them to relegate it to *after* other envelopes.

Frankly, I find this somewhat unconvincing: when they open the envelope, they will find out soon enough that the message is commercial. Therefore, why not use that envelope to create a favourable frame of mind? (I would enter a caveat though: if a prospect has received a stream of mailings from you with envelope messages on them, then there is no reason why a blank one should not, by way of contrast, prove very effective.)

America's best direct mail copywriter, the late Bill Jayme, once told me that the envelope message was to start telling people what the subject was, so he didn't have to waste time doing so once they opened the envelope – he could get on with the persuasion. He also said rather more vividly that the envelope was 'the hot-pants on the hooker'.

I incline to his point of view. First of all, if there is some indication of what that envelope contains, of the subject it is going to cover, those who are not interested needn't waste any further time; whereas those who *are* will move forward into the package enthusiastically.

It has to be said that Bill Jayme had a substantial advantage in this area, because he wrote very, very ingenious envelope messages. For *Psychology Today* magazine: 'Do you lock the bathroom door behind you, even when there's no one else in the house?'

Or for a holiday magazine: 'How much should you tip when you're planning to steal the ashtray?'

My advice to you is: first to ask yourself 'would this message *deter* people?' Then 'would it *encourage* them?' If the answers are 'No' and 'Yes', run the message.

Anything you can do on the envelope to impart urgency is worthwhile. For that reason, many mailings may *start* by asking for action by suggesting you might miss something if you don't open the envelope. That's why you sometimes see mailing envelopes bearing stamps saying: 'Offer closes in 14 days, please open now.' Or: 'Dated documents inside.'

On one mailing aimed at travellers, I put on the reverse of the envelope: 'If you are travelling within the next 30 days, open now.' A very talented French direct marketing man, Bruno Manuel, once put a message on the envelope saying: 'Do not open until Christmas.' As he rightly surmised, this had precisely the opposite effect. People couldn't resist opening.

Sometimes the postal indicia used can lift response. In the UK, certainly, you are allowed to design (within certain guidelines) your own postal mark on the envelope. Attractive ones seem to lift response slightly.

It's difficult to predict what will or what won't work. Generally, a white envelope does better than a manila envelope; and a brightly coloured envelope will often do better than a white one. If, however, you wish your mailing to have a quasi-official appearance, then a manila envelope may be the best approach.

What is more, human beings are very strange. One client a few years ago tested an envelope which required the customer to buy their own stamp against his usual reply-paid envelope. Believe it or not, the reply-paid did not win this test. However, six months later in the same test to the same list, the figures were reversed. This sort of frustrating oddity makes strong men weep – and wise men test.

Personalisation and gimmicks

A while ago, I received a mailing containing two tombola tickets and a winners' list, which I opened to see if I had won or not. I had, of course. I pondered for a second before deciding I was not really interested in the wine being sold, and did not respond. Consumerists speak of gimmicks – especially sweepstakes, competitions, free gifts and heavy personalisation – as the latter day equivalent of the Bulgarian atrocities the great prime minister Mr Gladstone used to get so wound up about a century or more ago.

Harmless tricks that work

If we must look for social evils against which to pit ourselves, this sort of thing is a puny target indeed. Such devices are harmless tricks.

If you don't like them, you don't have to pay attention to them, just as if you don't like obnoxious TV quiz programmes you don't have to watch them. Why people get so excited about them is a mystery to me; I very much doubt whether ordinary people give a hoot. Some say they insult people's intelligence. Many intelligent people would never dream of visiting a fair-ground, whereas others (I confess I am one) still get childish delight from being whirled around on the waltzer and terrified on the Ferris wheel.

Appropriately, Americans refer to many of these devices as 'bells and whistles': the sort of thing that used to attract attention to the circus when it visited town. I liken them to the fanfare at the beginning of a public event: they draw attention to what is about to come.

Attract attention

A certain type of personalisation falls into this category. When it was first tried it increased responses by as much as 50 per cent. People like to see their names. The bigger the better. So one mailer sent out an order form with the recipient's name in huge letters on it. He got hardly any responses. When he researched to find out why, he discovered that people loved the personali-sation so much they were pinning the order forms up on their walls.

Often, of course, a mailing will try to make the personalisation unob-trusive, so as to look as though it really is a personal message. This is seen by the recipient as a sign that the mailer has taken the trouble to address him by name. It is really courtesy.

However, the reason why all personalisation tends to work is simple. Byron put it one way many years ago: 'How sweet it is to see thy name in print.' But, let's face it, we like to be addressed by name and have our prefer-ences recognised. What, after all, is more gratifying than to walk into a restaurant and have the owner say: 'Good evening, Mr Bird. I have reserved your usual table by the window.' From the highest to the lowest, we all respond to this sort of thing.

All these attention-getting gimmicks are employed because they work. Take, for instance, plastic cards with your name on them showing through the envelope. We tested this years ago and found these cards increased response in one instance by 70 per cent. One of the card manufacturers claimed that they can sometimes increase response by as much as 200 per cent. Today you can personalise the copy, then direct people to a personalised website. This can triple sales.

Appropriate gimmicks often work. A few years ago, a Norwegian company had a problem. They had been looking for investors. Several mailings had been tried. All had failed. They had almost given up, but made one last attempt. They sent a mailing to tell people they had not gone out of business, were still there and still wanted money. Inside the envelope was a little plastic frog with a spring inside. When the envelope was opened the frog popped out. The message to the recipient was: 'Hop to it! Act now.' The little gimmick dramatised the thought of hopping to it, and also the thought that the company was still around.

Appropriate gimmicks work

The mailing was not targeted at giggling teenagers, but at financial organisations, and the subject was related to computers. It was a howling success when no less than *eight* previous mailings – all more serious – had failed.

Why gimmicks work

Many of these techniques were arrived at by thinking about people and how they behave. For instance, *Reader's Digest* arrived at the concept of the YES/NO alternative through reflecting upon the difference between those people who were replying to their mailings and those who weren't.

Obviously only a minority of people were really interested in what they had to offer and did order. The majority – maybe 90 per cent – didn't. People at the *Digest* wondered about these non-responders. There must have been many who were *willing* to respond but couldn't make their minds up. Thus was born the concept of YES/NO. The idea was to force people off the fence. And it worked. Of course, they got plenty of NOs; but they got more YESs too.

In my experience this is always the case. And it has the subsidiary benefit that next time you mail the same lot of people, you can eliminate the NO responses, save money and get a higher overall response. This is a *very* simple use of regression analysis.

The concept of YES/NO/ MAYBE

This concept was developed further by a copywriter called John Francis Tighe in America, who introduced the idea of YES, NO or MAYBE. He was selling a publication and the MAYBE sticker gave you the option of saying, 'Well, I'm not really sure, but send me a sample copy anyhow and I'll see what I think.' This also worked. In mailings for my own agency, I gave four options: Yes; No; Not now, but keep in touch; and Right idea, wrong person.

Equally, the sweepstake works because – who knows? – you might win. Just as, when you go to the fairground sideshow – who knows? – you might win a goldfish.

Any device which creates involvement helps. The stamps you peel off and stick on order forms work. So do little rub-offs and things that show through envelopes indicating that something interesting is happening inside. Equally, touches of humanity help, like handwritten notes in the margin.

Involvement devices work

Some forms of involvement device work for more than one reason. Take those stickers. The idea of taking the trouble to sign your name and commit yourself overtly to buying a particular product or service is much more painful (and takes more effort) than simply moving a sticker from point A to point B on an order form. This sort of psychological ploy works in every sort of market, not just amongst the hoi polloi. *Fortune* magazine, for instance, uses stickers. The only thing you have to take care with is the style of language and the look of the piece when using these approaches to more sophisticated audiences.

GRAYDON

Graydon UK Limited
Hygeia Building
66 College Road
Harrow
Middlesex HA1 1BE

T. +44 (0)20 8515 1400
F. +44 (0)20 8515 1499
mail@graydon.co.uk
www.graydon.co.uk

a - seed

How much credit should you give your clients?
"Not too much", says the financial director
"Not too little" say the sales people

Know how much credit to give — almost instantly — and make
everyone happier (especially yourself)

You know how it is.

Every day, you must decide how much credit to give to a
client or when you should re-adjust your credit policy.

I guess you analyse credit reports or you wait to see how
the client behaves over time. But what if *at the press of a
button* you could:

√ Know *exactly* how much credit you can safely allow
every client on your ledger

√ Download analysis and reports that tell all you need
to know in an easy-to-read format. For instance, how
risk is distributed across your portfolio; who are
your 'riskiest' or best customers; your aggregated
exposure across risk groups.

√ Be alerted instantly if change occurs in any client's
position

√ Have your database updated automatically with up-to-
the-second credit report information

Would this make your life a bit easier? Then what you need
is ePatrol. Others find it enormously valuable, as this
comment testifies:

"Bad debt provision has reduced by 85% since using
Graydon's information. We are very impressed with the

This letter plays on the emotions of the credit manager, pulled between conflicting demands.

ePatrol reports; these have proved to be very useful and cost effective."
Glenda Taylor MICM (Grad), Credit Manager, Muntons plc.

How do we do it? Every day - constantly - we update our records for each of the 4,536,213 UK limited companies and even unincorporated businesses on our database.

This is one of the largest databases in existence - but more importantly ePatrol is the only online ledger management tool that is *dynamically* updated 24/7. Whenever you log-in, whatever information you can possibly need is there, on your screen, right up to date.

And we understand what matters most to you. We monitor 28 "critical" events that affect credit risk, including:

- New accounts filed at Companies House
- Receiver appointed
- Winding-up petition presented
- Meeting of creditors
- County Court Judgments
- Director resignation
- Holding company change

What's more, your information comes in the most timely manner possible: we *pre-warn* you if a change occurs so you can immediately adjust your credit limits or arrange a quicker collection.

So with ePatrol you prevent bad debts in two ways:

1. You get up to date, comprehensive information when you need to take your initial decision
2. You know in advance when a customer is likely to become a problem.

Maybe now you're thinking, "That takes care of the financial director. What about the sales people?"

They want to know where the money is, so they can concentrate their efforts wisely. Now, at the press of a button you can tell them who has the money and where you can advance more credit.

You might be allowing only up to £10,000 credit to a customer. Our monthly credit guide might suggest you could extend it to £50,000. ePatrol shows the "gap" which can be exploited - and you know that more credit almost invariably means more sales.

If this sounds too good to be true, here are two other comments:

> "We were fully prepared for a difficult trading year (2003) but with ePatrol monitoring not only have we kept our bad debts to a minimum, we also achieved good DSO results. It is difficult to quantify exactly but maybe 1-2 days improvement. We are confident that we now have a watchful eye on critical changes taking place which we can instantly react to, and see ePatrol monitoring as an essential tool."
> *Barbara Smith, Credit Manager, Scott Bader Company Limited.*

> "Excellent value for money, it helps us as a company to monitor our customers' credit ratings and gives us very up to the minute information regarding their status. In our industry this is very useful, I have yet to see another service that offers such good value for money."
> *Sue Patton, Credit Manager, Scania (Great Britain) Limited.*

We could do all that for you, too. Test us. Arrange a free demonstration: we'll come and demonstrate what ePatrol can do for you. No hard sell, just a demonstration. You decide for yourself

Just fax back the enclosed slip to Peni Bennett on 0870 136 4462 - and we'll call you back.

Thanks,

Peni Bennett
Business Development Manager

P.S. Get a FREE copy of the Graydon Glossary of Credit Management Terms. Our clients find it invaluable. In fact they *buy* it at £16.99. It can be yours just for the cost of a fax. Why don't you make this the next thing you do?

→

Please fax back to Peni Bennett on 0870 136 4462 to claim your FREE copy of the Graydon Glossary of Credit Management Terms. Or simply send us back the slip below (I've enclosed a pre-paid envelope).

☐ Yes, I'd like to see ePatrol at work. Please call me on ....

☐ It sounds interesting and I'd like to know more. Please call me on ....

☐ Right idea, wrong person. Please contact my colleague .... on ....

☐ Right idea, wrong time. Please call me on .... in .... months.

Ref.No.: a - seed   Your name: Mr Drayton Bird

Company Name: Drayton Bird Associates

Notice how the recipient is given a choice. This increases responses and helps you to stop wasting money on people who aren't interested.

How many pieces?

I used to spend a lot of time lecturing each year, particularly for the Institute of Marketing near London. At virtually every session people used to question the need for a large number of pieces in an envelope. It is as natural as it is to question whether letters should be long.

My early adviser Bernie Silver showed me a mailing package out of which tumbled eight pieces (two of them different types of order form). I couldn't believe it. When I asked him for the reason, he laughed and said: 'One piece in the envelope means one chance to make a sale. Eight pieces means eight chances. They've got to say "no" eight times.'

This reasoning was validated for me many years later when I heard of some research conducted by one large company which learned that each piece in a mailing package is looked at for about three seconds before being discarded.

Recent research, where Ogilvy & Mather Direct filmed consumers (unbeknown to them) looking at direct mail, revealed that they tended to spend very little time on packages which only had one or two pieces in them. On the other hand, one of the pieces tested – a mailing for Dove soap, with a large number of pieces inside it, including a sample of the product – gained their attention for as long as five minutes.

Just as interesting, perhaps, is a simple look at the finances of direct mail. I am not going to give actual figures, since they keep changing because of inflation and obviously vary from country to country. However, the point is that the principal costs in a mailing are *fixed*. There's nothing you can do about them. You have the postage – a huge element. Then there's the envelopes. The list rental. Handling charges and other unavoidable overheads.

When you add up the figures, it may cost you only 35 per cent more to send out a 'rich' full colour all-dancing, all-singing package with lots of pieces than to send out a 'poor' two-colour affair. The question you have to ask yourself is: which will do better for the investment?

Unless you are only going for an enquiry – and certainly if you are going for a serious sale – the answer is usually the rich package. You're getting more opportunities to sell for your money, once people have opened the envelope. If they're *not* interested, they won't look properly at any of the pieces. If they are, they'll spend lots of time with them.

Your aim – to seize attention, and retain it – may not differ, but because of the ways in which people *experience* different types of communication, the way in which you actually go about this will.

Thus, a television commercial or radio commercial can only be seen or listened to from beginning to end. They are linear communications. But a press advertisement does *not* have to be seen in any particular order. Probably the headline will be seen first, in conjunction with the illustration. After that you can't guarantee where the eye goes. This is why you should make sure the layout is such that wherever the eye lights there is something worth seeing: a caption, an interesting little picture, some quote perhaps from an authority on the subject, an appealing guarantee – anything calculated to attract and retain interest.

Pieces working together

A mailing package presents the same problem on a larger scale. It may have as many pieces of paper in it as you wish, but you can't guarantee which will be looked at first, or how. One thing is certain: you'd better make sure that *every one* of those pieces of paper is planned carefully to attract attention.

If you have a singly-folded leaflet, the headline on the front and the illustration accompanying it must attract attention. But don't forget you can't *force* your reader to look at the *front* first. They may look at the back. Make sure there is something appealing there, too.

People start where they please

They may look at the order form first: make sure that's doing a selling job. And they will almost certainly read the letter. That, too, must do an effective job. US and German research some years ago suggested that more people start with the PS in the letter than anything else in the mailing. People start where they please.

It stands to reason that in this business, like any other, you will learn much by watching what others do. Looking at lots of mailing packages teaches a lot. You will soon notice how in successful mailings the various elements work in concert.

The brochure will normally describe the service and display the merchandise – it is like your shop. The accompanying letter will be the salesman, who shows you round and points out the finer aspects of what is on offer.

There may be a second letter (a 'lift' letter as it is known) from someone more impartial, giving you friendly advice. Or, like the shop manager reassuring you, saying 'Don't worry – we'll always do what we promised, you can depend on us. You can bring it back if you don't like it. We'll gladly exchange or refund.'

To add conviction there may be a testimonial sheet. Or some examples of how the product has helped others. Or a newspaper clipping. Or all of these.

Remember, a mailing (or insert or door-to-door piece) can contain anything you like – it's up to you to find out what works best.

Note that a letter in a mailing package should *look* like a letter, using typewriter or word processor script. Too many times printers produce them in a printer's type. That's not what your business letters come looking like. Why should mailing letters? One financial client tested the old-fashioned Courier type against Times. Courier got 60 per cent more replies, but in one case Times did better.

Avoid conflict within the message

Beware of messages which conflict with each other. The whole must have a cohesion and consistency. Many direct mail packages fail because the message on the envelope is not followed up logically once you open the package. The creative people have had another idea which they like just as much, and which they are unwilling to jettison. This is a common error to be guarded against.

Another common error is slavish adherence to the order AIDCA. The various components should be included, but need not necessarily come in precisely that order. As I've already indicated, you can ask for action on the envelope. (Though you would be very unwise if you did not start by attracting attention, and *crass* if you did not ask for action at the end.)

CREATIVITY IN ACTION

Inserts: quite similar to a mailing

I am often asked how you approach creating an insert, as opposed to a mailing or an advertisement or, for that matter, a TV commercial. I start by looking at the context. How likely is it that anybody is going to look at it in the first place? Is it going to be really difficult to attract attention? And, once you've attracted attention, what do you wish to do next?

How does an insert differ from a mailing? In my view, less than you might think. A mailing is pretty intrusive. The majority, even in a heavily mailed country like the United States, still get opened and read. The question is: with what degree of interest? It is here that your skill comes in.

An insert is not as intrusive. In an insert you will almost certainly have precisely the same overall message as you would in a mailing for the same product – save that it's all contained in one piece. (That is, unless you choose to make some sort of letter part of the insert – or even make a letter itself the insert, which has worked very often.)

What to do with an insert

As I have already suggested, there is no guarantee that anybody will look at what you have fondly designated as the front as opposed to the back. Both sides must work equally well, as with a leaflet in a mailing pack. This applies whether you are talking about a two-sided insert or a folded insert. In the case of the latter, however, the messages on the outside should be designed to encourage people to look inside. They have something in common with envelope messages for mailings.

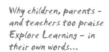

Equally, you could say that the outside of an insert can be viewed in much the same light as the headline of an advertisement. In both cases the task is to get people reading.

Think carefully about how your prospect or customer will look at that communication. By doing that you will be able to visualise what you ought to do. For instance, pick up the insert. Look at it. Would you want to open it? If you were the prospect, what do you think you would do if you received something like that? Then apply the same rules as to an ad or a mailing – does it contain all the elements of persuasion in AIDCA?

I have observed elsewhere that research will tell you a great deal about how people are likely to pick up and read your communications. It does not cost much to arrange for typical prospects to sit and look at your insert while you watch. Even asking a colleague to do so will reveal something.

The telephone

I am concentrating here for the most part on print media: direct mail, advertising and inserts – and particularly on the major problems of getting ideas and gaining attention.

With the telephone, there is no problem gaining people's attention. When the phone rings they pick it up. Or, if it's an inbound telephone call, they have taken the initiative themselves. They are interested to hear what you are going to say anyhow.

However, the telephone is unique: it is a two-way medium. It is also very expensive. You are paying all that money because, as long as you are polite, people will listen to what you have to say. So make sure they get the right message. This means, above all, having a professional script, delivered professionally. Relying on amateurs is not likely to work. (More on this in the chapter on media.)

The telephone is a two-way medium

Telephone scripts allow for interruptions and reactions. This is not an inconvenience: it is a great opportunity as long as the script is planned properly.

Scripts are in effect divided in two. First there is the script as planned. Then there is a series of pre-planned answers to questions and objections. The script evolves as it is used, being adapted according to the reactions it receives. And of course, the whole thing is often done on a computer screen.

My advice on telephone is to go to professionals. To begin with, get them to do the job for you, and then at the very least get them to train your own people.

The two biggest telephone sins: treating people like morons; and not giving them a chance to reply. If you simply read out a script without allowing for any reaction, you learn nothing. You might just as well send out a mail shot. The best telephone people are often 'resting' actors.

Catalogues: the visual reigns

Catalogues, being entirely visual, are apparently the medium with least in common with the telephone but they have a similarity when it comes to the creative approach. That is, you don't have to worry about getting attention. Usually they have either been requested or they are received with pleasure.

Keep people interested

The challenge, therefore, just as with the phone, is to exploit that attention – to *keep* people interested.

In one other respect, catalogues differ from most other media apart from posters. The pictures are more important than the words. However, every word must count. Trying to describe the product in the minimum number of words, every one of which must justify its place, is splendid training. It takes exceptional professionalism to do it well. Few can.

It also takes exceptional professionalism to come up with an unusual catalogue approach. Often because catalogues are thrown together as cheaply as possible, the result is what you would expect: rubbish. But paying a little more, and spending more time thinking about how you can differentiate yourself is of exceptional importance. It really will pay off for you.

For instance, the Banana Republic Catalogue in the United States was the foundation of a business which was exceptionally successful in mail order, then moved into retail, and is now international. This was achieved by breaking most of the accepted rules for catalogues. Thus, drawings were used, rather than photographs. There was a lot of copy, developing a narrative line based upon an imaginary republic. The catalogue was entertaining, as well as selling.

The best catalogues seem to develop their own style and tone of voice. They are often chatty, friendly, frank – like a good salesman in a shop. Here's an extract from the Land's End catalogue to show you what I mean.

Good catalogue copy

When we first offered a Mesh Knit Polo shirt back in the 1970s, some suggested that we embroider some little logo on our garment, citing the competition's fondness for equines, canines or reptiles: 'Why don't you follow their lead?' they asked.

Frankly, we thought – and still think – that the competition should follow our lead, and pay more attention to the things that really make a garment better.

Things like fabric. We use only 100 per cent cotton that is combed for softness and treated to reduce shrinkage. Or color – we offer nineteen, each and every one created with superior, fiber reactive dyes. These dyes bond chemically to the molecules in the cotton, giving you colors that don't fade away after only a couple of trips through the washing machine.

As you can see, this is very persuasive copy. It is also beguiling and even witty.

This leads me into the first of 16 suggestions for improving your catalogue.

1 Find a way to make your catalogue different

Certainly make it different visually, and try to make it different verbally, too. Develop a *character* for it.

2 Catalogues should not be impersonal

Some of them read as though they are produced by computer. Your catalogue should have an introductory letter to establish a relationship between company and buyer. The letter is best as a separate piece, not just a printed section inside the body of the catalogue.

3 Position is vital

Your letter, for instance, will almost certainly do better bound on to the front cover, just revealing the merchandise beneath, rather than looking like a printed piece inside the front cover. Your order form – better bound in than floating loose – should be constructed so that it is easily seen.

4 The cover is your prime selling spot

Tests show that whatever is on there will sell at least three times as well as if it were in the body of the catalogue. So you have to have good reason not to use the cover for merchandise.

5 Space is at a premium in a catalogue

Areas given over to 'mood' shots are usually not selling. Build mood into your overall treatment, don't just ladle it in at intervals – it's wasted space.

6 Don't underestimate the number of items you can get on a page

Properly planned, it can accommodate more than you think. Pages with few items usually won't make as much money as those with many – so you must have good reason for reducing numbers, eg a product that sells extremely well.

7 Create changes of pace and interest

Put in little 'hot' spots that make people open up on certain pages – like pages with heavier weight paper, gatefold pages and, of course, the order-form pages. Testimonials will also add interest, especially if you put people's faces in them.

8 Every catalogue entry should be a 'mini-ad', with its own headline

That's because your catalogue can point to what will work for you in ads or mailings. Beware, however: some items that do well in a catalogue don't do well on their own. I don't know why. Maybe they're just gregarious.

9 Use the same style for your catalogue as you would use for other communications

One client of ours used to use a different style of copy, headline, photographic treatment and even typography for his catalogue to the one he used for his ads. He could never understand why items that did well in one medium so rarely did well in others; nor why he got relatively poor results from his catalogue when sent to his ad respondents. People who have responded to one style of presentation will not necessarily react well to another.

10 Photographs usually, but not always, do better than illustrations

They are more credible. If using illustrations, make sure they give a very detailed impression of the products. The principal reason why some prefer illustrations is that they add character.

11 Pay great attention to the order form and how it is planned

Making it easy to order, just by checking a few items and having the customer's name already filled in, will have a critical effect on results. Study the order forms of good catalogues.

12 Reminding people how to order frequently throughout the catalogue pays

When they've seen something, they want it *now*.

13 Great care must be taken to ensure that the captions (and prices) are easily related to items

It's infuriating for people when they have to *hunt* for information.

14 Catalogue results can be boosted enormously (sometimes over 50 per cent) by the use of contests and sweepstakes

15 For reasons of finance and logistics, it usually pays to use as few photographers or illustrators as possible

16 Tell people to order on every page. The more you ask, the more you get

Broadcast media

What you can do in broadcast media is affected clearly by the very limited time those media allow. That time is itself governed by another factor: you have to allow a sufficient period within the commercial to give details of how to respond.

Television is watched with a fair degree of attention by its audience. This is one of the reasons for its power. You don't have to do anything *particularly* startling to attract attention. (Though this doesn't mean you shouldn't try.) The challenge is, having opened the commercial, to build people's interest. **Build people's interest**

Here are three basic things to remember about TV or radio (bearing in mind that radio is TV without pictures). Here, once again, you're trying to create pictures inside people's minds.

First, you must seek a single, simple, central idea. **A single, simple, central idea**

Rosser Reeves in his book *Reality in Advertising* uses the expression 'there's only so much room in the box'. People can rarely take on board more than one simple idea in a commercial. You may buttress it with supporting facts, but don't try to introduce any conflicting thoughts.

For example, *Reader's Digest* for some years used a brief commercial to tell people that a mailing was going to come through their door offering them a chance to win a sweepstake. In the UK the simple idea here was to put a former newscaster in front of the camera and let him tell people. This gave the whole thing credibility. The only time we moved away from the central shot of this newscaster was when showing the mailing coming through the door. Similarly, Publishers Clearing House in the United States uses scenes of happy winners getting a giant cheque.

If you look at the commercial I have illustrated for Time-Life (see pages 291–92), you will see that the simple idea is just to put a lot of scary things on the screen in a logical sequence, which demonstrate the content of the books being sold.

TV is a demonstration medium

This brings me to the second cardinal principle: never forget that TV is a *demonstration medium*. In the case of the commercials I have mentioned above, the first commercial demonstrates the mailing arriving through your door; the second one demonstrates the content of the book. Indeed, the very first successful television commercials were made by somebody taking street corner hucksters selling food processors and similar gadgets through demonstration, and sticking a camera in front of them. It worked beautifully.

In the case of radio, demonstration is perhaps best used when selling record collections, which are clearly made for the medium.

Entertainment should be derived from the sell

The third thing to remember is that if you are going to be entertaining, that entertainment should derive from the sell. It should not be inappropriate. Thus, in the case of the food processors I have just mentioned, after doing straightforward pitches for the product, it was decided to try using somebody *entertaining* to demonstrate the products. The agency very wisely didn't build in entertainment for its own sake: they got a celebrity, Richard Simmons, to do the commercials. He was quite funny, but he was talking all the time about the product.

When *Reader's Digest* tried to run a funny commercial with speeded-up film of people running to the post box to post their entries, the gimmick overcame the idea. It didn't work.

Here are some points likely to make your commercials better:

Pointers for effective TV

- Are you really exploiting the medium? For instance, if you're on TV, is it truly visual, or just words set to pictures? If you're on radio, is it just words or are you using the medium properly to conjure up images in people's minds?
- Is there a key visual or sound which acts as an mnemonic device to fix in the memory? Have you repeated it?
- Is the product the hero – or is the execution?
- If there's music, is it relevant or just gloss? The same applies to any visual device. Everything should be essential to making the commercial work better.
- Do you get straight to the point? You have limited time: get people involved instantly. In particular, a dramatic opening at the beginning of radio commercials to set them aside from the tapestry of sound – a loud noise, a fanfare – are obvious things. A challenging statement is another, or some tricky form of delivery like somebody speaking very fast.
- Does the product or service solve a problem? If so, is it shown clearly?
- Have you made it clear this is a direct offer? Preferably at the beginning, so people know they have to take note of somewhere to reply to.

TWO SECRET INGREDIENTS

Two ingredients for successful creative work are rare – yet perhaps most powerful of all. They are *genuine* involvement and *enthusiasm*.

Illustration	*Video*	*Audio – Male voice over*
	Man's hand stroking a glowing rabbit's foot.	'A rabbit's foot, carried luck …
	Man at table knocks over salt shaker and throws pinch of salt over his left shoulder.	a pinch of salt, tossed over the shoulder …
	Black cat in front of fire place hesitates, meows, runs out of frame.	a sense of foreboding at the sight of a black cat …
	Woman's hand mirror falling to the floor. It shatters; fluttering calendar page showing Friday 13th; knuckles knock on wood.	Are they harmless superstitions – or reminders of a darker time when the world was young, nature seemed all-powerful, and humble charms were man's best protection against unknown evil?
	'Wizard's worktable' filled with books and occult objects. Cover opens by itself, pages begin flipping quickly by. Camera moves in on werewolf illustration.	Enter The Enchanted World … a spellbinding series from Time-Life Books that probes the forgotten origins of the world's strangest curiosities.
	Book visuals: Dragons; Dwarfs; Fairies and Elves; Night Creatures.	In each lavishly illustrated volume, you'll move through storybook lands where the original endings to the tales of childhood weren't always happy ones.
	Darkened hallway. Wind stirs curtains … a ghostly figure moves towards you from far down the hall.	The Enchanted World takes you back to a time when restless apparitions drifted through darkened hallways …'
	Book visuals: Ghosts.	*Female reading passage:* 'Some ghosts were nothing more than cold spots on floors or shadows in corners. Others took human form.'

Figure 10.2 Time-Life Books' 'Enchanted World'

Robed figure laying down Tarot cards.

Male voice over:
A time when men who called themselves sorcerers used the Tarot to prophesy the future ...

Male reading passage:
The Hanged Man, dangling from a gallows, was a sign of life in suspension, while the Death card indicated change ...

Male voice over:
and a time when malevolent creatures were thought to stalk the night in search of hapless victims.

Traveller on foot at night on shadowy path. As he passes large tree, 3 pairs of eyes watch him.

Book visuals: Book of Christmas; Night Creatures.

Female reading passage:
Unwise was the wayfarer who journeyed by night
...

for in the shadows greedy eyes glittered, claws curled, teeth clicked.

Wizards & Witches volume stands centre screen.

Male voice over:
Begin your journey through The Enchanted World with Wizards & Witches. Examine it free for 10 days. If you keep it, other volumes will follow, one about every other month ... Spells & Bindings ... Ghosts ... and Water Spirits.

Gnarled hand with large signet ring closes open volume on table, hesitates – and knocks wooden surface.

So enter the Enchanted World ... where anything is possible, and a little luck never hurts.

(The remainder of the commercial was devoted to instructions on how to respond)

Figure 10.2 (continued)

You encounter these most often amongst copywriters who happen to be the proprietors of their own businesses. My favourite example (but then I am biased) comes from my mother. At the age of 67 she started running a charity which rescued homeless animals. I kept on telling her she ought to write to her supporters because she had spent all her money on this project and was getting desperate. So at the age of 71 she finally wrote her first piece of direct mail copy. I reproduce it below in its entirety.

Show genuine involvement and enthusiasm

Dear Animal Lover,
We are about to reach our second Christmas as a recognised charity. During this year and nine months we have rescued and homed over 925 cats and kittens, along with a number of dogs and puppies.

A wonderful example from my mum

We have, with your help, been able to improve our cattery and the cats are now, for the first time, able to scent the fresh air and see the blue sky. Originally we had 8 spacious cages, two storeys high, down one side. With the help of donations and money raised by members at charity functions, we undertook the much-needed improvements.

We decided to close in August for two weeks except to the most needy cases, in order to carry out these alterations.

Firstly we built another 8 cages on the opposite side of the cattery, all with a removable perspex sneeze barrier, power point and electrically heated bed. We then added a false ceiling for heat conservation. The rough concrete floor was covered with smooth asphalt for easy cleaning. At one end of the cattery the old garage doors were replaced by toughened patio-type doors to let in more light and these are left open when weather permits for extra ventilation. They now lead onto a high, walled-in 'adventure playground' which is escape-proof and fitted with platforms and a peep-hole.

Our second smaller cattery is next in line for up-grading.

I would like to add that except for the asphalt floor and the brickwork on the outside run, all this work was done by members and members' families.

We are now very proud of our cattery and, most important of all, it must add to the comfort of the cats while they are with us.

In March of this year we started to run an active neutering plan for the cats which come to us. Under this scheme we have neutered approximately 120 she-cats and 40 toms.

I would like to take this opportunity to thank you for your generosity for without your help we could not survive. As you will appreciate, our vets' and feeding bills are colossal and we have to struggle to keep our heads above water. Our members work hard and continuously, for nearly all have another job so their time is limited.

Finally, have a wonderful Christmas and a happy and healthy New Year.

Every one of these letters that went out raised £5. I sent the letter to David Ogilvy. He wrote back: 'Hire your mother.'

Why is it so good? Clearly, first of all it comes from the *heart* – the enthusiasm and urgency shine through. Second, she gave the *facts* because she was so intimately involved. You can see the whole letter is peppered with

Enthusiasm and urgency shine through

details which add verisimilitude. And you can also see that her love for animals comes out in phrases like: 'for the first time, [the cats are] able to scent the fresh air and see the blue sky' – phrases that conjure up vivid pictures; pictures that move you to action.

The professional – the *condottiere* as it were, who is writing because he has been hired to write on somebody else's behalf – finds it difficult to summon up this degree of enthusiasm or to acquire this depth of knowledge. But the ability to do so distinguishes the outstanding writer from the also-ran.

Take pride in your craft

Where does this ability come from? In my view, from an emotional determination, born of pride in one's craft, to align oneself totally with the client's interests and do the very best job possible. This is an egotistical characteristic. It is the belief that one has the mysterious power to persuade other people to do what you want them to do.

Few people have it; but that does not mean to say it cannot be nurtured in you, and I am certain that a clear understanding of what you should and shouldn't do to get good creative work is utterly essential.

For that reason, the next chapter will deal with *lists* of what works and what doesn't – and why.

Finding and expressing ideas well

Points to remember

- A proven technique:
  - Research.
  - Enlist the help of your subconscious.
  - Ask others.
  - Panic common!
- Be disciplined; have a structure: AIDCA.
- Study the context – and adapt: poor creative fails to.
- What do you know about the prospect?.
- National differences matter little if benefits universal.
- Business versus consumer differences overstated.
- Media vary; principles don't.
- Try adapting a success in one medium to another.
- AIDCA not always in that order – but you must gain attention.
- Benefits and news work best.
- Beware cleverness.
- Curiosity only works if relevant.
- Good headlines often lurk in copy.
- Keep them interested: think what they would want to know next.
- Don't skimp on argument: use all relevant detail.

- Samples – or word pictures.
- People suspicious – conviction vital.
  - Be appropriate.
  - Beware superlatives.
  - Don't treat prospects like halfwits.
  - Be specific; give specifications; omit nothing relevant.
  - Try to write in the present, not *will*, *can*, *might*, or *could*.
  - Make it seem easy.
  - Restate benefits before asking for action.
- Emotion beats reason.
- Long headlines work.
- Good envelope message encourages opening.
- Personalisation and gimmicks often pay.
- Why many pieces? Fixed versus variable costs.
- Content of message must be consistent.
- What would you do? Try simple research.
- Telephone – two ways: use pros.
- Catalogues: 16 rules for success.
- Broadcast:
  - Be simple.
  - Demonstrate.
  - Don't let entertainment drown selling.
- Enthusiasm and pride are the keys.

11

How to Make Your Creative Work *Virtually* Foolproof

*'There's no safety in numbers,
or anything else.'*
James Thurber

For many years I lived way out in the country in an old house.

One day, on my way up our long, overgrown drive, I glimpsed a sinuous, agile creature less than a foot long which darted into the undergrowth, then swiftly popped out its head to peep at us. It was a weasel. A cynic might describe the weasel as the patron animal of a certain type of copywriter.

'Weasel' in our business means a word or expression the reader may not even notice, which modifies the meaning of what is written to make it sound better than it is. Weasels are designed to mislead without actually lying.

Mislead without actually lying

The word *virtually*, which I used in this chapter title, is an example; or the phrase 'up to'; or the word 'helps'. The latter is often used when making claims about beauty products, such as 'helps give you younger looking skin'. (Even 'younger looking' is a weasel: people notice 'younger', but not 'looking'.)

Weasels work because people believe what they want to believe. That's one of the great truths of selling. However, when I read the other day about a new computer programme called 'Headliner' – described as 'thought processing software ... a series of linked databases for ideas', which writes headlines for you, I did not want to believe it.

My brain goes numb when I hear of such devices, but once I have penetrated the jargon and understood what they are, I usually recover my sang-froid.

I cannot believe anyone will ever invent a machine that can produce good weasels; nor can I imagine any machine that can generate imaginative ideas – or for that matter evaluate them. And since everything we do in our business is based on getting and judging ideas, 'I am encouraged to go on', as Harold Ross of the *New Yorker* used to say.

If you have ever had to assess creative work, you know how hard it is; almost as hard as thinking it up – but not nearly as much fun. No matter how tactful you are, the people who had the idea will never thank you for anything short of pure adulation.

One reason many people find it hard to separate the sheep from the goats in creative work is that it's so easy to judge subjectively. Do you like the picture? Do you find the headline ingenious? Are you titillated by the snide remarks made about your competitors in the copy? All these are easy things to say 'yes' or 'no' to. Because people have no *objective* criteria, they tend to fall back on what they like – often what they find original, strange or funny.

The reason is that if you spend a lot of time (as we do) looking at selling communications, you become blasé. 'Oh! Not another headline announcing a new product' ... 'God! Not another free offer.' You've seen it all before – and you don't want to see it again.

Beware of becoming blasé

So you look for something different. Unfortunately, there is little evidence to suggest that something different necessarily sells, as we have already learned from the Ogilvy research mentioned at the beginning of Chapter 5. Your customers prefer you to be relevant, not clever or entertaining.

So, beware the siren call of the original.

Never is this truer than in headlines. For instance, I once received a mailing from Barclaycard to tell me I could use my card to get money out of cash machines all over the world. You might think a sensible heading to the leaflet would be: 'Now your card can get you cash anywhere in the world'.

Nothing of the sort. The heading said: 'The shape of things to come'. This was neither relevant nor original – indeed, it managed to be dull, whilst obscuring entirely what I wanted to know. The writer had undoubtedly started out by trying to be clever.

Of course, you can be as original as you like in general advertising – unless you have an interest in raising sales. A significant proportion of people in general advertising are interested above all in gaining awards. Indeed, research in Britain in 1991 revealed that the majority of creative directors believed aesthetic effect mattered more than sales results. And marketing directors often want to run commercials which their relatives and their friends at the golf club will applaud.

Unfortunately, their friends are not necessarily likely to be the same sort of people as our customers. What is greeted with squeals of delight by sophisticates of the communications industry may be greeted with an uninterested yawn by those who cough up the lolly. Worse, it can ruin your business.

A few years ago a UK retail chain hired world-famous Richard Avedon to take pictures around which they would create some advertisements. His work was superb – and rightly acclaimed. He took a beautiful black model and posed her in stunning and bizarre make-up. The campaign was showered with awards – and sales plummeted. The agency lost the account. The client could measure the sales, and didn't want to go broke.

Because direct marketing reveals what works and what doesn't (often in a way which upsets sensitive folk like me) bitter experience has given me a pretty comprehensive idea of what works and what doesn't. I have put together a series of laundry lists, therefore, to help you create more effective work, or if you are judging work, to judge it better.

There is no guaranteed success

I must warn you, though, that like most failsafe methods, these lists don't guarantee success. No two creative problems are identical; every market differs slightly from every other market; but the principles that make for success are usually the same. You are far more likely to succeed by using these lists; and when you decide not to follow their advice, at any rate you will do so *knowingly*, for good reasons. That's where your commonsense comes in.

Why formulae work

Despite what I have said already, you may still wonder whether working like this – to what is really a series of formulae – can help in something so quirky and personal as having ideas. Well, let's go back to the old definition of advertising being 'Salesmanship in print'. This is all very well, but face-to-face selling allows you to do things that are impossible when you cannot actually *see* the reactions of your audience.

For instance, I was once making a speech in Brisbane, Australia, at the height of summer when the air conditioning stopped working. I could immediately witness what effect this had on my audience: it put them to sleep. So I livened up my presentation.

You can't see the reaction of somebody receiving your direct mail shot or looking at your advertisement. You don't know what's going through their minds. And you can't vary your approach to fit in with their reaction. Once that mailing shot has gone out, it has gone out. Once that commercial runs, you can't change it.

The exception is telephone selling. You can quickly evaluate the way people react to particular lines in a telephone script, and alter it accordingly. But even the phone is very deceptive. You might be talking to somebody on the telephone, and saying something you find very witty. The person on the other end may misunderstand it – being unable to see the expression on your face – and even take it as an insult. Indeed, because I have a strange sense of humour, this has happened to me more than once.

A salesperson with a strong personality can break all the rules and still succeed. Twenty-odd years ago I sent a man up to Birmingham to sell £3,000-worth of fire extinguishers. He was so ill prepared he didn't even know how much they cost – and had to ring me up to find out. But his personality overcame his lack of preparedness: he came back with the order.

You can't hope for miracles like that when addressing people in print or broadcast. You need a logical sequence of argument. One that offends nobody, convinces as many as possible, and leaves out nothing which will help you achieve your objectives. For that you do need a formula – a set of rules.

A logical sequence is key

You will notice that some of the points listed here are mentioned elsewhere in the book. This is because these lists are not just to be looked at but to be *referred* to. I am trying to include everything that's relevant. In any case, even though I'm very familiar with all these points myself, I still forget them very often – so they bear repetition.

A famous copywriter was once asked how he apportioned his time. He said: 'I spend 90 per cent of my time thinking about how to approach the prospect before I even start writing. And of the remaining 10 per cent, I spend about half the time writing the envelope message and the beginning of the letter. The rest is easy.'

When you see an ad or mailing you may be struck by the compelling language, the brilliant visual, the elegant typography. All these things, if they are effective, come not simply from technique, but in the first place from how the communication has been planned in advance. Like the inner structure, deep foundations and steel, which support a building.

All this comes from proper preparation and careful evaluation of what you have done before you send it out.

Proper preparation and careful evaluation are key

For this reason, the first of my lists is perhaps the most important. Not only the most important, but also the most neglected, because as I have already pointed out, people are often far too inclined to get on with the job before they should even start it. That's simply because writing and drawing can be much more fun than hard thinking.

TWENTY-FIVE POINTERS BEFORE YOU WRITE A WORD OR SKETCH A LAYOUT

Not only should most of the work be done before you actually start writing or drawing; it is also at this point that most things could go wrong. The questions I am about to cover are those which should all be incorporated in a comprehensive brief – but rarely are.

1 What is the background?

What's going on in your business; what's happening in the market? By outlining this you will get a clearer picture of the problems and opportunities you face. Information about relevant reading and people worth talking to is always valuable.

Get a clearer picture

2 What is the objective?

Gather names? Provide qualified leads? Make firm sales? Get free trials? Different objectives require different solutions. To give one obvious example, it requires a great deal more copy to sell something expensive than to get a weakly qualified enquiry.

3 How much can you afford?

This should not be arbitrary but related to what you think can be achieved: what percentage response you anticipate, or how many replies – both of which must be related to the margin you have allowed yourself; which in turn is related to how much you are prepared to pay to get an enquiry or customer.

4 When is it wanted?

Obvious – but never lose sight of the deadline. One common mistake is to leave the delivery of the work to the last minute, which doesn't give time for it to be properly reviewed and considered. This is particularly common in agencies, where there are many jokes about the work being handed to the account executive as he gets into the taxi to go to the client's offices.

5 Are you clear on the positioning?

What will your message tell the prospect about your product or service? Does it fit in with your positioning? Or does it conflict?

6 Who are you selling to?

What are their hopes, fears, likes, dislikes, needs? Are they male or female? Young or old? Rich or poor?

Until you know these facts, you will not know what tone to adopt, let alone what to say. Try to visualise them, and think how they would talk, where they would live, and what they would do for a living, or for fun.

As discussed in the chapter on planning, 'who?' may well be the most important question of all in our business.

When considering your prospects, it is often worth dividing them into two types. First, the *natural* prospect. The person who is an obvious target for this product. Second, people who might be *persuaded* to buy. Beware of trying to kid yourself that what you are selling appeals to the whole wide world. This is extremely unlikely. To all intents and purposes, if you have covered these two groups, you've done all you should do. The best person to focus on is the perfect prospect.

7 What is it? And what does it do?

You'll remember I commented in the last chapter on how often people fail to describe what is being sold accurately. This often happens because an accurate description has not been written down at the start. Make sure it is.

Describe the product accurately

8 What need in your prospect does your product or service fulfil?

Here are nine basic human motivations. How many of them are relevant to your product or service?

People like to: make money, save money, save time and effort, help their families, feel secure, impress others, gain pleasure, improve themselves and belong to a group.

Common human motivations

You might be surprised at how many of these motivations can justify a purchase. Consider our old friend the American Express Card. I have calculated that every one of those human needs, save perhaps self-improvement, can be met to some degree through the range of benefits offered to card-members.

9 What makes it so special?

Interrogate your product or service. How does it differ from alternatives? Is it better, worse, cheaper, dearer? Is there something new about it? Does it replace anything? And what does it compete with? All these factors will give you an idea of what to say and – equally important – what to *avoid* saying, or to argue against. Included under this heading of what makes something special can be some peculiarity to do with the way the product was discovered, or its background.

What to say and what to *avoid*

For example, I mentioned earlier a new kind of spark plug which was sold a few years ago. One interesting thing about this was that it was discovered by a World War II test pilot. Keep an eye open for something interesting like this.

10 What benefits are you offering?

We covered this to some degree in the previous chapter. It is a very common error to talk to prospects about the characteristics of a product rather than the benefits: what it *is* rather than what it *does*.

What it *is* and what it *does*

Thus, when I was advertising the Business Ideas Letter, I could have said in my ad: 'Gives news of how other people are making money'. That was the characteristic of the newsletter. But the *benefit* was expressed in a very successful ad that said: 'Make up to £50 a week in your spare time.'

11 What do you consider the most important benefit?

Is there a unique benefit?

If you can find one that is unique, that would be ideal, since you would have no competition. Often what you are looking for is a single benefit or a combination of benefits which you consider to be appealing.

A good example is the calorie-coded Kathie Webber cookery cards for which I have reproduced advertisements in this book. The combination was learning to cook and health. When you have such a strong combination you may express them in more than one way – as I did.

12 Is there a good offer or incentive?

The words 'offer' and 'incentive' are interchangeable: they mean what we are prepared to give if the customer will act. Don't confuse this with a benefit, as some people do.

Always justify your offer

Always justify your offer. If you give something away without explanation, people assume – quite reasonably – that the cost is coming out of the value of the product they pay for. By implication you are degrading your product or service.

There are a number of possible explanations: eg, this is a slack time of year, so we are making an offer to keep our factories busy; or there is a recession, so we are prepared to offer a lower price; or we are willing to take less margin to gain extra business; or we're making an offer to get you as a new customer.

Thus when the Consumers' Association started using sweepstakes in the UK, they told the truth: sweepstakes attract so many people they are a cheaper way of recruiting new members – so you as a member of the Association ultimately benefit because they have lowered marketing costs.

Always try to link the offer or incentive to the desired action. Thus, you will give something if people reply quickly, or buy an extra item, or recommend a friend. The simplest reason for giving something I can recall is simply to say that people will receive something free 'just for reading this letter'. Here are 19 offers you can make:

Nineteen offers that work

- Free trial.
- Easy terms.
- Pay no interest – or less interest.
- Free gift for ordering.
- Free gift whether you keep product or not.
- Sweepstakes entry.
- No deposit.
- Nominal deposit.
- Temporary price offer.
- Buy now – pay in a few months, eg pay for your Christmas gifts in January.

- Sale.
- Two for one, and variations of this.
- End of stock close-out.
- Mystery gift.
- More than one gift.
- Discount or gift for quantity.
- Discount or gift for buying in a certain period.
- Double your money-back guarantee. (You must always check on the nature of the guarantee for a product or service.)
- We'll buy back from you after a certain period. (Sometimes used for investment products.)

Don't just say something is free, or cheap. Sell it. Make it sound desirable. And, as questioned, explain why you are offering it.

Sell your incentive – and justify it

Once you have discovered the most important benefit you offer, settled upon your positioning, determined your target audience and how best to reach them, it is the offer which will make most difference.

One reason why it pays to put the offer at the beginning of the communication is because, as I have already pointed out, offers serve *three* purposes: first to get people interested enough to read; second to get them eager to respond. If you put an offer up front and you don't think it's going to make somebody start reading, it probably isn't good enough. The third reason why incentives work is that they give people an excuse, assuaging their guilt about buying.

There are two types of offer. One is an offer logically related to your product. For instance when encouraging people to enquire about a financial service, then a booklet on how to organise your finances is not out of place.

The second kind of offer has *universal* appeal, to match products which are of appeal. Take the *Reader's Digest*, for example. Their potential readers can be interested in practically anything, and come from all walks of life. One extremely successful offer for them was miniature rose bushes. Others that seem to do well include clocks, watches, calculators and luggage. Everyone wants to know the time, to work out things; and most people travel.

The importance of the offer is difficult to overestimate. I would go so far as to say – indeed I have often said in public – that if you were to set aside a little time each day to think up new offers, you would become obscenely rich faster than you might believe possible.

One offer I liked was made by Procter & Gamble for Crest toothpaste in the United States. They ran television commercials inviting people to join a scheme whereby they would go to a nominated dentist and have their teeth checked. They were then required to use Crest toothpaste for six months, before having a further check up. If the toothpaste did not live up to everything claimed for it, they could get back the money they had spent on it during that period.

13 If you cannot make a good offer, can you say something very interesting or threaten a penalty?

Here are some examples.

Other ways to encourage replies

- New improved product.
- News item related to your product.
- Prices are about to rise. Buy now. (An extremely powerful motivator.)
- We don't know how long we can hold this offer open ... prices *may* rise.
- Lots of powerful testimonials. Once, when unable to say anything else about a slimming product, I just filled a page full of testimonials. It worked exceptionally well.
- We're repeating this offer because it was such a smash hit last time.
- We only have a certain number in stock.
- Specially imported from somewhere else where it was a great success. (More convincing than you might think: a margarine called Krona became a best seller in England largely because commercials told how it had been a sensation in Australia – a land famous for its *butter*.)

All the offers, or 'non-offers' mentioned in the last two points, are relevant when planning follow-up mailings to enquirers or past customers. This is important to remember. There is more profit lying dormant in enquiry lists and customer files than most firms imagine.

14 What lists, media or database selection will be used?

What happened previously?

Have they been used in the past and if so what happened? Is there any group of people who seem exceptionally responsive, or unresponsive? This will usually give you a clue to the motivations of those you are communicating with, and help you find new appeals for special groups.

15 What tests are you conducting?

Thinking up possible tests is itself a natural route to good creative ideas.

16 Put the product or service to the test

How to learn interesting things

Let somebody who would be interested buy it. See what they think. If you are selling a service, put it to the test. This will often reveal interesting things – like the fact that it is not very well run, or the staff don't return telephone calls

– or even answer them. Similarly, an amazing number of firms send out requested literature slowly or not at all.

17 Examples of previous promotions – those that did well and those that didn't

To see how relevant this is, let me tell you something that happened less than 24 hours before I wrote this passage.

I was discussing with a friend an offer two of my creative colleagues had devised which I think will do a tremendous job for the brand in question but probably won't get a very high level of response. He revealed that he had tried a similar offer for the same client three years previously and it had produced only an average response.

What has been done before?

I imagine that this fact lies buried somewhere in my client's files, but nobody thought to tell me. It certainly would have made a difference to our approach.

18 What about competitive material?

Surprisingly few briefs tell you what the competition is doing or give examples of their creative work. If marketing is, as is often suggested, like warfare, then this is like going into battle without knowing anything about your enemy's dispositions or previous victories and defeats.

19 Proofs and testimonials

Many – perhaps most – creative communications simply do not convince sufficiently. As I mentioned above, testimonials are extremely powerful, and any reputable company normally gets testimonials automatically from satisfied customers. They should be carefully collected.

You can encourage testimonials, by asking people to tell you what they think, or by using questionnaires. You can ask them to rank your service from one to five – that sort of thing. Often you can find scientific or impartial proof that what you say is true.

Ask people to tell you what they think

All these things give your product or service credibility – which is immensely valuable. The same applies to other sources of comment like celebrity endorsements and media comments. If you have any public relations running, then you must get good write ups or broadcast comment. Use them.

20 What about complaints?

A while ago I did some seminars in Australasia. We used questionnaires to gauge the audience's reaction, and I was delighted to see that 98 per cent thought that our performance was either good or excellent. However I

**Do better
next time**

learned more from the 2 per cent who disagreed. It helped me do better next time.

The same applies when selling. Find out what people *don't* like, then you know what objections to overcome. Obviously some objections are from cranks and must be ignored. But often you gain useful knowledge.

21 Any physical restrictions?

**Neglected
details cost
money**

This is so obvious I am embarrassed to mention it. Sometimes there are restrictions for one reason or other on the size or shape of envelopes or advertisements. It is no use the agency coming up with some brilliant full page idea when the client has stated quite clearly that they want small ads. A few years ago a mailing produced by one of the largest agencies in the world, for one of the best known clients in a particular field, lost them the account. It was brilliant but, unfortunately, it didn't fit through a lot of letter boxes.

22 What are the terms of the guarantee?

**Where
guarantees
work best**

Sometimes, as already observed, the guarantee can be of critical importance. Even if it is only there as a matter of reassurance, one needs to be aware of the exact terms. Money back guarantees are very persuasive when you are making a hard to believe claim. Conversely, firms with very high reputations have seen their responses decline if they have emphasised the money back guarantee. Up to that point the reader has always assumed they will do exactly what they promised: emphasis on the guarantee raises doubts.

23 How do people pay or reply?

**Make it easy
to pay**

Again, something so obvious it would hardly seem worth mentioning. Yet, for instance, telling people that they can pay by fax quoting their credit card number used to have a very significant impact on your orders and profitability. In a campaign in 1990 in Hong Kong 28 per cent of all orders came in by fax.

It is also useful to know how people have ordered in the past. How many order by telephone? Is there an 0800 number to make it easy for them? – that sort of thing. And now a huge percentage of orders and replies come via the internet – and people tend to look at your website before they decide whether to reply or not.

24 What style guidelines are there?

**When
certain
approaches
work better**

Some companies have a very clear style that they aim for. When I worked for the Franklin Mint, I quickly noticed that they had a unique way of writing and organising their copy. I had to master this before I could write copy for them, because not only did they adhere to this style of language: their customers had grown used to it, and probably would have been put off by anything else. I have seen cases in insurance where responses were affected by how closely the creative approach fitted in with what customers expect from an insurance company. Approaches that looked 'commercial' worked less well than those with a quasi-official appearance.

Some companies have strong views on humour. American Express, for instance, do not like humorous approaches. I think they are right: money is not funny. People kill for it.

25 Sacred cows

Often an agency comes up with what it thinks is a splendid approach to a problem, only for the client to say that the company doesn't believe in that sort of thing. One area is that of making specific comparisons with other companies. Some organisations love attacking their competition. Some consider it most ungentlemanly. As I have already indicated, I believe it depends on how you do it.

However, if the company has any constraints of this nature, the agency should be told about them in advance. This will save a lot of trouble.

Tell the agency your plans in advance

PLANNING YOUR CREATIVE TREATMENT

Back in 1957 when I came into the advertising business, the people who wrote and the people who drew were segregated. Generally I would write my copy and then it would be taken along to the studio, where somebody would put pictures to it. It was rare for us to spend much time talking about what we wanted to do. We worked in isolation.

In direct marketing agencies this segregation was given added force because copy has always been seen in our business as more important than art. Now, it is accepted that two people talking together and exchanging ideas are often more fruitful than each working in isolation. Indeed, it has now reached the stage where agencies frequently wish to hire a team rather than an individual. I think this is just as rigid as approaching the matter the other way.

The end of segregation

Whether you are a team, or a lonely individual, here is a list of points to refer to as you work towards a good creative treatment.

1 Your safest opening (though not always the best) is your prime benefit and incentive

On the envelope of a mailing. At the beginning of your letter. At the start of your brochure. At the commencement of your commercial. On the phone, too, once you have told the prospect who you arc and what you are talking about, the benefit and offer are normally the first things you talk about. (Assuming your prospect has agreed to listen to you.)

The benefit and the offer normally come first

2 Tricky, clever openings rarely work

Get to the point

Remember, the average ad is seen for perhaps two seconds, and each piece in a mailing package may be picked up and scanned briefly before the prospect decides to read or not. An *instant* statement, *instantly* comprehensible, is most likely to work.

Thus, one of the most effective headlines ever written in the insurance business is: 'Cash if you die. Cash if you don't'. Nothing clever about that, but it certainly got to the point.

But don't forget, teasers – as long as they are relevant – often work well on envelopes. As do broken messages, like the first half of a recipe, to which you can only find the conclusion by opening the envelope.

This ad was ten times better than the one it replaced because it made a clear, simple promise – and said a lot more.

3 Seek a dramatic central idea; preferably one that works in words and pictures

'Unless your campaign contains a big idea, it will pass like a ship in the night,' said David Ogilvy. I have already quoted one such idea in the point above. Another was produced for a Xerox mailing which incorporated a stopwatch to dramatise the speed with which the product would be delivered (illustrated on page 220).

     If you can have an idea which is both visual and written, perfect! And if that word-picture combination *demonstrates* – as the stopwatch did – even better (see point 5). Finding a strong idea is vital. That's why you shouldn't just settle for the first one you come across. If you only examine one idea, it's a little like buying one lottery ticket, when for very little more you could get ten – and multiply your chances. Seek plenty of alternatives. Work hard!

Word-picture combinations are perfect

4 Is it the right length?

When asked how long copy should be, an Indian colleague said: 'How much string do you need to wrap a parcel?'

     The length should fit the objective. A complete sale takes more persuasion than an enquiry. An enquiry about something important, where big money is involved or a difficult decision has to be made, calls for more copy than where the matter is trivial. Obviously it's easier to sell something cheap than to sell something expensive, just as it's easier to sell a new product with no competition than an old product with lots of competition. However, a new product may require a lot of explanation if it is unfamiliar, whilst a well known product will require little.

The length should fit the objective

     One thing to remember is the impact of the brand name. If it is famous, you will require less persuasive copy than if it is unheard of.

     Because long copy almost always outpulls short, bad writers often write far too much. All you have to do is give *every* sensible reason why your prospects would want to act and overcome *every* reasonable objection to acting. Never use a single word more than required. And don't forget, get rid of unnecessary adjectives – 'exciting', 'fantastic' and the like.

5 Can you give a test drive?

When preparing your work, remember what I said earlier: what do salespeople do? A salesperson would try to demonstrate the product. Good communications do the same thing, in words or in pictures or both. Sometimes a direct mail pack can *literally* demonstrate the product – as in the burnt letter featured in the last chapter. Nothing convinces more than an involving demonstration.

Demonstrate the product

6 If your name is well known, feature it strongly

As I have pointed out to you, this could double your response. But make sure it is well known. Most people can only remember about three brands in a product category, until they are prompted. Even then they can usually only remember about seven.

Lead with the benefit and offer

For this reason, if your company is not well known, you may find it pays to lead your letters with your benefit and offer (your 'headline') and put your letterhead at the *base* of the page.

7 In mailings, give great thought to the envelope

Remember the shape, the texture, the colour can all influence response. When wondering whether you should have a message on the envelope, remember that *normally* the answer is 'yes'. The editor of 'Who's Mailing What' in the US analysed the most successful mailings in that country. Over 70 per cent had envelope messages. And don't forget that texture, colour, shape and brand names are all envelope 'messages'.

The most successful mailings in the US

Remember, the offer, or a hint of it, should usually go on the envelope, together with an indication that people must reply quickly.

Don't forget that envelopes have fronts and backs and insides. If there's a window envelope, there's a space behind that. That can be used also.

Some mailers use the entire inside of the envelope to put testimonials on. I have also seen it used as an additional order form.

8 The letter is the key element in direct mail, the most personal part of the communication

The letter comments, amplifies, makes more human, 'sells' the facts in the other material.

People like getting letters

People expect to receive a letter. They like getting letters. If you can't afford a costly mailing, then leave out the brochure, not the letter. (On one occasion an American insurance company left a beautiful horoscope brochure out of a birthday mailing to customers by accident. Sales jumped 25 per cent.)

You can get the best of both worlds by illustrating your letter – but make sure it's still in the letter 'convention'. Test a typewriter-style font.

9 How many pieces should there be in a mailing?

The letter is the salesperson – the brochure is the store

The principle here is similar to that on length of copy. The more you have to say or can say, very often the more pieces you can usefully put in. The common analogy is that the letter is the salesperson, whilst the brochure is like the store. This is not exactly true, but the brochure is probably going to put over the same arguments as the letter with illustrations and in a slightly different tone – it's just less personal.

It may be that you find the need for other pieces. Suppose you have a lot of testimonials or press comments: these could go on another piece of material. Suppose you have decided to have a sweepstake; that may be featured in a further piece. I have already mentioned the lift letter which reminds people that the offer is so good they shouldn't turn it down (page 282).

These letters used to cause some amusement when first introduced. They always said on the outside: 'Only open this if you are thinking of saying *no* to this offer.' Inside the copy would begin: 'Frankly, I am amazed ...' whereupon the writer would express his astonishment that anyone should turn down such a great opportunity.

If you want to see how an elaborate mailing should be put together, look at one by *Reader's Digest* or by *Time-Life*.

Overly sophisticated marketing people are cynical about such mailings. But every element has been tested and retested year after year.

They are probably not selling the same sort of product as you, but if you examine them carefully you will pick up a great deal about what to do and what not to do. One thing you should note particularly when looking at *Reader's Digest* material is how careful they are to tell – very often at the *beginning* of a letter – how easy it is to respond and exactly how to do so.

How to learn what to do

You will also notice that they lay overwhelming emphasis on the *incentive*. Having done their best to create a good product, and having a fine reputation, they know as long as they illustrate and describe the product appealingly, *the* critical factor is the incentive.

ELEVEN UNCREATIVE (BUT TESTED) WAYS TO MAKE YOUR LAYOUT WORK HARDER

I have pursued my career so far without being able to draw anything except a cartoon of my dog. Thus, I may seem little-qualified to comment on good or bad art direction. But I am heartened by the fact that many art directors aren't too impressive when it comes to draughtsmanship. The reason for this is that visual *ideas* and *good design* matter most.

Visual ideas and good design matter most

Unfortunately, just as most copywriters direct a turgid stream of clichés at their unfortunate readers, so most art directors hanker after self-defeating layout formats. If you look through any publication, you will see that over half the ads fly in the face of tested principles of visual comprehension. Or, to put it in another way, they are hard to take in and hard to read.

Self-defeating layout formats

God knows, it's hard enough trying to entice people into paying attention to your message without making them struggle to wade through it.

Accordingly, here are some *facts* about what makes for easy visual comprehension. These statements are not based on opinion, but upon research into what works and what doesn't. In particular, I would like to acknowledge the work of Colin Wheildon of New South Wales University. For two years he conducted research into the effect of layout upon comprehension. He worked with 224 subjects to discover what they found easy to read and comprehend, and what they didn't. Then he carried on for a few years more, just to make certain, and wrote an excellent book called *Type & Layout: How typography and design can get your message across – or get in the way.*

I don't suggest you follow these guidelines slavishly. But why ignore them unless you have to?

First, here are ways to make life easier for the reader to take in your message:

1 Easy-to-read typefaces

Most daily newspapers are set in serif type, in caps and lower case. The type will be roman, and most of it is set in black on white rather than reversed out. Most of the body will be in upper and lower case, not capitals. This is because these things are all easy to read. And that is because:

- The serifs – or little feet – at the bottom of letters line up to keep the eye moving horizontally along the line of type, rather than straying below to the next line. That's why if you wish to use sans-serif faces, you should have heavy leading between each line.
- The eye recognises shapes more than letters and a word in capitals has less shape than the word in caps and lower case.
- The eye finds it tiring to read reversed out type in any great volume. Reversing out of copy has been known to *halve* response.

The eye does not find it difficult to read serif italic type, by the way.

Use sans-serif in moderation

Let me emphasise, this is not a plea for the wholesale banishment of sans-serif faces, capitals or reversing out. I am merely suggesting you use these in moderation.

Wheildon found that on an A4 page sans-serif type reduced comprehension from 67 per cent to 12 per cent. Imagine losing such a percentage of your sales!

2 Clear contrast

Just as reversed out type is difficult to read, type set over tints or textures or colours, so that it does not stand out clearly, is even more difficult to read.

Ensure people can read the type easily

Equally, very small type is not a good idea: lots of people (including me) can't read it very easily. Indeed, around one person in ten has poor eyesight. And when you consider that the difference between success and failure for an ad may well be 10 per cent, that's worth thinking about. And don't forget, older people, who have more money, have worse eyesight.

3 Don't change typefaces unnecessarily

Constant changes in typeface are ugly. If they are in a headline, they are also confusing: your eye doesn't like constantly having to readjust.

4 Narrow measure

You will note in your newspaper or magazine that the words are set in narrow columns. That's because the eye likes to travel down the centre of a column if it can, rather than having to go back and forth all the time.

If possible, don't set to a measure wider than about 50 characters. (You may ask why this book isn't set that way. Well, frankly, I don't know, but many paperbacks are set to a much narrower measure.)

5 Long unbroken blocks of type are hard to read

Big blocks of type are daunting. To the reader they look like great trudges through the desert. Moreover, when the eye first looks at a layout, it tends to flit around like a butterfly before settling.

For that reason, you should break up your copy with lots of crossheads, subheads, and changes of width. This makes it interesting to look at. It also enables the reader to learn the essence of your message from the subsidiary headings, which should make it interesting enough for him or her to want to start reading the body copy.

Break up your copy

To encourage readers to do this, it's often a good idea to have an explanatory subhead after the headline leading into the copy. A 'dropped' – ie oversized – initial capital letter also encourages readership.

6 Try to justify your columns

Comprehension goes down if the edges of columns, either left or right, are unjustified – that is to say, ragged. Once again, this is because the eye has to work harder.

Don't make the eye work harder

7 Huge headings are stupid

Art directors love them. But people do not read these things from the other side of the room. Nor do they have arms 10 feet long. Large headings are a waste of space and a waste of time.

Don't waste space

What reduces readership

8 A headline should be a headline, not a baseline

Sometimes people design clever layouts where the headline is beneath the body copy. They turn them into baselines. You will not be surprised that all this does is stop people from reading the copy at all. Wheildon found readership was greatly reduced as a result of this practice.

9 Don't mislead the reader's eye

The eye is lazy

The reason for the last point is that putting the headline below the copy *misleads* the reader; and the eye is lazy: gravity forces it down, not up. In the same way, illustrative elements which point out of the layout – like people's feet, or the direction in which they look – lead the reader's eye out of the advertisement. Also, illustrations which block off a column halfway up the page discourage the reader from travelling further down. The eye may simply go straight to the top of the next column, thus omitting the section *beneath* the illustration.

10 Make the coupon easy to cut out

Don't maroon it in the middle of a page so that people have to make four cuts to get it out. And don't give it a fancy shape. The origami school of coupon cutting has never flourished.

I once saw an advertisement prepared by a very well known agency in which the coupon was designed in the shape of the product. Ninety per cent of the (very few) respondents had gone to the trouble of cutting out this bizarre shaped coupon. I wondered how many couldn't be bothered. (And don't print your coupon on a funny colour on which it's impossible to read anything, or make it tiny. Both are more common than you might imagine.)

11 Lay out your letters

Use serif face and give them shape

Just as advertisements should be laid out to be interesting to the eye, so should letters. You should always use a serif face for ease of reading).

So indent at the beginning of each paragraph, indent whole sections and use numbered points or asterisks, just as you should in long-copy advertisements and brochures.

The use of second colour, 'handwritten' notes in the margins, underlinings and the *occasional* word in capitals can all add variety and interest for eye and brain. I don't think you should justify both sides of a letter. It looks unnatural.

... and two qualifications

I lay down so many rules that I realise I am in danger of being seen as an old curmudgeon. That's why I am at pains from time to time to emphasise that I am certainly not always right.

When considering layout and typography one has to say that views certainly vary. A traditional one – that typography is an art or science to help you communicate better – has been questioned. This questioning arises from one of two ways of thinking; and sometimes both. These are:

● That the typography itself by its appearance (usually bizarre, novel or even downright ugly) signals to the potential reader something about the nature of the product or merchandise or communication.

Unusual typography sends a signal

Thus, on launching a publication designed to appeal to young, unconventional people (or at any rate people wishing to conform to a different convention) magazines have deliberately formulated a typographical style which flies in the face of just about every fundamental typographical given.

Classic examples of this are magazines aimed at young people. Here, typographical styles – sans-serifs, reverse outs, all sorts of eclectic design features – are used to signal non-conformity and rebellion. It often seems to work. The typography in effect is saying: 'Do you like to be different? Do you like to break the rules? Then join us!'

In a way, such layouts have established their own new form of non-conformist conformity.

One of the consequences of this form of typography is of course that to read such stuff you have to make a real effort. Which leads us to the second theory of the new typography:

● You should be required to make a deliberate effort to penetrate the message. This extra effort means that the reader is more likely to take it in and relate to it more effectively by being more involved.

Encourage greater involvement

Candidly, I have no research to support either of these theses. Nevertheless, perhaps there is a certain logic behind them. And I certainly believe you should be aware of them. In any case, I think it is quite possible to combine unconventional approaches with legibility.

Colin Wheildon is so emphatic about serif type being better, but the research he conducted was only into printed material; nobody has done similar studies of how type affects people when viewed on a computer screen. There is a theory that the screen makes the serifs very indistinct, so they don't do their job, but nobody has proved this. Amazon mixes serif with sans-serif, which is probably the answer, but yet again testing will tell you what works best.

Captions are very important: they are heavily read.

This classic layout is by far the easiest for readers to follow.

This subhead makes transition into the body copy easier for the reader.

Dropped initial caps like this also lure people into the body of the copy.

Moreover, a short first paragraph like the one above makes it easier for people to get started on your story. And there are other things to remember.

For example, readers find it easier to take in short words, sentences and paragraphs - with the latter containing only one or two thoughts.

Why is this?

Because people are not really concentrating when they read copy, and won't make the effort to grasp difficult thoughts - even if they are intelligent, which many aren't.

Crossheads tell the story

Breaking your copy up with crossheads makes it far more digestible for the reader than one unbroken block of words.

The crosshead should not be clever or tricksy, but should communicate and encapsulate the story for people whose eyes are hovering over your ad.

Many people imagine that advertisements are read religiously from start to finish. Would that it were so! In fact, readers tend to start where they please, and stop reading when they please. Very few advertisements indeed get read in full.

Bold elements attract

We use bold elements - headings, illustrations, the like - to lead people into the advertisement. For that reason, all these elements must work very hard. Unless one of them catches the eye, your ad will fail.

The most important element is the headline/picture combination. Together they should communicate almost instantly what the advertisement is all about, and if possible demonstrate the benefits.

This is utterly vital, because research years ago revealed two important facts: first, most advertisements are never seen for longer than two or three seconds; and second, that most are never read beyond the headline.

Captions important

After headline and picture the things that people's eyes generally turn to most are captions. As children we learned to read by looking at pictures with explanations under them. So it is very unwise to have a picture without a caption.

Sometimes, of course, the headline itself acts as a caption. Generally speaking, if you cannot find anything interesting to say about your picture, then the chances are it is not a good picture.

Bold coupons help

One element which will actually increase readership of your advertisement is the presence of the coupon. What is more, the bolder the coupon, the higher the readership and the response is likely to be.

Pay no attention to languid aesthetes who tell you that coupons will kill your image. I have yet to see any evidence to suggest this is so.

Sample coupon
Return address for the coupon
Name
Address
Postcode
Telephone no.

Figure 11.1 Layout styles

Reversed out copy kills readership - though many people don't know it.

A reversed-out full page charity ad doubled response when it was reset in black on white.

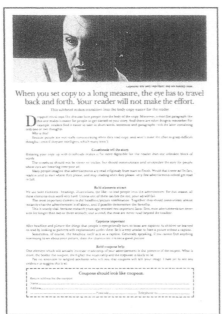

When you set copy to a long measure, the eye has to travel back and forth. Your reader will not make the effort.

This subhead makes transition into the body copy easier for the reader.

Don't block off two columns like this. People won't keep reading below the illustration

When the headline is placed below copy, many cannot be bothered to move their eyes up to start reading.

Figure 11.1 (continued)

A badly positioned coupon can reduce response

If you set your copy in sans serif type you pay a heavy price indeed

CAPS ARE DIFFICULT TO READ BECAUSE THE EYE RECOGNISES SHAPES - NOT INDIVIDUAL LETTERS

Justified - OK

Ranged Left - harder

Ranged Right - Very hard

Centred - Crazy

Figure 11.1 (continued)

Authorised and Regulated by the Financial Services Authority. Registered in England and Wales 3509545.
Directors: Adam Norris, Peter K. Hargreaves FCA, Stephen P. Lansdown FCA,
M. Theresa Barry BSc, Nigel J. Bence BA (Hons).
Hargreaves Lansdown Pensions Direct Ltd; Registered office at address shown.

HARGREAVES LANSDOWN

Pensions Direct Limited

Kendal House
4 Brighton Mews
Clifton, Bristol
BS8 2NX

Telephone: 0800 138 2121
Fax: 01 17 98 09 820
www.hargreaveslansdown.co.uk

Would you like to make more of your pension fund?

If like many people your personal pension fund is one of your largest assets, I expect you are eager to give it the potential to generate the best retirement income possible?

If so, you may be keen to learn more about what is becoming an extremely popular choice for the astute investor – a self invested personal pension.

Self Invested Personal Pensions (SIPPs)
Despite the name, there is nothing complicated about a self invested personal pension. It is simply a tax efficient pension wrapper that gives you far greater flexibility to invest your pension where you wish than a conventional personal pension plan.

Where can I invest?
Investing in a SIPP can be as simple or sophisticated as you like. If you are busy, you may wish to leave the main investment decisions to top fund managers such as Fidelity, Jupiter and New Star to name but a few. Alternatively you can make all the decisions yourself and trade in stocks and shares from the UK, Europe and the USA as well as in numerous other investments.

So how do I choose the right investments?
Before you take out a SIPP our investment research team will provide you with excellent information to enable you to make your own investment decisions. Once your SIPP has been set up you will receive regular valuations with sector analysis and brief comments on most of the investments you hold plus regular information on new investment opportunities.

But aren't SIPPs expensive?
Traditionally yes, but not any more. Our Vantage SIPP for example has no set up fee, no transfer in fee and if you invest in a choice of over 800 funds we charge no annual fee. You will also receive an extremely competitive interest rate for any money you hold in cash.

PTO

Figure 11.2 The type-face, courier, repeatedly gets better results than more modern faces.

THIRTEEN ATTENTION-GRABBERS

Just as there are proven rules which make replying easier, there are many facts known about what tends to attract attention. Here are thirteen to remember:

1 'Busy' layouts often seem to pull better than 'neat' ones

In one split-run test on catalogue pages, a 'busy' layout out-pulled a neat one by 14 per cent. So it seems those little flashes and panels that art directors loathe add interest. Where you can introduce them without making the layout look like a dog's dinner, why not do so?

2 Vary shapes, sizes and colours

Just as the eye is bored with regular shapes, people lose interest if all the elements in a mailing package are the same size and the same colour, or if all the mailings in a sequence are to the same format.

Vary your colours, vary your shapes, vary your sizes in individual communications and sequences. Try a huge typewriter face, or a giant order form – or a Lilliputian letter.

Experiment!

3 Of all illustrative techniques, the cartoon attracts most attention

However, see my comment below about photographs before you put cartoons in all your ads.

4 One large picture attracts more attention than lots of small ones

5 A picture of somebody staring out of the page at you attracts attention

People look at people: and men look at men more than at women – and vice versa. Similarly, women look most at babies.

6 Colour will attract attention

But it is only appropriate where the product itself demands colour to convey its appeal. In a series of tests we conducted to sell records, colour was *not* cost-effective in four cases out of five.

7 Putting something odd into a picture will attract attention

One famous campaign which did this was David Ogilvy's for Hathaway shirts, in which the model always wore a black eye-patch.

8 Too many extraneous props divert attention

So, make the product the hero. This is particularly important in TV commercials. Make sure your *actor* is not more interesting than his *pitch*.

Even in an ordinary ad you can get some surprising results from using eye-catching props. I recall a campaign 40 years ago for a curtain material in which a cute teddy bear was used as a prop. More people wanted to know where to get the bear than where to get the product.

Make sure the product is the hero

9 Extreme close-ups of a product attract attention

But make sure they are not so close that you cannot identify the product.

Make sure you can identify the product

10 Be careful where you put your headline

Tests with an eye camera revealed that the eye tends to settle naturally around the middle of the page. So don't put your headline at the top of the space, above the picture. Put it below. In a series of four tests, we found that response went up by between 27 per cent and 105 per cent in the latter case.

Where does the eye settle?

11 Use tables and graphs when conveying complex information

Tables definitely increase response where relevant. In an insurance mailing, response increased when the size of the benefit table was doubled.

12 It pays to use layout styles that make coupons look 'valuable'

Use the sort of designs that you see on currency.

Attention grabbers

13 But will they believe what they see?

Point 12 shows how a visual signal can make your message more convincing. Often, even if people are attracted by what they see, and find it easy to take in, they still may not believe what you say. Good art direction can do much to help.

- Photographs are more convincing than drawn illustrations. I learned many years ago that a photograph can sometimes increase response by over 50 per cent.

  This is hardly surprising when you think about it, yet frequently people use illustrative techniques for no reason other than personal preference. Short of sending a sample, nothing can be more convincing than photography.

- 'Before and after' pictures are very persuasive. Seek opportunities to use them. People believe what they want to believe – and a before and after is a wonderful way to dramatise it. So much so that on more than one occasion I have even seen before and after *drawings* – clearly not realistic – work well.

- Positive 'reward' pictures tend to work better than negative 'problem' pictures. This is not surprising. Most people like rewards more than threats. A classic instance of this is insurance advertising; telling people about the dreadful things that will happen to their family if they die is not as effective as displaying how much their family will get.

  The only area where negative approaches seem to work is in pharmaceutical products and the like. For instance, advertisements with themes revolving around the words: 'Oh, my aching back!'

- Don't use illustrations that do nothing. That may sound a strange thing to say, but if you look through many advertisements the product is merely *shown* when, with a little effort, it could have been *demonstrated*.

  I have touched upon the importance of demonstrations in TV. But it is equally true that a still picture which demonstrates the product works better than one which doesn't.

A consistent visual tone is vital

- A consistent visual tone is vital. I have already talked about the importance of positioning. This positioning must be respected in everything you do, everything you say – and that includes the 'look' of the things you do. Otherwise people get confused – and you start to lose conviction.

  Why should this be? Imagine if each time you saw a salesman he had a totally different appearance. One day wearing a sober suit. The next appearing in jeans and T-shirt. One day speaking quietly and sincerely. The next day bubbling with superlatives.

  Either approach might work well, depending on what he was selling. But alternating between the two is confusing and diminishes conviction.

- Break down the product or service visually. Show the fine details of the way it is finished, or put in panels which show different aspects of a service or product.

  You can show the fine stitching on a suit. Or illustrate in a series of shots precisely how a customer's query is dealt with. Or show the various points in a kitchen where craftsmanship is superior.

  All these things convince people they are getting good value for money, and that you have taken trouble to provide it.

Faces add credibility

- Showing the faces of people who give testimonials, and reproducing those testimonials in facsimile adds credibility. You should also put in their signatures if possible, and – if their statements are used in headings – put quote marks around them. This increases response.

● Don't use pictures just for the sake of it. Often, particularly in the financial field, illustrations are there for no reason. Ask: why is this here? What is it doing?

TRICKS AND TECHNIQUES THAT KEEP PEOPLE READING

In the 1940s a man called Rudolph Flesch devoted a great deal of time to discovering what makes for easier reading. Many of the hints that follow come from him.

Here are seven writer's tricks that keep people reading.

1 Use short sentences. They are easier to read and understand

The easiest sentence to read is eight words. The average length of sentence for easy reading is 16 words. Any sentence longer than 32 words tends to be hard to read.

2 Use short paragraphs

Make sure each paragraph contains just one thought, if possible. People don't read copy with great attention. Selling messages are driftwood on the surface of life.

Include one thought per paragraph

Try to make the first paragraph in any piece short – preferably only one sentence long. This is particularly important if the piece itself is very long. That first short sentence makes it easier to get into.

3 Count the number of times the word 'you' is used in your copy

There is a direct relationship, Flesch discovered, between effective selling and the use of that word. Talk about your prospect, not yourself. Certainly the word 'you' should occur at least two to three times as often as any reference to 'I' or 'we'.

Talk about your prospect

4 Use guile to keep people reading

End a column or page half-way through a sentence so people have to keep going. Eg 'This week we are offering a special discount of ... Next page, please.' (Always be polite enough to ask people to keep reading.)

Break up sentences

5 Use 'carrier' words and phrases at the ends and beginnings of sentences and paragraphs

Keep people reading

Once you have got people reading, you want to keep them moving. So anything you can do to signal that some added, interesting information is coming up is a good idea. Good tricks include: ending and beginning paragraphs with questions, so that the reader clearly has to read on to find out the answers. Other tricks include starting sentences and paragraphs with words like 'Also ...', 'Moreover ...', 'For instance ...', 'What is more ...', 'And ...'.

The secret is to read through what you have written and, as you come to the break between paragraphs, ask yourself if anything tempts people to keep reading.

6 Don't use pompous Latinisations

Be yourself

Use short, Anglo-Saxon based words. Don't say 'momentarily' when you mean 'soon'. When you use 'posh' words – the kind you would not use in your ordinary conversation – you become false. You also become obscure.

When writing, be yourself.

7 Don't use three words where one will do

Use simple language

'Now' is much better than 'At this point in time'. An 'emergency situation' is 'an emergency'.

Nobody has time to meander through your copy. They are more concerned about their dog being ill, or the wife playing around with the man next door, or the rent being due.

A digression here. Jerry della Femina, author of the best book I have read about what it feels like to work in advertising (*From Those Wonderful Folk who Gave you Pearl Harbor*) described his idea of the perfect ad. It goes:

Have you a dollar and have you piles? Send us your dollar and we'll cure your piles. Or keep your dollar and keep your piles.

This is a wonderful example of simple, effective language, apart from being funny.

One very important point. It is far easier to over-write and then cut than under-write and expand. Why, I do not know, but it is.

CHARITY ADVERTISING: A SPECIAL CASE

In reviewing charity advertising, you must remember that it has its own peculiar demands and its own particular problems.

People are usually tempted to dramatise the *miseries* of the particular situation. They're even tempted to be clever – I gave the instance earlier on of fresh food flying into Biafra daily. I also quoted the Dr Barnardo's case of the frightening truth about the new adoption shops.

I can think of others equally unsuccessful: 'Colin will be eight years old for the rest of his life' – referring to a retarded child. And: 'How Snow White and the 57 dwarfs helped Martin talk' – an involved story about a pantomime.

The secret of successful charity advertising starts with realising that in this area, perhaps more than any other, emotion is all important. People give from their hearts, not their heads. Thus, a headline I wrote a few years ago: 'How much would you pay to give a lost little girl a start in life?' did very well. Other headlines that have done well include: 'Won't you play Santa to a lonely little girl?', 'This Christmas help make a blind man see. £10.' Or: 'For £7.64 you can buy her safe water for life.'

Here are some guidelines for charity messages:

People give from their hearts, not their heads

1 Ask for a specific sum

Thus, for Save the Children: 'Won't you give £10 to save 10 children's lives?' Asking people to give generously is simply not enough. Talking about deadly perils is not enough either. You must tell people how much money is needed as well as how much you hope they will give. Eg: 'It costs £2,500 every three months to provide drugs.' Or: '2,000 doses of antibiotic cost just £42.'

2 Three critical elements

Successful headlines often contain three elements. For instance, in the headline I quoted above for Save the Children, we have:

- a problem (children's lives need to be saved);
- a solution the reader can supply, and thus feel good (you can save the children's lives);
- something which makes it sound easy (£10 is not a lot of money).

3 Come right out with it

Don't be cowardly about asking for money. Always ask people for more than you think they are likely to give. They won't feel insulted – on the contrary. And you will probably raise the average value per donation.

Ask for more money

4 Be personal

People give to people – individual people – not causes. That is why it is a good idea to feature a particular person in the advertisement. And have them looking at the recipient.

Feature a person

5 Sound the alarm

Emergencies are the best source of revenue. If you can make a situation sound like an emergency, do so. If there *is* an emergency, then for goodness sake shout from the rooftops.

6 Christmas spirit

Christmas is the time when people give most. At that time *always* include the word 'Christmas' in your headlines. It focuses people's minds.

7 Be precise

Tell people what their money will do

Tell people what their money will do, and how much money is necessary. For instance, UK tax rates went down under Margaret Thatcher. Good news for everyone – except the charities, because charities can claim back from the Government the tax that the donor would have had to pay. Thus, where previously the top rate of tax was 60 per cent, it became 40 per cent. Ergo: a drop in revenue for charities.

A mailing I saw to donors from one charity explained this problem but did not *quantify* it. It was not precise. It didn't say how much money this charity was actually likely to lose as a result of this change in the law. This is a fatal error.

8 Suggest an amount

Put specific sums in the coupon or order form starting with the highest sum and going down to the lowest, that people can give – plus a box with a blank so they can give any other sum they choose.

9 Be amateur-seeming

Look cheap

People like charities to use their money wisely. That's why you should mention how little money is wasted on administration; and why charity ads very often work better if they are set by the newspaper, and look cheap.

In a series of tests for Help the Aged, we found that setting our ads in reproduction typewriter face significantly lifted response.

WHAT TO WATCH FOR IN BROADCAST

Many things that go wrong in broadcast are quite simple. Many stem from the fact that time is limited. People who are used to writing direct mail, or long copy, find it very hard to adjust to the needs of broadcast.

That's why my first point – though apparently a very obvious one – is extremely important.

1 Don't over-write

The number of words you can get into a commercial is normally no more than three times the number of seconds.

2 Don't cheat when timing

Because people like to cram as much as they can into a commercial, they cheat when reading it out to time it. They gabble, and don't allow for the silences that will occur in that commercial. Don't do this.

Allow for silences

3 How long should it be?

Have you arbitrarily selected a particular commercial length, or are you suiting the length to the objective? If all you want is a simple enquiry, you need no more than 10 seconds. If you wish to sell something, you're very unlikely to be able to do it in under 90 seconds.

Suit the length to the objective

4 Poor presentation

Explaining to people who don't understand the medium what a commercial is going to look like is hard. Traditionally storyboards have been used. These are a series of frames, each with a description of the action and the script under them. Most people find this hard to take in. Other alternatives have been to use 'animatics' – stills which a camera roams over to give an illusion of action, accompanied by a soundtrack. That's easy to understand but expensive.

In the early stages of presenting commercials, I counsel you to do so by *describing* them. Tell the story, merely showing one or two key visuals. Trying to go through a series of 10 to 12 frames, explaining what's going on in each frame and also reading the script, is very difficult indeed.

Present by describing

5 Don't sell too literally

In the need to convey the wonders of the brilliant idea you've dreamed up, you may be tempted to produce very detailed visuals, or write very detailed treatments. (A treatment is a description of the commercial without the actual script.)

Being too detailed often creates a problem. When the commercial is finally produced, the client may say: 'But in the third frame you presented originally, you had a large rock on the right – why isn't it there now?'

Avoid too much detail

6 Choosing the production company

The choice of production company – and in particular director – is crucial. Pricing can vary phenomenally. But your judgement should not be on price alone: it should start with looking at a show reel, assessing whether a particular director can do a good job for you and – most important – asking yourself if you can get on with him or her. Then think about price.

Pricing can vary phenomenally

7 Missing out on key stages

Be there at every key stage

Once you have recovered from the thrill of dreaming up your epic, you may be tempted to skip out boring but essential details that have to be gone through as this dream becomes reality. You must make sure you're present at every key stage, without actually getting in the way.

It is particularly tempting to skip pre-production discussions. But working out how long it's going to take to produce your commercial and what's going to be needed is very important.

8 Don't be daunted

Stick to your plan

There's such a mystique about the broadcast media that sometimes people are reluctant to say to the director: 'This isn't what I had in mind.' The director himself may pose as an expert, not merely on directing, but on copywriting. Don't let this happen. I promise that if things go wrong, you'll carry the can before the director does. Make sure your original vision is retained, unless you are quite sure the changes suggested really are improvements.

9 Pay attention to editing

Editing sounds a very technical business. It isn't. Spending time watching while somebody edits a commercial, making sure you get what you want and you don't get what you don't (without trying to be bossy) is essential. Many great directors have started out as editors. You can't make good commercials unless you pay attention to editing.

10 Approach it step by step

Because of the mystique I have referred to, and because you may not be familiar with making commercials, the process will seem terribly complicated.

It isn't really. It simply has to be approached with the same care as anything else. It's just that you have a different set of things to worry about.

Personally, my overwhelming feeling about broadcast is that it can be extremely tedious (on the set, as far as I can make out, the only person who ever has fun is the director). Despite this it's a tremendous challenge. What is more, it is increasingly important in our business.

Five things to re-check

Broadcast may have its own demands, but it is not *all* that different from any other medium. What you're trying to do is the same. You're trying to attract attention and lead people through to a sale.

However, here are five things I would look out for with particular attention in reviewing your broadcast ideas.

1 What's the idea? Is it *really* a big idea?
2 Is the *technique* stronger than the content? Are you relying upon dancing and singing rather than the strength of the idea?
3 If you switched the sound off, would the pictures communicate the idea? And vice versa? Neither of these things is essential – but they sure help.
4 Are you using 'supers' – words over the screen which communicate the benefits? These can be very powerful and certainly increase memorability.
5 Do the scenes flow logically one after another? If they don't, you're in trouble. The thing may jar or be incomprehensible.

Things to look out for

A simple way to find out is to get somebody in off the street and ask them whether they understand what the commercial is all about. It sounds obvious – but few people think of doing it. I did this once for a commercial I thought was too fast to be comprehensible. It wasn't and it sold a shipload – literally – of previously unsaleable Philips radios.

NOW THAT YOU THINK IT'S PERFECT HAVE YOU FORGOTTEN ANYTHING?

Most of our communications are rather like aeroplanes. Whether it's a commercial, a mailing shot or an advertisement, once it's gone out, that's it. You can't call in 3 million pieces of paper because you just had a good idea. You can't stop the printing presses to change your headlines.

So it's vital that after you think you've finished creating or perfecting your message, you check again to make sure you haven't missed something out. This admonition is not just to the writer and the art director; it is addressed with particular force to those of you with orderly minds – the account handler and the client. Writers and art directors often get carried away. And as a former colleague of mine in India, Mani Ayer, once observed: 'The obvious is always overlooked.'

'The obvious is always overlooked'

Here are areas I think you should pay particular attention to – especially when you think you've done everything. (You won't be surprised that I have mentioned some of them before.)

1 Have you included every convincing reason for responding?

Go back to your planning stage and make sure it's all included. (But don't forget that if you are only going for an enquiry, you don't have to tell the full story ... just enough to get your prospect keenly interested.)

Be convincing

2 Is there anything you've taken for granted?

Mention everything

Your guarantee, your money-back offer, even the fact that you are selling direct?

These things may be boring to you through familiarity but they are important to your sale. That's perhaps why a common omission is describing and showing the product properly. I once forgot to say whether a magazine was weekly or monthly.

3 Have you built in maximum credibility?

Your prospect cannot see you or the trouble you take to deliver the perfect product.

So ensure that you have made full use of testimonials, third-party opinion, independent research. Where claims are hard to believe, emphasis given to money-back offers (even the simple words 'or all your money back instantly' prominently placed) can make a great deal of difference.

4 Do your pictures show what your words say?

Illustrate the benefit of the product

Research shows many advertisements confuse because the pictures illustrate some phrase in the headline, rather than the benefit of the product. One of my favourite examples was an advertisement for Xerox where the headline suggested it was 'ahead of the field'. The illustration actually showed a field – with a field mouse.

5 Is it all logical?

Describe each paragraph

Re-check that the package is consistent. Don't have three or four ideas which are slightly contradictory (even if each is good, they may counteract each other). Make sure you follow one theme. And, equally, make sure that in each piece there is a logical flow. Write a phrase describing each paragraph, and see if the sequence makes sense.

6 Are you going all out for telephone calls or website log-ins?

They will form a substantial proportion of your replies. Feature and illustrate the phone and website address boldly.

7 Have you paid sufficient attention to the ordering mechanism?

Repeatedly tests show that:

- The more time you give to the ordering instructions in a commercial, the more response you get.
- The more size and prominence you devote to the coupon, the more replies you get. The same applies to phone numbers and website addresses.
- The larger the order form in a mailing, the greater the response. In one case, response to an insurance mailing rose by 25 per cent after the order form was doubled in size.

On occasion I have spent hours writing and rewriting an order form to get it right. It is well worth spending such time to ensure that the instructions on how to order are full, clear and easy to understand. Ask somebody unconnected with the job to read through the order form, and see whether they understand what to do. **Ensure instructions are easily understood**

Ensure the address is in more than one place in the advertisement or mailing pack. (It might pay to put it on *every* piece of a mailing pack.)

Finally, remember people often put the order form or coupon aside to be sent off later – then forget. So it's important to restate the benefits and offer in full there. **Restate the benefits and offer**

8 Have you built in a sufficient sense of urgency?

Can you in some way mention the time factor right at the beginning – even on the envelope? Have you given people reason to act: time incentives, gifts for speedy action, or threats of imminent price rises? **Give people reason to act**

You'll be surprised what even the simplest gift does. As I was rewriting this paragraph I read a letter from an academic publisher who told me that to his great surprise a simple pocket calculator costing him £2 had increased his orders by 20 per cent for a book costing £50.

9 Are you getting as much as you can out of it?

I am not proposing that you cram everything to the limit. But look through your layout to see you have wasted no space unnecessarily. Weigh your mailing pack: maybe you can include some extra telling element without going over the postal limit. Don't be afraid of putting lots of stuff on your webpage. **Don't waste space**

10 Have you edited and polished sufficiently?

Write with fury; but correct with care. Look at your layout sternly and settle for nothing less than the very best you can do. The finished article will always reflect the work you put in. **Correct with care**

11 Don't be proud

Show what you have created to others. Try it out on them. You are not a genius. For instance:

- Get someone to read it aloud: does it *sound* good?
- Check it with someone who's not too bright – or even someone who doesn't like you. They will give you a fairly honest opinion.

Accept criticism

All truly professional creative people accept criticisms – even if they don't welcome them. Remember what Napoleon said: 'There is somebody who knows more than anybody ... and that is everybody.'

12 Re-examine the brief

The last thing of all. Go back to the brief. Have you met it?

Please use these checklists

While I was working on this book I read an article about the humorist S J Perelman. He was a great perfectionist. When somebody asked him how many drafts he went through to create a piece, he replied 'Thirty-seven'. I am afraid I am not as perfectionist as him. Ten is usually enough for me. Probably if I tried harder I would be a better writer.

It may be that you, dear reader, are one of those rare human beings who can produce perfect work every time. Or you may find it demeaning to subject your work to a mechanical process like a list of dos and don'ts.

All I can say is that I have found it *does* pay to subject your work to the kind of analysis I have outlined on the previous pages. Though I must emphasise that *first* you must let your fancy fly free. Be generous with your thinking. Try everything from the straightforward to the crazy.

I believe you will find these checklists not only concentrate your mind and give direction to your work: they will actually *help* you get ideas.

'Search the world and steal the best'

There's an old saying I'm particularly fond of. It is: 'Search the world and steal the best.' Well, after 40 years in this business, the lists above cover just about all I've learned, and all I've stolen. Be my guest. There is no honour amongst thieves – especially when it comes to ideas. I hope my list helps you.

One word of warning. Everything I have said has proved true for someone. Most of it will prove true for you. But not all of it. And not always.

Making sure your creative works

Points to remember

- Are you too blasé? You are not your customer.
- Why formulae work.
- Check what goes into a complete brief.
- How to plan your creative.
- Safest openings: benefit and incentive.
- Beware tricky stuff.
- Look for dramatic ideas – words *and* pictures.
- The right length?
- 'Test drive'.
- Feature strong name or brand.
- Remember role of envelope and letter.
- How many pieces?
- Don't ignore what makes type and layout communicate better.
- Never follow rules slavishly.
- 13 attention-grabbers.
- What keeps people reading.
- Charity is different: nine suggestions.
- 10 hints on broadcast.
- A final checklist.

12

How to Test – and Evaluate Your Results

'One must be a God to be able to tell
successes from failures without
making a mistake.'

Anton Chekhov

'To find a Prince, you have to kiss an
awful lot of frogs.'

Seen on a lapel badge at the time of the
marriage of Prince Charles and
Lady Diana Spencer

At the start of this book I revealed how one thing attracted me to direct marketing: you could *know* what worked and didn't, rather than guessing or relying on someone else's opinion. However, it is quite impossible to predict with any certainty *exactly* what a particular piece will do.

Elements of
a classic test
This was brought home to me in a way I have never forgotten when a former colleague, Stewart Pearson, devised a series of tests for a client we then had called Comp-U-Card. We were not at all sure which of 12 lists would work best for us, and what was the best price to charge. We tried three – £12.50 a year, £15 a year and £20 a year.

I was eager to test something I had tried when I owned the Business Ideas Letter: delayed bank mandate. What would happen if we allowed people three months to test the service before they were committed?

We also wanted to know what was the best time to mail people. I had a number of creative ideas I wanted to test, such as what difference it might make if we tried a bright yellow envelope instead of a white one. And finally, the client wanted to test whether people were prepared to respond on the phone without the facility of an 0800 number. So we tested three different response alternatives: telephone on its own; mail on its own; or a choice.

The results were salutary. The best list did six times better than the worst; the best offer – the highest price with a delayed bank mandate – produced three times as much money as the lowest with no delay. If we mailed at the best time of the year we did twice as well as at the worst time of the year.

Test results can surprise

The yellow envelope increased response 20 per cent, and a sticker which you could place on the order form to indicate acceptance, rather than having to sign, worked well too. In fact, these two elements together increased response by 35 per cent.

The best combination of all the above factors was, in theory, 58 times more responsive than the worst. (I'll explain later why it wouldn't be so in practice.) This is the most spectacular example I've ever seen of the power of testing.

I discovered in a very personal and distressing way what happens if you don't test, back in 1968. That was the year that my partner and I bought the Business Ideas Letter.

One of our first ideas was to mail 50,000 people who had previously enquired about the publication but not yet subscribed. I had reviewed the previous publisher's promotions and decided he had missed this obvious opportunity. I was also buoyed up by the confidence born of almost complete ignorance, which convinced me he knew far less about direct mail than I did. (He is now much richer than I.)

My youthful folly

My partner and I concocted a mailing so splendid and so much better than anything previously done that we decided to dispense with testing and send out to the complete enquiry list. True, it was a little close to Christmas to mail. On the other hand, the mailing was so good that it couldn't fail. So we went ahead.

It was an expensive mailing, because it included a copy of the newsletter itself – which many publishers have since been kind enough to inform me is almost invariably a mistake. Few publications live up to the claims you can make for them.

It was *the* most expensive mailing I have ever sent out in my life. It proved a complete disaster and cost us so much money that it took a year for our business to recover.

This inspired piece of commercial nonsense shows why you should *always* test if you can. A 50,000 mailing is a mere bagatelle to a large company. But it is enough to ruin a small one. And time after time I have learned that no matter how much experience one has, it is almost impossible to foretell the results of anything. One reason is that we lead very different lives and have very different interests to most of our customers. We find it hard to put ourselves in their shoes and predict how they will react.

In the case of the tests we conducted for Comp-U-Card, several results came as a complete surprise to me, and in particular I was astonished that the highest price produced the most money. I was puzzled that offering the option of phone or post did not work as well as post alone. I was also a little surprised at who were the best prospects. You might imagine that the people most eager to save money would be those who have the least to spare. On the contrary, affluent professionals proved our best prospects.

The American publication, *Direct Marketing*, used to ask readers to predict the results of split-run tests. After over 30 years in this business I used to get almost as many wrong as I got right. I doubt if you would do better.

Test, don't assume

The moral is: *test*, don't *assume*.

TESTING: THE FIRST DUTY

I suggested at the start of this book that once you have isolated your prospect or customer as an individual, two activities will govern your success: testing, and building a continuing relationship with your customers.

Both are important, but you will never even start a relationship if you can't recruit the customer at the right price. Moreover, once customers are recruited, they will never prove as profitable to you as they might unless you test your communications to make sure they bring in the maximum return.

So testing is your *first duty*. Apart from anything else, it will ensure you don't lose money – which is what you have to worry about first.

A friend once worked on the Buick account in Detroit. I asked him why their advertising was always such boastful piffle. He explained: 'Every year the agency works flat out for months, producing hundreds of ideas. All the layouts are pinned up on a wall. The client comes in and chooses the ones he likes. Usually the ones that make him feel good about his company.'

Judging by the fact that much General Motors advertising is boastful to this day, maybe they still do it in much the same way. It has done much to make them fail. But there is no need to produce your advertising like that. There is no need to spend days speculating about how the public will respond (whether the client likes it or not), if you *test*.

Claude Hopkins

The man who said the final word on testing – over 60 years ago – was Claude Hopkins. I have mentioned him a number of times already in this book because anybody in the business of marketing ought to know who he was. Sadly, many people don't. Let me tell you a little of his story here.

If the advertising business ever produced a full-blown genius, Claude Hopkins may have been the man. Certainly his employer must have thought so: he was being paid $168,000 a year (plus bonus) back in the 1900s – and in those days you paid no tax. By the end of his career in the 1920s, he was allowed to fill in his own salary cheque. John O'Toole, a former chief executive of Foote, Cone & Belding – the lineal successor of Hopkins' agency, Lord & Thomas – commented that Hopkins was cheap at the price, despite his enormous salary.

Hopkins helped build Lord & Thomas into the largest agency in the world. He wrote a short book entitled *Scientific Advertising* in 1924. In some ways it remains the best book ever written on the subject – and the briefest.

The best book ever written

Hopkins learned his trade in the mail order business, then applied what he had learned to general advertising. Although he was a copywriter, he did not restrict himself to writing copy, or even advertising. Thus, for example, he resuscitated the business of the Bex Bissell carpet sweeper company when he suggested to them that instead of having a wooden handle on their sweepers, they offer consumers a choice of colours.

For a suet company he had the splendid wheeze of baking the world's largest cake and placing it in the window of a Chicago department store.

He introduced putting 'buried' offers in the body copy of his advertisements so that he could measure which were most read. He also started putting coupons in advertisements that people could take to the retailer to redeem. His thinking was behind many of the techniques now taken for granted (or sometimes neglected).

'Buried' offers

He was the man behind the success of famous brands like Schlitz beer, Pepsodent, Chevrolet, and many others. Shrewdly, he used to take shares in the companies he wrote for, and became even more wealthy.

The school for advertising

Hopkins recommended mail order as the school from which one must graduate before hoping to succeed. (He also said he shifted to general advertising because it was easier to make money in.)

'There, false theories melt like snowflakes in the sun,' he observed of mail order, and conclusively: 'Almost any question can be answered, cheaply, quickly and finally by a test campaign. Go to the court of last resort – the buyers of your product.'

If you would like a free PDF of *Scientific Advertising*, e-mail me at Drayton@Draytonbird.com and I shall send it to you. It will be a very wise investment, for it only takes an hour or so to read, and once you have done so you will know far more about this business than almost everyone you meet. I mean that.

Free book for you

I am going to devote *two* chapters to testing, because I am astonished how little people know about it, appalled at how little they value it and alarmed that many who are new to direct marketing neglect it almost entirely.

I started this chapter with the story of my own blunder because it shows that even people who ought to know better (and I had read Hopkins long before that) make silly mistakes.

In my experience, you can almost always tell the difference between a really professional direct marketer and an amateur by how much testing they do. When asked to define the perfect client in three words at a conference in 1980, I said without hesitation: 'Willingness to test.'

The perfect client

But willingness to test is not enough. If you don't know how to test, and how to read results, you can get into a great deal of trouble. A little learning, they say, is a dangerous thing. In our business it can be downright catastrophic.

My former partner, Brian Thomas, was once taking over a seminar on direct mail for the Institute of Marketing. He was handed the previous lecturer's notes as a reference. He read them carefully. One section he read several times, because he could not believe what it said.

'If you have two letters and you want to know which will do better, conduct a test,' said these notes. 'Take a hundred copies of each and mail them out to your list. The one that does better is the one to go ahead with.'

This is such a parody of the truth that it verges on the criminal. Indeed, if you were to act on it all the time, you would be committing commercial suicide. When I deal (very briefly!) with statistics, you will see why. But if the man who gave the advice (a respected consultant, by the way) knew anything about the mathematics of testing, he would never have committed such a crass error. For such a test to be reliable, you would have to be anticipating a response of over 40 per cent to your letters. As rare as sunstroke in Manchester.

Dangerous rules

If people would only test more, they would never say or believe the things they do. In our business it is so easy to end a discussion with a fine generalisation, or take it for granted that because someone else has said it, then it must be true.

This is not so. Moreover, what may work for someone else with their product may not work for you.

For example, ads that look like the paper's editorial work well for charities or language courses, but I'd be amazed if they worked for expensive collectables. Equally, many direct marketers assume an incentive will always increase response. It usually does, but one company offering mortgages found free offers *reduced* reponse. One magazine tested three premiums and all three lowered response.

Another cherished belief amongst experts is that an envelope message will always increase response. Not if it's a stupid one. One of my clients tested a blank envelope against a singularly inane one produced by my agency. It did 25 per cent better.

Think carefully before you apply the 'rules'. Thus, in the cases I have just cited, cheap offers which do not reflect the quality of a magazine will depress response. Silly envelope messages will put people off rather than encourage them to start reading. So you must test. The knowledge you gain will make your marketing more effective than your competitors' and your knowledge greater even than that of some experts.

In his direct marketing book, Ed Nash, to take one example, states that your message must look different from its environment. 'The first law of layout is to be noticed.'

Ed Nash claims to be the 'Master Strategist' of direct marketing, yet the exact reverse of his first law of layout is, in my experience, often true. I have found time and again, not just with charity advertising, but with record advertising and consumer durable advertising that, on the contrary, a very good principle of layout is to blend into your environment.

A very good principle of layout

I have just commented on this, but here is a better authority. The late Richard V Benson, regarded by many as the pre-eminent US direct marketing consultant, expressed the view that an editorial ad will increase readership by between 500 per cent and 600 per cent. I do not know whether this is true or not; but I do know that when we started running editorial-style ads (see page 340) for our retail client Magnet, people came into the stores and commented on what 'good write ups' we were getting. This was although they were all clearly headed, at the insistence of the publications, by the word 'Advertisement'.

In the magazine *British Reader* a Young & Rubicam creative director suggested in 1987 that consumers had become so sophisticated they were no longer 'fooled' by editorial layouts. And indeed that being constantly exposed to advertising layout formats has made the readers prefer them. That was an interesting opinion. My views are not opinion. They come from experience and testing.

Claude Hopkins pointed out the truth long ago: 'Some advocate large type and big headlines. Yet they do not admire salesmen who talk in loud voices. Others look for something queer and unusual. They want ads distinctive in style or illustration. Would you want that in a salesman?'

'Do nothing to merely interest, amuse or attract. That is not your province. Do only that which wins the people you are after in the cheapest possible way.'

'Would you want that in a salesman?'

But does that mean *all* your ads should melt into the background by aping the editorial style? Does it mean that I am right, and others wrong? No: it means you must test, and find out what works for *you*, and *your* product.

FOURTEEN WAYS YOU CAN LEARN BY TESTING

It does not matter what media you are in, or how much you spend; you can test, observe your results, and learn from them. Some methods are far more statistically reliable than others. But *all* are better than just using your own judgement.

1 The A/B split

Many publications are printed on cylinders with each cylinder printing more than one copy of a given page on it. So it is possible for a cylinder to carry different advertisements on the same page of a publication.

New "Low Emissivity" double glazing works 52% better

Tests show "Magnashield" retains more heat — works as well as triple glazing yet costs little more than ordinary double glazing

by OWEN MATHER

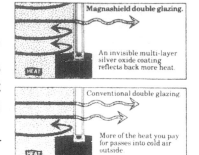

YOU can now buy a new kind of double glazing which works as well as the triple glazing that fights the cold in freezing Scandinavian winters.

The secret? A multi-layer coating containing silver oxide between the two panes of glass. This coating is so thin you can't see it, but gives the glazing what scientists call *low emissivity*.

It lets out less of the heat you pay for, yet allows the sun's rays through the glazing, and traps the warmth for longer inside your home.

Scientific tests conducted on a typical 3-bedroomed house prove low emissivity "Magnashield" performs 52.46% better than ordinary double glazing.

Slash your fuel bills

"Magnashield" costs only a fraction more than ordinary double glazing. Yet tests indicate the difference in cost between "Magnashield" and ordinary double glazing could be paid back over as little as 9 months.

"The price is low because we make it ourselves and sell it direct," says *Magnet Southerns Chairman, Tom Duxbury. "This is a big advance on ordinary double glazing – we believe it will cut fuel bills by an extra 15%. It cost us £7.0 million to build a facility. But since it's better, we thought we should offer it to our customers."*

"Magnashield" is only available through Magnet Southerns stores.

You are unlikely to see this new kind of double glazing elsewhere. That's because the manufacturing plant to produce it is very costly. So a company wanting to make it needs a huge volume of sales. Each week many thousands of double glazed patio doors and windows are sold through Magnet Southerns stores. That's why the company could afford the investment.

Free brochure tells more

If you'd like to know more about "Magnashield," visit your nearest Magnet Southerns store. At the same time you can pick up a **free** copy of their 116 page, full colour brochure.

This brochure tells you not only of "Magnashield" but other Magnet Southerns' exclusive products. They are Britain's biggest manufacturers of doors and have a wide range of their own craftsman-made kitchens. Many customers particularly like their free computerised kitchen and bedroom planning service.

Virtually everything you buy at Magnet Southerns is made by their own craftsmen and sold direct to you. This keeps the quality up and prices down. Check for yourself. Come into a Magnet Southerns store.

There are 250 stores throughout the country where you can see "Magnashield" window units and doors for yourself.

Figure 12.1 Magnet 'editorial' advertisement (not a direct ad, but applying the principles I learned from direct results)

Thus, you can have the publication printed so that one half of the copies have one piece of copy, and the other half a different one. This is called an A/B split.

In some cases you can have a four-way split. But the reason why these splits are so valuable is that the copies of the publication bearing the advertisements you wish to test come off the presses alternately in the case of an A/B split, or in sequence in the case of a four-way split.

In this way you get very close to statistical perfection. There can be no geographical or other bias, and each newsagent is delivered a pile of papers with alternate examples of the advertisements you are testing.

Getting close to statistical perfection

Newspapers normally charge you for arranging a split-run, but when you realise that one ad may be two or three times as effective as another, this is a small price to pay.

It was through split-run tests that we found out some fascinating (and valuable) information about Dr Barnardo's, the child care charity.

My friend Harold Sumption knows more about charity advertising than anyone I have ever met. He told me: 'People don't like the idea of charities squandering their donations on expensive advertising. They like to feel everything is done on a shoestring, by voluntary workers. The best ads look as though they were put together late at night by a group of dedicated amateurs on somebody's kitchen table.'

What works for charities

I had also learned that the Linguaphone company found their paper-set ads outpulled trade-set ads by about 25 per cent. Moreover, years previously, I had tested paper-set editorial style ads for washing machines. They had consistently done better than ads that looked like ads. (And the newspaper will typeset your ad free, whereas trade setting is very expensive.)

However, when we started work on Barnardo's, our creative director, John Watson, and his art director, Chris Albert, hated the idea of having our ads look ugly. In the end we arranged some split-run tests. The paper-set ads outpulled the trade-set ones by between 60 per cent and 250 per cent.

2 Split-run inserts

The weakness of the A/B split is that in most publications you can only test two things at a time – occasionally four. But the ability to *insert* material which you have had preprinted yourself into publications gives you far more flexibility.

Greater flexibility

What is more, since inserts get higher rates of reply than advertisements, you don't need as many copies of an insert to get a statistically reliable response level. I shall explain why in more detail later. But several benefits result.

In the first place, you can usually afford to test several publications at the same time, thus finding out which media are likely to do best for you. In the second place, you can test a variety of different creative approaches. So you can acquire a great deal of knowledge very quickly.

The drawbacks of the insert are that the initial print cost will almost certainly be greater than most ads, so you must balance this expense against the benefits.

Time, too, is an important factor. It can be infuriating to wait for a magazine carrying your insert to publish; and then to have to wait again until a sufficient percentage of the results is in before you project.

You must beware of making hasty decisions on the basis of early insert results. A few years ago, when testing a series of inserts for a knitting-card club, we made a costly error. In the early run of responses, one of these inserts was doing very well. Copy deadlines were looming, so we prepared an ad based on this insert. As further results came in, it turned out the early winner was not in fact by any means the best insert. Another one did much better. But by the time we learned we were wrong, it was too late to do anything.

So, although the insert may be a more flexible medium for testing, a daily newspaper split-run gives you a shorter copy date with results that come in much sooner than with a monthly or weekly magazine. In a fast moving world, that can be important.

3 Split-run mailings

This is the third major test bed and in some ways the most valuable.

The most valuable test

That is because there is a wide range of outside lists available for you to test and you have your own database which can be segmented according to any number of variables. In this way you can test new lists, new approaches, and the effect of particular approaches upon particular segments.

This latter is particularly important. For instance, in the United States our agency tested a service which helped the business customer arrange his finances better. Response was good when targeted generally to business people. Then, the creative approaches were varied to approach each profession with a special appeal. Responses increased dramatically – in some cases by over 200 per cent. The only exception was when mailing accountants. Predictably, they didn't see any need for advice on the subject on which they consider themselves experts.

Fundamentally, you can divide mailing tests into tests of new *lists* and tests of new *approaches*. But you must remember two things.

- Always test a new list with your existing, proven package – or 'banker'. This is obvious sense. If you try new copy, you will never know whether it was the new list or the new copy that worked.
- By the same token, every time you test new copy, make sure it is tested against your 'banker'. You can't rely on comparing what your 'banker' did last time out and what a new piece of copy does this time out. The timing can make a lot of difference (as you saw in the Comp-U-Card test, where it doubled response).

What I am saying here is: don't test two variables simultaneously. You will rightly reply that this is obvious, but I can tell you that otherwise very bright people do this quite often. For this reason, I shall be restating the point in a different way in the next chapter. It is extremely important.

Don't test two variables simultaneously

4 Geographical splits

Most publications don't offer A/B split facilities, but they may publish different geographical editions. This enables you to test many ads simultaneously in different parts of the country.

The problem is, of course, that different areas respond very differently, so you have to allow for that when testing.

You can do this in two ways.

- Break down your customer file and response records by geographical areas. Monitor the results. You can then relate your own historical experience of geographical variations to the number of replies coming in from the various regional editions of the publication.

  Monitor results

  Don't forget, though, that you have to allow for the *relative* circulation in each geographical area of the particular publication you are using. This can also cause misleading bias because it may differ from the geographical bias amongst your own customers or the population at large.
- If you *rotate* your copy region by region, so that each piece of copy appears in each region, you can then make allowances for such biases.

  Thus, first you run ad A in the north, and ad B in the south on week one. Then you do it the other way round on week two. Add the results of the two tests together and you have a fair reading. Rotating more than once will make this more reliable.

  However, bearing in mind that you should always look for big differences, not small ones, worthwhile results should emerge quite clearly.

5 Telescope testing

If you have statistical indications, you may already have worked out another, very valuable form of test: valuable because it enables you to learn faster.

Learn faster

This is a test in one publication using both a geographical split and an A/B split simultaneously. For example, if you test ads X and Y on an A/B basis in the southern editions, whilst splitting X and Z in the north, you should have a good indication as to which of the three ads is best. To be sure, you repeat the process, rotating the tests so as to eliminate any possible geographical bias.

To learn more, you then take the winning ad and use it as a control against two more ads, in the same way.

Note that you must have one ad in *both* geographical areas, as a control.

This method enables you to learn even faster – and is particularly useful with publications which have many geographical editions.

6 Your own database

You already know that the customers you seek are similar to the ones you already have. That's why your own database – apart from being the cheapest and most accessible test medium – is probably the most valuable one. For one thing, your customers are almost invariably the most responsive group of people you can reach, so you are far less likely to lose money with them.

As your knowledge grows, you will constantly be able to compare the response you get from your own customer file against what you get on the same offer made to other lists, or in outside media. So once you have tested an offer to your list, you can project roughly what it will do elsewhere.

The cheapest way to test

Unquestionably the cheapest way to test a new offer is to try it as a 'bounce back'. That is, an insert when sending out merchandise or welcoming people to your service. There's no extra postage; the people receiving it are the hottest of buyers. This is the very best time to catch them because they are (I trust) happy with what you have sent them: you will get a very high response. This means small numbers of inserts will suffice. Sometimes, you can put together a modest leaflet to test several possible offers simultaneously.

In the same way, an insert placed in one of your regular communications to your customers – a statement for instance – is also a very cheap and effective test medium.

In all these cases you can often use existing printed inserts and save money. Many forget this and waste money needlessly.

Once again, I must nag you with another warning. Make sure you express your offers to your list in the same way you plan to express them when going outside. It's no use using one headline and illustration to your list, and then being amazed that it doesn't pull well outside with a new headline and illustration. That's a *new* test. Obvious – but all too often ignored.

7 An ad catalogue

This is another way of reaching your customers to find out what might work outside – because, as I have already said, what works in your catalogue should do well with similar people you seek. However, this form of testing is indicative rather than decisive.

The catalogue is a medium with its own peculiarities. A product which works in a catalogue may not work on its own.

However, although what works in a catalogue doesn't *always* work elsewhere, often it does. And if you find something sells *extremely* well in a catalogue, it ought to work elsewhere.

Some companies have catalogues made up of reproductions of all their advertisements. This is a very, very inexpensive way of putting together a catalogue. It will also make it easier for you to insert a new product in the accepted format within your catalogue.

I must say, however, that this is not normally the best format for a catalogue. Catalogues, as I remarked in the creative section, tend to do better when there are several items on a page. This format makes it more difficult to test the validity of such products. Nevertheless, if you have a catalogue, then it is foolish not to use it as a test medium. (And if you don't have *some* sort of catalogue, try one.)

Choose the best format

8 Questionnaire

The questionnaire, in my view, is the Cinderella of direct marketing. A humble, drab, unexciting drudge which has now become transformed into the key to many direct marketing activities.

The Cinderella of direct marketing

You will already have concluded that direct marketing revolves around acquiring knowledge about customers and prospects and then deploying it effectively. What better way to acquire knowledge than simply to ask your customers and prospects? Sophisticated direct marketers have known this for years. One of my clients had a sequence of over 20 tests, the first of which was a questionnaire, before launching any product.

You cannot normally base your final marketing decisions on the responses to a questionnaire. Like the responses to a catalogue, they merely indicate what might happen. But in the early stages they are of enormous value in setting you off on the right track. As I suggested in Chapter 4, to find out what you ought to sell, start by asking your existing customers. You will learn a great deal.

Ask your existing customers

Constructing a questionnaire mailing or e-mail requires a knowledge of research, for it is a combined research document and mail shot. Too many are seduced into selling at the same time, thus eroding the validity of the responses.

To your own list, a well written letter with a questionnaire should pull 50 per cent or more – depending on the closeness of the relationship between you and your customers. But you *must* emphasise that you are asking them to give you advice that will help you serve them better in the future. 'Help us to help you' is the appropriate theme.

Properly written, such questionnaires do not even require inducements to be completed, though many companies offer a modest gift. Some adopt the ingenious and worthy ploy of making a gift to charity for each response.

This subject of a series of mailings to pre-test your product or service calls for lengthy treatment beyond the scope of this book. However, it is well worth your attention because it is the key to a *systematic* approach to selling which almost eliminates the possibility of large-scale loss.

Parenthetically, I would say that were you to employ even *half* the techniques I have recommended in this chapter so far, you would be working more scientifically than the majority of today's established direct marketers.

Some of the smarter 'new' direct marketers have started using the questionnaire to fine effect. One ingenious use of the technique was made by my colleagues in the United States who initiated a great 'debate' on that matter of consuming interest to all Americans: chocolates. Was a new product a *cookie* or a *candy*? This was the burning question respondents were asked to vote upon. A very simple form of questionnaire, but nevertheless taking advantage of the fact that people like to answer questions.

This is not testing, but it is interesting as a way of suggesting that you think very carefully about the potential of the questionnaire.

The questionnaire is, of course, the method used to build proprietary databases – a subject covered in Chapter 9.

9 Radio and TV

In Britain, radio was little used by direct marketers for many years. The quality of radio commercials in this country is generally low.

TV, on the other hand, where creatively many feel that British advertising is better than any in the world, is a fast-growing direct medium marketer. And as I observed in Chapter 7, the advent of cable and satellite TV channels has changed the picture completely.

As test media, TV and radio have a great advantage: speed of response. Their disadvantage is that translating what works on television or radio into print is difficult.

Radio is an ideal test medium. Production costs are low. The tape of a commercial can be altered so that you can easily and cheaply insert or delete phrases. And one thing we have learned in this business is that particular phrases can make a phenomenal difference. Moreover, many small radio stations charge relatively little for time.

Because of its low cost, even though it may not be potentially the most profitable medium, I think radio has a lot going for it. You may make little, but you won't lose much. And you could learn a lot fast.

The object is to *learn*, not to make a profit

One thing you should never forget is that the aim is to *learn*, not to make a profit. A test that loses you money today may tell you enough to make you a fortune tomorrow. Too many people try to test *and* make money. That is nice when it happens (which is often) but it is not the primary object of the exercise and is shortsighted.

Now there are many TV channels, testing is not nearly as costly as it used to be. An inexpensive commercial shown off-peak on a small channel makes an economic test.

You cannot conduct a true split-run test on TV and radio. You can, however, arrange geographical splits (particularly useful in conjunction with regional issues of the TV papers). And you can alternate commercials and achieve much the same effect, using different phone numbers or addresses, or referring to different advertisements in the commercials.

The US direct marketing man Lester Wunderman has the credit for inventing a technique known as the 'Gold Box', which helps in testing. On the TV commercial, mention is made of a box in the advertisement which – if you tick it – entitles you to a free gift when sending in your order. No mention is made of this in the ad so you can measure how many of the people who saw the commercial were motivated to reply to the ad: how much 'uplift' the commercial gave.

The 'Gold Box' technique

10 Small ad tests

The small advertisement is a much under-utilised test medium. Yet it can be immensely valuable. Most old-time advertising pioneers like John Caples learned their first rules from small ads.

The only difference between a small ad and a large one is size. Every element a large ad can have, a small one can have. A headline to attract attention, with maybe a small picture to illustrate it. Copy to make you want to buy. Mention of a premium. And a demand for action, with possibly even a coupon if the ad is above a certain size.

You can't split-run small ads (most media won't allow for splits on sizes smaller than 20cm double column). But you can *alternate* them day after day for a couple of weeks to get a reading. This also applies to classifieds – the most cost-effective spaces of all.

Alternate to get a valid reading

11 Shrinking your ads

You may want to test a number of large ads. But you could well be appalled at the cost of full-scale tests. Once again, think about small ads.

Shrink your large ads, retaining the same elements. You already know from pages 118–19 that a quarter page can be twice as cost-effective as a full page; you already know the headline is by far the most important element in the ad. So retain the significant factors you think the large ads have, and test them smaller.

Retain the same elements

Many people are reluctant to run small ads. They rue the fact that they won't make as much money. I rejoice that they can't *lose* as much money. So should you.

12 The telephone

What a valuable tool this is, for testing *and* research!

Obviously, it is very easy to split-run appeals on the phone. What is more, good telephone people will be able to tell you, within *hours* very often, which appeals are hitting the mark.

Get results in a matter of hours

Moreover, as I have already indicated, if you want to find out about how people reacted to your products or your mailing, getting on the phone to them is the fastest way. (And very salutary it is, too, when your readers say with one universal voice: 'What mailing?' Humility is a fine quality to engender in copywriters.)

Frankly, I am astonished at how little use is made of the telephone for these purposes. I can see no good reason why, after a mailing has gone out (particularly if it hasn't done well), people do not instantly get on the telephone and ask: *why*?

In a very short time you'll find out. Though you must be very careful to let people tell you their real opinions, not what you wish to hear.

13 E-mail

This book is largely based on commonsense. It seems commonsense to me that e-mail is an excellent test medium because it is quick and cheap; and since most people use e-mails nowadays, I imagine motivations vary little between those who do and those who don't. Accordingly, propositions that work in this medium should work elsewhere. I say 'propositions' because what makes the most difference in e-mails is, as a rule, the name of the sender – followed by the subject line, which may or may not be the proposition itself.

But the great thing about e-mail is that it is amazingly cheap and quick. Not only can you send e-mails quickly: the responses come in very fast too. You could send out 1,000 e-mails, with two alternative propositions or subject lines, before lunch and know whether one approach is significantly better than the other before you go to bed. Later in this chapter I point out why you may be wise to repeat this test.

14 Deduction

There is one more way of finding things out from looking at your results. It is called deduction or – in this book – commonsense.

When we were evaluating the first-year results for the Dr Barnardo appeals, we had a wide variety of ads and media to compare. Looking at the figures, a bright media planner working with us observed a significant difference in the results for ads which had coupons in them, and those that didn't. For most ads at that time, ads *with* coupons pulled about 20 per cent to 25 per cent more than ads without. In this case, consistently, ads with *no* coupons were doing better than ads with. In some cases over 50 per cent better.

What works for some doesn't work for others

Once again, we had learned that what works for some clients does not work for others. Why? I think the coupon acted, for the reader, like the donation box of a charity worker collecting on the street. If you don't want to give, you cross the road to avoid it – you miser, you!

Following this, we set up some split-run tests to see whether taking the name Barnardo's in the ads and setting it small, instead of as a display logo, would get us better results. It did not. From this I deduced that people are happy to read about the good work Barnardo's does, but put off by that rattling collector's box. However, once they've read they do give, thankfully.

There is an important postscript to this story which illuminates yet another instance where I was wrong about something. Upon reading the results of the tests of coupon versus no coupon, I immediately instructed everybody to eliminate all coupons from Barnardo's advertising.

I was forced very quickly to rescind this direction, when somebody more intelligent than I pointed out that one of the objects of the advertising was to recruit names and addresses. Eliminating the coupon was discouraging people from doing this. So the coupons were reinstated.

A FAIR TEST?

People read test results, or even set up tests, in a way that suits their own predilections.

The subject of coupons reminds me of a story I heard about Joe Sugarman of JS & A in the United States. You may recall that his ads didn't carry them. This always surprised me until I realised that his market was a very special one, dealing for the most part with gadgets and superfluities for the fairly wealthy American. Things like language translating machines and other electronic marvels.

I recall him saying at the European Direct Marketing Symposium at Montreux in 1979 that his best medium was *The Wall Street Journal*. Virtually everybody he sold to had a telephone and a credit card, so they bought by using the two.

However, he was challenged upon one occasion about the dropping of the coupon. He replied to the challenge by setting up a test. He ran one ad with a coupon and no phone number; and one with a phone number and no coupon.

If this story is true, it was a pointless test. The real question is, as you will already have realised, what happens when you run a coupon *and* a phone number as against a phone number and address alone. A mutual friend tells me that after reading this book, Joe agreed with me – and said this had cost him a lot of money.

A pointless test

(As a matter of interest, the coupon, because it signals there is a direct offer, tends to boost response if it is boldly outlined or made bigger. Even a dotted line around an ad will boost response. A simple flash stating 'This is a direct offer' helped one company to increase their responses. Moreover, the coupon itself will increase readership – but that is another subject dealt with elsewhere.)

To revert to my point about using judgement – or commonsense – in evaluating tests, you may imagine that the best way to test whether coupons did or did not help Barnardo's would have been to use split-run tests. The problem was that we were not *expecting* the result that occurred and it was against all our previous experience – against the 'rules'. We had never considered testing.

It is worth bringing out one other issue about coupons. In a split-run, if one ad has a coupon and another doesn't, then the ad without the coupon has more space for the copy. This means it could be made more effective by using the additional space – so the split itself is invalid: it doesn't compare like with like.

The only way to do this is to pay the publication to run a piece of ordinary news copy in the space that would have been occupied by the coupon. This would be extremely expensive – even if the newspaper could be persuaded to cooperate. In the case of Barnardo's, the results were so overwhelmingly decisive that this was not a problem. However, this issue can crop up in other ways.

On one occasion we wished to discover for a client whether we could squeeze a full-page ad which ran across five columns into four columns. We arranged to run a column of editorial copy (which we wrote ourselves) down the fifth column, and conducted the split.

The results were quite clear: there was no difference between the four columns and the five columns. Once again, we had to look carefully at the results before deciding what to do next. In practice, we discovered that the rates we could get for full pages by careful media negotiation meant it was not worth bothering with the smaller space although in theory it was more economic.

Evaluate carefully

What I am saying is: first get your results, then evaluate them – very carefully. This is the subject I am about to go into, but not before making one simple point. This is that the simplest type of test is what I call 'have a go' testing. Sometimes you don't have the time or the money or even the media available to test. The temptation then is to be negative – not to try something new. Don't give in to it. Always try something new if it looks like a good idea. Every now and then you will come up with a winner.

A TRUE AND PROPER RECORD

I have been left speechless more than once by the way otherwise sophisticated companies keep (or fail to keep) their advertising records. One famous computer company could do practically anything, it seemed, except tell you what the results were. One big publisher had no record of results at all.

Once the excitement of running the ad is over, people are often quite happy to leave it to the office junior to keep the record of what happened. If the results are bad, everyone wants to forget. If the results are good, why waste time working out just how good they were? So another year of potential knowledge is lost.

Yet keeping records is no great affair. Most mail order companies have a system. You can work one out quite simply. It merely needs to record *everything* about the particular communication and *everything* about the results.

It has to be a true and proper record. It doesn't matter whether you keep it on paper or on computer: accuracy and detail count.

- A copy of the mailing, insert, ad or details of the commercial.
- Details of when and where it appeared, or was mailed.
- How it was posted, and how people were asked to reply. Reply-paid, stamped, first class, second class, no stamp, telephone, Freephone, website and so forth.
- Weather and any political or heavy news events or holiday period that might have affected results.
- Position of ad. Whether it backed on to another coupon. The same consideration applies to inserts: how many other inserts did it go out with? What was the environment?
- Results day by day and cumulatively.
- Conversion rates day by day and cumulatively.
- Anything else your commonsense tells you is relevant. When you see a result which seems to you bizarre or unexpected, take a closer look. Take a good look at the publication and all the other circumstances surrounding that particular result. You may find something you had not bargained for – like a competitor's ad or mailing on the same day.

Your results are the most valuable thing in your office apart from your mailing list. They are your map of where you have been, and your compass to where you should go. *Don't* leave them to the office dogsbody. Keep an eye on them constantly.

Follow-up conversions and customer behaviour

You will find results exert a hypnotic effect on you, like racehorse form guides for gamblers. So although you must study them, don't waste time poring over them in the hope that they will look any better. They never do.

However, a word to the wise. You must return to your results regularly, because – as I pointed out when talking about one of my businesses which failed – what may at first sight appear to be happening could be misleading. For instance, advertisement A may be producing twice as many enquiries as advertisement B, and three times as many enquiries as advertisement C.

When you come later to analyse the conversion into *sales*, you may discover that in fact advertisements B and C are converting much better than advertisement A. You may then conclude that advertisement B is your best bet.

The same principle applies to mailings. For direct selling of insurance we once created a mailing which produced far fewer responses but three times as many sales. You must keep your eye on the value of those sales over time. It may then emerge that advertisement C is in fact the most effective of all because it produces sales of a far greater *average value*, or customers who tend to *spend more*, over a period.

This leads on, of course, to the next question – how *soon* do you know enough to be able to act upon your results?

How soon can you tell?

Inexperienced people expect all the replies to come in immediately. They don't. One spends frustrating days (or even weeks) trying to guess what the eventual results will be. However, there is a point with most response figures when sufficient numbers are in for you to be able to judge the eventual total.

Every medium is different

You will find that every medium is different, but *all* media have a response pattern. That is, after a certain period a certain percentage of your replies will normally have come in. And by and large this pattern does not vary much from ad to ad or mailing to mailing.

The only variation I have noticed is that the most successful 'pullers' seem to do better than average. They have a longer period during which they pull, reach a higher peak, and keep near that peak for longer. The flops reach a peak sooner, and tail off faster.

The problem is that every business appears to have slightly different figures on this, just as every medium does. You will have to find out what is true for you. But essentially the principle is that the more immediate the nature of the medium, the quicker the responses.

Obviously, on the phone they are instant. E-mail responses are very quick. In broadcast media, after a week you'll have had the overwhelming majority of your replies. The daily paper may produce a third of its response after a week. For a weekly, it may take a fortnight to reach that point. For a monthly it may take three weeks – and so on.

In the same way, your direct mail responses will come in faster or more slowly depending on whether you mailed first class or second, and whether you had a first class or second class reply vehicle. You could have half your replies in after a fortnight – or only a fifth. Catalogue orders are even slower. They take months to come in.

To add another piece of uncertainty, orders come in more slowly than enquiries (a decision to enquire is obviously easier to make).

Every case different

If all this sounds as though I can't tell you what's likely to happen, you're right. Every case is different.

In addition, whilst your postal service may be very keen to develop direct mail, they could well have great problems in maintaining the quality of the service. So day-to-day results may be very erratic.

The important thing is that the response pattern does not tend to change. You can rely on it, except when major news events depress response.

The other important thing to remember is **the results must be read carefully**.

Let me give you another example. It comes from one of the world's most famous companies, and I won't embarrass them by naming any names. This just goes to show how easily you can make mistakes.

Crazy mathematics

When they came to see us, we asked if they had tested personalisation. 'Yes,' they replied. 'It doesn't work for us.' We were surprised. We asked what the results were. 'It cost us an extra 15 per cent. And it only pulled an extra 15 per cent.'

They had not been thinking properly: 15 per cent extra response brought in infinitely more in money than the 15 per cent added mailing costs. In the intervening period they had lost a fortune in potential revenue.

As a child, I was an appalling mathematician. This business has made me quite a passable one. But to get a true understanding of this vital subject, I would suggest you read Julian Simon's book, *How to Start and Operate a Mail Order Business*, which gives a splendid exposition of this, and all the other mathematical aspects of this business.

His book (unlike many other worthy volumes on this business) makes a very complex business fairly easy to understand; though it can never be everyone's idea of a ripping read.

Nothing is foolproof

The British Prime Minister Disraeli said: 'There are three kinds of lies. Lies. Damned lies. And statistics.'

Sadly, statistics are all we have to go on when evaluating test results. Even more sadly, they aren't foolproof. There's no *absolute* guarantee that the results of your test will be replicated when, in the case of a mailing, you project your test on to larger numbers; or in the case of an ad, you re-run it in the same medium.

This is not just because of other factors (like changes in the weather, or the news, or public interest). It is because testing – oddly enough – is just like gambling. It is a matter of *probability*, not *certainty*.

A matter of *probability*, not *certainty*

However, the degree of probability is such that you can predict what is going to happen with a high level of confidence.

Thus, when you play roulette, each new spin of the wheel has no relationship to the last: it is as though every time, the wheel is being spun for the first time. This means that, although you may have had an odd number fifty times on the run, there is no logical reason why the next spin will come up even. However, there is a very high degree of *probability* that it will, and probability is what we are concerned with.

So, with ads and mailings, you want to know what *degree* of certainty you can act on. This is determined by the number of test packages that go out in a mailing and the ratio between that number and the expected level of response. Or, in the case of an ad or insert, the number of replies that come in and how large the margin of difference is between the winner and the loser.

- In the case of a mailing, the greater the number mailed, and the higher the response rate, the greater the probability that such a response will be repeated on a second mailing to the same list. The result one can most rely on is a high response to a large mailing. The least reliable result would be a low response to a small list.
- In the case of an advertisement, the same principle applies. A small number of responses to a publication with a low circulation is not to be relied on; and vice versa.

There are special probability tables which tell you how much you can rely on the results you get and the sizes of sample you need. Most people like to be 95 per cent certain that the result they got will repeat itself on another occasion. These tables tell you to within what percentage variation such a repeated result is likely.

For example, suppose you expect a 20 per cent response to your mailing. If you mail out 16,972 pieces, the result should be 95 per cent certain of being accurate to within 0.25 per cent either way. Nineteen times out of 20, it should fall within 1.75 per cent to 2.25 per cent.

I have reproduced such a table on the next page. As you can see, tests involving small numbers and modest rates are a complete waste. You either need a small number with an extraordinary high response rate for the result to be relied upon for future planning: or where the response is low, you must mail out a lot of pieces.

Ensure your sample size is large enough

The moral is that you must make your sample size large enough. Even then, there will be rare occasions when the results aren't to be trusted. This is why experienced mailers never just conduct one test and then 'roll out' in the millions. I'll say more on this below.

What if you are split-testing an advertisement, or an insert? Then, the criterion is the number of replies to each half of a two-way split. The more replies you get, the more you can rely on the difference between the two halves of the response.

Thus, if you only get 100 replies in total, the result is not to be trusted unless there is a difference of more than 20 per cent between the two ads. Whereas if you get 500 replies in total, then a 10 per cent difference should be

Table 12.1 Minimum sample size

95% Confidence Level
Expected Percentage Response from Mailing

Allowable Plus or Minus error on Expected % Response	0.5%	1.0%	1.5%	2.0%	2.5%	3.0%	3.5%	4.0%
.05	86,255	152,100	227,000	301,200	374,600	477,200	519,000	590,100
.1	19,100	38,000	56,800	75,300	93,600	111,800	129,800	147,500
.2	4,800	9,500	14,200	18,800	23,400	27,900	32,400	36,900
.3	2,100	4,200	6,300	8,400	10,400	12,400	14,400	16,400
.4	1,300	2,400	3,500	4,700	5,900	7,000	8,100	9,200
.5	800	1,500	2,300	3,000	3,700	4,500	5,200	5,900
.6	–	1,000	1,600	2,100	2,600	3,100	3,600	4,100
.7	–	–	–	–	–	2,300	2,600	3,000
.8	–	–	–	–	–	–	2,000	2,300
.9	–	–	–	–	–	–	1,600	1,800
1.0	–	–	–	–	–	–	1,300	1,500

The Institute of Direct Marketing©

Table 12.2 Significance factors in Split-Run Testing

95% Confidence Level

Total Response (ie Test A plus Test B)	Significance Factor (% needed for winner to be significant)	Winner	Loser	% Gain
50	64.24	33	17	+94%
100	60.00	60	40	+50%
500	54.47	273	227	+20%
1,000	53.16	532	468	+14%
10,000	51.00	5,100	4,900	+4%
100,000	50.31	50,310	46,690	+1%

The Institute of Direct Marketing©

reliable. So if one ad pulls 275 replies, and the other only 225, you can be 95 per cent sure that it is better.

But *don't* conclude that it is exactly 20 per cent better. We are talking about probabilities, not certainties. To get a clear idea of the difference, you would have to retest several times. Once again, to give you an idea of what I'm talking about I have reproduced a table.

I am indebted to my friends at the UK Institute of Direct Marketing for these tables.

Small numbers demand repeats

People ask me: 'What do we do about direct mail testing in our market? The lists are very small. To get one of your statistically valid test results we'd have to use the entire mailing list.'

The answer is that if you have, say, a list of 10,000 names then remember, first of all, you are looking for tests which are likely to yield big differences – 30 per cent or more. Accordingly, take a small sample of 1,000 and split it into two and mail it. Then repeat the same process with the same test and the same numbers. Then repeat it again. The result you get on the first test will not be statistically valid, but it should reveal which mailing is actually better than the other – remembering, again, that we are talking about *big* differences.

The benefit of repetition

The second mailing will give you a closer insight into the difference, and the third a further confirmation. You could draw the analogy with the way that artillery fires 'ranging shots' in order to bracket a target.

The idea of repetition is a sound one in any case. Nobody with any commonsense will spend a fortune just on the basis of one test. Ours is a business for cautious people.

Suppose you have a quarter of a million names. Take a small sample – say 10,000 pieces – and see what happens. Then, run a second-flight test with a larger sample of 50,000 before you go the whole hog.

Test the *best* segments first

Where you have segments of a list to test, some more responsive than others, you will obviously test the *best* segments first: the better buyers, more recent buyers, more frequent buyers.

I think you will find this pragmatic approach safest and more practical. But your initial test results (and quantity mailed) should be reviewed and determined in conjunction with the mysterious tables 12.1 and 12.2.

Frankly, I find the whole thing rather like alchemy or examining the entrails of chickens for portents. And I still can't understand why it always seems that however well the test does, the roll-out is never quite as good.

WHAT TESTING ACHIEVED FOR ME

Three hundred years ago, George Savile, Marquis of Halifax, wrote: 'Hope is generally a wrong guide, though it is very good company along the way.'

Too many people run their companies on hope, when they should be testing. But a willingness – no, an *enthusiasm* – for testing can achieve great things.

When we first set up in business as Trenear-Harvey, Bird & Watson, we tested two mailings. They determined for us what business we should be in. Then we tried testing telephone follow-ups. We found they got us in to see nearly every single person we wrote to; and nearly 50 per cent gave us work. We tried mailing *without* telephone follow-up. It got us a 3 per cent response. Ads didn't pay well either.

Tests to use when setting up a business

But our first telephone follow-ups gave us a client who stayed with us until we resigned the account eight years later. They came to see us at our accommodation address. They were not interested in how splendid our offices were. They just wanted to test us. They gave us two packages to work on.

Neither came out on top when tested. But both did well enough to convince the client that they had found a new source of creative ideas. They gave us more tests. And more again.

Eventually, we handled virtually all their business. Our work for them ran all over the world. More importantly, in the late 1970s, over a period of five inflationary years, this company's cost of recruiting new customers was virtually unaffected by inflation. In effect, this was a halving of the real cost; a result only possible because of a continual test programme. Every idea worth trying that we put up, this client tried. That gave us more of a chance, and them more of a chance.

If you rely on testing, you don't have to worry about creative flair, or guesswork. Your customers will tell *you*.

Your customers will tell *you*

In the next chapter, we'll look at some of the things you can test and some of the things you might learn.

Testing: the basics

Points to remember

- Elements of a revealing test.
- Expect surprises.
- Always test – no need to guess.
- 'Buried' offers – a forgotten idea that works.
- Get *Scientific Advertising* free – and read it. Just e-mail and ask me, drayton@draytonbird.com.
- Beware following the rules too closely: different things work for different firms and products.
- 14 ways to learn: refer to them when planning.

- Your opinions must not colour results – ensure they're genuine.
- Keep a proper record, or you're lost.
- Follow up initial results – a lead is rarely worth what you think.
- The difference between probability and certainty.
- Confidence levels and significance factors determined by numbers.
- Repetition when you have small numbers.

13

Testing Versus Research – and Other Matters

'The golden rule is that there are no golden rules.'
George Bernard Shaw

'Always challenge dogma.'
Leonard Freeman

By now, I hope, you will have been persuaded of the virtues of testing. But these virtues should not blind you to the value of research.

I get rather irritated at the lack of imagination shown by some direct marketers. If you tell them a PS generally increases response, they immediately assume *every* letter in *every* mailing should have one. If you point out that reversed-out type is harder to read than black and white, they assume you must *never* use reversed type. And, once converted to the joys of testing, many – as is common with converts – become equally dogmatic: 'There's no need to do any research; testing tells us all we need to know.'

This is silly. Testing usually tells you what works and what doesn't – but rarely *why*. You have to deduce. You cannot be sure. Research, on the other hand, will give you strong indications as to how people are likely to react, and why.

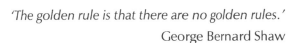

Testing tells you what works and what doesn't

If you put people in laboratory conditions you can see how they look at things and read them. You can find out whether the sequence is easy for them to follow and, in a mailing, what order they read pieces in. (After opening the envelope they tend to turn first to the order form to see what they are in for.) Research, too, will tell you whether they *understand* what you're trying to say.

On one occasion we changed the sequence of pages in a mailing because we discovered that prospects were not reading them in the way we thought they would. On another, we learned that – contrary to what consumers *say* – they will spend five or even ten times more time on a detailed, multiple-piece mailing package than on a short letter and order form such as they always claim they prefer.

By conducting *post hoc* research you can often find out why some people didn't reply, why some did, and what kind of people they were. In one case, for British Telecom we tested two alternative mailings. Both pulled very well, with almost identical results. Each was successful: but why?

Research revealed that one mailing appealed greatly to people with organised, tidy minds and of a conventional disposition. The other appealed to more adventurous and unconventional types. So we could use *both* approaches – and get a better eventual result.

Let me emphasise, though, that you must be careful when assessing research results. You can only base your views on what people actually do, rather than on what they say they do. Thus, repeatedly, consumers and businessmen with one universal voice say they don't read long letters. In my experience and that of every colleague I have spoken to all over the world, nine times out of ten a longer letter making the same proposition will substantially outpull a short one. Of course, the lower cost of a short letter may make it more profitable – but that is a different subject.

Time spent on reconnaissance is seldom wasted

Another research red herring is free gifts and sweepstakes. Once again, people deny they are influenced by these things – yet in practice they usually are. So don't expect research to tell you how people will behave. You can, though, learn quite a lot about their *motivations* and even *how* they behave.

In short, as the general said: 'Time spent on reconnaissance is seldom wasted.'

I applaud all kinds of research, but I must emphasise that people cannot tell you what they will buy until you ask them to part with money. One company used to get their customers into halls in groups, then show them potential products and get their opinions. They would then rank the possible products in order of appeal. After the session, the products were displayed at the end of the hall, and customers were allowed to take away the sample of their choice.

The first interesting thing the company discovered was that the customers *never* chose the products to take away that they said they preferred in the discussion. And the second interesting thing was that an infallible guide to what would sell (these were fairly simple folk) was to leave samples out on the table until the company cleaners arrived. The ones which were stolen most generally turned out to be best sellers.

The truth is that people will tell you they like the product they think they *ought* to like. But when they have to buy or even get a free gift, they choose what they really like.

For that reason, the right way to start establishing how products are likely to do is to go through a simple sequence. First, write to people asking them which of a list of products, briefly described, they find most appealing. Then choose the products that come out best, and write sample mailings or e-mails for each one. Test these mailings on your list, making it clear that customers will be able to buy the product later if and when it comes out, and giving a price, so that the offer is a real one. Then you choose the one or two products that do best, and start selling them seriously to your customers.

That's a very simplified description of a subject that deserves a lot of consideration. But one thing I would like to emphasise – and I make no apologies for saying this more than once, in different ways in the course of this book, because it is a mistake people *persist* in making – don't ask your customers (or anyone else, for that matter) what they 'think' of an ad or mailing. They are not critics. They are buyers. Even experts usually guess wrong. The ads people like are rarely (in fact almost *never*) the ones that do best.

What you really want to know about your messages is: do people understand them? And do they think the product in question would be useful to them, or is worth the price? All useful information to give you some idea (but no certainty) as to what is likely to happen.

Things research simply cannot tell you

TESTS THAT GAINED AN ACCOUNT

The subject of long letters and sweepstakes brings me to a true story about *Reader's Digest*, which is amongst the most determined and committed testers of all. For my own part I am very glad this is the case. For as a result of tests over 25 years ago, Trenear-Harvey, Bird & Watson gained the *Reader's Digest* account.

When we set out in business, we wrote to *Reader's Digest*, amongst others, offering our services. The marketing director replied politely, saying the company had a large internal creative department, and hardly needed us.

However, a year later they called us in and asked us to present our work. Afterwards, we were invited to prepare some work for an encyclopaedia. They gave us samples of the pages and a descriptive brochure to work from.

This was probably the most challenging project we had yet been offered. If we could get a chance to work for *Reader's Digest* it would be a feather in our caps. Apart from anything else, the company never used outside agencies to work on their merchandise.

Fired with enthusiasm, we went away and worked on the mailing package. We brought it back on the due date, and waited for them to comment.

A week passed. Then another. Then they called us back. The job had been just a test. The encyclopaedia did not exist; it had been *invented* for the occasion to see how we (and four other companies, including what was then the world's biggest agency, J Walter Thompson) would fare. They congratulated us and told us they thought ours was the best stab at the project. My partner and I looked at each other. I knew he was thinking what I was thinking – 'We've done it – we've got the *Digest*. Champagne all round tonight.'

We were brought swiftly down to earth. The marketing director explained that now they would like us to do a *real* test. They had always had mixed results selling records off the page. They wanted us to prepare an ad for a split-run test against their own ad prepared in-house.

This, then, was the moment when we had to deliver the goods. Could we do better than the *Digest*'s own superb creative department which knew the business backwards?

We worked feverishly on our ad, and it was accepted as it stood. ('No point in getting you in if we don't take your advice', observed the client.) Then it went into test in an A/B split in the *Sun* newspaper. Before it ran, we had a chance to see the ad the *Digest* had prepared. It was a bold, hard-hitting ad. I thought we had no chance.

In the event, our ad outpulled theirs substantially. Which shows that even after all these years in the business, I still can't be sure – a pretty good argument for testing.

When the results came in, we *did* break out the champagne. Especially when Victor Ross, the *éminence grise* of the publication, wrote us a letter of congratulations.

Another test

But we still didn't have the business. We had to prepare *another* ad for *another* product, and do *another* split-run. Sometimes this business reminds me of the Greek myth of Sisyphus, who spent eternity rolling a huge boulder up a mountain.

Once again, we saw the *Digest*'s ad before the split-run took place. Once again, everyone in our 11-man (and woman) agency voted on which would win. Once again, I thought *they* would. And once again, I was wrong – thank goodness.

This time, we did get the business. J Walter Thompson were so interested that their managing director came to see whether we might make a suitable acquisition. It consoled me somewhat that he was no better at guessing split-run results than I, because we put him to the test in our conference room.

Only testing can give you the answer
The truth is that *only* testing can give you the answer. Throughout the period we held the *Reader's Digest* business, they kept testing their ads against ours – they only beat us twice in 12 years.

TWO LAWS OF TESTING

Obviously, if you wish, you can test anything at all. Thirty years ago in the first flush of enthusiasm I used to test obsessively.

I recall testing the headline: 'This fully automatic washing machine can be yours for the price of a twin tub'. I put the word 'New' in front of the headline, and results went up. Then I tried the word 'Now'. There was no difference. Then I tried 'Look'. Still no change.

I was fiddling with the headline; not really changing anything of substance. 'New', 'now' and 'look' all mean much the same thing. As I have already said, you must go for *big* results in testing.

When I tried a radical change, and wrote: 'This fully automatic washing machine can be in your home within seven days', I found a new approach. An approach no *better* than the other one ... but *different*. We could rotate the ads and get more life out of our media schedule and thus, more sales over the period.

From this experience, I drew a lesson; a lesson which leads us to the first two laws of testing. These are:

The first two laws of testing

1 Only test a *meaningful* factor.
2 Test *one* or test *all*.

Let's look at these two laws in a little detail.

First of all, if you don't test meaningful factors, you risk learning nothing valuable.

Test meaningful factors

What do I mean by meaningful? To answer that, you must use commonsense. A delegate at one of the courses I used to teach asked me whether we had ever tested the effect different *styles* of handwriting would have in a mailing package, where we had added facsimile handwritten notes on the letter.

I thought this was a fairly irrelevant question; and my suspicions of the questioner's intelligence quickened when he pursued the matter at boring length.

Commonsense tells you the thing you have to test is the handwriting itself – is its personal nature likely to increase your results? Obviously, you want to be sure the writing is legible, similar in style (if possible) to the signer of the letter, and that if it is a male writing it should look like a male – and vice versa.

Commonsense should tell you not to test different words that mean the same thing (as I tried to in my washing machine headlines.) Commonsense should tell you to test *real* differences.

For example, in my washing machine ad, we tested putting a baby next to the machine. Results increased. Then we tested putting a baby and parents against the baby alone. Enquiries *doubled*, to my amazement. We repeated the test, with the same results.

We could never have anticipated such results. Someone told me that the reason might be that an unguarded baby by a washing machine looked at risk. I expected the baby on its own to do better, because I had read that babies increase response. I was wrong. But the test *was* about something meaningful. This is how you get big results.

'Test one or test all'

Apart from looking for big results, you should not waste your tests. That is why I say: 'Test one or test all.' Testing *one* means just taking one element in your ad or mailing and altering it.

If you change more than one element, then whatever the result may be, you'll never know what caused it. Possibly some of the changes you made were helpful, and others not. But the changes might counteract each other. You might even have a situation where a new package or ad appeared to make no real difference, although amongst the changes you made one might *on its own* have improved response dramatically.

Testing *all* means taking the communication and changing it root and branch: adopting a totally new approach in the hope of a big breakthrough. The moral, I think, is: little changes, little differences; and vice versa.

Little changes, little differences

I have spent more time than I care to contemplate sitting in smoke-filled rooms speculating why one package worked and another failed. It can't happen if you follow the rules.

When to test what

When should you test one factor; and when should you test all?

Limit what you test

Many people whose judgement I respect believe that given the choice between testing one and testing all – because obviously there is a limit to the number of things you can test at any one time – testing a completely new package is wiser. However, although this radical route may give great gains, it can also fall flat on its face because you are eliminating all the tested elements you know work.

If you are only going to test one element, then make sure it is a really important one. A completely changed offer. A much larger envelope. A different type of paper.

Let me give you an example of a case where changing the incentive made a great deal of difference.

Many years ago, for the first time we managed to attract an insurance company to our little agency. The client said he wanted a new approach to his mailings. The new package I wrote was a great disappointment to him. The approach seemed very similar; the content almost identical. 'I came to you looking for a new approach', he said to me. 'You charged me handsomely and all I have is something that's much the same.'

He was quite right. The only major change we made was to alter the first month's terms on his offer, so that people got a month free, where previously they had to pay £1. And we featured this offer on the envelope, which had been blank. The style of presentation and writing was different, but otherwise the content was very similar.

It seemed to me the biggest *single* change we could make was to alter the offer. And it was commonsense – from numerous previous tests – that the offer would do better if featured on the envelope. There was no need to test that.

Our new package increased response by over 60 per cent.

Once again though, very often after you have sent out a mailing you can review it and, based upon experience, make changes that you are pretty sure will lift response. These things may not call for radical change, but cumulatively they may make a great deal of difference. They can produce a package which *looks* quite similar, but is substantially different. It obviously makes sense.

My suggestion is that each season some of your tests should be single changes to your current winner and others totally new *ideas*. Both are necessary.

A firm that sold clothes had consistently, year after year, tested small but significant changes to their 'banker'. Suddenly their results fell. No matter what they did to their successful mailing they didn't seem to be able to come up with the improved responses they needed.

They found themselves in this position because they had previously neglected to try really radical tests. They had a very uncomfortable couple of seasons.

STARTLING RESULTS

Somebody once observed that one of the joys of travel is never knowing what you will find around the corner. So it is with testing.

Before giving you some practical advice on what you ought to test, let me give you some examples of the startling things that can happen.

A great friend and long-time mail order businessman, used to run an ad for night-driving glasses. His original headline was 'End blinding headlight glare'. After a while, the ad began to tire, so he changed it. He added one word: 'instantly'. Results jumped 20 per cent.

After another year or so, the new headline began to tire. So he added two more words, to make his headline: 'End blinding headlight glare instantly – for good'. Once again, results went up about 20 per cent.

So you see, even a word or phrase can make a difference. Often, the difference between profit and loss. A good reason for testing copy constantly.

In a series of tests for a mail shot selling garden compost, the following were some of the fascinating results that occurred:

- The name was changed from Cumba to Humush: sales went up 24 per cent.
- The mailing address was changed to one in the same county for each area. A 22 per cent increase was recorded.
- An incentive was offered for a quantity order. Twenty-seven per cent more sales came in. When the premium was offered for quantity as long as the order came in within 24 days, sales leapt 23 per cent.
- When the premium was changed from a trowel to secateurs, 13 per cent in sales was added. And when the premium was guaranteed, an 8 per cent increase came in.

● Perhaps the most striking results occurred when copy was put on the envelope. 'Humush for better gardens' is hardly the most imaginative line I can recall; but it pushed sales up a good 32 per cent. Almost as remarkable, when the incentive copy was also put on the envelope, an extra 27 per cent came in. (I am in Ernest Palfrey's debt for this interesting information.)

Why test results don't 'add up'

If you review individual test results you might conclude that by adding together a series of 10 such tests you could increase the effectiveness of a given communication by many hundreds of per cent. This would be wonderful if it were so, but unfortunately it isn't – as a statistician would tell you.

Check out what really happens

What happens is that individual tests when put together in one package in this way cannibalise each other, as it were. Thus, if you take an ad or mailing and make three changes, each of which *individually* increases response by, say, 20 per cent, 30 per cent and 50 per cent you do *not* get a 100 per cent uplift in response. The total uplift will be much lower. It is extremely important, therefore, that you test your new package with all the changes against the old one and check what really happens before you start getting excited.

Some impressive results are possible when you test the *position* of a particular item within a mailing. My former partner Brian Thomas found that when an incentive in a catalogue mailing was presented as a wraparound on the cover, as compared with a loose leaflet, response jumped over 25 per cent.

On another occasion he was amazed to get 11 times as many 'Member-get-a-member' names *without* offering a free gift as had previously been possible *with* one.

Why should this have made such a great difference? Quite simply because Brian decided to feature that offer on the flap of the envelope the respondent had to use to send in the order – and he was writing to agents who used to send in orders practically every month. As a result, they could hardly ignore the message.

Small changes can be significant

As I have already noted, changes which may *appear* extremely small when described can make substantial differences. In order to understand why this is so you should always look at the packages or advertisements in question. What sounds like a small change can be quite significant – as in the example I have just quoted. For instance, an Italian mailer changed the background colour of a mailing for a collectable from maroon to grey. Response leapt by 50 per cent. The reason for this apparently trivial change having such a large effect was simply that it made the copy much more legible.

But the thing I would most like to impress upon you is that many changes cost very little – sometimes nothing. The important thing is that you decide to test, and you think carefully *what* to test. Which brings me to my next subject.

NINE TESTING OPPORTUNITIES

1 The product or positioning

Rosser Reeves once observed that 'a gifted product is mightier than the gifted pen'.

As we have seen, it helps to have a gifted incentive too. But improving your product will have more effect than anything else. That stands to reason. After all, your product or service *is* your business. Sometimes, though, you can change your product without changing your entire business. Here are two examples.

For many years I was involved in the swimming pool business, as marketing adviser, copywriter, or advertising agency. It's an interesting challenge, selling pools in the UK. Rather like selling central heating in Zaire.

My patient and persevering client Steve Liu of Azure Pools found that things were really getting too tough for comfort. So we had a thoughtful lunch. How could he get more leads? I put it to him that the only way would be to get a better product. Something that no one else in the UK market had. He agreed, and said he was working on it. Meantime, what could we do?

Improve the product

I asked him why he thought people bought swimming pools. He talked about status, and investment, and health. I suggested it was because people wanted to *swim*, which was *so* obvious it was easy to forget.

Accordingly, I asked him whether the pool would cost all that much more if it were a few feet longer – but narrower. 'Not a lot', he replied. 'It's the excavation and the labour that costs the money.' So I wrote an ad that said: 'Four Extra Feet of Swimming Pool, FREE'. That did the trick for a couple of seasons: just changing the product so we could make an offer.

By that time, Steve had arranged to import a new pool from the US, made of a different kind of plastic, which gave him a unique story to tell. That did even better, because it was a genuinely improved product.

Here's another example.

When my late partner Martin Topley and I were running the Business Ideas Letter, we were looking for a way to make it more appealing.

'People are gregarious animals', the saying goes. People love to belong. Could we create something more than the publication that people could relate to? Something that would give it added value. We started the Institute of Small Business, which offered free advice to would-be entrepreneurs. And we found – as many have done before and since – that a good way to make your service or product more appealing is to start a club.

Start a club

Frankly, we stumbled on the idea almost by accident. But we wrought better than we knew; for over 20 years later all the promotional material sent out by the publisher still sold membership of the Institute, not subscriptions to the publication. We were really altering the positioning of the product rather than the product itself.

Why not look at your product and the way it is presented to see what you might test?

2 Your offer or incentive

The power of a good offer

I have talked about this at length already but I return to it happily, since no matter how often I emphasise its power, people still underestimate it. It's quite amazing how much difference changes in incentive make. My first experience of this was, by coincidence, also with the Business Ideas Letter.

Instead of asking people to pay their subscriptions immediately, we suggested they send us a post-dated banker's order, so they could try the publication for three months without risk.

Results doubled. The same offer worked for our client Comp-U-Card, who I mentioned at the start of the previous chapter.

On the other hand, when a US charitable foundation tried selling membership by offering a free three-month trial, it didn't work. One more reason *always* to test. Just because it works for one product or service, it doesn't mean it will work for all. Or, as they say: different strokes for different folks.

The number of offers you can test is limited only by the power of your imagination.

I have already quoted the late Joe Karbo – a most exceptional copywriter – whose offer was: 'I'm so sure you'll like my book *The Lazy Man's Way To Get Rich* that I won't cash your cheque for 30 days.' The ads ran for over 20 years.

The power of the negative incentive

Some of my favourites include: 'If you don't like this pipe, smash it, and send back the pieces.' Or, 'If you don't like this book, rip off the cover and send it back for a full refund.' Or, 'Double your money back if not delighted.' I mentioned the penalty or negative incentive. The power of this is such that the Franklin Mint's marketing strategy depends upon it: they simply offer a product until a certain close date, after which no more will be sold. In my experience, telling people that they have to reply in seven days or by a certain date always increases response.

In short, before you test any creative execution, look to test your offer, because it could pay big dividends for you.

3 Price

Many years ago I worked for the late Mickey Barnes, an astute marketing man who rose to become the head of the famous SH Benson agency – only to preside over its demise.

He once said to me: '*Price* is creative.'

This struck me as loose use of language; but certainly price can have more effect on results than practically any other factor.

In the UK, it is illegal to run two advertisements simultaneously offering different prices – or if not illegal, frowned on by the newspapers, and thus almost impossible.

Why this should be is not clear to me. My neighbour and I shop differently. By buying at different times or in different shops we can buy the same branded products at different prices. However, there it is: you cannot conduct split-runs on price in the press.

But you can run split *mailing* tests on price, and it is very easy using the internet.

Price is subjective

Price is a subjective thing. What you consider a proper price may not seem so to your customers. Sometimes, your price may seem too high to them; but more often than you might imagine, it can actually seem too low. For Comp-U-Card the highest price did best.

You can often charge a very high price where the product you are offering has no direct competitor. The Franklin Mint and similar companies are constantly producing unique products. It is very difficult for a consumer to put a value on these. They are worth what people are prepared to pay for them. One of the cleverest methods of establishing the value of a product was developed by the Bradford Exchange. They have created a mini stock market of their own in collectable plates. As added reassurance they offered to buy the product back from the prospect at the price paid within a certain period after it was bought.

I recall years ago talking to a shrewd mail order operator who was selling imported American items in France, but almost always at a much higher price than in the US. I asked him the reason. He replied: 'Drayton, if it isn't expensive, how can it be any good?'

Ask your customers

So: don't just pick a price that seems right to you. Let your customers decide. Try three or four prices, and see which makes you most profit. Remember, too, that a higher price can always be slashed. It's not always so easy to raise a lower one – particularly as that low price has set a value in your customer's mind (and vice versa).

4 Discounting: what works?

Under price we must consider *discounting*. This can have radical effects on response. I once took part in a seminar on split-run testing. I learned a lot, and made new friends including Tony Arau, like so many successful people in our business, a former *Reader's Digest* man.

He showed a series of results relating to price offers. When one organisation slashed its membership price by 33 per cent, responses jumped from 0.65 per cent to 1.20 per cent, more than offsetting the loss of revenue on individual memberships. However, when he tried a half-price offer, it was not cost-effective.

Test different discounts

So test different discounts and test how you express those discounts.

A few years ago, our agency was asked to work on the sale of a new business publication. The only change (other than the copy) that we suggested was that the price be raised by 20 per cent, so that we could offer a discount to subscribers if they joined within a certain period. The product was not altered; the ad appeared in exactly the same media. The response was 20 times greater than the previous mailing. The only additional cost was our fee.

Here are several ways of saying the same thing. They will all get a different response. Because what is important is not what you *say* – it is what people *hear*.

- Save 50 per cent
- 50 per cent off
- Save £11

- Half price
- Buy one, get one FREE
- Two for £22

You might like to know that the 'Buy one, get one FREE' formulation works best, according to a friend who has conducted tests.

You can profitably spend many happy hours working out the many possible permutations of price offer. A sort of commercial crossword. Obviously, these permutations depend on what you are selling. Thus, a year's newsletter subscription can be expressed in many ways. £50 a year. Less than £1 a week. Under £2 an issue if it comes out fortnightly. Or, perhaps, 14p a day.

In one case, we tested whether you ought to include the post and packing charge in the price of a mail order product: eg £47 *plus* £2 postage and packing versus £49 *including* postage and packing.

The change did make a significant difference to response. But this depended upon the price level. Thus, if the addition of postage and packing were to bring the price above the £50 mark, then almost certainly quoting the price plus postage and packing will do better – eg £49 plus £2 postage and packing.

This is simply a matter of commonsense: psychologically £50 is clearly breaking a price barrier. The first time I got involved in price was when I proposed to a client that instead of charging £67 he charge £69 – since to the public it would make very little difference. This certainly proved to be so, and increased his profit margin substantially.

5 Incentives

A relevant premium rarely fails to pull added response above its cost. By relevant, I mean something likely to be of interest to your prospect – either of *universal* appeal, or appealing to people likely to be interested in a specific product. Thus, clocks seem to be of universal appeal, whereas garden shears only interest gardeners. A sundial might appeal to gardeners and homeowners.

Never give something for nothing

As we saw earlier, an incentive should be related to some action. Early buying. Buying in quantity. Giving another person's name. Never give something for nothing.

One client offered two mystery gifts to encourage lapsed agents to rejoin the clan: each for a different purpose. One was a gift for replying; one for replying quickly. Fingerhut Corporation in the United States used to offer four gifts to their prospects, and for all I know may now offer five, if they find it pays.

Incentives can be offered in steps. So much for buying £10 worth of a product. More for buying £20 worth, and so on. You can vary the incentive according to the level of a customer's loyalty, their interest in your product, where they live or what kind of people they are. Thus, a country dweller could be offered a different incentive to a town dweller; a gardener something different to an angler.

As we learned above, *changing* the premium can affect results quite dramatically, too. So test that as well. But of all the incentives the sweepstake seems to be most effective – though it is not legal in all countries.

I confess I cannot understand why sweepstakes do so well, not being a gambler myself (life is chancy enough already). However, they can increase responses dramatically when prominently featured.

So try a sweepstake, and don't be too worried about the fact that you may think your customers are too sophisticated to react to this sort of nonsense. Lots of ordinary people play the football pools each week. But lots of very rich people go to casinos in Monte Carlo, London and Las Vegas. Gambling is a universal source of amusement. What you have to do is try a *sophisticated* sweepstake.

Try a sweepstake

In Britain *The Times* managed to raise circulation substantially by offering what to all intents and purposes was little more than a simple gamble. The trick was that they called it 'Portfolio' and related it to share prices.

A word of warning, though. Incentives of this kind sometimes do not produce the same quality of respondents as a straightforward product sell.

It stands to reason that someone who has been induced to buy as a result of being attracted by big prizes in the sweepstake is less interested in the product itself. (Remember, for a sweepstake, in most countries your customer cannot be asked to buy anything or do anything: that is illegal. However, people always imagine that the buyer stands a better chance than the non-buyer.)

The thing to remember is that if people are brought in by this sort of device, they are likely to respond to the same sort of thing in the future. So when selling them something new, you will need to bear that in mind.

Contests are also a good incentive, with the advantage – in Britain, anyway – that people who enter a contest must buy something, and must exercise some 'skill or judgement' – however minimal – in entering. I suspect the quality of contest entrants is marginally higher than that of sweepstakes buyers, since some effort is required.

What about prize structure? I have always understood that the best structure is one where there is a very spectacular major prize, and lots of very small ones. In this way, you combine the large promise with the chance of as many people winning as possible. (Incidentally, the best prizes seem to be *things*, not money, for they dramatise the offer. But people tend to take the money if they win.)

Test and find out

Latterly, I have been told that, on the contrary, the best structure is just to have one big prize and no little ones. But this is a technical subject I am not competent to pronounce on. Test it and find out. A very powerful message is 'You may already have won ...'. This is achieved by issuing numbers to the people you mail, but holding the draw before the mailing.

Leisure Arts ran a mailing in which everybody won a prize. They could afford to offer a small prize to everybody because, as Lenny Joseph their UK boss once told me: 'We got 50 per cent response.'

6 Time and number closes

Act now

I always used to say that people fear to lose as much as they hope to gain. And I saw some research in 2005 which suggested that, at least in financial matters, the fear of loss is a greater motivator than the hope of gain. No wonder offers that encourage you to act now lest you miss an opportunity work so well.

Many offers can be linked to price. You can offer a price advantage if the customer orders by a certain time. You can offer the opportunity to avoid a price rise: an exceptionally powerful incentive.

Nearly 30 years ago, one of my clients – Solarbo – was selling bedrooms and kitchens which people had to put together themselves. At that time, the government had just increased the rate of value added tax. We offered to pay the extra VAT for the customer if the order came in within 30 days, with full cash payment.

Eighteen thousand letters went out. Orders worth £78,000 (a lot of money in those days) came in; with a nice boost for the company's cash flow, since usually many of their sales were on credit.

Another way of motivating people is to say that you only have a certain number of the item in stock. This is unquestionably effective. An arbitrary date by which applications or orders must be received works well, too. *Anything* which helps to move people out of their lethargy is worthwhile.

7 Your logistics

There are many physical things you can and should test. For example, in the area of media there are a number of significant test opportunities.

For three years the Metropolitan Opera Guild in New York tested television to recruit subscribers. They discovered that not only was television a very expensive way of producing results (for instance it cost $20,000 to produce an inexpensive commercial, with Placido Domingo appearing for nothing) but that the calibre of subscribers was not as high as those attracted through direct mail.

Direct mail, obviously, can tell a complete and convincing story; the TV operation as compared to direct mail produced a renewal rate from subscribers of 25 per cent as opposed to 75 per cent. One comment made was that responses on television tend to be more impulsive than those made through direct mail.

A client selling an investment course found that the quality of replies from advertisements and inserts was better than those produced by direct mail. My client's theory was that this was because prospects had to take the trouble to fill in their name and address, which was done for them in advance in the direct mail. But quite apart from testing media, there are a number of things you can do.

But quite apart from testing new media themselves there are a number of other things you can do.

- Test *timing*. Most people get their best results in January and February. But your product or service may be different.   **Some sensible tests**
- And what about days of the week? For years, I imagined that after Sunday, Saturday was the best day. The reason for this is that a long time ago, when the newspapers couldn't sell space on Saturdays, they inaugurated the Saturday bargain page.

    This page became associated with mail order offers, and in my mind was *the* mail order advertising day. Of course, on Saturday one could also usually negotiate discounts, which was a sweetener.

    In fact in the UK Tuesday is the best day for most people, followed by Wednesday, Thursday and Monday, then Friday, then Saturday. But for you, it may be different. In fact, one company selling to DIY buyers and small tradespeople *does* find Saturday the best day.
- Consider size of space. Are you better off having a larger space or two small ones scattered through the publication? Or one small one, flagging a larger one? You'll never know till you try. And don't forget, just because the figures indicate that small spaces are more cost-effective, this may not be the case for you. Your product may be of such interest to people and have so many benefits that a large space will more than pay for itself.
- How about taking your ad and trying it in the form of an insert in a magazine? Normally, it will pull far more than an ad – maybe three to five times as much.   **Try a different medium**
- Or, if you're running inserts already, try changing their format. An L-shaped insert with the reply-paid card on the foot of the 'L' often works as much as 50 per cent better than an oblong one. And a bound-in insert tends to do better than a loose one, as I have already mentioned.

    Then there are the myriad possibilities the internet has introduced, starting with e-mail. Try testing an e-mail version of your direct mail piece. One of the interesting things about this direct marketing business is that there are so *many* things to try, and you learn so much as you go.   **Try many variables**
- How about your ad's position? I cover this in my section on the media. This is critical. And certainly you should pay great attention to it. Moreover, the effect of position will vary according to your company and your product.

One of our clients finds that his left-hand-page ads tend to do badly. Another finds that the right or left hand makes no difference at all. Why don't you find out what works for you?

- Then there's the vast number of things you can do with catalogues. Every catalogue has its own personality. But where you place items in a catalogue has a radical effect on sales.

    Where is the order form? Is it laid out easily enough? Have you tried putting extra blank space in it that people can fill in to give you more orders? Some people find this increases sales automatically.

- What about your mailings? Are you testing enough new lists each season? Are you testing new formats?

- Are you testing the growing opportunities for inserting in other people's packages? In his *Mail Order Moonlighting*, Cecil Hoge, one of the pioneers of modern mail order in the United States, recommends this as the cheapest (and most cost-effective) way of getting started in business.

- And are you inserting enough material in your own fulfilment packs? Have you tested the optimum number of pieces? Have you tried simply filling up envelopes right to the postal limit?

So you see, in mere mechanical areas – nothing much to do with 'creativity' – there are huge test opportunities. Don't neglect them.

8 Creative

The way you say it

Sometimes it ain't what you say, it's the way that you say it. And this brings us to the subject of creative tests. Here, by definition, the possibilities are almost limitless, for what we are simply talking about is getting new ideas, or adapting old ones.

What's particularly valuable about creative changes (and particularly copy changes) is that not only can they produce the most surprising results, but often they cost little or nothing to make. In the ads for Pitney Bowes featured earlier in this book, the better advertisement was actually *cheaper* to run because it was in black and white, not colour.

9 Tricks

Involve the reader

Some of the most worthwhile tests fall rather between two stools. They are not quite creative; they are not simply mechanical. They involve thinking about techniques which of themselves attract attention. Tricks that intrigue.

For example there are yes/no stamps in all their various forms. People have found that having such stamps printed in gold can increase response. Others have tried not just stamps, but envelopes; one for your 'Yes', the other for your 'No' (the one you want people to use obviously being a pleasing affair; the other a nasty dun-coloured mess). There are yes/no vouchers, too.

All these things tend to work because they involve the reader and force a choice. In my experience, though you get more 'noes' than 'yesses', you do get more 'yesses' overall.

Then there is personalisation in all its various manifestations; cut-outs in envelopes; pop-ups. Or trying a miniature typeface on a miniature letter; or a giant type-face on a giant letter.

The actual *feel* of a package can make quite a difference. A friend tells me a giant publishing house tested making their insert slightly larger than other people's inserts, and using a heavier weight of paper. He believes that as a result their responses went up 20 per cent.

Years ago a paper company, Svecia Antiqua, arranged for a series of tests to determine what effect a different texture of stock has on responses. In a series of tests, it improved results by 15 per cent, 25 per cent, 32 per cent, 61 per cent and 92 per cent.

Simply changing the colour of an envelope can dramatically improve responses. In my experience, by as much as 20 per cent.

HOW MUCH SHOULD YOU TEST? AND WHEN?

Testing is the *kernel* of direct marketing. The truth is that every major direct marketing business that succeeds does so largely by testing – or a run of quite exceptional luck. Luck is not something to base a business on; if I were you I would try the safer route.

Testing is the kernel of direct marketing

If at the beginning of each season you were to see the number of tests scheduled by a major mail order company, you might be quite surprised. It could easily fill a sheet of A3 paper, typed quite closely. And these are *successful* companies with *successful* products. They know that testing is in some ways more important when you are doing well than when you are doing badly.

Complacency is a poor basis for long-term success. Yet I have often heard people reject a proposed test on the grounds that they were 'doing very well, thank you'. This is poor thinking. For it is precisely when you *are* successful that you should worry about possible competition.

That's why you must have a body of knowledge built up from testing which will beat that competition when it comes. Anyone can copy your idea. But nobody can steal your knowledge.

Build up a body of knowledge

Perhaps you recall the story of the victorious generals in ancient Rome who were allowed to ride in triumph through the streets of the city. Behind them in the victor's chariot a man was stationed. His job was to whisper at intervals: 'Remember, thou art human.'

No matter how well you are doing, the day will come when – perhaps for no reason you can fathom – your results suddenly slump. Your control mailing stops pulling. Your winning ad tires. That's when you'll be glad you've tested some alternatives.

When you are in trouble, it's natural to test. You have to, in order to succeed. But each year, no matter how well you are doing, you are wise to schedule a good 10 per cent of your budget to testing. More if you can afford it.

Often, it's a good idea to schedule tests for the off-season. In the summer you can get cheaper ad rates, for example. And having done your tests, you're ready to take advantage of the results when the best time of year comes round.

The best companies never stop testing.

Your test programme can be compared in many ways with the industrial investment programme of a great nation. Britain and the United States invest only a puny percentage of their gross national product in new plant and equipment each year, whereas Japan invests many times as much. We all know who's done best over the last 40 years.

A FAMOUS CASE-HISTORY

I started this chapter by telling how we became involved with *Reader's Digest*. Let me end it by reprinting a speech made by Tony Arau for a Florida Direct Marketing Day years ago. I think it is both amusing and educational. I hope you do too.

Tony's title for his speech was 'The world's most successful direct mail piece – and how it grew'.

The object of the mailing was to get new readers by offering a reduced-rate introductory subscription. The market was American families with telephones in selected areas.

150 million pennies

Probably the most famous direct mailing piece ever created was the highly successful 'Two Penny' mailing used by *Reader's Digest* in the 1950s.

The famous penny mailing

At the peak of its use it required so many pennies that conventional suppliers and banks couldn't supply the *Digest*'s needs (some 150 million pennies a year), so the *Digest* became the first private customer in the history of the US Mint.

But the famous penny mailing did not spring into being, full-blown all at one stroke of genius. And its history is instructive for everyone who plays a role in the creation of direct mail.

'If thou hast two pennies ...'

Back in the early 1950s, the *Digest*'s circulation director, Frank Herbert, wrote what remains today one of the simplest but most brilliant direct mail letters of all time. It was known at the *Digest* as 'The Persian Poet' letter, and it began like this:

Dear Reader:

An ancient Persian poet once wrote, 'If thou hast two pennies, spend one for bread, and with the other buy hyacinths for thy soul'.

The letter then went on and, obviously, suggested the *Reader's Digest* as a modern sort of hyacinth for one's spirit, proposing a short trial subscription as a way to discover the pleasures of the *Digest* for oneself.

It was first mailed in a plain, white nine-inch envelope; inside was a simple order card (with the *Digest*'s Pegasus logo faintly imprinted in the background); the letter was run in black and red on both sides of a single sheet; a small four-page, four-colour brochure was enclosed.

Since it was a typical *Digest* 'Send no money' offer, the order card had a business reply back.

Worked for several years

The letter worked for several years, undergoing minor modifications from time to time. At one point, the copy line 'If thou hast two pennies ...' was added to the envelope in an oriental sort of type.

When the *Digest*'s new book club began at around that time, the Persian Poet letter was successfully adapted for condensed book promotions, too.

Reader's Digest has always been rather paranoid about revealing results of its various promotional efforts (and, within reason, properly so) so actual figures cannot be used here.

But using a scale of 10 to 100 for comparisons, the original Persian Poet letter scored about 35. By adding copy to the outer envelope, sprucing up the order card and the like, response was eventually boosted to a 45 level.

Results improved bit by bit

Response slipped

But then, after several major mailings, response began to slip. It had drifted back to somewhere around the 40 level when Frank Herbert retired from the *Digest* and a young *Digest* copywriter named Walter Weintz found himself promoted to circulation director.

Weintz promptly began a series of vigorous copy tests to find a way to either strengthen or replace the fading Persian Poet mailing.

Results were generally disappointing until he tried a remarkably ugly, sort of gold coloured plastic 'Savings Token' – really the first of the *Digest*'s famous 'gimmick' mailings.

This brought response back to the 45 level, then up to the 50 level by using the token in combination with the Poet copy.

But Weintz felt that he had still not achieved the major new piece he was searching for. And then he thought of pennies.

Horrified management

Although the thought of mailing two pennies, twice a year, to nearly every American household with a telephone horrified *Digest* management, Weintz was given the go-ahead (the *Digest* is probably the greatest direct mail testing laboratory in the world).

The early penny tests took three basic approaches.

The first contained two pennies, tied directly to the Persian Poet copy concept (keep one penny to buy 'bread', send the other back to buy 'hyacinths for thy soul', the *Reader's Digest*).

The *Reader's Digest* breakthrough

A pocket was provided on the order card for return of the penny, and a business reply envelope was enclosed to carry the order card and penny, but the offer was the same, basic introductory subscription 'trial' offer.

Response jumped

Results were dramatic. On our scale of 10 to 100, response immediately jumped to somewhere around the 60 mark.

A version was also tried using a single penny (hoping to save $10 per thousand in the mail cost) – the copy modified to a simple 'here's your penny for hyacinths' approach. It did not do as well, pulling something like 50 on our scale.

Then the two-penny version was tried with a brand new offer, something of the order of 12 issues for $1.98, we'll bill you later for $2.00, and you keep the enclosed 2c as your 'change' in advance.

The basic copy and outer envelope were still a variation on the Persian Poet. But response jumped to something of the order of 75.

The *Digest* had its big breakthrough.

Later, the envelope copy was changed to a simple 'Here's your change', with the two pennies showing through a window beneath the copy, and response inched up another five or so.

Poet retired

Eventually, a version was tried using completely new straightforward copy, without any references to Persian Poets – and response went up another five or thereabouts. The Persian Poet, after several years of yeoman duty, had finally been retired.

The new two-penny mailing was successfully adapted for the *Digest*'s Condensed Book Club ('Your first book for only 8c – just send us a dime for convenience, and keep the enclosed 2c change, in advance'). And it was even used for a couple of the *Digest*'s one-shot book promotions.

Over the years, numerous attempts were made to improve on the basic two-penny piece. One, resurrecting the Persian Poet copy, was tested with two real Persian pennies (actually, they were bronze Lebanese piastres). Another, based on the philosophy that if 2c is good, 5c should be about twice as good, actually included a nickel 'change' in advance.

Both were comparative disasters. In fact, if anyone would like to start a coin collection featuring Lebanese piastres, the *Reader's Digest* can probably provide several thousand cheap.

Staying power

Good copy and good promotional concepts sometimes have an astonishing staying power.

Good copy and good concepts

When the *Digest* bought the RCA Victor Record Club, the first successful new promotional piece was a variation on the basic two-penny offer.

Several years later, *Life* magazine put together a very successful piece which used its own variation – a single penny, showing through a window, with the copy line 'Here's your change ... and here's your chance ... to see life ... to see the world ... to eyewitness great events'. And many other mailers have over the years used the penny technique in any of a number of different ways.

Historical footnote: Because the pennies cost more to return than they were worth, the *Digest* attempted to have the Post Office simply destroy undelivered mail. And because some people who didn't want to subscribe to the *Digest* felt uneasy about keeping the two pennies, the *Digest* ran a copy line urging people to keep the pennies, please, not to return them, even if they didn't want to take advantage of the *Digest*'s offer.

A footnote

But the Post Office informed the *Digest* that they could not legally destroy or dispose of the mail containing pennies – the *Digest* had to pay to have its undeliverable mail returned. And many people insisted on sending their pennies back.

So the *Digest* was stuck with a growing warehouseful of penny mailings – mailings that cost about 4c each to open and salvage the pennies from. It became both a problem and a mild embarrassment.

Then Al Cole, General Manager of the *Digest* and president of the Boys Clubs of America, made his major contribution to the penny game.

He knew the local Mt Kisco Boys Club was struggling to raise money to build a new club building, so he made the kids a deal: if they'd open the mail, shuck the pennies off the cards and separate them into two piles, the Boys Club could keep the pennies and return the cards to the *Digest* to be reused.

At the time, a staggering total of something like 50 million pennies was involved. And the Boys Club of Mt Kisco got its new club house.

Not bad for a cheap little 2c mailing piece.

A footnote to this story: The *Reader's Digest* is *still* using coins – not to mention stamps for the cost of your response – in their mailings. I have seen a UK charity use it, and my agency used it successfully for a private utility in the UK – it still works. Because, contrary to what some believe, human behaviour changes very little over the years – if at all.

Where research fails; what to test – and more

- Testing not a panacea: don't ignore research.
- See how people are likely to react – and why.
- Two laws:
  - Only test big things.
  - Test one thing – or everything.
- Small but significant changes make big differences.
- Results cannibalise each other.
- Nine good testing opportunities.
- Why testing is a good investment – and how much to do.
- Beware complacency: keep testing.
- A classic test history.
- Old tricks still work.

14

How to Choose Your Agency – and When to Do Without One

> *'Those who counsel do not pay.'*
> Flemish proverb

I once read an article by a Mr Ragu Chellan, in *The Times of India*, about choosing a computer. I have never met Mr Chellan, but I thought he gave a most apposite analogy; one which applies just as well to choosing an agency – or for that matter any supplier.

> Deciding to buy a computer is like deciding to get married – the Indian way. You look at a variety of models, you compare attributes, you make a mental checklist of the points you like and the points you don't like, you ask friends and family about the prospective spouse and you try to imagine the situation a few years ahead.

How to choose

He went on to point out that the first question is not how to buy, but *why*? Once again, remarkably appropriate whether you are considering an advertising agency or a mailing house. What precisely do you want to achieve?

Sometimes I wouldn't recommend an agency at all. The same may apply to a mailing house. If you have a small operation you are building from the ground floor up, you may decide to fulfil this function yourself.

In considering any supplier it is certainly wise to review all your options. Don't do a deal with the first kind face you meet. Don't just go and see one agency – have a look at several.

See several agencies

Certainly ask around. Consult friends, colleagues. Look through the trade press. Visit seminars and conferences to check out the available talent. I am astounded how few people do these things. Indeed, I sometimes think people make significant decisions about suppliers with less care than they would in choosing a new car. Some, because they are excessively grand, do not

Ask for a list of current clients

deign to take the basic step of going round and having a look at the premises of the people they are proposing to do business with. They deal with the whole thing as though they were hiring a chauffeur-driven limousine.

Very few bother to do the obvious: ask for a list of current clients and go and talk to some of them. Perhaps they are too shy.

One other point Mr Chellan made impressed me particularly. 'Try to imagine the situation a few years ahead.' When you choose an agency or any other supplier, then you must envisage what the future situation might be. If it's a small agency, are they going to be able to cope with your business as it grows? If they're large, and you intend to stay small, will you retain their interest? Do they have sufficient talent in depth – bright young people – to be able to handle your business over a period of time?

One consideration, of course, that applies to brides and to companies is perhaps the most important of all. Do you actually *like* the people you meet? Do you think you could develop a good relationship with them – a friendly one? You should certainly spend enough time with them to get some impression of what sort of people they are. And not just on a business basis, but if possible socially, too.

Madness at work

Madness at work

Some of the ways clients choose agencies beggar belief. I was recently asked to advise an agency pitching for a huge direct marketing account. Doing this in a business where results are all that matters is sheer folly anyhow, but here's what made things utterly ludicrous.

First a long list of agencies pitched to get on the short list by explaining what qualified them to handle the account. This made some sense, even if it wasted everybody's time and money. Then the short listed agencies pitched and – here's the madness – the two winning agencies put in bids to see who would charge less. So (in the questionable event that the judges got it right) the agency that was best could lose on price.

So this client might not actually get the best – just the cheapest. This is not even an intelligent way to choose toilet rolls, let alone agencies. What's more, one way or another, the winning agency will find a way to recoup the money, by delivering less or charging more in ways the client won't notice, so the savings are an illusion.

This client (a very famous one indeed) has pretty much invited the patients in to run the asylum. No wonder their results over the last couple of years have been catastrophic, to the point where they had to sell out.

Of course, since the only thing that really matters is results, the whole thing could (and should) be settled faster and less expensively by a series of tests. Indeed, it is hard to see how those judging the agencies could have much idea how well they might perform, because after decades in this business, I can't predict results with a high degree of certainty.

I might add that the results approach can be used in any kind of marketing. The founder of Revlon, for instance, used to test different propositions – and even prices – by testing two different but similar markets. But the real moral is simple. Results are what matter, not costs. You will never congratulate yourself on how much money you save if it doesn't work; and you won't give a damn about paying a little extra if it does.

AGENCY OR NOT?

Choosing an agency reminds me of a statement made by a French nineteenth century wit, Count Montrond: 'Beware first impressions; they are almost invariably good.' Agency people tend to be fairly articulate and often very charming, and are hardly inclined to wax lyrical about their failures when you come to call.

'Beware first impressions...'

So many factors may be involved in the final decision that it can prove something of a lottery. Here are my thoughts on the matter, having sat on both sides of the fence.

How easy is it to find a good agency? Very difficult, in my view. There is a great shortage of talent counterbalanced by a massive over supply of persuasive waffle. In some cases you may find you are educating the agency as much as they are you.

Unfortunately, agencies themselves are not always shrewd about selecting their clients. They are often so excited by the idea of getting any business that they will take on all accounts, no matter what size. In taking on more business than they can handle, or the sort of business they should not try to handle, they are often particularly shortsighted.

Agencies are not always shrewd

A few years ago a small client came to us because he was not satisfied with the service he was getting from a competitor. Had we been wise, we would have reflected that our competitor was a man who normally served his clients very well and declined the business. Foolishly, fired by the thought of taking the business away from our rival, we took it on. We soon learned we could no more afford to service it properly than our competitor. We lost money and so did our client because we had barely begun to understand his business before we mutually agreed to call it a day.

Certain businesses are so complex and work-intensive that only the client can understand the problems and produce the promotional material economically. This is typically the case with a large publishing organisation with many products selling to small, specialised markets.

Sometimes, too, your budget may be too small to make it profitable for a good agency. Yet although your business may not be large, your problems are just as important to you as a large company's – and, for the agency, just as demanding. Under those circumstances it's certainly no use dealing with a large agency. They have high overheads. They can't afford to employ top talent on your business. You might be able to locate a good *small* agency – but

Your budget may be too small

such gems are rare. What is more, unless your business is going to grow with them, they may prove short-term partners.

Under such circumstances, do it yourself: because you are the only one who cares enough. Do it entirely on your own or in conjunction with a freelance, but don't waste time with an agency. (You may be wondering what is a large budget and what is a small one. Unfortunately, there is no simple answer to this; it depends on the market. A million dollars a year is a big budget in Denmark. In New York it would be small. When looking at an agency, the best thing to do is to find out how large their average account is. If you are going to be a little fish in a big pond, beware.)

Don't be a little fish in a big pond

Why stay in-house?

Reader's Digest, which I have mentioned already, plans and creates its mailings in-house. A powerful argument in favour of the in-house operation.

In 1987, a survey of 12 advertisers by Ad Business Reports in America outlined their reasons for having in-house advertising units. They were:

Consider these reasons

- More control of the process.
- Greater confidentiality.
- More access to company people, products and customers.
- Better knowledge of product or service.
- Direct contact between writer and merchandiser.
- Less likelihood of information being misinterpreted as it is passed along.
- More involvement.
- Greater speed and flexibility. Eg one company took 100 photos, and set up two 16-page catalogues in 15 days for a trade show.
- Creativity which is as good – maybe better.

I hold no brief for either in-house or advertising-agency route – I have worked as an agent, and ran an in-house advertising department in the past.

Unquestionably you can get greater flexibility in-house. One US in-house advertising unit receives sales figures five times a day. Particularly in the retail business it is important to be able to make changes quickly. The market is very volatile. Something as simple as the weather can affect what is happening.

Economies can be made

In addition to the benefits cited above, economies can be made. For instance, you need no account executives to mediate between client and agency.

I believe the chief drawback of the in-house operation is that it is *introverted*: it is difficult for fresh thinking to emerge. That is where the relatively objective – if less well informed – agency's contribution can be beneficial.

The argument that creativity is as good, often better, is one I find hard to accept. I can think of little in-house creative work of very high calibre. This is because in-house operations tend to pay less money and attract less experienced talent. The challenge and variety of work in the agencies appeal more to young people. However, many talented people start out in-house – working on catalogue copy, for example, which is very good training.

Us and you

The average marketing man's wife, asked to define her idea of hell, would probably reply: 'A night out with my husband and a group of his colleagues.' Whenever two or three marketing people gather together, they talk nothing but shop. The agency world especially is very inward looking.

This navel-gazing comes out nowhere more strongly than in agency presentations. They stand up, thrilled to bits to have the opportunity to talk interminably about themselves, their philosophy, their theories, their staff, their agency's history ... and so on. This is also apparent on almost all agency websites, which are all 'about us'.

Beware navel-gazing

This agency weakness of talking about 'us' when the conversation should be about 'you' should be stamped out to the profit of all.

Whenever a prospective client comes to see us because he or she is 'looking around', my heart sinks. It gives you nothing to get your teeth into.

When client and prospective agency meet, the conversation should centre around the client's particular needs. Thus both parties are more likely to find satisfaction. The client will get a good idea of the way the agency approaches a problem. The agency will be able to display its prowess. Drivel will be minimised.

Apart from their views on your problem, the thing you want to know about an agency is how they have dealt with others. For this reason, a presentation of case-histories is worthwhile. (I would *insist* on them.)

Don't let the display be confined to vague befores and afters: 'Before it was like this; now it's like this, and didn't we do well.' Ask *why* changes were made. Look for the thinking more than the general impression. Insist on facts about results.

Learning what they did for others is almost certainly more useful than wondering what they might do for you – or speculative work, which I come to next. And if I were choosing an agency, I would ask whether anyone there has worked as a client or has general business experience. If nobody at your agency has ever faced the kind of decisions you face, their advice can only be based on abstract theory bolstered by what they have seen happen to other clients. Is that enough?

SPECULATIVE PRESENTATIONS

When Dr Barnardo's came to see my old agency, THB&W, they told us they had been looking at agencies for eight months, and had a short-list of five, who were putting up speculative work for nothing. Would we like to join them?

We declined. How could we possibly understand their organisation and activities in a couple of weeks?

Speculative presentations are a pernicious waste of time, emotion and money. They are just a sort of beauty parade. Generally I do not think you should request speculative work unless the agency understand your business very well. On the other hand, I see no reason that you should not give the agency a full brief on some problem that concerns you, and get them to make suggestions. This allows them to demonstrate their thinking ability, and gives you a fair insight into their calibre without the ruinous costs of full-scale creative work.

Where speculative creative work calls for more than a cursory skirmish, it ought to be paid for. If it costs nothing, what is it worth? In any case, why should my existing clients subsidise free work for you when they are paying me to work for them? We generally only work for nothing if we have idle hands, or an existing client requests it.

One must be honest, however, and admit that the thought of a fat, lucrative account or one with enormous potential erodes one's views on this. Nevertheless, the practice is wasteful; in the end, clients as a group pay for it one way or another.

Test against existing material

A sensible way to assess an agency is to pay them to create something you can test against the existing material. If you do this, it's a good idea to give the agency more than one test opportunity. A single test is like deciding a World Cup result on one penalty kick.

ORGANISATION AND PROCEDURE

Organisation charts have their place, but you really want to know precisely how an agency will *handle* your business. Ask them to show you how a job goes through from start to finish. Try and get an insight into their views on marketing *strategy*, too. Tactical direct marketing is all very well, but only good strategic thinking will build your business.

One thing you may find very confusing when meeting or dealing with agencies is the titles they deploy in such large numbers. Thus, you may well be taken aback when some beardless youth is presented to you as an *art director*.

It started back in the 1920s. Albert Lasker, then head of Lord & Thomas, the world's biggest advertising agency, noticed his people were not winning enough new business. He found a simple solution. He called his account executives in and told them that as from that moment they were all vice presidents. This had the desired effect: prospective clients thought they were dealing with important chaps and business poured in again.

This nifty little idea has been repeated over the years: there is a sort of inflationary spiral on titles. 'Director' in an agency often means little or nothing today.

For instance, when I came into the business over 40 years ago, an art director was very important. He or she was in charge of the visual output of the agency. Nowadays an art director is just about anybody with some slight visual facility. His or her job is to work with a copywriter to develop creative ideas that sell your product or service.

Indeed, don't be overly impressed with anybody presented to you as a 'director' in an agency without asking what they direct. Thus, you may meet an account director. This does not mean he is on the board of the company. It merely means he directs the handling of a client's business, or maybe several clients' businesses.

Above him there may well be a real-live board director. Don't be too impressed by that either: a while ago, one London advertising agency had a staff of 160 and 23 board directors. How much say do you imagine they could have had in running the business? Not a lot. Even when I became a brand director of the Ogilvy Group, a fairly big business, I thought there were too many (21) of us.

If you're introduced to a creative director, try to find out how many creative directors the agency has. A few years ago there just used to be one. Now some agencies have several. They report to a supremo who may be described as an executive creative director.

It's all harmless fun really; titles in advertising agencies, apart from being popular, don't cost as much as wage rises. But because of this love of titles, ask your agency for a chart which shows you who does what.

Who will actually work on my account?

One common complaint is that when pitching the agency naturally puts up its best possible team – which may not always be the one that will finally be working on your account. So you buy a Rolls-Royce and end up driving an old banger.

Some clients insist on meeting the team that will be handling their account right at the beginning. This is a fair request; but – as in so many things – a little commonsense must be brought to bear. The agency may not know who they will eventually assign, because they don't yet know or have your business. They would be crazy to hire people in advance.

When a new client with a new set of problems comes in, the best thing the agency can do is put its best brains on to the account. You would be mad to object.

Equally, once the agency has grasped your needs it can quite reasonably turn the account over to other personnel. Knowing what I do about agency finance, I know if the top people worked all the time on your business, the agency would go broke.

What you should ensure is that your business always has the interest of the people at the top; and that at least one of them is *personally* concerned about it. The minute you are disturbed about something, speak to that person. Don't sit in your office quietly festering.

Ensure senior people are involved

Remember, the agency principals are just as anxious as you for your success. If they don't appear to be, something is wrong. Either with the agency, or you.

The brief

Importance of the brief

The quality of the *thinking* that the agency delivers to you in a presentation will depend almost entirely upon the quality of the brief you give them. I cover this in the next chapter. At this point however, let me simply say that unless you have given the agency a detailed, complete brief on what you wish to achieve, and how you are thinking of going about it, the presentation will never be as good as it might be.

I cannot know *enough* about what it is you plan to do, how you run your business, what problems and opportunities you see. I cannot spend too much time meeting your sales people, your colleagues who understand how you operate. I am delighted to talk to your customers and find out why they buy whatever it is you sell. Every scrap of information you can give to me is worthwhile.

Unhappily, some clients see a presentation as an opportunity to find out whether the agency can guess what it is they want. It may give a wonderful feeling of power, and even a few moments of entertainment. But it is an almost complete waste of time.

The same sort of clients like to sit in godlike judgement on the agency, reviewing their puny efforts. This is also a waste of time. Discussion as between equals will get you *much* further.

A clear point of view is vital

The best agencies have a clear personality which derives from the people who run them, who choose kindred spirits to work for them, and also have a point of view about what constitutes good work.

When you have a clear view about the business, then you can explain it to your clients and to your co-workers. Everything can be assessed in the light of that view. When new clients come to see you, they know what it is they have come for.

Without such a clear view, you are rudderless, with no idea of where you wish to go, and no idea of how to get there. I think this is important – if only for the selfish reason that when I ran an agency I always preferred to know what I was selling to people and how it differed from the competition.

Agencies are difficult to evaluate

Agencies are difficult to evaluate in any case. At least if the agency consistently approaches problems with certain criteria in mind and goes about things in a certain way, the client has a feeling for the kind of agency he has chosen. This is easier than choosing agencies simply because they seem to be nice chaps and you like the look of their work, or even because they have lots of people working for them and offices all over the world.

Because there is a grave shortage of high calibre creative people, many agencies are forced to use freelancers. They have no choice. Nevertheless, I think having to go outside to whatever freelancer is available at the time means the agency is less likely to produce a consistent body of work: a recognisable product.

The only alternative is to train your own people in the fond hope that if you are nice to them they will stay with you. It works very well.

Presenting ideas

The point at which the agency starts to present the creative work is the moment when the client sits up (after his somnolent period during the media presentation).

Many agencies skate gaily over this period, relying on well-finished roughs and bright colours to get them through. And many clients will depart satisfied with the amount of work evidenced.

But finished roughs are not ideas. They are just executions. And the fact that the agency produced 20 of them will not make them any better than if they had come up with one brilliant idea on the back of an envelope.

The agency must be able to explain how and why they came up with a particular proposal. That is the crux of a presentation.

Some think elaborate charts and witty lines are the key. Being a bit of a wag myself, I enjoy making a presentation a lighthearted affair. But what you need to hear is why the agency arrived at a particular solution. If they cannot tell, the proposal is merely whistling in the dark. Throw it out and start again.

Far too often, the agency team does not include the people who did the thinking – the hairy art director and nervous writer round the corner. They may not have been invited to bring their uncouth personae to the meeting. They may be shy (a lot of creative people are better at expressing themselves on paper than in person).

My advice is to coax them out of retreat, offer them a drink (most creative people react to this like horses to carrots) and ask what they had in mind.

You may even establish that they don't exist: the work was done freelance outside. This begs the question how the agency expresses their approach to direct marketing when using outside people – see page 388.

One more point: waffle is endemic in presentations. Some clients judge thinking by the thickness of the report. All agencies know this. Good thinking is better thinking if someone has to compress it. Get your agency to write a brief executive summary. It will make them concentrate, and save you time.

Figures, and large claims

Practically everyone would like to know how well an agency is going to do for them in advance. At some point a client will ask: 'How many per cent do you think this will pull?' No agency likes to disappoint a client, and there is a natural tendency to come up with a figure, if only to satisfy the beast.

Don't settle for promises

Professional clients and agencies both know that results are to some degree in the lap of the gods. Too many factors can influence them. And, if the product is a new one, there is no real basis for comparing with previous experience. So, as a client, beware large claims about results. As an agent, don't make them.

To repeat, an agent should be able to explain what he or she is doing to make your mailing or ad work better. Has the agency put in a better incentive? Or a new way of personalising the package? Or a new format?

Don't settle for promises. You want *ideas*.

Entertainment

When I was young, my parents had a restaurant. My idea of a perfect job was one where I could go to fine restaurants every day. I cannot say that the reality live up to my dreams, but I've done a lot of entertaining.

Entertaining never gains or keeps business – or if it does, the business isn't worth having. Never entertain a client to say 'please'. Entertain to say 'thank you'. Or just for fun.

Never award or gain accounts through bribery. What can come through corruption can go the same way, and both parties have given hostages to fortune.

PLAYING THE FIELD

There is a longstanding tradition in our industry whereby clients quite happily put out work to several different agencies, as though they were all freelancers, or printers.

A building society talked to a partner of mine some years ago about the possibility of us working for them. Afterwards they said: 'We plan to to try out a number of agencies over a couple of years, and then settle on one we like.'

My partner was tempted (but restrained himself, being a tactful sort of fellow) to reply: 'Well, we plan to try a number of building societies in the same way and see how *we* get along.'

Very few clients like the idea of agencies dealing with their competitors, but feel they are immune from such strictures. This is arrogant twaddle. It is not only arrogant – it is a silly way to go about things.

Avoid lack of consistency

I am not saying it is a bad idea to give out the odd project before choosing an agency, and indeed afterwards, but you would be wise to have one agency doing most of your work. Otherwise you end up with a lack of consistency in your communications, no continuing relationship with people who are dedicated to you – and maybe very poor stuff. I don't see how you can maintain your positioning successfully if you are constantly dealing with too many different people.

It's unsettling to an agency if a client is constantly hobnobbing with other agencies or seeing their presentations. You are unlikely to get the best possible work from them.

Because of international alignments, my former agency used to work for two organisations we found particularly unrewarding. They both had a rich variety of faults, but they shared this one of dealing with several agencies at the same time.

Some clients think it smart to keep on threatening the agency, either overtly, or implicitly by seeing other agencies' presentations when they have no real intention of moving. They do this because they believe it keeps the agency 'on their toes'. I can tell you this is not the case. It simply makes the agency hate you.

The truth is that the analogy with marriage is appropriate. Why should I work caringly for you if you are not faithful to me? More importantly, how can I possibly master all the complexities of your business if you only give me *some* of the problems you have? It goes without saying that just as clients should stick to agencies, agencies should not speak to clients competing with their existing roster unless they are thinking of changing the client.

Be faithful to your agency

Of course, large organisations have many divisions and products. Different divisions will, rightly, deal with different agencies. But it is ludicrous for smaller companies to do the same thing. It often happens because it gives junior executives a feeling of power, but a second reason is economic: they can negotiate each time for the best possible price. I think this may be shortsighted. Mr Chellan, whom I quoted earlier, makes an interesting observation: 'Buying the cheapest may be the costliest decision you ever take.' Time spent thinking about saving a few pounds or dollars might be better spent thinking about how to make more. This leads me very neatly on to the subject of money.

HOW MUCH YOU SHOULD PAY

At one time when prospective clients came to see us, I used to dread the moment when the question came up: 'How much do you charge?' I would reply lamely: 'Well, it all depends – we don't have any standard arrangement with our clients, because they all ask us to do different things.' The reason for the difficulty is that direct marketing work can cover so many more things than simply creating and placing advertisements, as an advertising agency does.

Let me consider three basic ways of charging which I have found work for one type of client or another.

1 Charging by the hour

It is possible to charge by the hour with a different rate of charge for each person working on the account. It is wise in advance for the agency to give the client, once his requirements have been carefully discussed, a rough estimate of how much it is expected these fees will work out at per month.

It is also extremely wise to have an agreement *in advance* that the fee structure will be reviewed regularly: probably fairly quickly after the opening of the agreement, say three months. The reason for this is simple: when a client becomes engaged in direct marketing, very often he discovers more areas of his business where it can be applied. What looked like a sensible estimate to start with becomes unprofitable in two ways. First the agency doesn't make money. Second, they start skimping – and the service suffers.

2 Commission plus relevant fees

Where a client is spending a lot of money in the media, it is perfectly possible to work on commission. There will always be hard bargaining about this. I will only say that when a lot of money is being spent, 15 per cent commission is sometimes a high figure, but I have rarely seen an account really well handled by an agency on less than 10 per cent. To make a profit, the agency cuts corners. Some advertisers (particularly in the retail field) offer their agencies a much lower rate of commission. It tends to show in the quality of the work. In short, if you pay peanuts, you get monkeys.

If you pay peanuts, you get monkeys

Often, in addition to any commissionable revenue from the media, an agency will be preparing mailings, and helping in areas such as database building. If the budget is a very large one indeed, these activities can be covered by the commission. If not, an additional fee should be negotiated in advance, based upon hourly rates.

3 An agreed monthly fee

In some ways this is the method I prefer. The agency and client estimate in advance how much work is going to be required, and the agency quotes a figure. Once again this figure can and should be reviewed regularly. But it does give the agency the certainty of knowing what its revenue is likely to be over a period. This in turn enables the agency to plan better for your business.

Get the best possible deal

Consequently you should get the best possible deal on this basis, because most agencies are prepared to sacrifice a little bit of revenue for extra security.

Few look very deeply into the charges and the basis for these charges. If one company is charging more than another company – why?

For instance, a large agency may provide a very wide range of services, and consequently charge premium rates. You may be able to call upon the facilities, for instance, of a research department – something few direct agencies offer – or a proper media department. You may also be able to get database advice, and other services smaller agencies may not offer.

It really all depends on what you are looking for. There is an analogy with going on holiday. If all you are going to do is get up every morning at seven o'clock, go touring and not return until late at night, you hardly need an hotel with a very good restaurant. You won't be eating there.

When you are negotiating with your agency you might reflect upon one simple fact. That is that very few agency people – even the principals – get rich. Many clients do.

For this reason, you should not begrudge your agency a decent profit. Indeed, it might be a good idea to model yourself upon enlightened companies that go to a great deal of trouble – even to the point of reorganising their suppliers' businesses, in one famous case – to make sure they earn a good living.

Payment by results

Does this work? It seems a wonderful idea, and in theory it is. But in practice very few clients are both willing to work on a results basis and also willing to allow the agency to control all the factors that would govern those results. I will touch on this again in the next chapter.

In the advertising field, I note that clients are increasingly looking at this sort of approach. Some large companies have recently started proposing *bonuses* to their agencies in a reaction against the worldwide trend to cutting agency income. For instance, General Foods in the United States some years ago decided to compensate its agencies based upon performance. The company would pay 14.3 per cent commission for average work, 16.3 per cent for outstanding work, and 13.3 per cent for work judged unsatisfactory. The previous rate was 14.3 per cent.

'Satisfaction' is defined as how well particular brands sell. I think this approach is wholly laudable, and one or two other major US marketers have started to adopt something similar. Everything we know about individuals shows that companies that offer high incentives get better performance from their staff. I am sure the same thing should apply to clients and agencies.

High incentives get better performance

I look forward with pleasure to the first client who can show me how it can be operated effectively in our business. All I can say is that in the last three years, full of optimism, I have tried to make three of these deals work. None has.

MONEY AND TALENT

Creating a full-scale mailing package is just as hard as creating a TV commercial (having done both, I would say it is usually harder). Yet a TV campaign may net the agency commission on many millions of pounds of expenditure, whilst few mailing packages will command more than a few thousand pounds in fees.

As the weight of promotional expenditure shifts more and more towards direct marketing – which it is doing and will continue to do – then clients will find themselves paying increasingly higher fees. Indeed, since 1977 in my experience the fee paid for a mailing pack by a client to an agency has increased many-fold. Yet I still do not think clients are paying enough. It shows in the fact that (in my experience at any rate) people work longer hours and harder in direct marketing agencies than they do in general agencies. It shows in the fact that much of the material put out by direct marketing agencies is still very poor. Only money – and the talent that money will attract – will change this situation.

If as a client you try to get first-class work for second-class money, you will end up paying in other ways. Nobody can afford to have top-class talent working on your account for a £2,000 mailing package unless that talent is churning out the work as fast as the words and pictures come to mind.

TRY TO UNDERSTAND THE PROCESS

Hardly any clients bother to go to the agency and ask to be shown round and have the whole process of putting together their communications explained to them *in detail*.

What is the procedure when you have a complaint? What is the after-sales service like, so to speak? Who precisely are you going to deal with? Take my advice: find out in advance. Who is responsible for which aspects of your direct marketing?

Spend a couple of days at the agency

I would make it my business to spend a couple of days at the agency.

The more I think about this, the more it astonishes me. In all my years in the business I cannot recall *any* client at a reasonably senior level spending any considerable length of time inside an agency. And only two ever sent junior people to do so.

It's crazy really. You might be about to spend millions of pounds with these people, yet you never bother to learn about the intricacies of their business. You never understand as well as you might do why things go wrong when they go wrong – which they always do – and, often just as helpful, who to congratulate when they go right.

The most important piece of advice

I am moved to say that this is probably the most important single piece of advice I can give to you as a client. You will get to know the people in the agency. You will forge relationships with them. They will come to know, and respect you – if you deserve it. They may even end up liking you. They will *certainly* appreciate you taking the trouble.

It is revealing that the first client who did anything like this in my experience did not come himself but sent a junior (and stupid) minion to spend time with the agency. The minion was quite incapable of learning anything whatsoever from the experience. His boss thought sending someone was a good idea. But not good enough to choose someone important.

Which brings us to the next issue: once you've spent all this time finding the right agency, how do you keep that agency and build a good relationship with them?

How to choose an agency – if you need one

Points to remember

- Determine what you really want.
- Look to the long term.
- Do you like them?
- Results, not presentations.
- Agencies often take anything.
- Budget may not be enough for an agency.
- Choose one that fits your size.
- Nine reasons to stay in-house.
- Beware introversion.
- It's about your needs – not the agency's boasts.
- Ask how they've handled others.
- Insist on case-histories – and explanations.
- Speculative – why it pays to pay.
- How will they handle your business?
- Meaningless titles: who does the real work?
- The brief vital.
- A point of view.
- Ideas must be justified.
- Beware large claims.
- Entertainment – when it pays.
- Monogamy or polygamy.
- How to pay – alternatives that make sense.
- Low price often means worse work.
- The importance of understanding what's going on.

15

Client and Agency: the Unequal Partnership

'O world! world! world! thus is the poor agent despised.'

Shakespeare

THE IMPOSSIBLE DREAM

Two words are greatly misused by agencies talking to their clients. One is 'strategy' – usually applied to some minor subterfuge. The other is 'partnership' – referring to a legendary state of affairs, a nirvana of equality between client and agency.

In my years in the business I have rarely come across anything even approaching this. The reason is simple, and is encapsulated in the Flemish proverb quoted at the head of the previous chapter.

Yet not only agencies but also their clients refer to this partnership. Even notorious bullies pretend they treat their agencies as equals.

Personally I much prefer the straightforward attitude of one of my former clients who objected violently when a long article appeared in an advertising publication on his choice of agency. 'Why so much fuss about my choice of a new supplier?' he asked.

He was quite right. The agency *is* just a supplier. And curiously enough, this client, despite an attitude some might see as rather feudal, extended more of a true sense of equality to us than others I have seen, who pay lip-service to the dream of partnership.

Build a mutually respectful relationship Whether you consider you are in partnership with your agency or not, a mutually respectful relationship is well worth working for, particularly if your business is largely based upon direct marketing. Under those circumstances your communications may compose all, or nearly all, your marketing activity. So getting on well with those entrusted with preparing, placing or sending them out seems to make a lot of sense. In fact, most intelligent clients take a lot of trouble to keep their agencies happy; whilst *all* agencies, since it is their bread and butter, try to keep their clients happy.

In fact, when my partners and I set up Trenear-Harvey, Bird & Watson in 1977 we always swore we would never deal with any client unless one of the partners liked him, and we all believed the account was worthwhile. If any one of the partners thought any client was behaving badly, then we agreed he could resign the account without consulting the others.

In the event this never happened – though we came pretty close to it more than once.

Unfortunately, I have to confess, *liking* a client tends to have a direct relationship to the amount of money he or she has to expend. A client who spends little money and is a pain in the arse is easily despatched. On the other hand, where a client is spending many millions of pounds, the decision is not so easy. One is inclined to search very hard for redeeming features – usually successfully.

Ensuring a stable relationship

If choosing a new agency is difficult, keeping the relationship in good repair is possibly even more so. Yet it is important that this repair is maintained.

Some years ago, the Jerry Fields advertising employment agency in New York ran an advertisement, the headline of which said: 'At five o'clock, my inventory goes down the elevator.'

The point was that an agency's stock in trade is its staff. This is what you are paying for. It is very much in your interest that they like you. Yet relatively few clients have the intelligence to get to know the agency's people.

Get to know the agency's people

First, make sure you meet *all* the people working on your business. Not just the principals. The man who is running the agency may be very good at running agencies; this doesn't necessarily mean he is talented creatively, for instance.

For that reason, quite apart from the people who deal with you every day – the account handlers – make it your business to get to know the creative people. They come up with most of the ideas which will make you rich.

Agency people are human. For a client they like, they will work nights and weekends. For one who is arrogant and uncaring they will simply do enough to give them adequate professional satisfaction.

Take time to praise

It is a red letter day when a client takes the trouble to congratulate a creative team on their work. Few ever do it, but those who do are the ones who get the best work and the best results themselves.

The surprising thing is that it doesn't take a great deal of effort on your part. One of our clients at Ogilvy & Mather Direct won golden opinions by simply sending a note congratulating us on our efforts in helping him reach record sales, accompanied by a couple of cases of champagne. That little investment paid off for months and months. For a couple of hundred pounds he bought himself hundreds of thousands of pounds worth of extra commitment.

JOY RIDE?

Many people imagine working in an agency is a joy ride: a life spent dreaming up wacky ideas, punctuated by an endless series of splendid lunches and dinners.

This may be one reason why advertising does not enjoy particularly great respect amongst the community. UK research I saw some time ago indicated that the public – leaders of industry, members of parliament, the press and many others – all regard advertising as of less than average merit amongst a wide range of occupations.

This is sad, because we fulfil an essential, if humble, economic function. Certainly our life is not nearly as easy as you might think. In my experience people in our business tend to work far harder than most.

This is reflected in some revealing ways. For example, some years back a friend went through a list of all the directors of a well known Manchester advertising agency since the end of the Second World War. Not one lived to reach the statutory age of retirement, 60. In fact, I recall reading with some alarm shortly after getting my first job in an agency that the average life-span of the advertising man was 58.

Many factors conspire to make our life stressful. There is great instability, for although clients do not move their accounts with the frequency one might think after reading an issue of *Campaign* or *Advertising Age*, they do move them more than, for example, accountants' or lawyers' clients do. What's more, they move them for the oddest of reasons very often. More to the point, most agents spend (in fact waste) far more time than they should worrying that their clients *might* depart.

A business of constant deadlines

In addition, our business is one of constant deadlines. You have to plan everything well in advance to meet them – yet clients rarely keep to timetables. Despite this, the creative work *has* to be prepared by a certain date. Then it has to be reviewed to make sure it's OK. Then the client has to see it and everyone worries lest he change it – which he often does, losing more precious time.

Then, of course, there is the production process. The finding of the right photographer, illustrator or director, the selection of the appropriate models: a fruitful field for discussion – and more time ticking away. Then when it's all been done the client has to approve the finished product.

Finally the work appears – a point at which you would have thought we could all relax, having mutually agreed beforehand that what we are doing is right. Not at all. Many clients feel no compunction whatsoever about unilaterally foisting the responsibility for anything going wrong after the event on to the agent. A distressingly high percentage shamelessly lie about what they had or had not agreed to previously. In some cases they will do this despite clear documentary evidence to the contrary.

One fertile area for discussion is always the quality of reproduction in the press or print, or the calibre of the direction in the broadcast media. These are very much a matter of opinion, where any one person's view is as good as the other's.

And even then there is the post mortem to look forward to. The results can be pored over and the agency allocated any blame for the consequences.

You may feel from reading thus far – and indeed, when you read the rest of this chapter – that my views are partisan. Of course you are right: 'I can but speak of that which I do know', and what I know is based on 40 years of experience; but I would add that I have acted as a client on occasion and been astonished at the all-round incompetence, shallowness and arrogance of the average agency.

My views are partisan

Accordingly, if you are a client and you can put your hand on your heart and honestly say you are not guilty of any of the sins I am discussing, I would be astonished. If you are an agency man or woman, I am happy to declare you guilty without even the privilege of a trial.

TWO TYPES OF RELATIONSHIP

Are you familiar with the following two-liner?

'What time is it?'

'What time would you like it to be, JB?'

This old joke epitomises a common type of client–agency relationship, where the client is always right.

The client is always right

Years ago I acted as a consultant to a well known agency which held a very lucrative account on this basis. If the client said black was white, then the servile account director would leap to concur. The advertising was created on the basis of the client's whims; the account director was in a constant state of nervous panic, and very rarely sober after lunch.

How could he possibly handle the client's account on any logical basis when the only constant factor was his 'yes' to the client's every request? In the end, the agency lost the account and he lost his job.

The other type of relationship is well characterised in Robert Townsend's lively book *Up the Organisation*. He reports that when he ran the Avis Rent-a-Car business he had a plaque in his office on which was inscribed an excellent advertising philosophy.

It recorded quite simply that Avis would never know as much about advertising as the agency; and the agency would never know as much about car rental as Avis – and from this concluded that except in matters of fact, the company would always take its agency's advice.

As I suggested in the last chapter, although this would be a happy state of affairs, it is not really practical in direct marketing, even if it makes sense in advertising.

Intermingled

Many agents would be delighted if their clients accepted unquestioningly everything they proposed. And many clients would as a result go broke.

In the case of Avis, the agency was simply advising on what sort of advertising to run. Advertising is basically communications. Successful direct marketing involves to a greater degree many factors beyond the communication – factors which are crucial, like what prices to charge and what sort of offers to make. And it has to produce sales or responses that will be measured.

I have met clients who would be only too happy to have the agent take over the worry of finding the right product; deciding on the offer; seeking the incentive; buying it; dealing with the mailing house; finding the right company to computerise the list; setting up an adequate record system ... in fact, almost running the business for them.

But no wise client can afford to resign so many aspects of his or her business to the agency (though he or she ought to take advice and pay attention to it). That is, clients surrender their function to somebody who can never be as interested in the consequences as they are, and who moreover – if we're honest – has a vested interest in encouraging them to spend on promotion.

I also think it is unwise on the part of the agent to take on too much responsibility for the business. A friend who ran a successful direct marketing agency in London nearly went bankrupt as a result of undertaking many of these functions for his client. The volume of work involved made the account unprofitable; the problem being compounded when the client went broke – nearly carrying the agency with it.

Agencies' and clients' functions intermingle

The truth, of course, is that agencies' and clients' functions intermingle, it's hard to know where to draw the line between them. Indeed, on occasion my colleagues and I have become involved in all the functions mentioned above for one or other of our clients (though, happily, not all at the same time). As long as we are well paid and it is not seen as a permanent arrangement, we are happy to do so.

Direct marketing is, as you will have realised already, so fast-changing, moving into so many areas of business – and indeed society – that it's difficult to lay down any binding rules. Compare what happens when you go to consult an advertising agency. The relationship is relatively simple. The agency will plan, prepare and, if you wish, place advertisements for you in exchange for a commission or an agreed fee. You will find it easy to agree also on rates for additional services such as research.

The relationship you set up with your direct marketing agency could involve far more varied factors. But there are certain considerations I think you should be aware of when you are dealing with (or choosing) an agency. Accordingly, I have set out a list of the areas where I think agencies and clients should be particularly sensitive to each other.

WHERE THINGS GO WRONG AND HOW TO GET THEM RIGHT

Was it sod's law or Murphy's law that stated that anything that can possibly go wrong will? Either way, it is a law which applies with peculiar force to our business. I have noticed over the years nine areas where things go wrong most. They are:

Murphy's law

1 No agreement on the criteria whereby results will be assessed.
2 Not enough planning ahead – or time given to execute the plans.
3 Poor briefing.
4 Rotten communication of the brief.
5 Too many layers of decision-making.
6 Confusion about who gets the money – and how much.
7 Passing the buck on mistakes.
8 No clear contract between agency and client.
9 Mutual suspicion.

1 Judging the results

You are probably familiar with the old Chinese saying about a 1,000-mile journey beginning with but a single step. One thing is certain: you had better make sure that the first step is the right one. That means you must have a clear view of the objective.

Make sure your first step is right

Both agency and client must know what they are trying to achieve and by when, in terms of numbers and money. How much profit are you trying to make? How much money are you prepared to spend? How much is a customer worth to you?

Frequently I have seen any or all of these shrouded in secrecy. What they add up to is the very first of my points: have we an agreed criterion? How are you going to judge the performance at the end of the year? Both of you – agency and client – must know and *agree* in advance if you are to establish exactly how well you have done.

2 Planning – and time

To do a good job you need about six months from the time you first conceive of the need for a mailing to the moment it goes out. And whether you are considering a mailing or a series of advertisements or commercials, time is extremely important.

Don't rush

At Ogilvy & Mather Advertising, I recall it was a principle that the agency should always delay a presentation rather than produce work not up to snuff. That is wonderful in theory, but there are many occasions in direct marketing where you would have to ignore it for business reasons – like the need to meet a mailing date when results are known to be good, eg the New Year.

Nevertheless, the faster you need something to be done, the more likely it is there will be mistakes. The answer is either give more time, or pay a great deal more money. If you want to get a good job done fast, that means you will have to have the top creative people in the agency working on it. You'll need to pay double rates to studios, photographers, and process houses. Even then you will still run the risk of things going wrong.

The difficulty of thinking ahead

It is difficult to think ahead in a business that is constantly demanding on-the-spot reaction to an unpredictable marketplace. But if everything is done in a rush, allowing little time for planning, the agency is unlikely to be able to do more than *react* to the client's request. They will not initiate ideas as often as you would like, or they would wish to.

In any case, agencies are often tempted to take on more work than they can properly handle. Their little piggy eyes light up at the thought of increased revenue, when they should be thinking more about their existing clients. But if those clients are constantly inundating them with rush work, that essential thinking will never develop.

3 Vague briefs

I have already dealt with this subject when discussing the matter of choosing an agency. But of course, every job requires a brief. And I would like to emphasise here that by this I mean a *written* brief, not a verbal one. Verbal briefs are written on the wind, and invariably give rise to dispute and misunderstanding.

The type of verbal brief that is particularly infuriating is one where the creative people are invited to let their imagination run freely. Some clients think this is a glorious opportunity. On the contrary, just to say: 'Go and have an idea – any idea – as long as it's amusing, or entertaining, or selling' is far too vague. One needs to know exactly *what* one is requested to do.

Vague briefs result in vague work

Vague briefs result in vague work.

You should be able to give a brief which covers your objective, precisely stated, the background to the job, who you think the target prospects are, and how you think the job ought to be tackled.

Bad clients play the second-guessing game. The creative people sit wondering what the client wants. The client thinks he or she is putting them to the test. What he or she is actually doing is fooling about and wasting money and emotional energy better employed realising (or improving) whatever he or she has in mind.

Bad clients haven't considered what they want properly, so they keep fiddling with the brief.

Bad clients are weak. Their bosses keep changing the brief over their heads.

Bad agencies – and freelance creative people – put up with all this nonsense for *money*.

What it all ends up in is work produced for no reason with no objective and altered simply for the hell of it. That results in bankruptcy.

If I had to say what *the* most vital contribution to successful work is, it is probably ensuring that everyone is jointly agreed on the brief before the work begins.

If the brief is wrong, skimpy or misleading, this leads to the next problem: by definition, whatever was in the mind of that person conceiving the project is unlikely to be communicated well.

4 Poor communications

Agency executives often relay your requests inaccurately. This, of course, won't happen if you have a clear, written brief. But sometimes your brief is inadequate simply because the person who actually briefs the agency does not eventually *judge* the work. That's because a junior has been sent to do the leg work whilst somebody much more important is going to judge: someone who may decide the original brief was not right.

A common problem

You can well imagine how confusing and frustrating this is. And don't think it doesn't happen often. I can think of very few clients where this is not the rule rather than the exception. In fact, in the week I first wrote this, it occurred twice on work I was doing with large sophisticated companies.

5 Hydra-headed indecision

This brings me to the fifth of the areas where problems appear, which I would categorise as hydra-headed indecision. Frequently, clients have too many people involved in making decisions. And sadly it is much easier to say 'No' to something than to say 'Yes' – nobody can ever criticise you for something that doesn't run. Then there is an endless series of meetings and proposals – and an agency which simply doesn't give a damn. They will run anything you approve.

Too many people making decisions

One of the least satisfying clients I ever worked for suffered from having about 94 layers of management, each and every one of which got involved in the judging of creative work, and none of whom knew a thing about direct marketing.

The problem reached a point where one set of artwork had a dozen sets of corrections on it, all emanating from different places. The art director was about to refuse to work any more on the business. We suggested we would not work further with the client unless they paid double the fee, or ran their business sensibly. We parted company. What a relief! The client learned nothing from the exercise. They were even more indecisive with their new agency.

Ideally, decisions should be made by *one person* from *one department* with plenipotentiary power. And just one other senior person as a final arbiter. Otherwise, everything dissolves in duplication, chaos and misery.

6 It may be your money but it isn't theirs

The agency has all the responsibility, but none of the power

One of the principal factors that bedevil agency–client relationships is – not surprisingly – money. The agency has all the responsibility, but none of the power.

Clients may be spending millions of pounds a year. They spend it *through* the agency, and emotionally feel they are giving it to the agency. That kind of money one takes seriously, and expects a lot of service for.

The agency will have the responsibility for this money in almost every sense. Indeed, where the money is being placed through the media, an agent in this business (unlike any other agent in business) is a *legal principal*. That means that if there is no payment, it is to the agent that the media come for redress, not the client.

This is one of the things that give rise to not infrequent bankruptcy in the agency business – in addition to exacerbating the worries of the agent himself.

Yet although all this money is floating around, the agent will only see a percentage of it. Either a commission, or a fee. This does not alter the clients' feeling that they have invested the entire sum with the agent. This simple, if unjust, disparity explains why clients get so excited about their investment, whilst agencies can't really understand why.

Both parties should occasionally give thought to this.

7 Mistakes

You will have realised by now that it is not difficult to make mistakes. Every agency makes them. Every client does.

In fact, in our business mistakes sometimes seem to occur much more frequently than in, for instance, general advertising. This is partly because the technology is evolving very quickly; partly because in a fast-growing industry many of the people on either side of the client/agency divide are very inexperienced. And partly because the mistakes show up more easily: they are measurable.

Admit mistakes

Remember, only God is perfect. Don't kick your agency for mistakes. In most cases, they will be errors you acquiesced in, since you ought to OK everything that is done. Don't pass your guilt on to them. Share it!

When mistakes are made, the agency should admit to them promptly if it is responsible – and vice versa. It takes courage to say 'I was wrong'. The thing to concentrate on is making sure they don't happen again, by working together.

If you change agencies hoping your new agency will make fewer mistakes, don't put money on it. They will *certainly* make mistakes when learning your business.

Obviously, I am not saying you should stay with a bunch of half-wits. They won't get any better because you keep hoping they will. But if you have had a good relationship with an agency for years, and they perpetrate a number of awful gaffes, you are almost certainly better off sorting them out than going elsewhere.

8 Legalities

A wonderful feeling overcomes the agency when it wins a new account. Often the effect is so overpowering that mere details like getting a proper *contract* are forgotten.

I have lost a lot of money through not having proper contracts. **Get a proper contract**

Areas where things can go wrong include how much the artwork and the production should cost as a percentage of the expenditure; precisely when payments are due; how much work has been agreed to at the beginning of the contract (often clients get carried away, ask for more work, then decide they didn't really want it and won't pay for it); and finally, no clear indication of what is and is not going to be done by the agency for nothing. One tiny example is the cost of travelling to and from the client's establishment.

9 Mutual suspicion

I have worked in agencies where people sincerely believed the client started every morning determined to give the agency a hard time. I know this isn't so. I have very rarely met a client who did not want good work just as much as the agency. But the factors I have mentioned tend to create this air of confusion. This mistrust can cause the relationship between agency and client to break down.

How do you create an atmosphere of trust? First of all, you're honest. **Create an atmosphere of trust**
You say what you think and ask the agency to say what they think. This includes being honest with the agency when you're fed up. Tell them so. Tell them why.

Next, you *listen* to them. Make it clear to them that you value their opinion. If you treat your agency as an equal and confide in them – tell them what your goals are and what your problems are – the agency will identify with you and your ambitions, and feel obliged to perform well.

It is also important to tell them the *results*. Every client judges his **Give clear targets**
agency by results. Every agency likes to know how well the work is doing. If

not in actual figures, then by comparison. It spurs people on, and gives them something to aim for. Human beings like goals.

Years ago, a very good account handler quit because the client would never give him any details of his results. He found it too frustrating. When we saw the figures, we realised how right our account man was. They were dreadful. The client had no idea how much money they were losing.

Without knowledge of the results, your agency is struggling in the dark, and cannot help you.

Build relationships

If you pay attention to all these nine points I've mentioned, you can build a kind of partnership in our business which is so rare, yet so valuable.

If you look at the truly successful marketers – the Procter & Gambles, the General Foods, the Unilevers – you will find they rarely tend to switch agencies. They build *relationships* with agencies.

They realise that constantly switching is an uneconomic way to operate. Much of the money you are investing is being spent to teach a fresh set of people about your business. Far better to have an agency which already has the knowledge, and can spend its time (and your money) seeking better solutions.

That, after all, is what we are all in business for, isn't it?

OTHER TROUBLE SPOTS

Bitching sessions

Sometimes, the relationship between a client and an agency can become so fraught that it is decided to clear the air. Somebody (usually an enlightened person on the client side) says, 'Let's put your people and ours together and speak frankly about where we are not doing as well as we might – and see what happens'.

This type of meeting rarely works very well because of the nature of the relationship.

Be frank

Frequently the people on the agency side – all too conscious of where their money is coming from – are far less inclined to be frank than the people on the client side. Some agency people cynically regard the whole exercise as an opportunity for clients to vent their frustrations and use the agency as a scapegoat, after which they will go away happy.

Sometimes, conversely, the agency people are unwise enough to be extremely frank and tell the client exactly what they think. It can often be traumatic. Client personnel who are used to having the agency jump very high every time they say 'frog' are alarmed to discover that the people they have been dealing with for so long dislike them intensely, and find them an utter pain.

In my experience, sorting out differences is best accomplished by people above the level of the battle. Senior client and agency people speaking frankly about what's going on are able to unite happily as elders in condemning the follies of their juniors – and they actually have the power to do something about it.

Of course, the truth is that the only real solution is a relationship based on mutual respect: a respect which grows from an understanding on both sides of what each is trying to achieve, and what their respective difficulties are. This requires hard work, commitment and decent people.

A relationship based on mutual respect

Fearless advice

'To ask advice is in nine cases out of ten to tout for flattery', someone once said, and it often applies in our kind of business. If your agency always gives you advice you agree with, then either you are a genius and need no agency, or they are sycophants.

Agencies do a better job and clients benefit more if honest advice is given fearlessly, and accepted gratefully. In fact, I believe, the *major* service an agency should render to a client – apart from creating effective communications – is giving sound advice.

Give sound advice

Often in general advertising, bad advice is less overtly damaging. The clients may never discover that the puns they love in their ads are a waste of money. But if clients do something stupid and you don't tell them in our business, then the public soon will – by not buying.

You and your big mouth

I have been at some pains throughout this book to try and avoid any accusation of infallibility. However, I confess that I have – believe it or not – still a few more faults to confess to, which fit neatly under the category of 'How not to handle clients'.

Tact is one quality I must own up about. Even my best friend would never describe me as tactful. So to do at all well in this business I had to try and alter my personality for the better. I have not always been as successful as I would wish. My enormous mouth has got me into dreadful trouble, especially when combined with my matching ego.

Early on in my career I managed not once, but twice, to get involved in *client politics* with disastrous results barely averted.

Avoid client politics

First, I took pity on a travel courier working for one of my clients. What a dreadful job he had, I thought. And suggested to him that he bring his literary talents into the agency business. All with the best of intentions.

When he told his boss, that gentleman was not at all amused at my thoughtlessness – trying to seduce one of his best, most underpaid (and therefore profitable) people.

I should have learned from this. But a few short years later I suggested to the advertising manager of one client that his mendacity and incompetence were such that he ought to find another job.

His boss forgave me eventually, and became a valued client at our agency. But it was still a silly thing to do.

Never get entangled in the client's internal business. Be everyone's friend and keep your mouth shut.

Indiscretion

Shortly after we started Trenear-Harvey, Bird & Watson, John Watson and I nearly lost us our biggest account through not being discreet enough.

Confidentiality is vital

At a major international conference we quoted figures given to us by a third party about a separate division of our client's business which we did not handle. Confidentiality hardly occurred to us.

After all, the client had not given us the figures. In any case, the account in question was not actually ours. The client did not see it that way at all. He was observed to turn puce with rage. He approached us afterwards, at the top of his voice.

My partner got excited, and threatened *sotto voce* to thump him (thankfully he never heard; we kept the account).

Direct marketing companies are very nervous about their figures. Be careful.

Ego

Avoid arrogance

Arrogance is a major failing with people in our business. After I have three successes in a row, I begin to think I am God.

Fortunately, two things prevent this problem becoming too chronic. First, my competitors keep producing work I admire and envy. I realise there are a great many people out there – and they're getting better every day. Second, it's never too long before I write a flop and am recalled to reality.

The characteristic that gives me most problems is one I have never been able to resolve. Some people cannot put names to faces. Some cannot put faces to names. I can do neither. This makes it hard for me to avoid constantly offending clients.

The client/agency relationship

Points to remember

- Not an equal partnership – but respect important.
- Meet the people – make friends.
- Why agency work is a tough ride.
- Two types of relationship.
- Payment by results not as easy as you think.
- Nine areas where things go wrong.
- What to do when you have a problem.
- Frank advice.
- Indiscretion.
- Beware arrogance.

16

The Future of Marketing: Ten Predictions – and a Health Warning

'Those who ignore the lessons of the past are condemned to repeat them.'

George Santayana

Above- and below-the-line

When I entered advertising with such high hopes in the 1950s, I little realised I would end up in a ghetto located 'below-the-line'. This rather demeaning phrase refers, in the UK at any rate, to all promotional activities other than advertising. It apparently derives from the way accountants at Unilever used to lay out the annual budget plan: advertising at the top of the sheet, everything else at the bottom, beneath a line drawn on the paper.

We didn't draw any lines years ago. My first job was to write an ad selling a chain of restaurants. My second, a sales brochure for somebody's sausages. My third, a mailing to sell seed-cleaning machinery.

But if I could not foresee the mysterious line below which I was destined to sink, still less was I able to predict the remarkable way the mail order business I knew would become today's direct marketing. If anybody had told me that expenditure on direct marketing would be expected to overtake general advertising by the end of the 20th century, I would have been astounded.

1. Direct marketing will take over

Early in this book, which I first wrote 25 years ago, I described direct marketing – to my own satisfaction if no one else's – as 'any activity whereby you reach people directly or they respond to you directly'.

You're at the end of the book now, so you may not recall reading that, but you will certainly agree that it is a pretty wide definition. It includes any message that people can respond to directly and any direct message that they can respond to indirectly – by going to a store, for instance.

Most ads now carry postal or e-mail addresses, or phone numbers, but many are chiefly designed to influence attitudes. Many packs now carry phone numbers – usually free – for customers to call. However, this can be classified as customer service.

But however narrowly or widely you define it (and such quibbles are probably a waste of time), direct marketing is taking over. One reason is that all transactions made on the fastest-growing new medium ever – the internet – are direct. As I have already pointed out, this medium speeds up the direct marketing process, and often makes it much cheaper.

What works in DM usually works on the internet

2. The internet will disappoint its wilder advocates

Internet fanatics used to predict that it would completely replace other forms of communication. But new media rarely have this effect.

Even Bill Gates observed, during World Book Day in 1999, that print has advantages over web pages. It is easier to read and flick through, and is much more portable. I recall claims made for other new media which made perfect sense at the time, but were proven utterly wrong. Records were going to kill live concerts; television would destroy book reading; video catalogues would be the death of printed catalogues. And 20 years ago Xerox, then my clients, talked about – and worked hard on promoting – the paperless office.

When a book is serialised on television, its sales soar; when a record climbs the charts, thousands flock to hear the artist in person. Because life is often dull and business life is often *extremely* dull, we love the idea of sudden dramatic change. But change is usually gradual. Indeed, the influential American business thinker, Peter Drucker, suggested a while ago that new ideas generally take about 40 years to become pervasive.

Change is gradual

Take the use of the computer to build and exploit a database. It has been over 50 years since the *Reader's Digest* started using them – but how many marketers use them properly, even now?

3. Those who ignore direct marketing principles will perish

Soon, every serious business will use direct marketing, not just tactically to retain customers or cross sell, but as an essential tool to launch and maintain brands and businesses.

Major firms like Procter & Gamble – or my own clients, Mercedes – have made direct marketing respectable. Twenty years ago they thought it beneath them. Now they see it as vital, and are starting to exploit its full range of possibilities.

The many faces of DM

As we have seen, only gradually have marketers begun to understand the discipline. Many stumbled upon it by chance. Some were doing it unknowingly when they sent out direct mail spasmodically, phoned up prospects, or ran couponed ads.

Some sought a measurable return on their investment in enquiries or sales. Others wanted to know which messages and which media were most effective. And recently, fancy labels have lured many – as the following suggests:

> I'm still doing direct marketing … but I call it relationship marketing now. The clients hated 'direct' because it involved difficult stuff like doing ads that worked and getting sums right. They love relationship marketing. Even they can have a relationship.

That was from Graeme McCorkell, who founded one of Britain's first good direct marketing agencies and became Chairman of the Institute of Direct Marketing.

4. Direct marketing will be used more intelligently

Many now use direct marketing – but not very well. They will learn to.

Banks will wonder whether spending millions on mass advertising is always as wise as selling to one customer at a time through direct marketing. That is how MBNA became the fastest growing credit card company in the UK, leaving UK banks flatfooted.

Retailers, who used to focus on this week's sales compared to last week's, are beginning to realise they are better off making customers and keeping them for longer by talking directly. Most are building databases and trying to exploit them – often through loyalty programmes.

Loyalty or bribery?

Many of these are little more than long-term systems of bribery. Their real value derives from the information that they can throw up. But as playwright and journalist Keith Waterhouse once noted, 'The belief that knowledge is power is erroneous if there is nothing to be done with the knowledge that you have so expensively taken possession of'.

You need to reward individual customers appropriately rather than everyone indiscriminately. And, of course, offer them products and services based on what the database reveals. In this country, Tesco have done it well by launching new products and services based on what they have learned about their customers. Their great competitor, Sainsbury, did it badly. I've seen little sign so far of any intelligent use of their database.

Accountants and lawyers can see the benefits

One new group of direct marketers is particularly interesting: professional firms – accountants, lawyers and so on. Being very conservative, they are almost the last to realise that direct mail need not be 'junk', but is perfect if you can determine who your prospects are.

When advising a huge New York accountancy firm, I was astounded that a 'small' new client could be worth a million dollars in fees. A French international management consultancy told me their average client was worth several times more. Plenty of money for sending out intelligent, well-crafted messages to acquire and retain clients.

Most direct marketing is still aimed at the end-user or consumer, but often (as I observed early on in this book), shareholders, employees, wholesalers, members of the trade and intermediaries such as brokers are more pivotal to success. This will be increasingly recognised.

Direct marketing can influence any audience, be used by every kind of enterprise and deployed via any medium. Not *either* direct mail, direct response, the internet, telephone contact or door-to-door, but *all* of these in a variety of appropriate sequences and combinations.

5. Companies will not only build databases; they will use them properly

This is the moral of the comparison I made above between Tesco and Sainsbury. Tesco had the knowledge and used it. Sainsbury had the knowledge and didn't.

As you may recall, the database means that you can:

- analyse the characteristics of your customers to learn which are most profitable, then seek similar prospects;
- record the history of your relationship with particular customers or prospects so that you can say the right things to the right people at the right time, and in the right way.

Unfortunately, firms (and especially governments) have squandered millions on databases but too often found them impractical, or – worse – have not known how to use them. They have been seduced by an appealing concept without understanding its practicalities. They will start to get it right.

Learn how to use the database

The full benefit of your own medium – the database – is rarely appreciated. Compared with outside media such as television, it confers unique controllability. You can use a personal computer to manipulate data about segments within a database, perhaps overlaid with outside geographic or demographic information to plan and target more effectively.

Marketers are starting to realise they, not external service bureaux, should control such a powerful weapon. They will manage their database planning directly. Functions that they have been advised about by agencies can be carried out by themselves.

6. Business will learn the importance of customer value

Most firms manage their marketing to suit themselves, which is crazy.

Take budgets; a firm might take a percentage of turnover or overhead as the right marketing budget. Many are led by short-term thinking. Recognise any of the following?

'We need more sales volume; let's spend more money.'

Short-term thinking

'We have to send more profit to the US. Spend less on marketing.'

'Last year, we had a good year. Put up the budgets!' – or vice versa.

'Our new CEO wants to change the world. Increase marketing spend.'

Five years later, 'Our old CEO hasn't changed the world. How can we get better figures? Slash marketing budgets.'

Professional direct marketers (many are not, unfortunately) first ask how much the customer is worth. As you will recall from the relevant sections of this book, you can measure how long customers stay with you and how much profit they provide in that time, then discount the sum to determine what you can afford to recruit and retain a customer, whilst at the same time allowing for a profit.

This thinking will start to influence businesses without a direct marketing heritage – because it makes sense. As a matter of fact, I believe this could be one of the biggest contributions direct marketing makes to business as a whole, not just to marketing as a whole.

7. Marketers will realise all customers are not created equal – and act accordingly

The Pareto Principle is not new; we've discussed it in this book. However, it still is the case that many marketers have not properly explored its implications.

Direct marketing is perfect for reaching lucrative minorities. The classy direct marketing media, direct mail and the phone, are very costly per individual reached. But they are intrusive and memorable.

95% of advertising is forgotten

Again, as we have seen earlier, over 95 per cent of advertising messages are either not noticed or forgotten within 24 hours; but good direct mail is recalled weeks later. A simple one-page letter we prepared for a bank was recalled after a month by 92 per cent of recipients.

In future, intelligent marketers will concentrate more on directly reaching those customers most likely to be big spenders.

8. Marketers will use direct messages for more than just selling

Relevant, thoughtful messages, whether they sell or not, are a service to customers.

Even a questionnaire or phone call asking the customer's opinion can be flattering. Besides being a good form of market research, it increases sales. I have seen more than one firm with poor service retain customers in this way.

This applies to inbound as well as outbound messages. An 0800 number on a pack is a service to customers who appreciate being able to ring up and ask about things that interest or trouble them. The questionnaire (in print or on the internet) allows you to ask the customer's permission to talk again.

Make sure you keep your customers

These things keep customers with you, spending more; what is more, they are far more profitable than trawling for new customers. As you know, it is several times easier to sell to the customer you've got than someone identical who is not a customer.

Direct marketers learned that years ago, but most other firms are only now realising it.

9. The mythical 'line' will be erased – and about time, too.

As I mentioned earlier, when I started in advertising, nobody spoke of above or below the line. It's a shame they started to, because it doesn't exist in customers' minds. They don't care how you categorise your messages.

When I was writing ads or salespeople's brochures or mailings, I was writing different types of message to different audiences with different objectives. In every case I was talking to customers or potential customers. Just as I had to alter my style to fit the needs of different clients, why should I not be able to adapt to each task?

Adapt to different tasks

Again, as we have seen, if all your messages work in concert, great synergy results. The same tone of voice and look, careful timing, consistent positioning, result in two plus two plus two making seven or eight.

10. Marketers will stop claiming to love customers, and act like they mean it

That dire new piece of jargon, 'customer-centric', reflects a truth: the customer should be at the centre of our world.

The customer is the centre of our world

When experts waffle about 'customer relationship management' (more dire jargon) we should remember that really customers manage us – right out of business, if we're not careful.

LITTLE MORE COMPETENCE

One reason I have never believed that direct marketing would conquer the world is very simple. There simply aren't enough good people around to handle the volume of expenditure involved.

Poor calibre of work is a problem

One of the great current problems in our industry, quite simply, is the poor calibre of much of our work. Just about anywhere I go in the world, if I am interviewed by a trade paper or newspaper, the question always arises in one form or another – what do you think about junk mail?

Direct marketers loathe the idea of being seen as producers of junk mail. So much so that a while ago a British magazine – *Direct Response* – held a competition amongst its readers to find a more agreeable phrase for what they produced. Of course, the truth is if people think the mail we send out is junk, then there is not much we can do to alter that view or that expression, apart from improving the quality of that mail.

HONESTY

Another thing we could do is to start being a little bit more honest with people. All over the world, customers dislike a lot of the ploys we make use of. They may not lose sleep over them, but they do get irritated.

For instance, in a survey by the American Specialty Advertising Association International, it was revealed that 85 per cent of business managers had recently been contacted by somebody who told them they had won a valuable prize – as long as they agreed to buy something.

These shrewd, perceptive business folk, it would seem, fell for this knavish trick. Twenty-two per cent did buy something. Of these, 64 per cent later decided their decision was not necessarily all that smart. They thought the products they'd bought were of inferior quality. Sixty-two per cent thought they were overpriced. And 7 per cent of the poor souls never received a product at all.

How to attain respectability

Until our business outlaws this sort of thing, direct marketing is unlikely to attain respectability. It will still seem to some extent the province of a bunch of fast-talking rogues, and the internet has a prodigious number of scams, especially on eBay. Moreover, low educational standards are making it harder and harder to find competent personnel. Until we recruit better people – first-class people – train them better and improve our behaviour, I do not see how serious marketers are going to pour the vast sums of money into direct marketing which are predicted.

Happily, we are trying to encourage virtue amongst the industry as a more palatable alternative to being legislated into honesty. Typical are the

Mail and telephone preference schemes

various mail and telephone preference schemes whereby customers can have their names removed from mailing lists. And the good news is, according to the only figures I have seen, that whatever they may say, only a very small percentage of people at the moment dislike receiving direct mail or e-mails enough to do something about it. Most are prepared to put up with the occasional irritant in exchange for the valuable information they often receive. However, the more intrusive the medium the more strongly they feel, so telephone preference schemes have proved very popular.

But, as I say, until we have an industry with the kind of reputation which encourages really talented people in large numbers, and has the intelligence to invest in properly educating those people, we will never meet the challenge posed by the future.

Invest in education

That's one reason why I'm sceptical about the degree to which direct marketing is likely to take over. The other is that marketing itself is changing. The marketing of the future will not be broken down into different specialities working independently of each other. Tomorrow's world will be a world of integrated marketing: 'maxi-marketing', as it is tagged in an excellent book with that title by Stan Rapp and Tom Collins.

Because ours is, above all, an age of specialisation, direct marketing has come to be regarded as a discipline unto itself. It has been seen, particularly by advertising agencies, as an adjunct to their other activities. They have felt they should be able to supply this particular facility to their clients. This, of course, is quite correct.

But because many of the new direct marketers on both agency and client side have come from a background of advertising or conventional marketing, many see direct marketing and its relationship to the other disciplines in a different way. This illustrates what I mean:

> What agencies are doing is not new, but now they are really moving into it [non-advertising developments]. The advertising agency is still the centre of the group – that is the flashy part; and then they are putting out a net to try to find ways of catching up all of that spending.
>
> So it ends up that the direct marketing unit is saying 'Why not put more money into direct marketing?' whereas the advertising people say: 'You need to spend more on advertising.' That is not the consultancy we need.

This comes from an article which appeared in *Advertising Age* as long ago as 1988. The speaker: Michael Reinarz, director of visual communications for Nestlé.

He went on to say:

> What could be the agency 10 or 15 years from now? I would not see the agency being the centre part. They may not even be called advertising agencies. A core business, a communication consultancy, does that coordination. It gets involved in understanding what your long-term and medium-term objectives are on brands and products.
>
> They understand what profitability you are after, and within that they will recommend how you should split your money. Then once they have done that, they use those specialist units.

Here we are 19 years on, and it hasn't happened yet. A good example of possible developments is a programme I mentioned earlier for Crest toothpaste in the United States.

This programme uses television to get a direct response and the mail to follow up, but it involves what one can almost describe as 'the trade', in the form of dentists. It doesn't matter to me whether this programme is sales promotion, direct marketing or advertising. What matters is: will it work? (I have no idea whether it worked or not).

Tomorrow's marketing is going to call for people who understand the *totality* of business. People who have allegiance not to general advertising, or direct marketing or any of the other disciplines. People who are solely concerned (as they should be) with doing a better total marketing job.

A total marketing job

In any case, try as you will to draw rigid demarcation lines between one discipline and another, it's impossible. Nor, when marketing is changing so fast, is it wise. To me the important thing is to arrange our marketing to suit not our own definition, but our customers'. And as I suggested at the beginning of this book, you cannot arrange anything to suit your customers other than by trying to treat them as individuals and endeavouring, in the first place, to find out what each individual wants.

Technology has made the growth of direct marketing possible. And similar technology is transforming many other areas of business. For instance it has long been possible for people reaching supermarket checkouts to be offered incentives as they leave which relate to what they have purchased. So the idea of reaching people as individuals and dealing with them in a way based upon what you know about them is not restricted to the world of direct marketing. It's happening everywhere.

Reaching people as individuals

FULL CIRCLE

I believe – and I hope – that in the future, people will be expected to do exactly what I was expected to do back in 1957 in my first job. They'll be expected to work within every marketing discipline. They will be expected to understand the role of all communications tools. Some people seem to think the intellectual challenge of doing this is too great; that specialisation will always rule. I do not.

Of course there will always be those who are better at one thing than another. But those who succeed will be those who try to *understand* everything. And this is true of those planning marketing, as well as those executing it. People will be increasingly concerned when preparing direct marketing communications to project an appropriate image: not merely to reflect that created by the general advertising, but help build it. Those preparing general advertising will see it as part of their natural role to try and help enrich the database.

Try to understand everything

In short, I believe that tomorrow's marketing world will look surprisingly similar to yesterday's. That the approach of pioneers like Claude Hopkins, who saw no boundaries between one discipline and another, will return. I believe that the present era of specialisation is little more than a blind alley. I think it's time we all got back on the right track.

The future

> ### Points to remember
>
> - The lunacy of the line.
> - Direct marketing taking over.
> - Internet overclaims.
> - Ignorance of direct most unwise.
> - More intelligent DM.
> - Databases used properly.
> - Customer value appreciated.
> - Varying customer values acknowledged.
> - More than just selling.
> - *Real* customer care, not just talk.
> - Shortage of talent.
> - Greater honesty essential.
> - More scrutiny, higher standards.
> - Back to the future.

Index

NB: numbers in *italics* indicate figures or tables

Lightning Source UK Ltd.
Milton Keynes UK
UKOW07f1611220915

259060UK00015B/100/P